REALISM AND RELATIVISM

Philosophical Issues Volume 12

Edited by Ernest Sosa and Enrique Villanueva

Blackwell Publishing | Boston MA & Oxford UK

Blackwell Publishing, Inc.
350 Main Street
Malden, MA 02148 USA

Blackwell Publishing, Ltd.
108 Cowley Road
Oxford OX4 1JF
United Kingdom

Library of Congress Cataloging-in-Publication Data has been applied for.

ISBN 0-631233-84-9
ISSN 1533-6077

Contents

I. Metaphysics and Logic

II. Metaethics

Editorial Preface

This volume includes main papers delivered at the 13th SOFIA conference, held in Oaxaca, Mexico, in January of 2001, as well as papers invited specifically for the volume. We express our gratitude to the following institutions and persons for supporting the conference: the Ministry of Education of Mexico (SEP-SESIC anexo de ejecucion 98-18-09-160-191); to the Instituto de Investigaciones Juridicas of the National Autonomous University of Mexico (UNAM); and, finally, to Lourdes Valdivia.

Ernest Sosa and *Enrique Villanueva*
Co-Editors

REALISM AND RELATIVISM

Akeel Bilgrami
Columbia University

Discussions of realism and relativism often proceed as if these are starkly opposed doctrines. I want to begin by observing that on one, by now classical, understanding of those terms ('realism', 'relativism'), the two doctrines in fact *share* some rather conspicuous philosophical assumptions. If that is really so, then there may be another doctrine, which is neither of these, since it opposes these shared assumptions. And, of course, therefore—as in so much of philosophy—a question will arise of any such position, whether it is to be most illuminatingly classified under a different name altogether, or whether, by the very way in which such a position comes to light, one is given the right to say that there was something not quite inevitable about the initial classification of doctrines and that there is instead a more illuminating non-arbitrary reclassification in which the position can without prejudice claim for itself at least one of the initial terms—in this case, 'realism'—though of course not any longer in the classically understood sense of that term. This sort of dialectical situation is common in philosophy, when distinctions among doctrines are drawn, contested, and re-drawn. I must apologize at the outset for producing yet another paper in philosophy of this rather routine sort.

The paper aims at advancing the cause of such a distinct position, a position properly describable as at once 'realist' and 'pragmatist', but unlike current positions held by fellow-critics of classical realism (such as, say, Davidson and Putnam and Rorty), providing a more credible and appealing epistemology than they do.

This position, which I am describing as both realist and pragmatist, will be contrasted in this paper with two other realist doctrines which owe in one way or another to Cartesian conceptions of reality and truth. The first, which will be discussed in section I, I will call 'classical realism' and it is the one which shares some assumptions with the doctrine of relativism. By questioning those assumptions, an argument against both classical realism and relativism will be presented there. The second I will call the 'residual Cartesian realism', and it is the position that some contemporary critics of classical realism, such as Davidson, have embraced, and it will be discussed in Sections II and III of the paper. The pragmatism espoused in the paper gets most fully motivated by way of contrast with this second realist doctrine. Finally, I will be arguing. in Section IV. that the realist element in this pragmatism is initially hidden from view primarily because, at first sight, it seems as if it really is a doctrine that must imply relativism rather than realism, but a closer look at the argument provided in Section I against relativism makes clear that no such thing is implied.

I

Let's then begin with the relations between realism and relativism.

First, realism. The standard and by now classical characterization of it, often discussed under the label 'the absolute conception of reality' owes to Descartes, and is intimately tied to the sort of radical scepticism that he thought possible in his early *Meditations.*[1] On the basis of arguments invoking the deliberately exaggerated idea of our comprehensive deception by dreams or by malign intervention, Descartes argued for the possibility that all the propositions by which we purport to describe reality (and therefore all our beliefs) are false, and this last was supposed to indicate the idea of a reality that was superlatively independent and therefore wholly ulterior to and remote from our knowing powers and wholly beyond the power of the propositions we employ, to describe. Thus a reality, unconstrained and 'absolute' in its very conception.

Key to such a realism, as we have just seen, is the conclusion that it is possible that all our beliefs can be false. Familiar modern versions of this ideal of realism have expressed it with more scientific glosses of the fictional intervention which makes such comprehensive error possible: mad scientists manipulating brains-in-vats.

Next, relativism. In his brilliant and celebrated paper, "On the Very Idea of a Conceptual Scheme",[2] Donald Davidson argues that conceptual relativism is the doctrine that the truth of beliefs or of propositions is relative to a point of view or, as he calls it following Kuhn and others, relative to a 'conceptual scheme', and he says that this idea of relativism is coherent only if one can make sense of the idea that different points of view have no common coordinate system on which they can be plotted. If differences of conceptual schemes always *do* have such an underlying common coordinate system, then that undermines the point of seeing them as 'different' and, in turn, undermines the very idea of a conceptual scheme. If that is undermined, there is no scope for relativization of truth to anything, and therefore no relativism. So relativism, the idea that there are radically different conceptual schemes to which truth must be relativized, requires the idea that there can be conceptual schemes *without* a common coordinate system on which they can be plotted. Davidson then adds that this latter idea, in turn, can only amount to one of two things. It can mean: 1) there are subjects with beliefs expressible in language, which when their language is interpreted, they turn out to be such that they have mostly false beliefs, by the lights of the interpreter. Or it can mean 2) there are subjects with beliefs expressible in language, and whose beliefs the interpreter grants to be mostly true, but whose language is not interpretable. Davidson argues against both possibilities, and in doing so claims to have repudiated relativism.

But before elaborating the arguments, I want to remark on the proximity in which 1) stands to the characterization given earlier of the standard, and by now classical, doctrine of realism. If relativism as a doctrine turns on the intelligibility of the idea mentioned in 1), i.e., the idea of mostly false beliefs, and realism as a doctrine turns on the intelligibility of the idea of wholly false beliefs, then if the latter condition (wholly false beliefs) held, so would the former (mostly false beliefs). That brings to the surface the large and conspicuous assumption *shared* by what are always presented as two *opposed* doctrines. Both relativism and realism assume that someone's beliefs can be mostly or wholly false. (I will further below deal with the protest that relativism is defined by the idea of beliefs which are false by the lights of an interpreter, whereas realism is defined by the idea of beliefs which are false, simpliciter.)

So far I have said that only 1) is shared by both realist and relativist. But, in fact 2), the other defining feature of relativism, can also be seen to figure in the kind of realism we are discussing. Let me bring this out by looking at Davidson's argument.

The argument against 1) rests on his familiar claim that interpreting someone to have any false beliefs requires that a background of true beliefs also be attributed to him. Thus, for instance, it is not possible to interpret someone as believing (what, let's say, by our—the interpreters'—lights, is false) that there are ghosts, without also interpreting him as at least believing (what, let's say, by our—the interpreters'—lights, is true) that people die. This is so because otherwise it would put into doubt that we were right in the initial belief we interpreted him as having, viz., the belief that it is *ghosts* that there are.[3] (Of course, it is not denied that there might be other false beliefs too that might be involved in identifying the initial false belief about ghosts, but Davidson's point is that intelligibility of interpretation requires that somewhere in this burgeoning network of interconnected beliefs required to identify these false beliefs, there will be beliefs that, by the interpreters' lights, are true.) To repeat, this argument therefore establishes that all our beliefs cannot be false, by claiming to show that for any to be false, some others must be true.

The argument presupposes that what is true is determined by what the interpreter believes, what he or she takes to be true. And it might be claimed that this is not a realist way of proceeding, in the first place. The realist is always going to ask, why might not the interpreter herself have things completely wrong? True and false by the interpreter's lights, he might say, is not true and false. Davidson's response will be that if it is the case that the interpreter has things completely wrong, she will have to be *interpreted* as having beliefs that are completely false, and this will have to be so by some (other) interpreter's lights. But he has already shown by his argument discussed above that if she is interpreted at all, she cannot be interpreted to be completely wrong in this way. Thus, no one can fail to share beliefs with all others, so long as they are interpretable one by the other. It is therefore not really possible or interesting according to Davidson to try and pull apart the notion of 'false' beliefs from the notion of 'unshared' beliefs between interpreter and speaker, (nor, by the same token, 'true' beliefs from 'shared' beliefs.)

And it is here that the question then arises: were we even to grant that if someone is interpreted at all they must come out as having many true beliefs, what if someone is simply not interpretable by another, what if he is completely opaque. This is just 2) above. So by a brisk dialectic, 2) is also shown to be implicated in any notion of realism which takes 1) or the possibility of comprehensive error as an assumption.

Davidson argues against this possibility of exploiting 2) to shore up 1), by saying that even God, an omniscient Being and Interpreter, would have to interpret someone as having true beliefs. Being omniscient, He cannot fail to know what someone believes and says, so He cannot find anyone opaque and uninterpretable as 2) suggests, and yet if He is genuinely interpreting, He must (as the original argument goes) find the agent being interpreted to have true beliefs by his lights. Thus 1) is still false. So uninterpretability cannot be a way of objecting to the conclusion that every agent has true beliefs, if he or she has any false ones.[4]

This is not a good argument, as it stands. The trouble with this appeal to an omniscient interpreter to repudiate the difficulty raised by invoking 2) to counter the original argument against 1) is that the appeal is exploiting two somewhat contradictory ideas. On the one hand, such an interpreter is defined as knowing everything including what everyone believes, on the other hand the argument requires that He interpret to know another's beliefs. If He knows everything, He ought not to be required to interpret to know, it might rightly be protested. And it's not as if interpretation is in the end what *underlies* what He does know, as it is, according to Davidson, in our (ordinary mortals') case when two speakers know the same language and do not explicitly interpret one another. When I, an English-speaker, know what my English-speaking wife means and believes, I do not have to carry out the sort of interpretation (radical interpretation) which, according to Davidson, requires that I make her come out as having many true beliefs. But all the same, it is Davidson's (and Quine's) point that radical interpretation underlies what we know about our fellow English speakers in such cases. As Quine once said, "radical translation begins at home". But the omniscient Interpreter is *not* like us in this regard; His sort of knowledge is *defining* of him, and unlike as between speakers of the same natural language, interpretation does not implicitly underlie what he knows without explicit interpretation. So there is something suspect about Davidson's appeal to both omniscience and underlying radical interpretation in the same argument.

A better argument (one which modifies the argument Davidson actually gives) against those who invoke uninterpretability in this way would be to say something different. In fact it is the only response an anti-relativist and anti-classical realist can give to someone who invokes uninterpretability to come to a relativist or classical realist conclusion. The response is: if someone is completely opaque, then all that shows is that *we should keep trying to interpret him*. The idea that someone is known to be a thinker with thoughts and is in principle not interpretable needs some sort of impossibility theorem to support it. Without such an impossibility theorem, there is no instruction to give, but: keep trying.

Impossibility *theorem* there perhaps is not, but we could simply have Cartesians saying, (as Tom Nagel does say) that it is *conceivable* that there is a sort of super-knower who knows all truths, and he is to us as we are to non-human animals.[5] We simply do not have anything like the conceptual repertoire that he has, the conceptual repertoire to get things right. So he is not interpretable by us at all. And if that is conceivable, it is also conceivable that we have things completely wrong because our concepts are too impoverished to get them right. But the possibility that we get things completely wrong is just the possibility claimed by 1). Thus again 2) very quickly comes to nest with 1) by providing support for what 1) claims, viz., it is possible that all our beliefs are false, and providing support therefore for a defining condition of classical realism. Proof of this lies in what Nagel is asking us to conceive. It's not as if what he is asking us to conceive is like some ordinary matter of conceiving someone being more ignorant than others (what I am to an advanced physicist, say). He is not asking us to conceive that we know some of the things that the super-knower knows, but he knows a lot more, just as I know some of the things that an advanced physicist knows, but she knows a lot more. That would not be of any consequence to a philosophical issue. Rather, what he asks us to conceive is that our relation to the super-knower is quite literally analogous to what animals are to us, where none of the concepts deployed by the super-knower to think and describe the world accurately are learnable by us, given our limitations. Such a super-knower obviously would not be interpretable by us. His beliefs which ex hypothesi truly describe reality are such that we do not share any of them. Thus we may grant to Davidson that interpretation requires shared beliefs and concepts but insist that not every thinker is interpretable by us. In particular, such a super-knower is not. Hence, Davidson's argument via the demands of interpretation is ineffective, and the claim 1) above, viz., that all of our beliefs can be false, still haunts us. The Nagelian fantasy underlying 2) shows how 2) can be used to support 1), and in fact must be used to support 1), if 1) is to hold up against the modified Davidsonian argument just given.

Davidson might persist and say that it is quite unclear that we have any right to say that it is thoughts exactly, or beliefs, that this super-knower has, if we do not share any beliefs or concepts at all with him. The idea of thoughts or beliefs is *our* idea, he might say. We are supposed to be using the idea, and we don't even know what it is we mean when we attribute thoughts to the super-knower. What we mean by this idea, by 'thoughts' is something that emerges in our notion of interpreting others, and that is precisely what, we are told by this Nagelian fantasy, we cannot do with the super-knower.

But the Nagelian response to this might simply be to say. "Yes, we do know what we mean when we say the super-knower has thoughts or beliefs, which we cannot interpret at all. We mean that he has intentional states of mind that are the sorts of things that are capable of being true and false, that have truth-conditions; it's just that we do not know what his thoughts are." The sugges-tion, then, is that we give a criterion for what a thought or belief is (a truth value bearing state of mind), but we insist that we cannot detect in this case of the Nagelian super-knower, that the criterion applies. It is in principle undis-coverable that this criterion applies to such a creature, but that should be no bar to supposing that it *does* apply to him. To demand that one must in principle be able to discover that the criterion applies before we can suppose that it does apply is to make a question-begging anti-realist demand, one precisely being opposed by the classical realist and the absolute conception of reality presup-posed by Descartes.

At last, then, the presupposition in Descartes that is being questioned by the (modified) Davidsonian argument is now out in the open. In Davidsonian terms, the presupposition emerges via semantic ascent. An absolute conception of reality is a conception of reality which may be accurately described in the thoughts or sayings of someone who, for all we know, is not interpretable by us at all, even in principle; and to deny that he has thoughts because we cannot in-terpret him is to give up on the realist assumption that for applicability of the criterion by which we define what a thought is, there need be no demand that we in principle be able to discover that it applies or fails to apply. In particular, we may not know whether it applies or fails to apply to the super-knower, but it may nevertheless be the case that it does apply to him, that he does have thoughts.

The point of interest in this way (via semantic ascent) of bringing out the Cartesian assumption of the "absolute" conception of reality, is that this con-ception is (at least implicitly) poised to stand in opposition to the main con-clusion of Wittgenstein's extended remarks on the impossibility of a private language. Wittgenstein's conclusion was precisely that we do not have a con-cept or meaning if we do not in principle have any idea when it is correct to apply it and when it is not. In the case of the super-knower's thoughts, we are being told just what Wittgenstein wants to rule out, that we have a right to say that he has thoughts even though (ex hypothesi) we could never detect that this is a correct or incorrect application of the term 'thought' to him.[6]

And notice one final thing. What Wittgenstein wanted to rule out is the intelligibility of the idea of meaning or thoughts that are not publicly available in principle to another (and therefore in particular unavailable to the David-sonian interpreter) and the idea of such undiscoverable thoughts is just a *special instance* of a more general idea, the idea of a reality that is in principle unknowable—Descartes' absolute conception of reality. The thesis of the principled publicness of thought and the thesis known as anti-realism (or at any rate an anti-classical realism) are related to each other as species to genus.

This discussion began by pointing out how *relativism* might be characterized by a commitment to either 1) or 2). It then tried to show that 1) is an assumption of *realism* as well, and then, with just a little dialectic, that 2) also supports, and indeed must support realism, if 1) is to support it. Thus both relativism and classical realism share two large assumptions. Finally, a somewhat modified and fortified Davidsonian strategy against these assumptions 1) and 2), was shown to be effective so long as one took for granted the publicness of thought.

However because, as we just saw, the denial of the publicness of thought and language is just a special case of the assumptions of classical realism, there is no non-question begging way of showing that meanings and thoughts are public, i.e., without denying 1) and 2) which realism and relativism take for granted. And equally there is no non-question begging way for the realist and relativist to show that it is wrong to demand that thoughts and meanings be public, i.e., to show it without assuming their own 1) and 2).

I rather suspect that for all the highly sophisticated philosophy that has been expended on it, this is the situation (the question-beggingness on both sides) we have always been in, in our discussions of this entire subject. What we have here (and have always had) is an abiding impasse in philosophy, one of the largest and most vexing of its perennial frustrations.

But recognition of the impasse need not put an end to philosophizing in this region. Given the impasse, we can turn to other philosophical tasks, taking one or other side on the dispute and thereby frankly and openly begging the question in one or other direction. If in taking one side of the dispute, interesting and fresh explorations with attractive conclusions emerge, then adopting that side of the dispute will have paid off, and to that extent would in retrospect seem a justified and non-arbitrary decision. The rest of this paper will from this point on assume, with Wittgenstein, that thought and meaning are public, and that therefore both relativism and realism in the classical sense are operating with two untenable assumptions (i.e., 1) and 2)).

Having done this, it will now address the following question. Taking it that *relativism* has definitively and *unsurvivably* been repudiated by the untenability of 1) and 2) which define it, is there any notion of *realism* which *does survive* the untenability of 1) and 2) which also define *it*? The untenability of 1) and 2) has shown that the 'absolute' conception of reality in the classical picture is wrong, and for that to have been shown means we have admitted into our conception of reality some elements which do not make it quite so absolute, which do not allow it to be so ulterior to our epistemological status as believers and inquirers. So the question is how shall we think of this surviving realism, if there is one, such that it squares with a credible epistemology.

II

In my dialectic so far, classical realism (and relativism) are supposed to have been repudiated by an argument which undermined an assumption which they both share, viz. that it is possible that all our beliefs are false. It is interesting to note that in Descartes himself there is *another* conception of realism, (a 'residual' Cartesian realism, let's call it) which turns not on this assumption at all, but another, one which generates a different form of scepticism than the radical and comprehensive one expressed by the assumption just undermined by the Davidsonian argument. It is a realism that unfortunately *Davidson himself*, and many other philosophers today who like him are critical of classical realism, quite readily accept. Let me state this residual Cartesian realist position in this section, and argue against it in the next.

In Descartes' early *Meditations*, the driving thought is that nothing in our experiences gives us the epistemological right to claims to knowledge of the external world. But the force of this thought is split by his own argument to generate two quite different forms of scepticism, each of which presuppose somewhat different realist ideas. The first takes the form of claiming that, given the absence of this epistemological right, *all* our beliefs about the external world might be false, and hence we lack knowledge of the external world. The second form of scepticism about the external world (the one I want to now focus on) concludes (from the arguments of the same text) that *no given* belief about the external world can be firmly claimed to be true and to amount to knowledge.

The second is different from the first because it is possible to grant the second scepticism and not grant the first. If the first form of scepticism were true, then of course the second would also be true. If all our beliefs about the external world might be false, then any given one might be false. But it is often thought that things are not so obvious the other way round. If any given belief about the external world might always be false, despite our best epistemological efforts, it is still thought arguable that it does not follow from this that all our beliefs about the external world could be false.

Any strategy opposing the first form of scepticism (while granting the second form of scepticism) about the external world, therefore, needs to show that the passage from the idea that any given belief of ours about the external world might fail to be knowledge to the idea that all our beliefs about the external world might so fail, is illicit. The second form of scepticism, however, will only be countered if for any given belief about the external world we are able to show that it can be claimed to amount to knowledge. The thought, "Well, we are happy to allow that any given belief about the external world is not knowledge but that does not mean that all are not" does not even take up the difficulty, as it is seen by the second form of scepticism. It concedes it at the outset.

We have in Section I of this paper looked at the realism underlying the first form of scepticism in Descartes, and called it 'classical realism'. What notion of realism underlies the second form of scepticism? It does not assume

1) and 2) which define 'classical' realism. Rather it is just the idea of a notion of truth, which is such that *we can never know which of any (empirical) belief of ours is true*. This is different from 1) because it can grant that some, and very likely many, of our beliefs are true, and in fact Davidson's argument against 1) is supposed to have established that. It only claims that truth is such, that we never know when in particular we have attained it, even if we know that many of our beliefs are true. It is, to coin a phrase, 'an epistemologically blind' notion of truth. And it defines a realism distinct from the classical one that the modified Davidsonian argument of the last section has rejected. Nothing in that argument, nothing about the publicness of thought and meaning, can help to show that this form of realism is wrong. And it better not do so, because as I said Davidson himself has explicitly embraced this epistemologically blind notion of truth and the realism it points to, describing it as the 'objectivity of truth'.[7] In doing so, Davidson has not really gotten out of the clutches of an essentially Cartesian picture, and has merely convinced himself that he has by focusing on only one form of scepticism and realism in Descartes—the classical one which he successfully rejects by the argument of the last section.

In the rest of this paper, I want very briefly to argue for two things. First, that this other notion of truth (and the 'residual' realism it entails) is quite as bad as 'classical realism', even if it does not fall afoul of the same argument as given in Section I. It is quite as bad because it generates an equally unsatisfactory epistemology. Having argued this I want to briefly sketch an alternative position on realism and the objectivity of truth, one that might properly be regarded as 'pragmatist', and I want to claim—returning to a point made in the first section—that if Davidson has been right to reject relativism by his argument there, then that very same argument gives him the space to occupy this much more credible epistemology rather than the quite different space he in fact occupies in embracing this epistemologically blind notion of truth and its residual Cartesian realism.

III

A view of truth and realism which has it that we can never know when one of our beliefs is true, does not encourage a plausible epistemology for a very simple reason. It makes truth fall outside of the targets of inquiry. Truth is no longer something we can aim for, not something we can intend to attain. This is not because such a view makes truth impossible to attain. If it did that, it would obviously remove truth from the targets of inquiry since we cannot intend to attain what we know it is impossible to attain. But it's because of something almost as bad. Though it allows that truth is possible to attain, and in fact though it is even compatible with the Davidsonian position (discussed in Section I) that it is not only possible but that it will and must be attained in the case of most of our beliefs, it nevertheless remains that it makes us blind as to when we have attained it. We never can tell or know which of our beliefs is true. We can never know when it is in any particular case that we have attained the truth. Under such circumstances, inquiry into or the search for truth would always be like sending a message in a bottle out to sea, making all success in the search something like a fluke or a bonus, something over which we have no control. What sort of notion of inquiry into truth is that? What kind of an epistemology is that? Why would one even set up truth as a goal, under such circumstances?

It is for this reason that pragmatists balk at such a realist conception of truth, even if it is less extreme than the classical realist conception discussed in Section I. From the pragmatist point of view it is still caught up in retrograde ways with elements of Cartesian scepticism, not the ones which give rise to classical realism, but close cousins of it, and generative of an equally unattractive scepticism, if a somewhat different one.

I've mentioned the pragmatists, but notice that once we see things this way, once we see clearly that this realism is connected with Cartesian scepticism of this second variety, we can see that its not just pragmatism but certain well-known responses to this variety of scepticism, owing to G. E. Moore, J. L. Austin, and Wittgenstein, which can be counted as opponents of such a realism as well. Moore famously claimed that there *are* particular beliefs and statements (his example was the belief about the presence of one's hand under certain routinely obtaining circumstances) which are such that they are not susceptible to this variety of scepticism, and so presumably that there is no question of not knowing that they are true, when they are. I will return to Austin and Wittgenstein a little later. I mention all this only to make clear that there is nothing novel or eccentric about opposing the widespread commitment to such a realist notion of truth, and it is not merely done by a fringe of pragmatists. An opposition to it is implied by a long cast of opponents of a certain variety of scepticism, with which this realist notion of truth is closely linked.

All the same 'pragmatism' remains a good label for making explicit the metaphilosophy involved in one's dissatisfaction with a notion of truth which yields an epistemology in which truth cannot be a goal of inquiry—for such a notion makes truth fall outside of what can make a difference to *practice*. It is the pragmatists who have always from the outset proposed that what does not make a difference to practice does not make a difference to philosophy. At any rate, given our interests in this paper, it does not make a difference to epistemology. We have seen that this realist notion of truth makes truth fall outside of the aims of inquiry, and inquiry is the one general practice which is central to epistemology.

In saying that bad Cartesian epistemologies may be opposed by stressing practice, as pragmatists do, and by seeing inquiry as the central practice of epistemology, I am doing two different things.

First, I am assuming that philosophy itself is not an inquiry, in the requisite sense. Thus it won't do to say that the logical possibility of any given empirical belief of ours being false (on the basis of Cartesian hypotheses about evil demons and brains in vats) is relevant to and makes a difference to *some* sort of inquiry, *philosophical* inquiry. The point about invoking practice was to bring in as a criterion for what is good philosophy, the concept of inquiry as a cognitive practice, relevance to which will be crucial in judging what is good *in philosophy*, and in epistemology in particular. Hence, to then say that philosophy itself is an inquiry, would be to altogether miss the point of setting up such a criterion. (There may also be reasons, quite apart from the point-missing just mentioned, reasons familiar from Wittgenstein, for resisting the idea that philosophy is an inquiry. For Wittgenstein philosophers did not engage in inquiry any more than they engaged in what ordinary people think about in their ordinary reflection. Both inquiry as scientists pursue it, and the plain thought of ordinary people uncontaminated by philosophy, are to be distinguished from the sort of thing philosophy is, the sort of thing which encourages all sorts of confusions and distortions and misrepresentations of what goes on in 'inquiry' properly so called as well as in ordinary thought. Philosophy thus stands *apart* both from ordinary reflection and from inquiry, and should not be thought of as a case or a version of one of these. And to this we can add that once we see traditional philosophy in this light—as the source of confusion by adopting a mode of thinking, whose confusions arise *because* it departs from both our ordinary responses and from 'inquiry', properly so-called—we might then fruitfully do what pragmatists suggest: propose a criterion which constrains philosophy so as to minimize these confusions, viz., "Don't admit anything that does not make a difference to inquiry." Wittgenstein himself made other proposals, having more to do with the charms of ordinary language, about which I am much more sceptical and about which we need not concern ourselves here.)

Second, in stressing practice as I have, I am not avowing those crude forms of pragmatism which take it that truth must be characterized in terms of practices and values that are *not cognitive* practices and values, but rather practices which essentially involve the *applications* of cognitive and theoretical conclusions (such as, say, in engineering or medicine) and therefore values that speak to the *usefulness* of our theoretical and cognitive pursuits in some sort of *practical* terms. That is a caricature of pragmatism, no doubt encouraged by some reckless remarks of some pragmatists, but by no means compulsory for those embracing a pragmatist epistemology in order to respond to one of the essentially Cartesian versions of realism, as we are.[8] The strategy of the response we are pursuing shuns this caricature by bringing to centre-stage *only* the *cognitive* practice of inquirers, and claims that any characterization of the notion of truth and of philosophical doctrines such as realism should restrict itself to what does make a difference to inquiry so conceived, i.e., merely as a cognitive practice.

How, then, may one do better by way of characterizing truth in a way that retains its direct relevance to the goals of inquiry, so conceived? (Some care is being taken to use the word 'characterizing' instead of 'defining'. One can happily join those who think that 'truth' cannot be defined, as we shall see later, and still make the claim that it characterized in such a way that it remain a goal of inquiry.[9])

Truth remains a goal of inquiry only if there is no place to doubt the truth of beliefs on grounds that are *general* and *purely philosophical* in ways that Descartes made famous and familiar. Comprehensive illusion or dream, intervening malign genies or mad scientists, are all hypotheses contrived to conclude only this: it is logically possible that any particular (empirical) belief of ours is false. But inquirers are not moved by logical possibilities. They are only moved if some reason or evidence is offered for doubting some *particular* belief on particular grounds relevant to *that* belief.[10] The logical possibility of a particular empirical belief being false is something it shares with all such beliefs, and so that possibility lacks the particularity of grounds for doubt that move the inquirer. Fanciful hypotheses about malign genies and brains in vats, for which there is no particular ground in any particular case, can be wheeled in to make vivid the logical possibility of the falsehood of empirical belief *in general*. The inquirer may grant such a possibility and proceed exactly as she would have proceeded anyway. It makes no difference to her, qua inquirer.

Some efforts at going beyond Cartesian style arguments and the notion of truth it presupposes, have not, in the end, avoided the problem in Descartes that we are discussing.

Putnam, for instance, who is sensitive to the point that we must stress the role of inquiry in characterizing truth, tries to do better than the conception presupposed by Descartes, but he so *idealizes* the notion of inquiry in the characterization, that it is not clear that the notion of truth which emerges *can* make any difference to practice as it is carried out in any *actual* inquiry. For Putnam, truth becomes the omnibus deliverance of inquiry in the ideal limit, inquiry at the end of time, so any given inquirer at any actual given time and point of inquiry will just as surely worry, not now perhaps about the logical possibility of being wrong in holding any of his (empirical) beliefs, but about the possibility that any of the beliefs he now holds will be judged false in the ideal limit of inquiry. The fact is, however, that such a generalized doubt about the truth of one's beliefs is just as bad as the Cartesian doubt, since it cannot make a difference to inquiry at any given actual point of time.

Apart from Putnam's unsatisfactory version of the appeal to pragmatism, there is another strategy which also tries to show that any given belief may be false without appealing to malign interventions or comprehensive dreams. It looks instead to meta-inductive arguments to make the case. But these strategies too are bootless. It is bootless to try to make the case by saying that we have been wrong in the past, so we are very likely to be wrong in at least some of the beliefs we currently hold. Even if, on the basis of this argument, an inquirer conceded the claim that some of her beliefs are bound to be false, that preface-paradoxical concession would still not be a concession to anything that made a difference to her inquiry. Unless she had evidence or grounds to think any *particular* belief or set of beliefs were put into doubt, she would proceed with inquiry just as before. Thinking that *some* beliefs (in the general sense of 'some or other' beliefs) are bound to be false would make no odds. What beliefs she took to be certain, the inquirer would continue to take to be certain and proceed with inquiry without any doubt about these, without any anxiety or concession at all that they might be false, even if she conceded on meta-inductive grounds that some of her beliefs are bound to be false.

So far I have been making negative remarks about Descartes and some other ways of thinking of truth, which fall short of the pragmatist conception as I am presenting it. To turn to a more positive set of remarks about this pragmatist conception now, let's first just declare that our doubt-free beliefs would possess the property, *truth*. We can then, as a perfectly accurate description of the procedure of inquiry, point out that taking these beliefs for granted, inquirers look at other states of mind about which they are not certain ('hypotheses'), but which it is the point of inquiry to ascertain whether they are to be included in the set of beliefs which possess this property of truth or to discard them as not belonging there. (It may be all right to call these other states of mind 'beliefs' as well, but we would then need to be very careful to distinguish between two senses of 'belief', one of which possesses the property of truth and the other which merely takes the form of supposals and hypotheses and conjectures, the question of whose truth is inquiry's large and governing motivation to answer. Confusion, however, may best be avoided by calling them something different, simply 'hypotheses' and not 'beliefs'.)

A picture of the relations between truth and belief and inquiry along these lines would find no need to say with Davidson (and puzzlingly Rorty,[11] even though he has long declared himself a pragmatist) that truth is not a goal of inquiry because it is not something we know we have achieved in any particular case. We *do* know when we have achieved it, and where we do, we proceed to take for granted these beliefs that possess truth, and use them as a standard and guide in our inquiries about other states of mind such as hypotheses. Such a picture was well-stated by Quine and he explicitly mentions it as a picture that departs from Descartes: "Unlike Descartes, *we own and use* our beliefs of the moment... Within our own totally evolving doctrine, we can judge *truth*...."[12] (my emphasis)

If we *do* know we have achieved truth when we have, and if we *can* make it a goal of inquiry, a crucial question arises as to how we should think of its *objectivity*. Doesn't the objectivity of truth require precisely that it must be divorced altogether from our epistemic reach and become, just as Davidson says, something that is beyond us to know if we have achieved it?

It is notorious that notions such as objectivity, just as much as 'realism', are multiply understood. And so the question is, can this pragmatist position we are promoting claim for its understanding of truth, the property of 'objectivity', as it is understood in at least some senses of the term?

Here is a sense in which we certainly can. A Tarskian T-sentence (say, " 'Hanse has accepted a bribe' is true if and only if Hanse has accepted a bribe"), even for this pragmatist position, still captures something central about the notion of truth. What is that? I have said that the idea of taking beliefs (as opposed to hypotheses) for granted in inquiry is just the familiar idea of a background theory which provides the standard by which we judge truth in a particular case or by which we assess an hypothesis on the question of its truth. Quine was clear about this point too, and in the same passage as the one quoted earlier says: "It is rather when we turn back into the midst of an actually present theory... that we can and do sensibly speak of this or that sentence as true... To say that the statement 'Brutus killed Caesar:' is true or that 'The atomic weight of sodium is 23' is true, is in effect simply to say that Brutus killed Caesar, or that the atomic weight of sodium is 23. [Here Quine in a footnote explicitly cites Tarski and his T-sentences for a way of developing this point]...the truth of attributions are made from the point of view of the same surrounding body of theory."

When the surrounding body of theory or beliefs is doing its work, what does the Tarskian T-sentence of (as Quine puts it) "this or that sentence" capture? It captures the fact that something *correct* is going on, something *true* is stated by the sentence "Hanse has accepted a bribe", if Hanse has indeed accepted a bribe. The appeal to Tarski therefore is not, as it is sometimes thought, an appeal to something bland and insubstantial regarding truth. This is because, if what I have just said about them is right, it is not something bland and insubstantial that is being stated by such T-sentences. It's not as if some mere syntactic device of removing quotations is all that is effected, nor as others think, something merely of a piece with bringing to light that the predicate 'is true' has the function of summarizing the unspoken detail packed into such statements as "Whatever Plato said is true." T-sentences cannot possibly be insubstantial in this way, if the kind of *correctness* they capture, the kind of correctness involved in uttering the sentence "Hanse has accepted a bribe" when Hanse has accepted a bribe, is just the correctness that *inquiry aims for*. It thus has the full prestige and normativity of 'substantial' truth. The fact that disquotation can be understood as capturing something as substantial as the goal of inquiry is proof that there is nothing insubstantial in this way of characterizing truth.

Now, it must be admitted of course that if the ideal of the objectivity of truth is one in which the correctness involved goes *beyond* the kind of correctness which I have just identified as being captured in T-sentences, then Davidson will be justified in sticking with his own picture of the relation between truth, belief, and inquiry, i.e., that inquiry does not have the truth of beliefs as a goal. What would that more demanding correctness be? Presumably it would be something like this: the normative (normative, because of the word 'correct' used above in characterizing the role of T-sentences) relatedness of our beliefs to things in the world would have to be a relatedness of our beliefs to things, *not* as they figure in our world view, but quite *independent* of our world view. Such an independence of the things to which our beliefs are related in this correctness relation would explain why (for Descartes, Davidson and many others) we do *not* have any grip on when we have attained truth in any particular case.

I am assuming instead with Quine (Quine explicitly says this in the first quotation from him above) and others (such as McDowell, from one of whose fine essays[13] I have taken the phrase "normative relatedness of our beliefs to things as they figure in our world view") that this sort of independence is exactly what is being rejected by the idea that we *use* our own beliefs as a standard in inquiry. To say we use them in this way is just to say that they constitute the world view within which specific beliefs (or hypotheses) are judged (or assessed) for truth. It is quite crucial to understand that Quine in his talk of such *use* of our beliefs and McDowell in his talk of truth as a normative relatedness of our beliefs (or sentences) to things *as they figure in our world view* are making the same point in their different ways. Here is the relation between their two ways of making the point. It is because we think of *our beliefs* as providing the standard of *truth* in inquiry, that the sentence we employ on the right hand side of a T-sentence refers to things as they figure *in our world view*, and not independent of our world view.

What sort of *independence* remains, once we *reject* the idea that truth is a normative relatedness of our beliefs to things *independent* of our world view? This is a question that Davidson and many others caught up in a realism still moored to elements in Descartes, are bound to ask us. How can there be any independence, they will ask, if the standard of correctness comes from our beliefs themselves? (This question is a cousin of a host of complaints usually sounded against pragmatist epistemologies—and also in a slightly different form against Moorean, Austinian, Wittgensteinian epistemologies—complaints such as "In stressing inquiry, this pragmatism has stressed the inquirer's point of view, but how can *truth* be characterized from a point of view? It is the point of truth that it is independent of points of view" and "Isn't what is being offered by pragmatists just a theory of *belief*, or at most belief justified by inquiry?" It cannot therefore be a characterization of the notion of *truth* or of the doctrine of *realism*, notions and doctrines which must go beyond belief, however justified belief may be by inquiry.)

In answering the original question about independence we will have said something relevant to all these related complaints. The answer to the question about independence is this. The standard of correctness provided by our beliefs in inquiry is such that we know that, were we to suppose that we judge something true which is not dictated by these standards, we would be wrong to do so. If an inquirer believes that Hanse has accepted a bribe, if this particular belief meets the standards of correctness that are dictated by the background beliefs in use in inquiry, then the inquirer will say that *were* he to believe otherwise he would believe something false. The correctness involved here thus does meet *a* requirement of independence from belief (though not all requirements obviously, in particular not ones motivated by the Cartesian picture we are opposing) because it makes clear that the truth of this belief would not be threatened at all, if he believed its opposite. That (opposite) belief would be false. Inquiry's standards of correctness make that independence-conferring outcome perfectly available.

When I wrote some of these things in a recent essay,[14] Rorty responded by saying that I am trying to *define* truth in terms of beliefs that we as inquirers hold to be certain, and recoiled from the thought not only because he thinks it is the wrong definition, but because it is wrong to think that one can define truth. But I nowhere claimed then, nor do I now claim, that I am defining truth. I could not possibly have been defining truth in terms of belief in saying the sorts of pragmatist things I said, since presumably if truth was *defined* in terms of one's beliefs, then something like the Euthyphro scenario would hold. Our beliefs would not be tracking the truth, but rather they would be determining what is true. But no such idea of non-tracking or non-independence follows from what I said. 'Truth is what inquirers believe', if it is intended as a *definitional* slogan, would imply that inquirers believe *all the truths there are*. That absurd and extreme conclusion is indeed anti-realist, and it is what follows from taking truth to be *defined* in terms of belief. But not only is the pragmatist happy to grant that inquirers are massively ignorant of any number of the indefinite number of truths there are, he insists on it. So if this absurd and extreme conclusion does not follow from what I did say, (viz., roughly that what inquirers believe—as opposed to hypothesize—is true and known to be true by them, and it sets the standard by which their inquiries are carried out, and specific truths are then judged) then that is proof that I was not defining truth at all. I, along with Quine and McDowell, for the reasons I am giving, rather than define truth, are merely characterizing it in terms of a kind of normative relatedness of our beliefs to things as they figure 'in our world view'. In doing so, we are all characterizing a substantial notion of truth, a normative notion, a goal of inquiry, and not merely a 'minimalist' notion with no substantialist aspirations. Moreover, as I've been saying, that the normative relatedness is to things as they figure '*in our world view*' does not undermine the idea of the objectivity of truth, the idea of the independence of truth from belief. However it is independence only in the sense carried by disavowing the absurd anti-realist conclusion that we have just seen to be implied by the claim that doubt-free beliefs (or a 'world-view') *define* truth. And it is also independence in the somewhat stronger sense mentioned in the previous paragraph. That such notions of independence should not be even stronger, i.e., that truth should *not* be characterized as a kind of normative relatedness to things that are *independent of our world view*, may of course disappoint those who are still barking around the Cartesian kennel even after having come out of it, as Davidson and Rorty are with their ideal of the objectivity of truth. But an epistemology in which truth remains a goal of inquiry and continues to provide a norm and a goal which we know to be fulfilled when it is fulfilled, is a gain that should more than compensate for a disappointment along those lines.

The weaker independence just expounded which pragmatism provides still makes clear that no idealism is entailed by these pragmatist ideas, ideas which are present too in figures such as Moore, Austin and Wittgenstein.

I said something about Moore earlier, and promised to say more about Austin and Wittgenstein. Let me conclude this section by saying something about these antecedents and allies, before returning in the next section to conclude with some remarks again about the initial theme of the relation between realism and relativism.

Austin, like Moore, presents his opposition to the realism we are rejecting by criticizing the notion of knowledge that its implied variety of scepticism in Descartes promotes. He says: "The expression 'When you know, you can't be wrong' is perfectly good sense. You are prohibited from saying 'I know it is so, but I may be wrong'...." This conveys in terms of the concept of knowledge, rather than truth, the shortcomings of the epistemology which has it that we never know when one of our beliefs is true.[15] Austin also says a little later "Being aware that you may be mistaken doesn't mean merely being aware that you are a fallible human being; it means that you may be mistaken in this case."[16] We have been making this point by saying that being aware that one is fallible in general but not being aware of (having any evidence of) any actual fault in any particular case makes no difference to inquiry, and therefore is of no interest to practice, in the only sense of practice that is relevant to epistemology.

Wittgenstein is a trickier case. He too thinks that there are some beliefs which we take for granted in inquiry, and whose truth is something quite secure, and we do not ever think that we may be wrong in believing them or that they may be false. He calls these 'hinge' propositions For instance, he says "...the questions that we raise and our doubts depend on the fact that some propositions are exempt from doubt, are as it were, like hinges on which those turn. That is to say that it is the logic of our scientific investigations that certain things are indeed not doubted." (pp. 341–343). This is the point we have been making, when we said that there are broadly speaking, two relevant kinds of cognitive states of mind, beliefs and hypotheses, and scientific investigation targets the latter and in doing so takes for granted the former in the background as providing the standard by which the investigation is carried out. Without beliefs, we would not know how to assess the deliverances of such investigation. And what provides the standard (our beliefs) is something we 'own and use' and is not something we can doubt or think *might* be false (in any interesting epistemological sense, as opposed to a logical sense). So the notion of 'hinge' propositions (what in this paper I am simply calling 'beliefs', as opposed to hypotheses) is very much present in the picture of epistemology presented as an alternative in this section to the residual Cartesian epistemology presented in Section II.

Wittgenstein, however, goes on to spoil the good point I have cited above by adding that hinge propositions are never questionable or revisable, that they involve some notion of necessity, at least of a conventional kind, if not some other. That further thought is not a pragmatist thought. Just because a hinge proposition cannot be doubted on the basis of *general* philosophical grounds of the sort found in the early Cartesian Meditations, just because the logical possibility of their being false does not translate into an epistemically interesting possibility, in no way suggests that they cannot be revised if *particular* evidence against any particular one of them comes in. They are not abiding and necessary truths just because they are used as a standard during inquiry. So though I am taking Wittgenstein to be an antecedent of this pragmatism in having seen the importance of not doubting what we use in inquiry, while we are using it, his conception of the propositions or beliefs we do not doubt is not the same as the one being presented here because for him they are not revisable at all on the basis of evidence, not the *sort of things* which can be revised on the basis of evidence. Thus hinges for him are not empirical beliefs at all, not beliefs such as "Here is a hand", "the earth is round", etc. They are much more general, and apparently in some sense or other, necessary truths, such as 'there is a material world'.[17] On the picture presented here, the hinges of inquiry are all of the ordinary and scientific empirical beliefs (such as the two mentioned above) which we do not doubt and take for granted in the ordinary circumstances in which we find ourselves. But these latter are certainly revisable under extraordinary circumstances, if specific evidence comes in against their credibility for the inquirer.

The revisability of the 'hinges' of inquiry, therefore, is central to a pragmatist epistemology which rejects the residual Cartesian realism we are considering. And so a few questions about revisability arise which must be considered now. Since some of these questions relate importantly to the topic of relativism, which is one half of the subject of this paper, I will conclude now by a brief discussion of relativism and realism again.

IV

I have said two things that are perfectly compatible. First, that an inquirer's beliefs are true and are fully known by her to be true and are used by her as standards relevant in her inquiry regarding hypotheses. Second that an inquirer's beliefs are revisable by her. As Quine says in the same passage cited earlier, "Within our own evolving doctrine, we can judge truth...*subject to correction*, but that goes without saying." (my emphasis)

The possibility of correction does not spoil the idea that it is *truth* we are possessed of earlier, before the revision. Austin too say this explicitly in the same essay cited earlier.[18] But somebody may question this, arguing that something like relativism follows from the pragmatism I am espousing. And in fact Quine's remark is explicitly made by him in the context of the worry that, if we say that we do possess the truth in our body of beliefs, and know ourselves to do so, and *use* those beliefs in the ways I have been stressing, then someone may think that this must inevitably leads to relativism. He asks "Have we now so lowered our sights as to settle for a relativistic doctrine of truth, rating the statements of each theory as true for that theory and brooking no higher criticism?" And he replies with some of the words I have cited before, "Not so. The saving consideration is that we continue to take seriously our own particular...theory...Unlike Descartes, we own and use our beliefs of the moment... Within our own totally evolving doctrine, we can judge truth...subject to correction, but that goes without saying."

But we are moving too quickly here, and a serious difficulty posed by revision for the pragmatism we are espousing must be addressed before Quine's reply can stick.

What is it exactly that is happening when one revises a doctrine (or some part of a doctrine) that is said to be possessed of (and known to be possessed of) the property of truth? We are, of course, judging p at one time, and not-p at a later time. And, it is also, of course, from the point of view of the doctrine at one time that p is judged true, and from the point of view of the revised doctrine at a later time, that not-p is judged true. But, given the pragmatism sketched in the last section, shouldn't this amount to saying that the *truth* of the judgements is relative to the doctrines of the earlier and later time respectively, i.e., just what relativism says? In other words, since, for the pragmatism sketched, it was so urgent to say that inquirers' beliefs actually *possess* the property of truth, and are not merely thought to do so by the inquirers, is there not a threat that it will fall into saying that both p and not-p are *true*? And is not the intolerability of saying that only removed by making pragmatism pass over into relativism? The whole point of relativism is to be unperturbed by the disagreement over *truth* between two believers, relativizing the truth of the disagreed upon belief to each of their points of view. It allows that each is right (not merely thinks himself right). But each is only right relative to their doctrine.

The problem before us is that the pragmatist position being espoused here seems to imply that two people or (taking the case of revision) one person at different times, who hold contradictory beliefs, both have truth on their side. If an inquirer's beliefs held with certainty (unlike his hypotheses) are not epistemically segregated from truths, then it would seem that something like this *is* implied. But that (like any contradiction) is intolerable, and can only be made tolerable if the truth of the relevant belief of each inquirer is relative to his current doctrine. (It should be obvious that it is intolerable not in the sense that there is irrationality of any kind when *two* people make contradictory claims. So it's not really from the point of view of the notion of *rationality* that one is driven to find it intolerable, but rather from the point of view of the notion of truth. *Truth*, because it is the world which cannot be such that both are right.)

Notice what is happening here. Everyone, both the pragmatist and his opponents, may well agree that truth is *judged* relative to the current doctrine.

But his opponents are saying that when the pragmatist of Section III above claimed that there was to be no epistemological segregation of confident judgement (belief) from truth, he was saying much more than this innocuous thing which all may agree upon. He was saying not merely that truth is *judged* relative to the current doctrine, but that *truth* is relative to the current doctrine. It is this last which is (the despised) relativism. In being committed to the idea that we never know when any belief of ours is true, this opponent of pragmatism has no such relativist worries pressing on his position, since he thinks that confident judgement does not amount to truth itself, and so he can without any such worries grant that we *judge* truth relative to our current doctrine, without granting that *truth* is relative to it.

Is there really a worry here for the pragmatist which his opponent avoids? Quine denies that there is any such worry in the quoted passage, claiming that, even for the pragmatist, revision is perfectly compatible with the idea that truth is not relative at all. On what grounds can he claim this? He does not mention any grounds, and seems to think it obvious—as he says in the quotation above, "it goes without saying". But he was perhaps wrong to make it seem so obvious, as if no philosophy or argument was necessary to show it. To show it, it will be necessary to return to some of the points made in Section I.

What has to be shown to stave off relativism is that in those cases when two inquirers contradict one another on some matter (or when a verdict at a later inquiry-stage contradicts the verdict of an earlier inquiry-stage), *it is every bit as bad* and intolerable as when the same inquirer contradicts himself at a one and the same stage of his inquiry. Every bit as bad, in the sense that in those cases too we want to say that only one of the contradictory beliefs is true. But how may *a pragmatist* give herself the right to say this? Her opponent can easily give himself the right by saying that since belief (or confident judgement of truth) and truth are *epistemologically segregated*, only one of these two contradictory verdicts is right, even though these inquirers or inquirer-stages, *do not know which*. Its just this way of thinking about truth, a way of thinking that is happy with the idea of 'do not know which', that pragmatism has been complaining about in the last section, in the critique of residual Cartesian realism. It does not seem so easy for her therefore to give herself the same right. If she insists that contradiction is just as bad in these cases as it is in the single inquirer at a single stage of inquiry, she would seem to be abandoning the pragmatist *denial* of such a segregation which had been argued for in section III.

Let's deal with this problem in two stages. First, notice that the pragmatist is certainly not abandoning the denial of the segregation we argued for in Section III if she says that it is intolerable that the *same* inquirer at the *same stage* of inquiry contradicts himself. Even the opponent of pragmatism will grant that nothing pragmatist is being abandoned when the pragmatist says that. What this opponent is insisting, however, is that the case of two inquirers and the case of revision, i.e., of two inquiry-stages, are not like the case of the same inquirer at the same stage of inquiry. In these cases, the opponent of pragmatism will insist that the pragmatist is not in a position to say that contradiction is intolerable without abandoning the pragmatism. And the opponent will claim that the only way the pragmatist can get out of this is by saying that the truth of each contradictory belief or judgement is relative to a different doctrine, so they are not in the end contradictory. Pragmatism thus implies relativism, the opponent will say. So the pragmatist has to find an argument to show that these cases are in fact, in all important and relevant respects, just like the case of the single inquirer at a single stage of inquiry.

And so we move to the second stage, and this paper's punch-line. That these other cases are just like the single inquirer at a single stage of inquiry is indeed the *entire point* of Davidson's argument against the very idea of a conceptual scheme which was presented in Section I. I will not rehearse the argument here which was presented there in detail, but merely recall that the argument's conclusion was that the very idea of a conceptual scheme does not make any sense at all. So there is *nothing* to which truth can be relativized. It is the precise force of this argument therefore that two people contradicting one another, or two inquiry-stages contradicting one another, is *quite as bad* (from the point of view of truth, that is, and not rationality) as one inquirer contradicting himself at the same stage of inquiry. The argument has this force because it has shown that two inquirers or two inquirer-stages and their body of beliefs *cannot be elevated to two 'conceptual schemes'*, where conceptual schemes are just the sorts of things that lack a coordinate system underlying them. If the argument presented at length in Section I showed that there is always such an underlying coordinate system, then there are no conceptual schemes to which truth can be relativized. And the pragmatist, *appealing also to just this argument*, may insist that his position does not entail that he must deny the intolerability (from the point of view of truth) of two inquirers or two inquiry-stages contradicting each other. He can, just as much as the realist with anti-pragmatist and residual Cartesian inclinations, insist that only one of these contradictory claims is right.

The upshot is that when it is reported that two inquirers or two inquirer-stages *confidently judge* respectively that p and not-p, relative to their doctrines or background sets of beliefs, there is no scope to make this harmless report slide into the quite different and relativistic point that the *truth* of p and not-p is relative to their respective doctrines or background sets of beliefs. Such a slide is blocked, despite the fact that the pragmatist denies the segregation of confident judgement from truth, because the pragmatist has now (by Davidson's argument) been given the resources to say that only one of these two contradictory beliefs of the two inquirers or inquirer-stages is right, just as much as he has the resources to say it of two contradictory beliefs of one inquirer at a single stage of inquiry. The doctrines or sets of beliefs of these two inquirers or inquirer-stages do not and cannot amount to two conceptual schemes. There is nothing therefore to which the truth of p and not-p can be relativized. One *could* express the thought we have arrived at by saying that the pragmatist has been given the resources to say that only one of them is right because since there are no 'different' conceptual schemes, they are both part of a single conceptual scheme, just as much as the single inquirer at one and the same stage of inquiry is part of a single conceptual scheme. All inquirers, all inquirer-stages, are part of a single conceptual scheme. Therefore, contradiction within one inquirer, contradictory judgements by two inquirers, contradictory judgements issuing out of revision made by an inquirer from one stage of his inquiry to the next, are all just as intolerable from the point of view of truth. But Davidson's preferred way to say it is to say something slightly different. He does not say that there is always only one conceptual scheme. He instead says: if there are no *different* conceptual schemes, there are *no* conceptual schemes. The very idea of a conceptual scheme is mistaken. However one says it, the outcome is the same anti-relativist one.

The idea that one should always insist that one of two contradictory beliefs is right is of course a *realist* idea that we have arrived at by appending Davidson's anti-*relativist* argument to pragmatism. But it's a realist idea which, unlike the classical realist idea and the residual Cartesian realist idea, allows us to embrace a more intuitively satisfying epistemology, an epistemology in which one need never deny that we seek truth in inquiry, nor deny that we achieve it from time to time, nor go around with a pervasive diffidence (diffidence, in the sense captured in "we never know when any given belief of ours is true") about the beliefs (as opposed to hypotheses) one has. In other words, a realism by which each of two disagreed inquirers can say *as realists*, "Only one of us is right," and then *as pragmatists* add from the corners of their mouth, but with no diffidence at all, "And I am."

Summing up, then, where does all this leave us on the question of realism and relativism?

It is the claim of this Section IV of the paper that if the *classical* realism of Descartes' absolute conception of reality (along with relativism, with which it shares a crucial assumption) was successfully refuted by the argument presented in Section I, then the second and residual form of Cartesian realism presented in Section II cannot claim any advantage over the far more attractive pragmatist realism (more attractive because it promotes a more credible epistemology) presented in Section III. This is because the only reason to think that it might have any advantage over the pragmatist version of realism is that the latter seemed susceptible to a kind of relativism. But since it was precisely the force of the argument of Section I that it not only refuted classical realism but also refuted at the same time the kind of relativism with which it shares a crucial assumption, that advantage is illusory. The pragmatist can appeal to that argument, as we have just done in the present section, to show that no such relativism threatens her, despite her rejection of the residual Cartesian realism of Section II.

It is a pity that Davidson does not see the force of his own argument, presented in Section I, as allowing him the space to occupy a far more plausible epistemology than the residual Cartesian one that he rests with. He is happy to rest with the thought that not all our beliefs can be false, thinking that that is enough to keep the Cartesian sceptic at bay. He therefore aggressively asserts that once we have established that not all our beliefs can be false, we must add that we never know which ones among them are true. Truth, of this kind, is still realist truth of course, if not quite that of the absolute conception of reality. In embracing it, Davidson completely neglects the fact that a quite distinct and just as crippling sceptical Cartesian position is entailed by it, a scepticism which remains unhurt by his argument presented in Section I, a scepticism which Moore, Austin, Wittgenstein, and the pragmatists are all resisting, the one which says that we are never given the right to claim that any particular belief amounts to knowledge, even if have the general right to the general claim that we have a great deal of knowledge. But he need not have gone on to assert this residual Cartesian position. If I am right in this last section, *his own argument* with its combined and integrated force against classical realism *and* relativism allows him to assert an alternative position, a pragmatism, with no concessions to Cartesian scepticism of any variety, with no concessions—despite appearances—to relativism of any sort, and moreover a position (as was shown in Section III) which may properly also call itself a 'realism' because it satisfies basic realist demands, once they are shorn off from extreme and gratuitous Cartesian notions of the sort of independence truth and reality are supposed to have from our position as inquirers.

I have singled out Davidson for the most discussion because it is particularly ironic and frustrating that someone who has provided an argument against relativism which makes no appeal to Cartesian realism of any variety in the course of giving the argument, someone who has provided therefore an argument which helps us see that in opposing relativism we do not have to embrace any realism of a sort that implies an unattractive epistemology, should then have failed to arrive at a much more satisfying realism, a realism that integrates itself with a far more attractive epistemology. But it's not just Davidson—Putnam, Rorty, and all the other philosophers who are opposed to one or other versions of Cartesian epistemology and the realisms they presuppose, should all prize such an integration that pragmatism in this form provides. Yet, as I said earlier, Putnam ties truth to unnecessarily idealized conceptions of warranted assertiblity, and Rorty has given up the idea that truth is in any sense a goal of inquiry, seeking to replace it by notions of justification and warranted assertiblity. None of those options seem necessary or attractive, once this pragmatist version of realism comes to light.

Notes

1. René Descartes, *Meditations on First Philosophy*, translated by John Cottingham, (Cambridge, England: Cambridge University Press, 1986).
2. In Donald Davidson, *Inquiries into Truth and Interpretation*, (Oxford: Oxford University Press, 1984).

3. It would seem that there is an element of analyticity presupposed in the argument, at the point where one assumes a certain sort of connection between the very notion of ghosts and the belief that people die. But some weaker connection than the despised analyticity may be just as good to work the trick (and in fact there had better be one since Davidson has himself denied any truck with analyticity.) Perhaps it is enough that for the initial belief that there are ghosts to be properly attributed, it's not so much that any specific defining belief is also required to be attributed in each and every case where that belief is attributed to an agent in interpretation. Different agents may have different concepts of what a ghost is (of what the term 'ghost' means) and so there is no canonical belief or set of beliefs defining of ghosts. To stretch this point a little further, particular agents may have different concepts of what a ghost is at different times of speaking. Thus, the concept may differ from person to person, even from occasion to occasion, and so there is no analyticity, merely highly localized and idiolectical use of words and deployment of concepts. *But still* some background of true beliefs (by the interpreters' lights) is required to be attributed to identify any given agent's belief about any particular sort of thing (such as ghosts) at any given time, and that is enough to ward off the comprehensive scepticism.

4. This argument is given in a subsequent paper entitled "The Method of Truth and Metaphysics", *Inquiries into Truth and Interpretation* (Oxford University Press, 1984).

5. See Chapter VI in Thomas Nagel, *The View from Nowhere*, (New York: Oxford University Press, 1986).

6. Ludwig Wittgenstein, *Philosophical Investigations*, (Blackwell 1953). Because the point in Davidson emerges by semantic ascent, it seems to say something higher-order than what is usually found in Wittgenstein, but the philosophical significance is the same. In Wittgenstein the point is usually expressed by saying that a particular thought or the meaning of any particular term must be such that the criterion for its attribution or use is something we can tell has been applied correctly when it has been. Because of the semantic ascent involved in Davidson's reply to the idea of a super-knower, it's not any particular thought or meaning of which this philosophical point is made but about the application of the criteria for the term 'thought' (or 'meaning') itself.

7. See Donald Davidson, "Truth Rehabilitated" in *Rorty and his Critics*, edited by Robert Brandom, (Blackwell, 2000).

8. In "Truth Rehabilitated" (see last footnote), Davidson's characterization of pragmatism comes close to this caricature. The pragmatism being sketched in the present paper by contrast is ignoring a host of what I, in the text above, have called 'reckless' remarks made by pragmatists over decades which encourage this caricature. In doing so it is really going back to the pragmatism to be found in Peirce's classic paper "The Fixation of Belief". That extraordinarily profound paper has been an inspiration for the sort of pragmatism that has come over decades to be associated with Columbia's Philosophy Department (which was—lest it's forgotten—for years John Dewey's department) thanks to the determined advocacy of Isaac Levi who has himself shaped a highly original philosophy of belief revision out of it. I am happy to see this paper of mine and others I have been writing on the subject over the years as contributing in minor ways to the propagation of what might as well be

called "Columbia Pragmatism" against a range of other less attractive epistemologies in the field. My debt to this paper by Peirce and to Levi should be apparent to those who have read them.

9. Rorty in his reply to my essay in the volume mentioned in footnote 7 suggests that I had tried to define truth in that essay. See below for more on this misreading.

10. A certain amount of holism may enter, of course, which would make one doubt a number of implied beliefs if evidence is encountered against any one. But this would still be different from the logical possibility of empirical beliefs being false, giving rise to doubts of a general and comprehensive kind regarding all such beliefs.

11. In his "Is Truth a Goal of Enquiry"? Davidson *Vs* Wright", *Philosophical Quarterly*, vol. 45, no. 180, July 1995. Rorty quite fails to see the attractions of the pragmatism being presented here, and like Davidson is happy to give up the idea (an idea that is preserved in the pragmatism being presented here) that truth is a goal of inquiry. See also his paper mentioned in footnote 9.

12. W. V. Quine, *Word and Object* (MIT Press, 1960), pp. 24–45.

13. See John McDowell's essay "Towards Rehabilitating Objectivity" in the volume mentioned in footnote 7.

14. See my contribution to the volume mentioned in footnote 7 and Rorty's reply to it.

15. There may be a temptation to drive a wedge between knowledge and truth here, allowing that Austin is right about knowledge but disallowing us our criticism of Davidson and Rorty on truth. This wedge would be based on some separation of the concept of knowledge from that of truth, a move that I think should be regarded with great suspicion, a suspicion which I will not articulate now.

16. Austin, "Other Minds," *Philosophical Papers*, (Oxford University Press, 1960) p. 98.

17. Crispin Wright, "Facts and Certainty," *British Academy Lecture*, 1985.

18. See the discussion of 'goldfinches' on p. 88–89 in the essay mentioned in footnote 16.

Philosophical Issues, 12, Realism and Relativism, 2002

UNDERDETERMINATION AND REALISM

Michael Devitt
The Graduate Center, The City University of New York

1. Introduction

The underdetermination of theories by evidence often leads to skepticism about the theories and hence to antirealism about the worlds described by the theories. At its most extreme, this skepticism is about "Commonsense Realism," about our knowledge of the observable world of stones, trees, cats, and the like. This skepticism must spread to "Scientific Realism," to our knowledge of the unobservable world of atoms, viruses, photons, and the like. But underdetermination sometimes leads to a less extreme view aimed only at Scientific Realism: against a background acceptance of realism about the observable world, realism about unobservables is rejected.

The underdetermination theses that concern us claim that a theory (belief) has rivals that stand in some sort of equivalence relation to it with respect to certain evidence. The theses vary with the equivalence relation and with the evidence. In particular, sometimes the relation is deductive and sometimes ampliative; and sometimes the evidence is the actual given evidence and sometimes it is some sort of possible evidence.

There are two dimensions to the realisms that are challenged by underdetermination. "The existence dimension" of Commonsense Realism is a commitment to the existence of most observables such as stones, trees, and cats and to these entities having, for the most part, the properties attributed to them by science and commonsense. The existence dimension of Scientific Realism is a similar commitment about such unobservables as atoms, viruses, and photons. Typically, idealists, the traditional opponent of realists, have not denied this dimension; or, at least, have not straightforwardly denied it. What they have typically denied in response to the skeptical challenge is "the independence dimension." According to some idealists, the entities identified by the first dimension are made up of mental items, "ideas" or "sense data," and so are not external to the mind. In recent times, under the influence of Kant, another sort of idealist has been much more common. According to these idealists, the entities are not, in a certain respect, "objective": they depend for their existence and nature on the cognitive activities and capacities of our minds. Realists reject all such mind dependencies. Relations between minds and those entities are limited to familiar causal interactions long noted by the folk: we throw stones, plant trees, kick cats, and so on. We could say a lot more to make these doctrines precise and I have done so elsewhere.[1] But these definitions will suffice for our purposes.

In part I, I will consider whether underdetermination has any consequence for Commonsense Realism. If it does, this must spread to Scientific Realism. In part II, I will consider whether underdetermination has any consequence for Scientific Realism alone.

I. Underdetermination and Commonsense Realism

2. Extreme Skepticism

In the *First Meditation* Descartes famously doubted the evidence of his senses. We can see this as an argument about underdetermination. Descartes believes that he is sitting by the fire. But perhaps he is suffering from an illusion, perhaps he is dreaming, perhaps he is being stimulated by an evil demon. There seem to be a range of alternative hypotheses to Descartes' belief, each equally compatible with the evidence available to him: his belief is underdetermined by the sensory evidence.

This is the first step in the argument of the extreme skeptic. We do not need to imagine evil demons and the like to find support for this underdetermination: it is supported by our psychological and neurophysiological theories of perception. Consider this example: I look in front of me and come to believe that there is a cat there. Our scientific explanation of this is roughly: the cat reflects light waves which provide stimulus to my retina causing sensory neurons to fire leading to my belief. But that scientific account also tells us that the cat is not necessary for the belief, for a multitude of reasons. The cat is not necessary for the light waves that strike the retina: the waves might have other causes. The light waves are not necessary for the stimulus: there are other ways of providing that stimulus. Similarly the stimulus is not necessary for the neuron firings and those firings are not necessary for the belief. So the belief has a range of rivals that are compatible with the sensory evidence.

Let us call beliefs like Descartes' and mine—beliefs about the external environment caused by perception—"observational beliefs." We seem to have established the following basic underdetermination thesis:

DG1: Any observational belief has rivals that are equally compatible with the actual given sensory evidence for that belief.

The 'G' in this name indicates that the thesis concerns *the actual given* evidence. In part II we will be concerned with underdetermination theses that concern *possible* evidence, theses named with a 'P'. I shall explain the 'D' in the name in a moment.

DG1 needs some clarification. What exactly is "the sensory evidence"? We might take it to be the perceptual experiences themselves, but then it is not clear what it is for an observational belief to be "compatible with" the evidence. If we suppose that perceptual experiences produced beliefs about ideas or sense data then we could take beliefs about about them to be the sensory evidence; for example, the belief that the sense datum I am now perceiving is cat-like. But the supposition is controversial at best. We can be more ontologically cautious, taking the sensory evidence to be beliefs, prompted by perceptual experience, about how things appear (with no commitment to mental entities); for example, the belief that it appears to me that there is a cat in front of me. Then we can take DG1 to be claiming that this belief is logically consistent not only with the belief that there is a cat in front of me but with many other beliefs. That is surely true.

We move to the second step in the extreme skeptic's argument. Given DG1, how could an observational belief be justified? What basis is there for eliminating rivals that are equally compatible with the evidence? The skeptic's position is that there is no basis. She infers the troubling epistemological thesis:

AG1: Any observational belief has rivals that are equally supported by the actual given sensory evidence for that belief.[2]

DG1 is concerned with the *deductive* relation of *logical compatibility* between the sensory evidence and observational beliefs; hence the 'D' in its name. AG1 is a much stronger underdetermination thesis because it is concerned with the *ampliative* relation of *epistemic support* between the sensory evidence and observational beliefs; hence the 'A' in its name.[3] If AG1 is correct, even ampliative inferences like induction and abduction (inference to the best explanation) do not provide a basis for preferring any observational belief over many alternative hypotheses. Indeed, the skeptic is dubious of all such inferences. Our observational beliefs about stones, trees, cats and the like are all unjustified. Commonsense Realism must be abandoned.

Suppose that we found some way to reject AG1 and justify our observational beliefs. We still have a way to go to escape extreme skepticism. We want to move from observational beliefs to singular beliefs about unobserved objects and to general beliefs that cover such objects; to take a boring but familiar example, we want to move from the evidence of many ravens all observed to be black to the belief that Oscar, an unobserved raven, is black, indeed to the "theory" that all ravens are black. The skeptical tradition once again presents us with an underdetermination problem:

DG2a: Any theory has rivals equally compatible with the actual given observational evidence for that theory.

This seems to be indubitably so. Thus our evidence of many sightings of ravens is compatible not only with the theory that all ravens are black but also with the theory that all ravens are black except the ones on island X which has never been investigated. Another related underdetermination thesis also causes trouble:

DG2b: Any theory has rivals that entail the same actual given observational evidence.

Thus the theories that all ravens are black and that they are all black except on X both entail our evidence of raven sightings.

These deductive underdetermination theses are the first step in the extreme skeptic's argument. She then, once again, infers an ampliative thesis. Given these deductive theses, how could a theory be justified? She arrives at another troubling epistemological thesis:

AG2: Any theory has rivals that are equally supported by the actual given observational evidence for that theory.

According to this ampliative underdetermination thesis, a theory enjoys no epistemic support over some of its rivals.[4] Our general beliefs about stones, trees, cats and the like are unjustified. Again Realism must be abandoned.

We note that the pattern of the skeptic's argument is:

Deductive underdetermination → ampliative underdetermination → antirealism.

Now, it might well be objected that my discussion does not do skepticism justice for it takes skepticism to be *committed* to AG1 and AG2. The cautious skeptic would avoid this commitment, like almost all others, simply putting the onus on the nonskeptic to undermine AG1 and AG2. I think this is a good objection but, in the end (section 8), we shall see that it makes no difference whether the skeptic is committed or not. Meanwhile, for convenience, I shall take the skeptic to be committed.

3. "First Philosophy" Responses

We could accept the inferences to AG1 and AG2 and give up on our knowledge of the world: we do not know what there is and what it is like. This abandons the existence dimension of Realism and is very unappealing. The traditional responses of "First Philosophy," were different.

One response started by seeking a more basic area of knowledge than (what I have called) our observational beliefs, an area that was not open to skeptical doubt and that could serve as a foundation for all or most claims to knowledge.

This foundation was found in the sensory evidence for our observational beliefs: we were thought to have indubitable knowledge of our own ideas (sense data); this knowledge was not underdetermined. Even if we go along with this highly dubious claim, we still have to get from this foundation to knowledge of the world of stones, trees, cats, and the like, thus rejecting AG1 and AG2. In attempting to solve this problem, foundationalists nearly always gave up the view that the world is external to the mind, thus abandoning the independence dimension of Realism. It was thought that only by constituting the world somehow out of ideas could we hope to save our knowledge of it. Realism leaves a "gap" between our ideas and the world that makes knowledge of the world impossible. Idealism closes the gap by bringing the world into the mind.

Another traditional response, currently much more popular, is also idealist. It seeks to reject AG1 and AG2 by taking the world to be partly constituted by the mind's imposition of concepts, theories, or languages. We can know about that world because we partly create it. Realism's independence dimension is abandoned once again.[5]

So the price of saving our knowledge in the face of underdetermination and skepticism was typically an idealist metaphysics of one sort or another. Even if we were prepared to pay the price of such a bizarre metaphysics, these responses would not be very convincing. Although First Philosophy aims to take skepticism seriously and hence meet the very demanding skeptical standards for rational belief, it often seems to fall short of those standards: it assumes what no self-respecting skeptic should allow (for example, indubitable knowledge of ideas). So even with an idealist metaphysics we still seem not to have the knowledge we want. I have argued for this, and against idealism, elsewhere (1991, 1997a, 1999, 2001a).

We are faced with a choice between skepticism and idealism. Surely something has gone seriously wrong. It is time to think again. I shall first make a Moorean response to the skeptical challenge, then a naturalistic one.

4. A Moorean Response

The disaster has come from the epistemological theses AG1 and AG2 which make Commonsense Realism untenable: we are supposed to doubt our commonsense beliefs in an external world. But why should we accept these skeptical theses? How much confidence should we have in a view that undermines Realism? Realism is a compelling doctrine almost universally held outside intellectual circles. From an early age we come to believe that such objects as stones, cats, and trees exist. Furthermore, we believe that these objects exist even when we are not perceiving them, and that they do not depend for their existence on our opinions nor on anything mental. This Realism about ordinary objects is confirmed day by day in our experience. It is central to our whole way of viewing the world, the very core of common sense. A Moorean point is appropriate: Realism is much more firmly based than the epistemological theses AG1 and AG2 that are thought to undermine it. We have started the argument in the wrong place: rather than using AG1 and AG2 as evidence against Realism, we should use Realism as evidence against AG1 and AG2. We should, as I like to say, "put metaphysics first."

Descartes puts us in an armchair and asks us to start by clearing our minds of all knowledge and doing some epistemology. The Moorean puts us in an armchair and asks us to start by assessing the evidence for Realism. In so doing we must resolutely decline to *theorize about* standards of good and bad evidence, for that epistemological path was what led to the disaster: we simply apply our ordinary evidential standards, just as we presumably did in childhood when we became Realists in the first place. Once we have done that, we turn to the epistemological theses AG1 and AG2. In assessing them we have little to go on but the skeptical argument that puts these theses at odds with Realism. We ask: Is it more likely that the theses are mistaken than that Realism is? Is it more likely that there is a flaw in the skeptical argument than that, contrary to what we have always supposed, we lack knowledge of the external world? The Moorean answers these questions with a resounding "Yes."

5. A Naturalistic Response

What else do we have to go on in assessing AG1 and AG2? DG1 does not *entail* AG1, nor do DG2a and DG2b *entail* AG2. Where can we look for more evidence? Not, First Philosophy assumes, to empirical science, for science itself is doubted by the extreme Cartesian skeptic. So the evidence must be of some nonempirical sort. Thus the various idealist positions that rejected the theses were thought to be, like mathematics and logic, known a priori. The a priori approach is the very essence of First Philosophy and its response to underdetermination. Reflecting from the comfort of armchairs First Philosophers decide what knowledge *must* be like, and from this infer what the world *must* be like. If the world were the way the Realist says it is, we could not know about it. Yet, it is typically thought, we surely do know about it. So the Realist cannot be right.

The Moorean response alone casts doubt on any such arguments. Given the strength of Realism, it is simply not plausible that we could know something a priori that undermined it, whether that something is the skeptic's AG1 and AG2 or the idealist's response to them. But the Moorean response is not, of course, sufficient. We need to do better and we can. Manifestly we could not have a priori knowledge damaging to Realism if we could not have a priori knowledge at all. According to Quinean naturalism, we could not: *there is no a priori knowledge.* There is only one way of knowing, the empirical way that is the basis of science (whatever that way may be); in Quine's vivid metaphor, the web of belief is seamless.[6] So we could not know AG1 and AG2 a priori because we could not know anything a priori.

Drawing on earlier works (1996, 1997b, 1998), I shall now present two arguments for this naturalism: first, we no longer have a strong motivation for thinking that there is any a priori knowledge; second, the idea of such knowledge is deeply obscure.

6. Lack of Motivation for the A Priori

It is overwhelmingly plausible that *some* knowledge is empirical, justified by experience. The radical, yet attractive, naturalistic thesis is that *all* knowledge is; there is only one way of knowing. This thesis faced an embarrassing problem that dogged empiricism: some truths—most notably those of mathematics and logic—did not seem open to empirical confirmation or disconfirmation, but rather to be known by armchair reflection.[7] It did not seem *possible* that such truths could be revised in the way that 'All swans are white' was by the sighting of black swans in Australia. Quine, following in the footsteps of Duhem, argued that we must break free of the naive picture of justification suggested by the swan example and view justification in a much more holistic way: beliefs, even whole theories, do not face the tribunal of experience alone, but in company of auxiliary theories, background assumptions, and the like. Much evidence for this "Duhem-Quine thesis" has been produced by the movement in philosophy of science inspired by Thomas Kuhn and Paul Feyerabend. In light of this, we have no reason to believe that whereas scientific laws, which are uncontroversially empirical, are confirmed in the holistic empirical way, the laws of logic and mathematics are not; no reason to believe that there is a principled basis for drawing a line between what can be known this way and what cannot; no reason to believe that there is a seam in the web of belief.

Quine is fond of an image taken from Otto Neurath. He likens our web of belief to a boat that we continually rebuild whilst staying afloat on it. We can rebuild any part of the boat but in so doing we must take a stand on the rest of the boat for the time being. So we cannot rebuild it all at once. Similarly, we can revise any part of our knowledge but in so doing we must accept the rest for the time being. So we cannot revise it all at once. And just as we should start rebuilding the boat by standing on the firmest parts, so also should we start rebuilding our web. So we normally take the propositions of logic and mathematics for granted in rebuilding our web. Still each of these propositions is in principle revisable in the face of experience: taking a stand on other such propositions, and much else besides, we might contemplate dropping the proposition.

In suggesting that mathematics is in this holistic way empirical, I do not mean to suggest that the epistemological problem of mathematics is even close to solution. How *could* it be since the *ontological* problem of mathematics— what mathematics is *about*—remains so intractable? The point is rather that we no longer have any reason to think that, if we solved the ontological problem, the epistemological problem would not be open to an empirical solution. The motivation to seek an a priori way of knowing is removed. This is so even though we do not have the rich details of the empirical way of knowing that we would like to have. For, what we do have is an intuitively clear and appealing general idea. It starts from the metaphysical assumption that it is the worldly fact that *p* that makes the belief that *p* true. The empiricist idea then is that experiences of the sort produced by that fact are essentially involved in the justification of the belief.

In a critique of my naturalism, Georges Rey has a lot of rhetorical fun mocking the remarks that Quine and I make about the empirical way of knowing and about the application of this way to logic and mathematics. He thinks that I am under "the illusion" that these remarks amount to "a serious theory" (1997: 146). I am not. I agree with Rey that "*no one yet has an adequate theory of our knowledge of much of anything*" (1998: 29). In any case, Rey's mockery is largely beside the point. Since we do not have a serious theory that covers even the easiest examples of empirical knowledge, the fact that we do not have one that covers the really difficult examples from logic and mathematics hardly reflects on the claim that these are empirical knowledge too. We all agree that there *is* an empirical way of knowing. Beyond that, the present argument against the a priori needs only the claim that the empirical way is holistic. *We have no reason to believe that a serious theory would show that, whereas empirical scientific laws are confirmed in the holistic empirical way, the laws of logic and mathematics are not.*

7. The Obscurity of the A Priori

The argument that a priori knowledge is unmotivated casts doubt on it but does not alone establish that there is none. We need also the second argument about the obscurity of a priori knowledge. This argument attempts to show that the a priori alternative to an empirical explanation of our knowledge of logic and mathematics, indeed of anything, is very unpromising. If this is right, we have a nice abduction: the *best* explanation of that knowledge is that it is empirical.

We are presented with a range of examples of what is claimed to be a priori knowledge. But what are we to make of this claim? What is the nature of a priori knowledge? We have the characterization: it is knowledge "*not* derived from experience" and so *not* justified in the above empirical way. Doubtless we can expand this negative characterization in a satisfactory way.[8] But what we need if we are to take the a priori way seriously is a *positive* characterization, not just a negative one. We need to describe a process for justifying a belief that does not give experience the role indicated above and that we have some reason for thinking is actual. We need some idea of what a priori knowledge *is* not just what it *isn't*.

Why? This question may seem particularly pressing since I have just agreed that we do not have a serious theory of the empirical way. However, there are two crucial differences in the epistemic status of the two ways. First, the existence of the empirical way is not in question: everyone believes in it.[9] In contrast, the existence of the a priori way is very much in question. Second, even though we do not have a serious theory of the empirical way, we do have an intuitively clear and appealing general idea of this way, of "learning from experience" (briefly described above). In contrast, we do not have the beginnings of an idea of what the a priori way might be; we lack not just a serious theory but *any idea at all*.

The difficulty in giving a positive characterization of a priori knowledge is well-demonstrated by the failure of traditional attempts based on analyticity. Let the example of allegedly a priori knowledge be our belief that all bachelors are unmarried. Before considering the process of justifying this belief, we need some metaphysical information: What fact makes the belief true? According to the tradition, the fact was one about the relation between the "concepts" making up the belief: the concept ⟨bachelor⟩ "includes" the concept ⟨unmarried⟩, thus making the belief analytic. This seemed promising for an account of a priori knowledge because it was thought that simply in virtue of *having* a concept, a person was in possession of a "tacit theory" *about* the concept; in virtue of having ⟨bachelor⟩, a person tacitly knows that ⟨bachelor⟩ includes ⟨unmarried⟩. So a person's conceptual competence gave her privileged "Cartesian" access to facts about the relations between concepts. The required nonempirical process of justification was thought to be one that exploited this access, a reflective process of inspecting the concepts to yield knowledge of the relations between them which in turn yielded such knowledge as that all bachelors are unmarried. This alleged process is that of "conceptual analysis."

I think that this story is better told speaking of meanings (or contents) rather than concepts. According to the "Representational Theory of the Mind" ("RTM") the belief that all bachelors are unmarried involves a mental representation—a token in the head—that means **ALL BACHELORS ARE UNMARRIED**.[10] One part of this representation, 'bachelor', means **BACHELOR** and another part, 'unmarried', means **UNMARRIED**. The story is that simply in virtue of being competent with the various representations—for example, being competent with 'bachelor'—a person has access by conceptual analysis to the fact:

1. 'Bachelor' means **ADULT UNMARRIED MALE** and so means the same as 'adult unmarried male'.

Hence she can reason along the following lines:

2. 'All bachelors are unmarried' means the same as 'All adult unmarried males are unmarried'.
3. 'All adult unmarried males are unmarried' is true.
4. So, 'All bachelors are unmarried' is true.

5. So, all bachelors are unmarried.

In some such way conceptual analysis was thought to yield a priori knowledge of the world.

But, even if we grant the Cartesian access to meanings that yields 1, this account fails as an account of our allegedly a priori knowledge of 5. For our knowledge of 5 depends also on our knowledge of 3. Where did the justification of 3 come from? It does no good to say, rightly, that 'All adult unmarried males are unmarried' is a logical truth (of the form 'All *FGH* are *G*'). For, what justifies logical truths? Logical truths were, of course, one of the main things that we were supposed to know a priori. Yet no satisfactory nonempirical account was ever given of how we could justify logical truths (nor, as a matter of interest, of how we could justify logical inferences like those involved in the above argument). Without such an account we have not described a nonempirical way of knowing.

In any case, we should not grant the Cartesian view that competence gives privileged access to meanings, despite its great popularity. There is a much more modest view of competence according to which it is an *ability or skill* that need not involve any tacit theory, any semantic propositional knowledge; it is knowledge-how not knowledge-that (1996). Why then should we believe the immodest Cartesian view, particularly since it is almost entirely unargued?

The meaning of a person's token is presumably constituted by relational properties of some sort: "internal" ones involving inferential relations among tokens and "external" ones involving certain direct causal relations to the world. Take one of those relations. Why suppose that, simply in virtue of the fact that her token has that relation, reflection must lead her to *believe that* it does? Even if reflection does, why suppose that, simply in virtue of the fact that the relation partly constitutes the meaning of her token, reflection must lead her to *believe that* it does? Most important of all, even if reflection did lead to these beliefs, why suppose that, simply in virtue of her competence, this process of belief formation *justifies* the beliefs, or gives them any special epistemic authority, and thus turns them into *knowledge*? Suppositions of this sort seem to be gratuitous. We need a plausible explanation of these allegedly nonempirical processes of belief formation and justification and some reasons for believing in them.

In his "Rationalist Manifesto" Laurence BonJour also rejects traditional attempts to explain apriority in terms of analyticity, finding them "entirely bankrupt" (1992: 69). For him, "a priori justification occurs when the mind directly or intuitively discerns or grasps or apprehends a necessary fact about the nature or structure of reality" (p. 56). He accepts that "the task of giving a really perspicuous account of such justification has hardly been begun" (p. 88). Quite so. And it seems to me that his later book (1998), despite its many subtleties, does not throw any significant light on where in his quasi-perceptual process of apprehending a necessary fact the justification is to be found.[11]

At this point, it remains a mystery what it would be for something to be known a priori. Any attempt to remove this mystery must find a path between the Scylla of describing something that is not a priori knowledge because its justification is empirical and the Charybdis of describing something that is not knowledge at all because it has no justification.[12] The evidence suggests that there is no such path.

In sum, the case against a priori knowledge is that history has shown that the notion is deeply obscure and Quine has shown that we don't need it.

8. Naturalism and the Underdetermination Arguments

We have been considering the underdetermination arguments against Commonsense Realism that involve the theses AG1 and AG2. The Moorean point is that it is simply not plausible that we could know these theses a priori given that they undermine a doctrine as well-established as Realism. The naturalistic point is that we could not know them a priori because there is no a priori. It is time now to consider these theses from a naturalistic perspective.

Naturalism is an over-arching epistemological doctrine claiming that the only way of knowing *anything* is the empirical way of science: for each area of knowledge x, naturalized x. When the area is physics, this yields naturalized physics, when the area is biology, it yields naturalized biology, and when the area is epistemology, it yields naturalized epistemology. Everyone believes in a naturalized physics. Everyone but a few benighted creationists in places like Kansas believe in a naturalized biology. But those in the tradition of First Philosophy do not believe in a naturalized epistemology. The radical consequence of naturalism is that philosophy, including epistemology, becomes continuous with science.

From this naturalistic perspective, the troubling epistemological theses, AG1 and AG2, have no special status. They have to be assessed empirically, contrary to the assumptions of First Philosophy, because there is no other way to assess them. As empirical theses, they do not compare in evidential support with our view of stones, trees, cats and the like. Experience has taught us a great deal about such objects but rather little about how we know about them. So epistemology is just the wrong place to start the argument: it is one of the weakest threads in the web of belief (cf. Neurath's boat). Instead, we should start with an empirical metaphysics and use that as the basis for our naturalized epistemology, as the basis for our empirical study of what we can know and how we can know it.[13] Instead of the traditional pattern of argument, exemplified by the underdetermination arguments against Realism,

a priori epistemology → a priori metaphysics,

we should follow the pattern,

empirical metaphysics → empirical epistemology.

The underdetermination arguments not only use the wrong methodology, they proceed in the wrong direction.

Proceeding empirically in the right direction, we start with metaphysics. Realism is then irresistable. Indeed, it faces no rival we should take seriously. We then turn to naturalized epistemology. This is a very difficult matter. Still, with Realism established, we already know that AG1 and AG2 are false. We can go a bit further. It is clear from scientific practice that we are entitled, despite DG1, to dismiss implausible theses like the evil demon one; and that we are usually entitled, despite the equivalence that a theory has with some rivals according to DG2a and DG2b, to prefer that theory to its rivals; we are entitled to believe that all ravens are black, for example. The epistemic standards implicit in scientific practice clearly give us these entitlements. We would like to know, of course, exactly what those standards are but it has proved notoriously difficult to say. Nevertheless, it is indubitable that, whatever the standards are, they give us these entitlements.

Finally, we must consider the objection raised in section 2. For convenience, we have taken the skeptic to be *committed* to AG1 and AG2. The objection is that this does not do the skeptic justice. The cautious skeptic would be dubious of these epistemological theses as of all other substantive theses. After all, she *is* a skeptic. Since she is not committed to the theses she is not committed to knowing them a priori. So what then is the nature of her challenge to Realism? She puts the onus on the Realist to justify his rejection of AG1 and AG2. She does not boldly assert the badness of ampliative inferences, thus embracing skeptical standards of justification. She simply points to these epistemic standards, which yield AG1 and AG2, and asks for a justification for ruling the standards out in favor of Realist alternatives that reject AG1 and AG2.

From our naturalistic perspective the challenge of this cautious skeptic is no more difficult to meet than that of the incautious one. For, what I have presented is just what the cautious skeptic wants: a case against AG1 and AG2 and against any epistemic standards that would sustain them. On the one hand, the strength of the case for Realism counts against them. On the other hand, the practices of science counts against them. And these practices are the only place to look in assessing epistemic standards because there is no a priori knowledge. These practices support the use of ampliative inferences for preferring a theory to many, if not all, of its rivals. Sometimes, of course, a theory will face a rival that cannot be ruled out in this way but it is not the case that *all* theories *always* face such rivals. Commonsense Realism is not threatened by the underdetermination that remains.

In conclusion, naturalism appeals to scientific practice to dismiss the skeptic's underdetermination theses AG1 and AG2. Any alternative way of dismissing extreme skepticism must rest on a priori knowledge. I have argued that there is no such knowledge. Even if there were, alternatives that rest on it have tended to involve bizarre metaphysics and to be otherwise unsatisfactory.

If the sort of underdetermination by the actual given evidence discussed in this part had threatened Commonsense Realism it would, of course, also have threatened Scientific Realism. But there is alleged to be a stronger form of underdetermination, underdetermination by the possible evidence, that is thought to challenge Scientific Realism alone. This challenge is associated with the empiricism. I now turn to it.

II. Underdetermination and Scientific Realism

9. The Argument from Empirical Equivalence

I begin by emphasizing that this new empiricist challenge to Scientific Realism arises only on the assumption that the old extreme skeptical one, discussed in part I, can be dealt with. For, unless there is an acceptable answer to that challenge to Commonsense Realism, hence challenge to Scientific Realism, the cause of Scientific Realism is already lost. If there is no basis for rejecting AG1 and AG2 and somehow or other allaying Cartesian doubts about the very clearest cases of knowledge of the observable world, then of course there can be no basis for believing in the unobservable world. We have seen that rejecting AG1 and AG2 requires the acceptance of some methods of ampliative inference, methods strong enough to rule out the likes of the evil-demon hypothesis and sustain hypotheses, including generalizations, that cover unobserved observables. I have argued that the basis of rejection is to be found in scientific practice. Others may reject this naturalistic view, claiming that the basis must be found a priori. But such disagreements are beside the present point. This point is that the new challenge arises only once we have, on whatever basis, accepted some ampliative methods of inference and put extreme skepticism behind us. Armed with those methods, whatever they may be, and confident enough about the observable world, empiricists think that there is a *further* problem believing what science says about unobservables.[14] So the challenge of the underdetermination argument to be considered in this part is not to refight the part I battle with extreme skepticism; it is to respond to this special skepticism about unobservables. We shall see that this point has not been kept firmly enough in mind.

The underdetermination argument we are to consider—really several arguments—is one of the most influential arguments against Scientific Realism.[15] The argument starts from the thesis that any theory that posits unobservables has "empirically equivalent" rivals. What does this amount to exactly? The basic idea is:

DP: Any theory positing unobservables has rivals that entail the same possible observational evidence.

This is a deductive underdetermination thesis like DG2b but differing in that it is concerned not only with the set of actual given observations entailed by a theory but with any possible observations entailed by it; hence the name 'DP'.

On the basis of DP, the empiricist infers the very strong ampliative underdetermination thesis:

AP: Any theory positing unobservables has rivals that are equally supported by all possible observational evidence for that theory.

Not only does no actual evidence support a theory over some of its rivals, no possible evidence does so. So what the theory says about the unobservable world can make no evidential difference. Surely, then, commitment to what the theory says is a piece of misguided metaphysics. Even with extreme skepticism behind us, Scientific Realism must be abandoned.[16]

There is disagreement over what counts as "possible evidence." In my initial assessment of AP I will take a liberal and, it seems to me, intuitive view of what counts. To mark this I will call the thesis "AP(1)." Quine and Bas van Fraassen have a more restricted view of possible evidence yielding a thesis that I will call "AP(r)" and consider in section 13.

Since the possible evidence must include the actual given evidence, AP(1) would entail AG2 *were it not for AP(1)'s limitation to theories positing unobservables*; so our part I rejection of AG2 would suffice to reject AP(1). It is only because of the limitation to theories positing unobservables that, even with extreme skepticism behind us, we must still be concerned about AP(1). We need a powerful argument to show why the limitation makes this difference. The argument from empirical equivalence is suppose to fulfil this need.

The argument from empirical equivalence is another illustration of the pattern:

Deductive undertermination $\rightarrow$ ampliative underdetermination $\rightarrow$ antirealism.

In the next section, I shall argue that this argument, as it stands, is a dismal failure. I shall go on to consider various reinterpretations that are intended to be in the spirit of the argument.

10. Algorithms for Empirical Equivalence

A good reason for believing DP is that there is an empiricist algorithm for constructing an equivalent rival to any theory T. Consider T_o, the theory that the observational consequences of T are true. T_o is obviously empirically equivalent to T. Still, it may not count as a rival because it is consistent with T. That is easily fixed: T^* is the theory that T_o is true but T is not. T^* is an empirically equivalent rival to T. So DP is established.

It is tempting to respond that T^* is produced by trickery and is not a *genuine* rival to T (Laudan and Leplin 1991; Hoefer and Rosenberg 1994). But this response seems question-begging and unconvincing, as Andre Kukla argues (1998: 66–81). A better response is that, in counting theories generated by the empiricist algorithm as rivals, DP is far too weak to sustain AP(1). For, with extreme skepticism behind us, we *are* justified in choosing T over T^*.

In considering this choice, the first half of T^*, T_o, is key. In van Fraassen's terminology, T_o is the claim that T is "empirically adequate." He has some famous remarks comparing this claim with the bolder claim that T is true: "the empirical adequacy of an empirical theory must always be more credible than its truth" (1985: 247); "it is not an epistemological principle that one may as well hang for a sheep as for a lamb" (p. 254). The extra boldness of T comes, of course, from its Realist commitment to certain truths about unobservables. Because van Fraassen thinks that T takes no further empirical risk than T_o, he claims that this extra boldness "is but empty strutting and posturing," a "display of courage not under fire"; (p. 255). We should prefer the weaker T_o.

Now if van Fraassen were right about this, no evidence could justify a move from T_o to the bolder T. So it could not justify a preference for T over its rival T^* ($= T_o$ & not-T). AP(1) would be established.

Here is a reason for thinking that van Fraassen is not right. If it were really the case that we were only ever justified in adopting the weakest theory compatible with the possible evidence for T, we would have to surrender to extreme skepticism. For, T_o is far from being the weakest such theory. For example, consider T_e, the theory that T is "experientially adequate." Where T_o claims that the observable world *is* as if T, T_e claims only that the observable world *appears to be* as if T. T_e is much weaker than T_o: it does not require that there be an observable world at all; perhaps an evil demon is at work. Those, like van Fraassen, who believe theories of the observable world are displaying courage not under fire all the time.[17]

This argument exemplifies one side of an important, and quite general, Realist strategy to defend unobservables against discrimination, to defend "unobservable rights."[18] The Realist starts by reminding the anti-Realist that the debate is not over extreme skepticism: it is agreed that we have knowledge of observables (sec 9). The Realist then examines the anti-Realist's justification for this knowledge. The above argument exemplifies the side of the strategy that attempts to show that if the case for skepticism about unobservables produced by the anti-Realist were good it would undermine her justification for knowledge of observables. So it cannot be good.

This is the negative side of the Realist strategy. There is also a positive side: attempting to show that the epistemology involved in justifying our knowledge of observables also supports knowledge of unobservables. We can apply this here too. Any methods of ampliative inference that support the move from T_θ to T_o and free us from extreme skepticism must justify the dismissal of the evil-demon hypothesis and a whole lot of others, and must support many hypotheses covering unobserved observables ('All ravens are black' and the like). Whether or not these methods alone support the further move to *T*, hence support Scientific Realism, they will surely justify the dismissal of *T*'s rival *T**, produced by the empiricist algorithm. And they will justify the dismissal of another empirically equivalent rival produced by Kukla's algorithm according to which the world changes when unobserved (1993). It would be nice to know, of course, what these methods are. But it is a strategic error for the Scientific Realist to attempt to say what they are in responding to the anti-Realist. For, the anti-Realist believes in observables and *whatever* ampliative inferences support that belief will justify the dismissal of the likes of *T**.

The anti-Realist might, of course, simply insist that inferences that work for observables do not work for unobservables. Certainly there is no logical inconsistency in this insistence.[19] Nevertheless, the insistence is epistemically arbitrary and unprincipled. The Realist need say no more.[20]

We conclude that DP cannot sustain AP(1): *T* is indeed justified over empirically equivalent rivals like *T**. If an argument from empirical equivalence is to work, it needs to start from a stronger equivalence thesis, one that does not count any theory as a rival to *T* that can be dismissed by whatever ampliative inferences support our knowledge of the observable world and avoid extreme skepticism. Let us say that the rivals that can be thus dismissed are not "genuine." *T** and the output of Kukla's algorithm are surely not genuine. Precisely how far we can go in thus dismissing rivals remains to be seen, of course, pending the details of how to avoid extreme skepticism. And, given the Realist strategy, the details that matters are the ones given by the anti-Realist.

In sum, once we keep firmly in mind that our task is not to refight the battle with extreme skepticism, the argument from DP obviously fails.

11. Reinterpreting the Thesis of Empirical Equivalence

DP is too weak to do the empiricist job. We need a reinterpretation of the thesis of empirical equivalence that restricts it to genuine rivals. The natural first stab simply adds 'genuine' to DP yielding:

> **EE1**: Any theory positing unobservables has genuine rivals that entail the same possible observational evidence.

(The talk of entailment makes this seem to be a deductive underdetermination thesis but the restriction to *genuine* rivals makes it partly ampliative. So it does not fit happily into my naming convention. I have not tried to force it.)

Whether or not EE1 is true, it is easy to see that it is inadequate to support AP(1). This inadequacy arises from the fact that any theory *T* is likely to entail few observations on its own and yet the conjunction of *T* with auxiliary hypotheses, theories of instruments, background assumptions, and so on—briefly, its conjunction with "auxiliaries"—is likely to entail many observations. *T* does not face the tribunal of experience alone (Duhem-Quine). By failing to take account of these joint consequences, EE1 leaves many ways in which evidence could favor T over its rivals, contrary to AP(1). To sustain AP(1) and challenge Scientific Realism, we need a still stronger reinterpretation of empirical equivalence.

Consider Laudan and Leplin's influential critique of the underdetermination argument (1991). They propose the thesis, "The Instability of Auxiliary Assumptions" according to which "auxiliary information providing premises for the derivation of observational consequences from theory is unstable in two respects: it is defeasible and it is augmentable" (p. 57).[21] As the accepted auxiliaries that can be conjoined with T change, so do its consequences. So, any determination of T's empirical consequence class "must be relativized to a particular state of science," the state that supplies the auxiliary hypotheses. Thus "any finding of empirical equivalence is both contextual and defeasible" (p. 58). To determine the consequences of T we need more than logic, we need to know which auxiliaries are acceptable, an "*inescapably epistemic*" matter (p. 59).

To avoid the consequences of this argument, Kukla (1993) proposed a reinterpretation along the following lines: for two theories to be empirically equivalent at time t is for them to entail the same observations when conjoined with At, the auxiliaries that are accepted at t. This yields:

EE2: Any theory positing unobservables has genuine rivals which are such that when it and any of the rivals are conjoined with At they entail the same possible observational evidence.

Set aside for a moment whether or not EE2 is any threat at all to Scientific Realism. It is clearly too weak to sustain the threat posed by AP(1). Let T be a theory and T' an empirically equivalent rival according to this interpretation. So $T\&At$ and $T'\&At$ entail the same observations. This sort of equivalence is *relative to At*, to the auxiliaries accepted at a certain time. It amounts to the claim that T and T' cannot be discriminated observationally if conjoined only with those auxiliaries. But this does not show that T and T' could not be distinguished when conjoined with *any* acceptable auxiliaries at *any* time. And that is what is needed, at least, to sustain the claim that T and T' cannot be discriminated by *any possible* evidence, as AP(1) requires. AP(1) demands a much stronger reinterpretation of the empirical equivalence: for two theories to be empirically equivalent is for them to entail the same observations when conjoined with any possible acceptable auxiliaries (cf. section 13 on the demands of AP(r)). This yields:

EE3: Any theory positing unobservables has genuine rivals which are such that when it and any of the rivals are conjoined with any possible acceptable auxiliaries they entail the same possible observational evidence.

If *T* and *T'* were thus related they would be empirically equivalent not just relative to certain auxiliaries but *tout court, absolutely* equivalent. Only then would they be observationally indiscriminable. So if a thesis of empirical equivalence is to support AP(1), it must be interpreted as EE3.

Laudan and Leplin's critique leads them to two somewhat different conclusions about the doctrine of empirical equivalence. They claim, (i), that the doctrine "loses all significance for epistemology" (1991: 57); and, (ii), that we have no reason to believe the doctrine (e.g., p. 55). (i) is an exaggeration. The truth underlying it is that EE2 cannot sustain AP(1). Still, we shall see (sec. 12) that were EE3, or even EE2, true, they would be epistemologically significant. I take Laudan and Leplin's main claim to be (ii). And what they have in mind is that we have no reason to believe EE3.[22] This is dead right. If *T* and *T'* cannot be discriminated observationally relative to, say, currently accepted auxiliaries, they may well be so relative to some future accepted auxiliaries. Some currently accepted auxiliaries may cease to be accepted and some new auxiliaries are likely to become accepted. This point becomes particularly persuasive, in my view (1991: 119), when we note our capacity to invent new instruments and experiments to test theories. With a new instrument and experiment comes new auxiliaries, including a theory of the instrument and assumptions about the experimental situation. Given that we can thus *create* evidence, the set of observational consequences of any theory seems totally open. Of course, there is *no guarantee* of successful discrimination by these means: a theory may really face a genuine empirically equivalent rival. Still, we are unlikely to have sufficient reason for believing this of any particular theory.[23] More importantly, we have *no reason at all* for believing it of *all* theories, as EE3 requires. We will seldom, if ever, have a basis for concluding that two genuine rivals are empirically equivalent in the absolute sense required by EE3.

Behind this argument lies the following Realist picture. *T* and *T'* describe different causal structures alleged to underlie the phenomena. We can manipulate the actual underlying structure to get observable effects. We have no reason to believe that we *could not* organize these manipulations so that, if the structure were as *T* says, the effects would be of one sort, whereas if the structure were as *T'* says, the effects would be of a different sort.

The argument against EE3 does not depend on any assumption about the breadth of *T*. So EE3 cannot be saved by taking it to apply to "total sciences" (Boyd 1984: 50). Should such a broad conjunction of theories seem to face an equivalent rival at a certain time, we are unlikely to have sufficient reason for believing that experimental developments will not enable us to discriminate the conjunction from its rival by supplying new auxiliaries. *There is no known limit to our capacity to generate acceptable auxiliaries.*

AP(1) would be a disaster for Scientific Realism but it needs a powerful argument. With extreme skepticism behind us, DP does not come close to providing the argument. Nor does EE1 because *it entirely overlooks the role of auxiliaries* in providing evidence. Nor does EE2 because *it does not take ap-*

propriate account of the role of auxiliaries. EE3 cannot provide the needed argument because *we have no reason to believe it.* I conclude that there is no powerful argument for AP(1). Still, there remain some loose ends to clear up.

12. Possible Consequences for Scientific Realism

Suppose, nonetheless, that EE3 were true. Would it then establish AP(1) and undermine Scientific Realism? It might well do so.[24] If EE3 were true, Realists would have to appeal to "nonempirical virtues" to choose between empirically equivalent theories. Empirical virtue is a matter of entailing (in conjunction with accepted auxiliaries) observational truths and not entailing observational falsehoods. The nonempirical virtues are explanatory power, simplicity, and the like. I think that the Realist is entitled to appeal to explanatory virtues, at least. But if it really were the case that all theories faced genuine rivals equally compatible with all possible evidence, the appeal to these virtues would seem epistemologically dubious.[25] For, in those circumstances, there could be no way to judge the empirical success of these virtues, no way to show, for example, that theories that provide the best explanation tend to be observationally confirmed. So the defense of Scientific Realism might well depend on there being no good reason for believing EE3.

What about EE2? It will not sustain AP(1), but perhaps it is otherwise threatening to Scientific Realism. So, first, we need to consider whether it is true; then, whether, if it were, it would undermine Realism.

There are surely some theories that face a genuine rival that is empirically equivalent relative to the accepted auxiliaries at a certain time. But do *all* theories face such rivals at that time, let alone at *all* times? EE2 *guarantees* that all theories do at all times. But the ampliative methods, whatever they may be, that support our knowledge of the observable world and avoid extreme skepticism will count many rivals as not genuine, so many as to make this guarantee seem baseless. How could we know a priori that a theory must always face such a genuine rival?

Suppose, nonetheless, that EE2 were true. So, if a theory T and its rivals are restricted to the accepted auxiliaries at a certain time, T could not be justified over some rivals on the basis only of the observations that the theories and auxiliaries entail and the ampliative methods that save us from extreme skepticism. So, without recourse to some further ampliative methods, T would be underdetermined by the evidence that the restriction allows into play. Of course, once new acceptable auxiliaries were discovered and the restriction changed, the further methods might well not be needed to justify T over those old rivals. So this underdetermination would not be as serious as AP(1), but it would be serious enough: at any time, we would not know what to be Realist about. But then perhaps the Realist *would be* entitled to the further ampliative methods that would remove this underdetermination. Given that the case for EE3 has not been made, I think that the Realist might be so entitled.[26]

We have no reason to believe EE2 or EE3 and so they cannot undermine Scientific Realism. However, if EE3 were true, it might well do so, and if EE2 were true, it could. Once we have set aside extreme skepticism then, contrary to received opinion, the nonempirical virtues are not central to defending Scientific Realism from the argument from empirical equivalence; the rejection of the equivalence thesis is.

13. Restricting Possible Evidence

In assessing AP and its consequences I have taken what seems to be an appropriately liberal view of what counts as "possible observational evidence," taking note of our capacity to create evidence by inventing new instruments and conducting new experiments; hence the name 'AP(l)'. Quine has a more restricted view reflecting, no doubt, his distaste for modality. He takes the possible evidence to be what would have been observed had there been an observer at each point of *actual* space-time (1970b: 179). This is also van Fraassen's view of the phenomena he wishes to save: all *actual* observable things and events, past, present and future, whether or not anyone in fact observes them (1980: 12, 60, 64). On this restricted view, acts of observation are the only nonactual aspects of possible evidence. On the liberal view, in contrast, the possible evidence includes many things that we do not do, but could have done, other than merely observing. If we had had more time, energy, and money perhaps we could have invented the right instruments and conducted the right experiments to discriminate between T and T'. There may be many differences between them which we never detected because we *passively observed* points of actual space-time where we could have *actively intervened* (Hacking 1983) to change what happened.

Let us make explicit what AP becomes on the restricted view of possible evidence:

AP(r): Any theory positing unobservables has rivals that are equally supported by all the actual truths about observables.

Quine may believe AP(r)[27] but, as Laudan points out (1996: 41–2), he offers no evidence for it. Yet it needs a powerful argument for much the same reason that AP(l) did (sec. 9). Since the actual truths about observables must include the observed truths, AP(r), like AP(l), would entail AG2 *were it not for its limitation to theories positing unobservables*. So our part I rejection of AG2 would suffice to reject AP(r). We need a powerful argument to show why, with extreme skepticism behind us, this limitation makes a difference. Set that aside for a moment.

What would the consequences be for Scientific Realism if AP(r) were true? In a previous work I found AP(r), in effect, "too weak for the task of undermining Realism" (1991: 121). Certainly, AP(r), unlike AP(l), would not show that we *could not* find evidence that would discriminate between a theory and its genuine rivals, just that we ran out of time before we did. So AP(r) would not show that commitment to a theory's unobservables was a piece of misguided metaphysics. But I overlooked that AP(r) would still be a problem for Realism because it would have the consequence that we would *never as a matter of fact* know what to be Realist about; we would *never as a matter of fact* be justified in preferring the unobservables of our chosen theory over those of its rivals. So the Realist must resist AP(r) as well as AP(l).

Where might we find an argument for AP(r)? Once again we must look to an empirical equivalence thesis. What thesis? We found no reason to believe EE3 but, in any case, its talk of "any possible acceptable auxiliary" would not recommend itself to the restricted view of possible evidence. On that view, any empirical equivalence thesis that is to support AP(r) must surely restrict the relevant auxiliaries to actual ones. And it will not be sufficient to restrict them to actual ones that are accepted "at any point of space-time" because some that are accepted at one point are later rejected; think, for example, of auxiliaries about the number of planets. It seems that we must restrict auxiliaries to the ones that are still standing "at the end of human inquiry"! This yields:

EE4: Any theory positing unobservables has genuine rivals which are such that when it and any of the rivals are conjoined with auxiliaries that are accepted at the end of human inquiry they entail the same possible observational evidence.

But why should we believe EE4? In discussing EE2 we found no reason to believe that all theories face genuine equivalent rivals relative to the auxiliaries at any time (sec. 12). So we have no reason to believe that all theories do relative to the auxiliaries at the end of human inquiry. We have no reason to believe even that *some* theories do. EE4 is baseless.

Suppose that EE4 were true? Would it sustain AP(r)? If not, would it be otherwise damaging to Scientific Realism? It is not clear that the answer to either question is "Yes." In thinking about these questions we should look, once again, for ampliative methods beyond those that save us from extreme skepticism.

In sum, AP(r), with its restricted view of the possible evidence, would threaten Scientific Realism, albeit not as badly as AP(l) with its liberal view. But AP(r), like AP(l), needs a powerful argument that it does not have. In particular it can get no support from the equivalence thesis EE4 because the thesis is baseless. And it is not clear that EE4 would support AP(r) or anti-Realism even if it were true.

14. Conclusion

In part I we considered the underdetermination theses AG1 and AG2 of extreme skepticism. If true these would count against nearly all our knowledge and hence undermine Commonsense and Scientific Realism. The traditional responses of First Philosophy to these theses rest on a priori knowledge. I argue that there is no such knowledge. Even if there were, these traditional responses tend to involve bizarre metaphysics and to be otherwise unsatisfactory. Instead, I urge a naturalistic response that appeals to scientific practice.

In part II we considered AP, the very strong thesis that scientific theories positing unobservables are underdetermined by *all possible* evidence. If AP were true it would threaten Scientific Realism even though Commonsense Realism was secure. There are two interpretations of AP, one with a liberal view of possible evidence, AP(l), and one with a restricted view, AP(r). On each interpretation, AP needs a powerful argument that it does not have. In particular empirical equivalence theses do not provide the argument either because we have no reason to believe them or because they would not support AP(l) and AP(r) if they were true, or both. The underdetermination argument against Scientific Realism turns out to be rather weak. To see this we need to keep firmly in mind that the argument only arises once extreme skepticism is behind us.[28]

Notes

1. 1991, 1997a, 1999. My definitions are unfashionable in not being, or even appearing to be, semantic. I argue that it is very important to disentangle the metaphysical doctrine of realism from any semantic doctrine.
2. Quine thinks this likely even given all the sensory evidence that there will ever be, "man's surface irritations even unto eternity" (1960: 23).
3. Larry Laudan emphasizes the importance of the distinction between the deductive and the ampliative in his helpful discussion of underdetermination theses (1996: ch. 2).
4. Laudan calls this "the nonuniqueness thesis". A stronger thesis, "the egalitarian thesis" claims that a theory enjoys no support over *all* of its rivals. He is sadly persuasive in attributing the latter thesis to Quine, Thomas Kuhn, and Mary Hesse (1996: 33–43).
5. For example, Kuhn 1970 (on which see Hoyningen-Huene 1993); Feyerabend 1975, 1981; Goodman 1978; Putnam 1981; Latour and Woolgar 1986.
6. See particularly Quine 1952: xi–xvii; 1961: 42–6. Quine uses 'naturalism' to stand for this epistemological doctrine. Others use it to stand for the reductive metaphysical doctrine like physicalism.
7. We are concerned whether there is a nonempirical way of *justifying* knowledge. We are not concerned whether there is a nonempirical *source* of knowledge, whether there is *innate* knowledge. Innate knowledge is sometimes called 'a priori' but that is not my usage. Naturalism is consistent with there being some innate knowledge (although I strongly doubt that there is). Naturalism simply insists that any such knowledge must be justified empirically: presumably, experiences of the worldly facts that are the subject of the innate knowledge must play a role via adaptation in the production of the knowledge.
8. See, for example, Kitcher 1980.
9. Rey (1998) even urges us to use it to show that there is an a priori way!
10. What exactly is *believing* according to RTM? The literature often seems to suggest that *believing* is a functional relation between agents and mental tokens. But there

are problems with this. I am inclined to think that we should not take it as a relation at all. We should take 'belief' to have a dual function, part relative term and part quantifier (2001b).

11. Hilary Kornblith (2000) raises another concern about BonJour's notion of the a priori: Can it do any epistemological work?

12. My objection (1997b, 1998) to Rey's attempt to give a reliablist characterization of the a priori (1997, 1998) is, in effect, that it falls victim to Charybdis.

13. Van Fraassen, in his critique of what he calls (independently), "Moorean Scientific Realism" (2000: 261–71), seems to misunderstand the naturalist's view of the relation of epistemology to science. It goes without saying that *epistemology* implies the methods of science. But van Fraassen seems to take the naturalist view to be that *basic science, or special sciences like biology, medicine, and psychology*, imply the methods of science, a view that van Fraassen rejects. But this is not the naturalist view. The naturalist view is that *epistemology is itself a special science*. As such it is no more simply implied by another science than is any other special science: it has the same sort of relative autonomy, and yet dependence on basic science, as other special sciences. Naturalized epistemology, like any special science, applies the usual methods of science, whatever they may be, mostly taking established science for granted, to investigate its special realm. In the case of epistemology that realm is those very methods of science. The aim is to discover empirically how we humans learn, and should learn, about the world (1991: 75–9). We have no reason to suppose that the methods that have yielded knowledge elsewhere cannot yield knowledge in epistemology.

14. This further problem should also concern somebody who takes an idealist path to rejecting AG1 and AG2. This idealist has, of course already abandoned the independence dimension of Scientific Realism but she should be as interested as the Realist in defending the existence dimension. She should be as interested in preserving the idea that science is more or less right about the unobservables even though, for her, these unobservables are not mind-independent. The existence dimension of Scientific Realism is challenged by this new underdetermination argument.

15. In my view (2002), another influential argument, the "pessimistic meta-induction," is more powerful although ultimately ineffective.

16. The argument has no one clear source. But see Duhem 1906, Quine 1960, 1961 ("Two Dogmas"), and 1975; van Fraassen 1980, Putnam 1983 ("Equivalence").

17. I develop this argument more thoroughly in my 1991: 150–3.

18. For examples of this strategy, see Boyd 1984, Churchland 1985, Gutting 1985, Musgrave 1985, Clendinnen 1989, Devitt 1991 (pp. 147–53), and Psillos 1999 (pp. 186–91). Van Fraassen 1985 responds to Churchland, Gutting, and Musgrave.

19. Kukla emphasizes this (1998: 25–6, 84).

20. However, I think that an examination of the epistemic significance of observation helps to bring out the arbitrariness (1991: 143–7).

21. See also Ellis 1985 and Devitt 1991: 117–21.

22. Note that this is not the claim that EE3 is "demonstratively false"; cf. Kukla 1998: 58.

23. For some theories where we may have sufficient reason, and for some past ones where we wrongly thought we had, see Psillos (1999: 166–8) and the works he cites.

24. Laudan and Leplin (1991: 63–8) think it would not, arguing that T can be indirectly supported over its rival by evidence that confirms another theory that entails T but not its rival; and that some consequences of T and its rival might support only T.

But, as Kukla points out (1998: 84–90), this argument begs the question: if EE3 really were true, this evidential support would seem to disappear.

25. I emphasize that since it has not been established that *all* theories do face such rivals, it might well be appropriate to appeal to explanatory virtues, or indeed to the evidential support mentioned by Laudan and Leplin (note 24), to prefer *some* theory that does face such a rival.

26. In a reply to Kukla 1993, Leplin and Laudan (1993: 10), in effect, doubt EE2 but in any case emphasize that EE3 is what matters to the underdetermination argument. Kukla disagrees, claiming, in effect, that EE2, when applied to total sciences, "brings in its train all the epistemological problems that were ever ascribed to the doctrine of EE" (1998: 64). According to my discussion EE2 would bring some epistemological problems if it were true, but they are not as extreme as those that would be brought by EE3 if it were true.

27. Quine starts, in effect, by saying that AP(r) is *conceivable* (1960: 22), which it surely is, and then moves on to the earlier-mentioned claim (note 2) that the somewhat different AG1 is *likely* even when the given evidence is "man's surface irritations even unto eternity" (1960: 23).

28. Comments on my 2002 by Andre Kukla, Jarrett Leplin, and David Papineau have helped me in writing this paper.

References

BonJour, Laurence. 1992. "A Rationalist Manifesto." In *Return of the A Priori: Canadian Journal of Philosophy, supp. vol.18*, Philip Hanson and Bruce Hunter, eds. Calgary: The University of Calgary Press: 53–88.

BonJour, Laurence. 1998. *In Defense of Pure Reason: A Rationalist Account of A Priori Justification*. Cambridge: Cambridge University Press.

Boyd, Richard N. 1984. "The Current Status of Scientific Realism." In *Scientific Realism*, Jarrett Leplin, ed. Berkeley: University of California Press: 41–82.

Churchland, Paul M. 1985. "The Ontological Status of Observables: In Praise of the Superempirical Virtues." In Churchland and Hooker 1985: 35–47.

Churchland, Paul M., and Clifford A. Hooker, eds. 1985. *Images of Science: Essays on Realism and Empiricism, with a Reply from Bas C. van Fraassen*. Chicago: University of Chicago Press.

Clendinnen, F. J. 1989. "Realism and the Underdetermination of Theory." *Synthese* 81: 63–90.

Devitt, Michael. 1991. *Realism and Truth*. 2nd edn (1st edn 1984). Oxford: Basil Blackwell.

Devitt, Michael. 1996. *Coming to Our Senses: A Naturalistic Defense of Semantic Localism*. New York: Cambridge University Press.

Devitt, Michael. 1997a. "Afterword." In a reprint of Devitt 1991. Princeton: Princeton University Press: 302–45.

Devitt, Michael. 1997b. "Responses to the Maribor Papers." In Jutronic 1997: 353–411.

Devitt, Michael. 1998. "Naturalism and the A Priori." *Philosophical Studies* 92: 45–65.

Devitt, Michael. 1999. "A Naturalistic Defense of Realism". In *Metaphysics: Contemporary Readings*, Steven D. Hales ed. Belmont, CA: Wadsworth Publishing Company (1999): 90–103.

Devitt, Michael. 2001a. "Incommensurability and the Priority of Metaphysics." In *Incommensurability and Related Matters*, P. Hoyningen-Huene and H. Sankey, eds. Dordrecht: Kluwer Academic Publishers: 143–57.

Devitt, Michael. 2001b. "Sustaining Actualism." In *Philosophical Perspectives, 15, Metaphysics, 2001*, James E. Tomberlin, ed. Cambridge MA: Blackwell Publishers: 415–19.

Devitt, Michael. 2002. "Scientific Realism." In *The Oxford Handbook of Contemporary Analytic Philosophy*, Frank Jackson and Michael Smith, eds. Oxford: Oxford University Press.

Duhem, P. 1906. *The Aim and Structure of Physical Theory*, trans. P. Wiener. Princeton: Princeton University Press (1954).

Ellis, Brian. 1985. "What Science Aims to Do." In Churchland and Hooker 1985: 48–74.

Feyerabend, Paul K. 1975. *Against Method*. London: New Left Books.

Feyerabend, Paul K. 1981. *Realism, Rationalism and Scientific Method: Philosophical Papers Volume 1*. Cambridge: Cambridge University Press.

Goodman, Nelson. 1978. *Ways of Worldmaking*. Indianapolis: Hackett Publishing Company.

Gutting, Gary. 1985. "Scientific Realism versus Constructive Empiricism: A Dialogue." In Churchland and Hooker 1985: 118–131.

Hacking, Ian. 1983. *Representing and Intervening: Introductory Topics in the Philosophy of Natural Science*. Cambridge: Cambridge University Press.

Hoefer, C. and A. Rosenberg. 1994. "Empirical Equivalence, Underdetermination, and Systems of the World." *Philosophy of Science* 61: 592–607.

Hoyningen-Huene, P. 1993. *Reconstructing Scientific Revolutions: Thomas S. Kuhn's Philosophy of Sciece*. Trans. A. T. Levine (German edn 1989). Chicago: University of Chicago Press.

Jutronic, Dunja, ed. 1997. *The Maribor Papers in Naturalized Semantics*, Maribor: Pedagoska fakulteta Maribor.

Kitcher, Philip. 1980. "A Priori Knowledge." *Philosophical Review* 76: 3–23.

Kornblith, Hilary. 2000. "The Impurity of Reason." *Pacific Philosophical Quarterly* 18: 67–89.

Kuhn, Thomas S. 1970: *The Structure of Scientific Revolutions*. 2nd edn (1st edn 1962). Chicago: Chicago University Press.

Kukla, Andre. 1993. "Laudan, Leplin, Empirical Equivalence, and Underdetermination." *Analysis* 53: 1–7.

Kukla, Andre. 1998. *Studies in Scientific Realism*. New York: Oxford University Press.

Latour, Bruno, and Steve Woolgar. 1986. *Laboratory Life: The Construction of Scientific Facts*. 2nd edn (1st edn 1979). Princeton: Princeton University Press.

Laudan, Larry. 1996, *Beyond Positivism and Relativism: Theory, Method and Evidence*. Boulder, CO: Westview Press.

Laudan, Larry, and Jarrett Leplin. 1991. "Empirical Equivalence and Underdetermination." *Journal of Philosophy* 88: 449–72. Reprinted in Laudan 1996. (Page references are to Laudan 1996.)

Leplin, Jarrett, and Larry Laudan. 1993. "Determination Underdeterred: Reply to Kukla." *Analysis* 53: 8–15.

Musgrave, Alan. 1985. "Realism versus Constructive Empiricism." In Churchland and Hooker 1985: 197–221.

Psillos, Stathis. 1999. *Scientific Realism: How Science Tracks Truth*. New York: Routledge.

Putnam, Hilary. 1981. *Reason, Truth and History*. Cambridge: Cambridge University Press.

Putnam, Hilary. 1983. *Realism and Reason: Philosophical Papers Volume 3*. Cambridge: Cambridge University Press.

Quine, W. V. 1952. *Methods of Logic*. London: Routledge & Kegan Paul.

Quine, W. V. 1960. *Word and Object*. Cambridge MA: MIT Press.

Quine, W.V. 1961. *From a Logical Point of View*. 2nd edn (1st edn, 1953). Cambridge, MA: Harvard University Press.

Quine, W. V. 1975. "On Empirically Equivalent Systems of the World." *Erkenntnis* 9: 313–28.

Rey, Georges. 1997. "Devitt's Naturalism: A Priori Resistance to the A Priori?" In Jutronic 1997: 141–54

Rey, Georges. 1998. "A Naturalistic A Priori." *Philosophical Studies* 92: 25–43.

Van Fraassen, Bas C. 1980. *The Scientific Image*. Oxford: The Clarendon Press.

Van Fraassen, Bas C. 1985. "Empiricism in the Philosophy of Science." In Churchland and Hooker 1985: 245–308.

Van Fraassen, Bas C. 2000. "The False Hopes of Traditional Epistemology." *Philosophy and Phenomenological Research* 40: 253–80.

QUANTIFIER VARIANCE AND REALISM

Eli Hirsch
Brandeis University

A pervasive theme in Hilary Putnam's writings for many years, running as a constant thread through various changes in his views about realism, is a doctrine that he calls "conceptual relativism", representative formulations of which are as follows:

> [A]ll situations have many different correct descriptions, and ... even descriptions that, taken holistically, convey the same information may differ in what they take to be 'objects' ... [T]here are many usable extensions of the notion of an object ...[1] [T]he logical primitives themselves, and in particular the notions of object and existence, have a multitude of different uses rather than one absolute 'meaning'.[2]

In these passages Putnam seems to be saying that the quantificational apparatus in our language and thought—such expressions as "thing", "object", "something", "(there) exists"—has a certain variability or plasticity. There is no necessity to use these expressions in one way rather than various other ways, for the world can be correctly described using a variety of concepts of "the existence of something". One of his favorite examples concerns a disagreement between mereologists and anti-mereologists as to how many objects there are in some domain.[3] Suppose we are evaluating the truth of the sentence, "There exists something that is composed of Clinton's nose and the Eiffel Tower". Mereologists will accept this sentence, whereas anti-mereologists will reject it. Putnam's doctrine of quantifier variance implies that the expression "there exists something" can be interpreted in a way that makes the sentence true or in a way that makes the sentence false. Since both interpretations are available to us, we have a choice between operating with a concept of "the existence of something" that satisfies the mereologist or operating with a different concept that satisfies the anti-mereologist.

The doctrine of quantifier variance may be philosophically unsettling. Our initial reaction may be that, if we are free to choose between different ways of conceiving of "the existence of something", then this threatens a robust realist sense that there are things in the world whose existence does not in any way depend on our language or thought. The nature and force of this threat is one of the topics of this paper.

Before proceeding let me emphasize that this paper is not an exercise in Putnam-exegesis. I take it as obvious that the doctrine of quantifier variance is a central part of Putnam's overall position, but I make no attempt here to trace Putnam's evolving views as to how this doctrine relates to different versions of realism. The possible threat to realism posed by this doctrine is something that I am trying to work through on my own terms, though I have little doubt that virtually every point I am going to make can be found somewhere in Putnam's writings.

I

I think we should begin by making sure to repudiate a thoroughly confused, though somehow tempting, formulation of what the threat to realism is: "Since, according to the doctrine of quantifier variance, our linguistic decisions determine whether or not there exists something composed of Clinton's nose and the Eiffel Tower, it evidently follows that this thing's existence or non-existence depends on our language and thought. If this point generalizes to every application of our concept of 'the existence of a thing'—as the doctrine seems to imply—then quantifier variance evidently conflicts with the realist idea of things existing independently of language and thought".

The fallacy in this formulation lies in the claim that the doctrine of quantifier variance implies that our linguistic decisions determine whether or not there exists something composed of Clinton's nose and the Eiffel Tower. What the doctrine does imply is that our linguistic decisions determine the meaning of the expression "there exists something"; hence, they determine the meaning of the sentence "There exists something composed of Clinton's nose and the Eiffel Tower". Hence, the truth or falsity of this sentence depends in part on our linguistic decisions. It is merely a use-mention confusion to conclude that whether or not there exists something composed of Clinton's nose and the Eiffel Tower depends on our linguistic decisions.

Consider the two sentences: "There exists something composed of Clinton's nose and the Eiffel Tower" and "Whether or not there exists something composed of Clinton's nose and the Eiffel Tower depends on our linguistic decisions". Quantifier variance implies that the expression "there exists something" can be interpreted in a way that makes the first sentence true or in a way that makes it false. But there is no relevant way to interpret "there exists something" that would make the second sentence true. The second sentence expresses an absurd form of linguistic idealism that is not at all implied by quantifier variance.

There is the familiar joke about how many tails a dog would have if the word "tail" were used to refer to legs—the correct answer, everyone seems to agree, is "one", because how many tails a dog has does not depend on our linguistic decisions. The meaning and truth-value of the sentence "A dog has one tail" depends on our linguistic decisions, but how many tails a dog has does not depend on our linguistic decisions. Why does it seem harder to grasp this point when we are talking about the meaning of quantifier expressions rather than a general term such as "tail"? I think that part of the difficulty stems from our wanting to say, when we are formulating the doctrine of quantifier variance, that the relevant variations would still leave us with a *kind of quantifier expression*, an expression that, as Putnam put it in the earlier quote, continues to signify *a notion of the existence of something*. This formulation may be misconstrued as implying that, although the meaning of the quantifier expressions and the notion of existence remain fixed, what we are somehow going to accomplish with our linguistic decision is to alter the truth-values of our existential claims. And that might indeed amount to a lunatic form of linguistic idealism. What needs to be stressed, however, is that the doctrine of quantifier variance only allows for the possibility of a *change in the meaning* of quantifier expressions, yielding a *different* or *extended* notion of existence; only in this way does the doctrine allow our linguistic decisions to affect the truth-values of existential sentences. Once the meaning of the quantifier is fixed there is no further effect that our decisions can have on the truth-values of typical existential sentences.

To say that even after there has been a change in the meaning of quantifier expressions we still have a "kind of quantifier expression" and a "notion of existence" is merely to indicate a degree of similarity between the concepts we started with and those we end up with. Nothing is being said here to imply the idealist view that what exists in the world depends on our linguistic or conceptual decisions. Suppose that I start out with the anti-mereologist's position that the sentence "There exists something composed of Clinton's nose and the Eiffel Tower" is false. If I accept quantifier variance I will allow that I can make intelligible to myself a change in the meaning of the expression "there exists something" which would have the effect of rendering the sentence true. I might characterize this change as simply "giving up the quantifier" and "giving up the notion of the existence of something", but it seems more natural to characterize it rather as "acquiring a new kind of quantifier" and "acquiring a new notion of the existence of something". The second characterization seems more natural because it seems clear that the imagined change in the meaning of the expression "there exists something" will leave the expression's general role in the language largely intact. In particular, the purely syntactic and formal logical properties of the expression will not be changed at all (the formal principles of quantificational logic will be unaltered). It therefore seems natural to follow Putnam in treating relevant variations in the meaning of such expressions as "there exists something" as yielding an altered quantificational apparatus and an altered concept of the existence of something.

If I start out with the anti-mereologist's stance, what exactly is involved in changing the meaning of the quantifier with the effect of making the mereologist's sentences come out true? There are important complications in the answer to this question that I will return to later, but the basic idea is quite simple. In general, we explain the meaning of a logical constant by describing the role it plays in determining the truth-conditions of sentences. Thus we explain the meaning of "and" by saying that sentences of the form "*p* and *q*" are true if and only if both the sentence "*p*" and the sentence "*q*" are true. If we were to explain some imagined change in the meaning of "and" we would do so by describing a change in the truth-conditions of sentences containing "and". Analogously we explain the relevant change in the meaning of the quantifier, which will render the mereologist's sentences true, roughly as follows: In the new meaning, any sentence of the form "There exists something composed of the *F*-thing and the *G*-thing" is true if the expression "the *F*-thing" refers to something and the expression "the *G*-thing" refers to something. We are here using the quantifier in one of its meanings to explain the other meaning. It is evidently not part of the doctrine of quantifier variance to claim that the meaning of the quantifier can be somehow analyzed or defined in terms not involving the quantifier—any more than the meaning of "and" can be analyzed or defined in terms not involving conjunction. The issue of quantifier variance should therefore not be conflated with familiar questions about the analyzability of (the criteria for) the identity or existence of a thing. Quantifier variance is not a matter of substituting one "definition" for another; it's a matter of substituting one range of truth-conditions for another.

II

I suspect that the deepest source of the illusion—and I am maintaining that it is an illusion—that quantifier variance conflicts with realism stems from the analogy we are led to draw between different kinds of quantifiers, the analogy, that is, that leads us to speak, not simply about eliminating the quantifier and the concept of existence, but about a variation that still leaves us with a different quantifier and a different concept of existence. Suppose, again, that I start out with the anti-mereologist's position that the sentence "There exists something composed of Clinton's nose and the Eiffel Tower" is false. In my use of "there exists something" a sentence of the form "There exists something composed of the *F*-thing and the *G*-thing" counts as true only if "the *F*-thing" and "the *G*-thing" refer to things that are connected (united) in some special ways. Let me call my use of "there exists something" the A-use. I now imagine a different use of "there exists something"—I will call this the M-use—in which a sentence of that form counts as true so long as "the *F*-thing" and "the *G*-thing" refer to things, no matter how they are connected. Now, how am I to describe in my language, the A-language, what is going on in the M-language?

When speakers of the M-language assert "There exists something composed of Clinton's nose and the Eiffel Tower" they speak the truth. That is implied by the semantic rule that has been explicitly laid down in my description of the truth-conditions in the M-language of sentences of the form "There exists something composed of the *F*-thing and the *G*-thing". I assume, however, that this explicit stipulation carries with it a natural way of filling in the truth-conditions for an indefinite variety of other sentences in the M-language. Take, for example, the sentence "There exists something that is now being touched by exactly two people". This sentence is not rendered true in my A-language by a situation in which one person is touching Clinton's nose and one person is touching the Eiffel Tower,[4] but my implicit assumption is that the sentence would be true in the M-language with respect to that situation. When I reflect on a range of examples of this sort I find myself tempted to say (in my A-language) something like the following: Although there doesn't exist anything composed of Clinton's nose and the Eiffel Tower, it's somehow *as if* there does exist such a thing relative to the M-language. This "as if" formulation is a simile; it is a way of expressing the felt holistic analogy between the A-use of the quantifier expressions and the M-use. As such it may be perfectly innocuous. But similes can often lead to metaphors, and metaphors, if we are not careful, can sometimes lead to lunacy. The move from simile to metaphor might take the form of simply dropping the words "as if" from the previous formulation. We then wind up saying, "Relative to the M-language, there exists something composed of Clinton's nose and the Eiffel Tower". As a metaphor this may still be okay; it may in fact qualify as what John Wisdom called an "illuminating paradox".[5] It can, however, turn into utter confusion and philosophical madness if one forgets that it is merely a metaphor. One may then wind up claiming that language or thought literally creates everything that exists, that nothing could exist if there were no people speaking or thinking. What we need to be clear about— and this may require a continual effort on our parts—is that the doctrine of quantifier variance does not imply any such idealist formulation.[6]

The push towards the simile and metaphor, and the accompanying risk of falling off the edge of idealist madness, is enhanced when we consider the following kind of sentence: "In the M-language the expression 'thing composed of Clinton's nose and the Eiffel Tower' refers to a thing composed of Clinton's nose and the Eiffel Tower". This sentence (about the M-language) cannot be true in my A-language. Since (as I say in my A-language) there isn't any thing composed of Clinton's nose and the Eiffel Tower, there can't be any such thing referred to by any expression in the M-language. But if we make the natural assumption that the truth-conditions for sentences in the M-language containing the word "refers" will respect the disquotational principle, then the previous sentence about the M-language, although false in the A-language, counts as true in the M-language. To take this one small step further, the sentence "In the M-language the expression 'thing composed of Clinton's nose and the Eiffel Tower' refers to something" counts as false in the A-language but true in the M-language.

As goes "existence" so goes "reference". The lesson here is that if we are imagining that the quantifier expressions in the M-language function differently from our A-quantifiers, then we can—and naturally will—imagine a cor-relative difference in the use of the word "refers". If we alter our concept of "a thing" then we alter our concept of "reference to a thing". But here especially we may feel impelled to say, "It's as if, relative to the M-language, there is something being referred to by the expression 'thing composed of Clinton's nose and the Eiffel Tower'". Again we must struggle to keep this simile in tow and not let it lead us into idealism.

III

Let me now briefly consider a few formulations that figure in the literature on realism and ask how they relate to quantifier variance. I will assume that these formulations are being posed in the A-language. (In the next section I will argue that people who speak plain English are in fact using the A-language, not the M-language.)

1. *The truth of a (contingent) statement in any language depends on what things exist and what properties these things have.* This claim is not threatened by quantifier variance. People who speak the M-language will have a different concept of "a thing" than mine, but the truth of their statements will depend on how it is with things in the world, in my (A-language) sense of "things in the world". For instance, if one person is touching Clinton's nose and another per-son is touching the Eiffel Tower, then the existence and properties of these things will render true the M-statement, "There exists a thing that is being touched by exactly two people".

Might there, however, be truths that do not depend on how things are, truths that are somehow not about things in my sense (or perhaps in any sense that I can make intelligible to myself)? I think that this question takes us into the vicinity of Kantian noumena and mysticism. It's not a question that I'm address-ing here.

This last question should, however, be distinguished from another one: Might there be things whose nature and unity I cannot understand? The doctrine of quantifier variance does not preclude there being such things.[7] (This relates to my earlier point that the doctrine is not to be confused with issues about the "analyzability" of existence and identity.)

2. *The truth of any (contingent) statement in any language depends on the existence and properties of the things referred to by the non-logical expres-sions in the statement.* This claim as it stands is immediately refuted by such sentences as "The average professor has fewer children than the average plumber", the truth of which evidently does not depend on there being any things referred to by the expressions "the average professor" and "the average plumber". Let's suppose, however, that this sentence can be viewed as in some sense "merely a transformation" of some other "basic" sentence. Claim 2 might then be roughly understood as saying that, in any language, the truth of a basic sen-tence depends on the existence and properties of the things referred to by the

non-logical expressions, and the truth of other sentences depends on their equivalence by way of transformation rules to some basic sentences.

Is claim 2 threatened by quantifier variance? If we suppose that the notion of "reference to a thing" is kept fixed to the language in which 2 is formulated (which I am now imagining to be the A-language), then I suspect that 2 is threatened. In terms of my A-concept of "reference to a thing" I cannot explain the truth of the M-statement "There exists a thing that exactly two people are touching" by appealing to the reference of "touching".[8] (Qunatifier variance might thus be said to induce a certain kind of systematic difference of meaning in the word "touching" and, by the same token, virtually any other general word.[9]) I might try to treat as "basic" only those sentences of the M-language that have the same truth-conditions as homophonic sentences in the A-language and derive the rest by transformations, but it is not obvious what such transformation rules would look like. Claim 2 requires that it be possible to formulate in my A-language something approximating to a Tarski-style theory of truth for the M-language, that is, very roughly put, a finitary account in terms of reference relations that yields for each of the indefinite number of M-sentences what the conditions are for its truth. It seems quite possible that this requirement can't be met.

If claim 2 constitutes a certain kind of "correspondence theory of truth" (what might be called a "referential correspondence theory") then this kind of correspondence theory may indeed fall to quantifier variance—assuming, again, that claim 2 is being formulated in the A-language and that what is meant by "reference to a thing" is kept fixed to this language. But I think it is therefore clear at this point that this kind of correspondence theory is not essential to a straightforward realist view of the world. The possible falsity of claim 2 does not threaten the basic realist idea (now being expressed in the A-language) that the world consists of things whose existence and properties are independent of language or consciousness.

Putnam takes Donald Davidson's animadversions against "the very idea of a conceptual scheme" to constitute a repudiation of quantifier variance.[10] I don't fully understand what Davidson is driving at in his talk against "conceptual schemes", but I doubt that it has really any definite connection to the issue of quantifier variance. Let us note that the M-language is "translatable" into my A-language in at least the following sense: For any M-sentence I can find an A-sentence with the same truth-conditions, where two sentences have the same truth-conditions if, relative to any context of utterance, they hold true with respect to the same possible situations.[11] This kind of intertranslatibility between the A-language and the M-language holds even if it's impossible to formulate in the A-language a finitary theory of truth for the M-language. ("For any M-sentence I can find an A-sentence with the same truth conditions" does not entail "There is a finitary truth-theory which yields, for any M-sentence, an A-sentence with the same truth-conditions".) It is indeed because of this intertranslatibility that the proponent of quantifier variance maintains that the two languages are equally capable of truthfully describing the world. I don't know, therefore, whether the A-language and the M-language qualify as "different conceptual schemes" in Davidson's sense. If they do, he has certainly said nothing to show why there couldn't be different conceptual schemes in this way.

Another idea associated with Davidson is that any (learnable) language must be describable in terms of (something approximating to) a Tarski-style truth-theory.[12] Interpreted in one way, this claim, too, is not threatened by quantifier variance. If it is possible to formulate in the A-language a truth-theory for the A-language, then it is possible to formulate in the M-language a truth-theory for the M-language, each theory being formulated in terms of each language's meaning of "reference to a thing". If, however, Davidson is claiming that it must be possible to formulate in our ("home") language a truth-theory for any possible language, this seems clearly untenable, for we can surely conceive of people whose sensory apparatus differs from ours to the extent that we cannot describe the truth-conditions of some of their sentences.[13]

A question that might be raised, however, is this: If we start out speaking the A-language (as I think we in fact do), and we are not able to formulate in this language a truth-theory for the M-language, how can we come to learn that language? How do we come to agree (as I assume we do) on the truth-conditions of an indefinite number of M-sentences? The answer is that we are relying on our shared sense of the analogy between our A-quantifier and the M-quantifier. Starting with the A-language I teach someone the M-language *ostensively*, by giving a few representative examples of how the M-language works. That anyone can then be expected to go on in the same way is part of what Putnam means when he says that our quantificational concepts admit of "many usable extensions".[14]

3. The truth of any (contingent) statement in any language depends on what the facts are in the world. This might also be put by saying that a statement's truth depends on *the way the world is*, the statement's being true only if the world is the way the statement says the world is. Claim 3 is another perennial version of "the correspondence theory of truth". Is it threatened by quantifier variance?

In the philosophical literature we find facts (as well as states-of-affairs, propositions, and properties) sometimes understood in a coarse-grained *unstructured* manner and sometimes in a fine-grained *structured* manner.[15] A structured fact is what Putnam describes—and rejects—as a "sentence-shaped thing in the world".[16] A fact in this sense is built up in a certain way out of things and properties (and perhaps logical operations). If we have logically equivalent sentences, such as "This is round" and "This is either round and red or round and not red", then each sentence expresses a different structured fact, or, as another alternative, they express the same structured fact but only one sentence (the first) succeeds (or succeeds better) in properly picturing the fact's structure. In the coarse-grained sense, however, these sentences express the same unstructured fact, and it therefore makes no sense to ask which sentence does better at depicting this fact.

If claim 3 is understood in terms of unstructured facts it does not conflict at all with quantifier variance. Quite the contrary, the basic idea of quantifier variance can be nicely formulated by saying that the same (unstructured) facts can be expressed using different concepts of "the existence of a thing", that statements involving different kinds of quantifiers can be equally true by virtue of the same (unstructured) facts in the world.

The notion of a structured fact does, however, raise certain problems for quantifier variance—but one must be careful not to misunderstand what these problems are. If I change what I mean by "a thing" then I must also change what I mean by "the way a fact is built up out of things and properties"; hence, I must change what I mean by "a structured fact". But, note carefully, that it does not follow that there are no structured facts independent of language— any more than it follows that there are no things independent of language. Indeed, when one looks at this carefully I think one sees that claim 3 can be sustained even if the facts on which the truth of statements depend are taken to be structured. I can say in my A-language that the truth of an M-statement depends on the structured facts, even though what I mean by "the structure of the facts" is not what a speaker of the M-language means.

A problem arises, however, if one wants to say that corresponding to any true statement in any language there is, as Putnam puts it, "a *unique* sentence-shaped thing in the world",[17] in other words, that each true sentence states one structured fact. How can we say which one that is? If we stick to our own language then we have the trivial disquotational formulation, "The sentence '*p*' states the structured fact that *p*", and perhaps we don't have to worry further about which structured facts are identical with which. But if I am speaking the A-language, how am I to say which structured fact is stated by the true M-sentence "There exists a thing that exactly two people are touching", when I am able to "translate" that sentence into a variety of structurally different sentences in my language having the same truth-conditions? I don't doubt that some moves might be made here (for instance, it might be suggested that it is indeterminate which structured fact, in my A-sense of "structured fact", the true M-sentence states), but I am inclined to agree with Putnam that, once we've accepted quantifier variance, there is no point in trying to hold onto language-shaped facts that are in the world independent of language. However, we can retain the notion of an unstructured fact. I think this is indeed our most basic notion of "reality", "the world", "the way it is", and this notion can remain invariant through any changes in our concept of "the things that exist".

IV

In the two passages quoted from Putnam at the outset of this paper he says in the first one that "there are many usable extensions of the notion of an object", and in the second that "the notions of object and existence have a multitude of different uses rather than one absolute 'meaning'". These two characterizations of quantifier variance are subtly different: the first seems to talk about the *possibility* of having different meanings attached to the quantifier, whereas the second seems to say that *in actuality* the quantifier is used with many different meanings. In the preceding discussion I was arguing in behalf of quantifier variance in the first sense, not the second; that is, I was arguing in behalf of *possible quantifier variance*, not *actual quantifier variance*.

In the discussion surrounding the second passage—the passage that seems to describe actual quantifier variance—Putnam criticizes an anti-mereologist who gives the following speech: "I know what you're talking about if by an object you mean a car, or a bee, or a human being, or a book, or the Eiffel Tower. I even understand it if you refer to my nose or the hood of my car as 'an object'. But when philosophers say that there is an 'object' consisting of *the Eiffel Tower and my nose*, that's just plain crazy. There simply is no such object. ... and it's crazy to suppose that every finite universe contains all the objects that those [mereologists] would invent, or, if you please, 'postulate'. You can't create objects by 'postulation' any more than you can bake a cake by 'postulation'".[18]

Now I am myself an anti-mereologist who considers the above speech to be quite reasonable. At least it seems reasonable if it is taken in the following spirit: "I assume we're all speaking plain English, and that we're employing the quantifier in the sense of plain English. Given that, I understand perfectly well what it means to talk (in plain English) about such things as cars, bees, human beings, books, and the Eiffel Tower, or even to talk about such marginal things as noses and car-hoods. But it's crazy to say (in plain English) that there exists something composed of my nose and the Eiffel Tower. And you can't create any such thing by 'postulating' it or by changing your language—that would be an absurd form of linguistic idealism". As a believer in possible quantifier variance I would add: "I can of course make intelligible to myself a possible language that differs from plain English in the meaning of its quantifier. In that imagined language the sentence 'There exists something that is composed of my nose and the Eiffel Tower' would be trivially true. If you're speaking that language for some reason, that's okay. Just don't pretend to be speaking plain English".

Putnam seems to reject this criticism of the mereologist because he thinks that, in plain English, there actually are different senses of the quantifier, and that the mereologist's claims are true in one of those plain English senses. It seems to me, however, that the linguistic evidence indicates that fluent speakers of English do not speak the mereologist's language. Speakers of English use what I was calling in previous sections the A-language; they do not use the M-language. My attitude towards the mereologist might be compared to the attitude that I and most current philosophers have towards the traditional epistemologist who says, "Only sense-data can be (strictly) perceived; physical objects cannot be perceived". Most philosophers would nowadays agree that the sense-data philosopher is saying something that is absurd. This is not to deny that we can imagine a use of "perceives" different from the one in plain English which would render the sense-data philosopher's remark true. Indeed, this philosopher's confusion might be characterized as "language gone on holiday"[19]; the philosopher has somehow confused himself into speaking a new language without realizing it. But confusion this is; the philosopher has made a mistake.

What holds for the sense-data philosopher holds as well, I think, for the mereologist. Putnam, it seems, doesn't see it that way. I'm quite sure he would agree with what I have said about sense-data philosophy, but he apparently views the issue of mereology differently. He says that if an anti-mereologist attacks the mereologist's view as being obviously wrong, then this shows that the anti-mereologist is a "metaphysical realist" who wrongly rejects Carnap's "principle of tolerance".[20] I think, however, that the attack can stem from the anti-mereologist's being a philosopher of common sense.

I think it's clear that Putnam's use of "metaphysical realism" has sometimes been confusing. I think he uses this term as the name of a certain attitude in metaphysics as much as the name of a definite philosophical position. To the extent that there is a position it is the denial of even the possibility of quantifier variance. Metaphysical realism says that there is somehow one metaphysically privileged sense of the quantifier, that any departure from this privileged sense would leave us without adequate resources to state the truth properly. There is, so to speak, the quantifier that God would use, and to get things metaphysically right, that's the quantifier we have to use. I think it is clear, however, that most people whom Putnam would call metaphysical realists have never heard of quantifier variance, and would not readily acknowledge that they have any special views about the necessity to use one kind of quantifier rather than another. It's their attitude when they philosophize that suggests that they tacitly deny the possibility of quantifier variance. What is the nature of this attitude? Putnam has characterized it in various ways throughout his writings, but I would like to put it as follows: these philosophers argue too much. They descend upon us as a legion of ontological lawyers, their briefcases overflowing with numerous arguments and counterarguments, a case for one entity, a case against another. Questions that appear to be trivial beyond the pale of conversation are somehow converted by them into occasions for deep theoretical debate. "Metaphysical realists" are afflicted with a kind of hyper-theoreticalness. I would certainly not claim that there is an inevitable connection between this affliction and the issue of quantifier variance, but I think that in many cases a potentially helpful diagnosis of the affliction would be roughly as follows: If whenever you make an existential claim in metaphysics you are tacitly or unconsciously assuming that the claim has to be couched in terms of a quantificational apparatus that is in some sense the uniquely right one—the one that God would use—then this assumption is likely to lead you to futile and interminable pseudo-theoretical arguments.

In his discussion of mereology Putnam implies that the proper remedy for the hyper-theoreticalness of "metaphysical realism" is Carnapian tolerance. I am suggesting that another remedy is "ordinary language philosophy" or an appeal to common sense. Each of these two remedies is appropriate in different cases. Carnapian tolerance is appropriate where an existential sentence being disputed by philosophers is actually vague or ambiguous in plain English (or whatever natural language the philosophers are speaking), and each disputant has in effect become attached to one permissible interpretation of the sentence. In this kind of case once the disputants realize that the quantifier admits of relevantly different interpretations in their language they should each say— thereby exhibiting Carnapian tolerance—that both of them are right, taking the quantifier in the relevantly different meanings. But there are other cases—and I think the case of mereology is an example—in which the disputed sentence admits of only one relevant meaning in plain English, and one of the disputants is saying something that—interpreted in plain English—is trivially absurd. What may prevent this disputant from simply acquiescing to ordinary usage and common sense is the implicit assumption that any question of ontology must be highly theoretical, because any such question turns on how to describe the world in terms of the metaphysically privileged sense of the quantifier. Once the possibility of quantifier variance is accepted, and the notion of a metaphysically privileged quantifier is abandoned, there is nothing to inhibit us from simply expressing the trivial common sense truth in terms of the quantifier we actually have in our language. In these kinds of examples acknowledging quantifier variance leads not to Carnapian tolerance but rather to the common-sense philosopher's ridicule of needless philosophical paradox.[21]

What may make it difficult for Putnam to see that the mereologist's position, stated in plain English, seems to be trivially absurd is the fact that there is a closely related position that is not absurd. If we have Clinton's nose and we have the Eiffel Tower then perhaps we also have the total quantity (or mass) of matter that composes these two things. To talk about *that matter* may seem tolerably correct in plain English. If so, there may be, in terms of plain English, something that can be said to consist of Clinton's nose and the Eiffel Tower. What needs to be understood, however, is that this is not the thing that mereologist's mean by "the sum of Clinton's nose and the Eiffel Tower". The matter that makes up the nose and the tower at one moment may not be exactly the same matter that makes up these objects at another moment; hence the matter cannot be identified with the mereologist's "sum" of the nose and the tower. Once this point is grasped I think it seems quite clear that there is no defensible interpretation of the plain English quantifier which would make true the sentence "There exists something that remains composed of Clinton's nose and the Eiffel Tower while these two objects alter their matter".

Perhaps the paradoxical effect of the mereologist's position is clearer if we consider non-contemporaneous objects, such as Socrates's nose and the Eiffel Tower, which the mereologist will say has a "sum". The paradox is still clearer when we add to the mereologist's position another doctrine that almost always goes together with it: the doctrine of temporal parts. If we have temporal parts and also mereological sums then we wind up with the position, familiar from Quine, Lewis, and many other philosophers, in which any set or series of bits of matter constitutes an object—that is, constitutes an object that can be said to occupy a place and to have ordinary qualities of shape, color, texture, and so on. Imagine that a tree stands in a certain yard, and that nothing extraordinary happens to it. Consider the succession of (stages of) bits of matter that make up the whole tree in the daytime and just the trunk during the nighttime. According to the position just mentioned this succession corresponds to an object on a par with the tree and the trunk. We could then give a name to such an object, say, "a shmree". A shmree, on this view, is a brown wooden object in the yard that loses its branches every night and regains them every morning. Surely to claim that there is such an object seems to violate common sense to the highest degree. Philosophers who are attracted to this view, I am suggesting, consciously or unconsciously reject the possibility of quantifier variance, and therefore take themselves to be engaged in some high-level theoretical speculation about whether the metaphysically privileged concept of existence—God's quantifier—would encompass shmrees. We who accept quantifier variance, on the other hand, consider the question about the existence of shmrees to be utterly trivial. It seems immediately clear that our ordinary concept of "a thing" renders the sentence "There is a thing in the yard that keeps gaining and losing branches" false. We can indeed make intelligible to ourselves a different concept of "a thing" which would render the sentence true, but, once we reject as unintelligible the idea of a metaphysically privileged concept of "a thing", there is no reason for us to resist acknowledging the concept that we in fact have. And, then, there is no reason to resist acknowledging the obvious and trivial truths that flow from that concept.

We can say, in the general spirit of ordinary language philosophy: It's obviously false to assert that there is a thing in the yard that gains and loses branches, because *that's not the way we talk*. But the appeal here to "the way we talk" is not to be misconstrued as suggesting the idealist view that, had we talked differently, there would have been something in the yard that gains and loses branches. The suggestion rather is that, had we talked differently, the sentence "There is a thing in the yard that gains and loses branches" would have been true. The appeal to "the way we talk" is a reminder that we have the concepts that we have and that, especially when we do philosophy, we need to remain responsible to the concepts we claim to be using, and not confuse ourselves into slipping inadvertently into a different way of talking.

If the denial of the possibility of quantifier variance leads to a certain kind of hyper-theoreticalness in ontology, the acceptance of quantifier variance leads to an attitude that might be called "ontological shallowness", or what Quine at one point calls "steadfast laymanship".[22] That is the attitude I am commending. What I have tried to explain is that, depending on what kind of case we are dealing with, ontological shallowness will either take the form of Carnapian tolerance or the form of insisting that the ontological judgments of common sense be respected in philosophy.

V

I am primarily concerned here with the ontology of physical objects—indeed, highly visible physical objects (roughly, what Austin called "moderate-sized dry goods"[23])—and the issue of quantifier variance with respect to that domain. I'm not addressing questions that involve abstract things (such as the familiar question whether numbers exist in the same sense as physical objects). I have maintained thus far that with respect to the domain of physical objects we can understand possible variations in the quantifier. Are there, however, examples of *actual* variations? Do we, in fact, when describing physical objects in plain English, alter the meaning of the quantifier?

Insofar as English is conceived of as an evolving language, whose major sortal-categories change somewhat from time to time, I'm inclined to think that this change carries with it some change in the meaning of "a thing", and therefore in the meaning of "the existence (and reference to) a thing". Moreover, insofar as a given speaker's repertoire of sortals changes over time, this may qualify as a change in the speaker's concept of "a thing" (modulo issues about the "communal" nature of each person's concepts). In any case, the "sortal-dependence" of our concept of "a thing" is an issue I have discussed at length elsewhere, and I will not try to add to it here.[24]

It's essential to distinguish between quantifier variance and what David Lewis calls quantifier *restriction*. Lewis points out that if, looking into the refrigerator, I assert, "There is no beer", I am restricting the quantifier to (the domain of) what is in the refrigerator. The unrestricted quantifier, by contrast, says what exists "strictly" or "*simpliciter*".[25] That the quantifier is often contextually restricted in the way that Lewis says may be granted by all. The question of quantifier variance, however, pertains to the unrestricted quantifier, to our concept of "existence *simpliciter*". We will see in a moment that Lewis, while often appealing in his work to restrictions on the quantifier, tacitly denies the possibility of there being variations in the unrestricted quantifier.

I have often heard it suggested—though not, to my knowledge, on the basis of anything Lewis himself says—that, once we acknowledge the phenomenon of quantifier restriction, it is no longer clear that the ontological commitments of Lewis and other philosophers, in favor of mereological sums and temporal parts, conflict with the views of common sense. Take, again, the sentence, "There exists a brown wooden thing in the yard that keeps losing its branches every night and gaining them back every morning". Lewis says that this sentence is true, and ordinary people say it is false. But that's because Lewis is using the quantifier unrestrictedly, whereas ordinary people are restricting the quantifier to the domain, roughly speaking, of "familiar bodies". So there is really no conflict, after all.

This suggestion is misguided, I think. Ordinary people must have a concept of "existence *simpliciter*". They must understand how to use the quantifier unrestrictedly; otherwise no such use could be part of the English language. With respect to the cited sentence, if we explain to ordinary people that the "brown wooden thing" in question need not be any kind of familiar thing, it need not be an interesting thing or the sort of thing one would normally talk about, they still regard the sentence as insanely false, though now qualified in absurdly irrelevant ways. For they take it for granted that there is no brown wooden thing in the yard *of any sort whatever* that keeps gaining and losing branches. They would in fact claim to be able to *see with their eyes* that this is the case. So there surely is the starkest conflict between the views of common sense and the ontological position of Lewis and other philosophers.

I've tried to indicate earlier that there is a certain general connection between the tacit rejection of quantifier variance and the tendency amongst many philosophers to reject the ontological judgments of common sense. In Lewis's case, however, there is a more specific connection between these two rejections. His main reason for believing in mereological sums, contrary (as he admits) to the views of common sense, is that he holds a certain view about quantifier vagueness that, as I will try to explain, comes out of his tacit rejection of quantifier variance.

Let me give an illustration to bring out Lewis's reasoning about mereological sums. Suppose we are constructing a very simple table out of a top and a leg. If we accept the common sense position, and do not believe in arbitrary mereological sums, we will say that at the beginning of this process, when the top and the leg were far apart (or, perhaps, when no one even had the plan to connect them), there wasn't any thing made up of the top and the leg. At the end of the process there is a thing, the table, made up of the top and the leg. Now, given the gradualness of this process (the gradualness, say, of driving a nail into a piece of wood or gluing two pieces of wood together), there must surely be a time at which it is indeterminate whether we have a table yet. At that time, then, it is indeterminate whether we have *anything* composed of the top and the leg.[26] But that, says Lewis, makes no sense. It can be indeterminate whether there exists something having a certain property only if there exists a thing such that it's indeterminate whether it has that property. In order for it to be indeterminate whether there exists something composed of the top and the leg, then, there must exist a thing such that it's indeterminate whether it is composed of the top and the leg. What thing could that be? It seems as if we are being led by the common sense view to say incoherently that there exists a certain thing such that it's indeterminate whether there exists that thing. "What is this thing such that it sort of is so, and sort of isn't, that there is any such thing?"[27]

The only coherent way to view the matter, Lewis concludes, is to assume, contrary to common sense, that at every point in the process there is something composed of the top and the leg. At some point in the process it may be indeterminate whether the thing composed of the top and the leg qualifies as a table. That's the only kind of indeterminateness that can make sense here. If we restrict the quantifier to tables (or "familiar objects") we can correctly say, "It's indeterminate whether there exists anything composed of the top and the leg", meaning that it's indeterminate whether the sum of the top and the leg is a table (or any other "familiar object".) But the quantifier can be restricted in that manner only against the background of arbitrary mereological sums.

The key assumption in Lewis's argument is the principle mentioned earlier: If it's indeterminate whether there exists something having a certain property, then there exists something such that it's indeterminate whether it has that property. If not for this principle we can simply say that it's indeterminate whether there exists something having the property of being composed of the top and the leg, though there isn't anything such that it's indeterminate whether it's composed of the top and the leg. So why should we accept this principle? If we deny the principle then we are saying that a sentence of the form "There exists something that is F" can be vague, not by virtue of the vagueness of the application of the term "F" to things, but by virtue of the vagueness of the rest of the sentence, that is, by virtue of the vagueness of the quantifier expression "there exists something". Lewis's argument depends on his denying the possibility that the quantifier can be vague.

Lewis is explicitly aware of this. And he tries to explain why the quantifier can't be vague as follows: "The only intelligible account of vagueness locates it in our thought and language.... Vagueness is semantic indecision. But not all of language is vague. The truth-functional connectives aren't.... Nor are the idioms of quantification, so long as they are unrestricted. How can any of these be vague? What would be the alternatives between which we haven't chosen?"[28]

I accept Lewis's assumption that vagueness is a matter of semantic indecision.[29] I won't say anything here about truth-functional connectives, but what is the problem Lewis is raising about the vagueness of the quantifier? Since the meaning of a logical constant is given by its role in determining the truth-conditions of sentences, the vagueness of the quantifier would consist in our semantic indecision with respect to the truth-conditions of certain sentences, for example, the sentence, "There exists something composed of the top and the leg". With respect to a situation in which the top and the leg are borderline attached, we are undecided about whether to count the sentence as true or false.

I can think of only one reason why Lewis rejects this explanation of the vagueness of the quantifier. The explanation requires us to be able to make sense of there being two possible meanings for the quantifier, the "precisifying" meaning that would make the sentence true and the one that would make it false. Quantifier vagueness requires the possibility of quantifier variance, and Lewis rejects the former because he rejects the latter.[30]

VI

In this final section I want to try to explain a bit further what I mean by commending a "shallow" approach to ontology. From the standpoint of shallow ontology Quine's portentous notion of "ontological commitment" already conveys an unfortunate aura of theoretical hype and pseudo-depth. One of the most striking characteristics of "deep ontology" is a certain kind of maddening modesty and caution in its formulations. Whereas the shallow ontologist will address a typical question of ontology either by shrugging it off with Carnapian tolerance for many different answers, or by insisting with Austinian glee that the answer is laughably trivial, the deep ontologist will tend to treat the question with the kind of somber speculative anxiety appropriate to matters of high theory. "All things considered, I am tentatively inclined to be ontologically committed to apple trees but not to apples".[31] The challenge for the shallow ontologist posed by this kind of formulation is how to keep a polite straight face while listening to it.

Even from the shallow perspective not every ontological question—within the domain of highly visible physical objects—can be quickly answered. Here is a good philosophical experiment: Look at your hand while you are clenching it, and ask yourself whether some object called a fist has come into existence. As shallow ontologists the first thought that must come to mind when we ask this question is this: *There can't be anything deep or theoretical here.* The facts are, so to speak, right in front of our eyes. Our task can only be to remind ourselves of relevant ways in which we describe these facts in our language. We might consider, for instance, comparisons and contrasts between how we talk about "making a table" and "making a fist". (For example, a table can be made and can be destroyed, but do we talk about "destroying a fist"?) Our task is to "*command a clear view* of the use of our words", as Wittgenstein put it,[32] that is, a clear view of how the relevant concepts operate. We're engaged in what Austin called "linguistic phenomenology", which need not always be an easy task.[33] Finally—and perhaps most importantly—we are open to the vagueness of "existence": The best answer might turn out to be that a fist sort of comes into existence and sort of doesn't.

The deep ontologist approaches this question in a very different spirit. She is engaged in the highly theoretical enterprise of deciding whether her "ontological commitments" should include fists that come into existence when hands are clenched. She will anguish over the "theoretical price" of having such things or not having them. She might eventually venture her best theoretical conjecture about whether fists come into existence. Or perhaps, after furrowing her brow for an appropriate period, she will simply announce that it "darkens the understanding" to suppose that fists keep popping in and out of existence.

Do the deep ontologists care about what common sense says? Sometimes they claim to be trying to balance the demands of common sense against the demands of philosophical theory.[34] The trouble is that theory seems always to win. When I consider the writings of some of the most prominent deep ontologists of recent years—Chisholm, Lewis, van Inwagen, just to mention three—I can rattle off many cases in which they veto a commonsensical judgment in behalf of a philosophical argument, but I would be hard pressed to recall an example in which the reverse happens. My impression is that, in matters of ontology, virtually any theoretical problem, however marginal or flimsy, if it cannot be adequately answered, suffices, by the lights of these philosophers, to trump the most deeply entrenched beliefs of common sense. For a shallow ontologist like me, the opposite is the case. Given any well entrenched ontological judgment of common sense (about highly visible physical objects), I could not imagine giving it up for the sake of some philosophical argument. If I had nothing more definite to say about the argument I would simply repeat Moore's famous point that the force of the common sense judgment shows that there must be something wrong with the argument (even if I don't know what it is).[35]

I am trying to roughly characterize two ways of approaching an ontological question, what I am calling the "shallow" and "deep" ways. This difference is no doubt partly a matter of intellectual temperament and style, but there is more to it than that. I'm especially interested here in how it relates to the issue of quantifier variance. Let me try to sketch now a general model that shows that common sense judgments of ontology must be taken very seriously. The model, it will be seen, presupposes the possibility of quantifier variance.

Suppose that two philosophers named Xstein and Ystein are engaged in an ontological dispute. I assume that both philosophers claim to be speaking plain English. We might attempt a certain strategy of semantic ascent. Perhaps both philosophers can be gotten to agree that there are two possible languages, call them Xglish and Yglish, such that every sentence asserted by Xstein is true in Xglish and every sentence asserted by Ystein is true in Yglish. Each philosopher agrees that he can understand what the truth-conditions are of the sentences in both languages, and that, in terms of those truth-conditions, he could express in either language everything (every unstructured fact) he wants to assert. In these circumstances, if it were known that Xstein is speaking Xglish and Ystein is speaking Yglish, then these philosophers could simply agree that both are speaking the truth in their respective languages. Of course, this happy result cannot be quite right, since each philosopher claims to be speaking English, which can't be both Xglish and Yglish.

Now suppose, further, that typical fluent speakers of English assert the sentences that Xstein asserts and reject the sentences that Ystein asserts. In other words, they assert sentences that are true in Xglish but false in Yglish. This would seem to be overwhelming evidence that the language they speak is Xglish, not Yglish. As usual, I am focused on sentences having to do with highly visible physical objects. By any reasonable standards of interpretation—for example, the standards explained by Lewis[36]—we ought to say that these people are uttering truths in Xglish, rather than that they are uttering falsehoods in Yglish.

We have concluded that English is Xglish. We have, therefore, also concluded that Xstein is right and Ystein is wrong. Since they both claim to be speaking English, it is Xstein, not Ystein, who is saying the truth in English. It appears that Ystein has allowed "language to go on holiday"; Ystein's philosophical theorizing has apparently confused him into in effect slipping into a language of his own creation, the language Yglish. Of the lamentable Ystein we must say, following Wittgenstein, that his theorizing has led him to "have a new conception and interpret it as seeing a new object [or seeing the absence of an old object]." [37]

As an illustration of this model: Let Lewish be the language in which all of David Lewis's ontological utterances (with respect to highly visible physical objects) are true; let Inwagish be the language in which all of Peter van Inwagen's ontological utterances are true; and let Shmenglish be the language in which the typical ontological utterances of non-philosophers are true. (By "true" I always mean "true in the strictest and most philosophical sense", whatever that is supposed to mean; and I am always assuming an unrestricted use of the quantifier.) The sentence "There exists a brown wooden thing in the yard that keeps gaining and losing branches" is true in Lewish but false in both Inwagish and Shmenglish. The sentence "There exists apples" is true in both Lewish and Shmenglish but false in Inwagish. And so on. I expect the reader to be able to fill in the truth-conditions of the indefinite number of sentences in these three languages.

Both Lewish and Inwagish correspond to Yglish, and Shmenglish corresponds to Xglish. Both Lewis and van Inwagen correspond to Ystein, and I—the shallow ontologist, who simply asserts the same sentences that are asserted by ordinary speakers of English—correspond to Xstein. The argument proceeds as before. Since the typical fluent speaker of English asserts sentences that are true in Shmenglish, but false in both Lewish and Inwagish, the evidence seems to be overwhelming that English is Shmenglish, not either Lewish or Inwagish. Therefore, I am right, and both Lewis and van Inwagen are wrong. Only my ontological sentences are true in English (= Shmenglish); theirs are not. Their sentences are true in either Lewish or Inwagish, but not in English, which is the language they both claim to be speaking.

It will be objected that something essential has been left out of my model. What about the theoretical arguments these philosophers give for their positions? Why haven't those arguments been taken into account?

But how *can* they be taken into account? That's my main point here. Those arguments have no obvious bearing on what has now become the critical question: whether English is Shmenglish. Remember, if English is Shmenglish, then it follows directly that both Lewis and van Inwagen are mistaken; that simply follows from the way Shmenglish has been defined. It appears now that all of the deep ontologist's theoretical maneuvers have no relevance to rebutting the seemingly obvious fact that English is Shmenglish.

I've already considered Lewis's argument about the vagueness of the quantifier. As another and more typical ontological argument, let's briefly consider

Lewis's reason for believing in temporal parts. Lewis's argument derives from a problem about what he calls "temporary intrinsics".[38] The problem, roughly put, is as follows. If an object can have a shape at one moment and lose it at another moment, as common sense says, then the shape is being treated logically and semantically as if it were a relation binding the object to a time. But shapes are intrinsic properties, not relations. The only way to hold onto the intrinsicness of shapes is to claim, contrary to common sense, that what has the shape is a temporal part of the object, and this temporal part never loses the shape.

Now I don't myself see this as a genuinely worrisome problem.[39] But I don't want to enter into the details of this issue. My point now is something else. How does Lewis's problem of temporary intrinsics bear on the question whether English is Shmenglish? Remember, once again, that if English is Shmenglish then it follows that Lewis is wrong in asserting (in English) that there are temporal parts. It is given that the following sentence, which Lewis holds to be false in English, but to which typical speakers of English assent, is true in Shmenglish: "A bent wooden stick can sometimes be straightened without any wooden thing going out of existence". In order for the problem of temporary intrinsics to show that English is not Shmenglish the problem would somehow have to be reflected in the speech behavior of typical fluent speakers of English, perhaps by their being disposed to assent to the sentence, "Shapes are intrinsic properties, and an intrinsic property cannot be treated logically and semantically as if it were a relation binding an object to a time". In all likelihood, only typical fluent speakers of English with philosophy degrees from Princeton would have any strong tendency to assent to this sentence. But, furthermore, whatever evidence Lewis might be able to marshal from the speech behavior of typical speakers of English vis-à-vis the problem of temporary intrinsics, this would have to be capable of defeating the overwhelming evidence that English is Shmenglish that derives from the unambiguous disposition of typical speakers to assent to countless sentences such as, "A bent wooden stick can sometimes be straightened without any wooden thing (of any sort whatever, whether familiar or not, interesting or not) going out of existence". I cannot see how Lewis could argue successfully that English is not Shmenglish, let alone argue successfully that English is Lewish.

I am aware that my argument from the Xstein-Ystein model requires various refinements—I intend to provide these elsewhere—but I think that the argument even in its sketchiest form indicates that there is something fundamentally incoherent in the attempt of philosophers to deny basic and seemingly trivial ontological beliefs of common sense.

The point at which my argument depends on quantifier variance is in its assumption that we have these three possible languages, Lewish, Inwagish, and Shmenglish, each with its own quantificational apparatus and concept of "the existence of a thing". A philosopher might try to block the argument by holding that Shmenglish is not a possible language. The burden would fall on this philosopher to explain why the seemingly most obvious interpretation of the language we speak is not a possibility. I don't see how this burden can be met.[40]

Notes

1. Hilary Putnam, "The Question of Realism" in *Words and Life* (Harvard University Press, Cambridge, Mass., 1994), pp. 304–305.
2. Hilary Putnam, "Truth and Convention: On Davidson's Refutation of Conceptual Relativism", *Dialectica*, Vol. 41 (1987), 69–77, at p. 71.
3. "Truth and Convention", pp. 70 ff.
4. Subject to a slight qualification to be made later.
5. John Wisdom, *Philosophy and Psychoanalysis* (University of California Press, Berkeley, 1969).
6. Ernest Sosa's "existential relativity" has it that things exist relative to conceptual schemes, but Sosa takes great pains to disassociate himself from the idealist claim that language or thought literally creates things. An important question considered in Sosa's discussion, which I'm bypassing here, is how "far down" quantifier variance can go. See Ernest Sosa, "Existential Relativity", *Midwest Studies in Philosophy*, 22 (1999), and my "Sosa's Existential Relativism", forthcoming in the Blackwell volume on *Sosa and His Critics*.
7. So the doctrine need not prevent us from agreeing with Thomas Nagel's claim in *The View from Nowhere* (Oxford University Press, N.Y., 1986), p. 98: "We can speak of 'all the things we can't describe', 'all the things we can't imagine', 'all the things humans can't conceive of', and, finally, 'all the things humans are constitutionally incapable of ever conceiving'."
8. I am perhaps making some sort of controversial assumption here related to the inscrutability of reference, or better put, the scrutability of non-reference, for it might be questioned whether some kind of ingenious reference scheme assigning a reference to "touching" might somehow do the trick. I'm quite sure that this is impossible, but perhaps I should limit myself to saying more cautiously that I don't see what such a scheme could be. See, further, my *Dividing Reality* (Oxford University Press, N.Y., 1993), pp. 102–109, and my "Objectivity Without Objects" in the *Proceedings of the Twentieth World Congress of Philosophy: Epistemology*, Vol. 5 (Philosophy Documentation Center, Bowling Green State University, 2000) .
9. There may yet be a sense in which the qualities (features, points of similarity) signified by general words remain the same despite quantifier variance. I am leaving a number of questions open here.
10. This seems to be Putnam's assumption in "Truth and Convention." See Donald Davidson, "On The Very Idea of a Conceptual Scheme", in *Inquiries into Truth and Interpretation* (Oxford University Press, London, 1984).
11. In other words, they have the same "character" in the sense of David Kaplan, "Demonstratives" in J. Almog, J. Perry, and H. K. Wettstein, eds., *Themes from Kaplan* (Oxford University Press, N.Y., 1989).
12. See *Inquiries into Truth and Interpretation*.
13. See Thomas Nagel's criticism of Davidson in *The View from Nowhere*, pp. 94–98.
14. "The Question of Realism", p. 305.

15. See George Bealer, *Quality and Concept* (Oxford University Press, N.Y., 1982), pp. 181–187, and David Lewis, *On the Plurality of Worlds* (Basil Blackwell Ltd, N.Y., 1986), p. 56. It must be borne in mind that I have defined the notion of "truth-conditions"—and consistently use it here—in the coarse-grained unstructured sense.

16. "The Question of Realism", p. 301.

17. "The Question of Realism", p. 301 (my emphasis).

18. "Truth and Convention", p. 72.

19. See Ludwig Wittgenstein, *Philosophical Investigations*, I, 38.

20. "Truth and Convention", p. 73.

21. I allude casually here to Carnapian tolerance because Putnam mentions it. I am not seriously discussing or defending Carnap's own thinking on these matters. He seemed to imply that realists ought to "tolerate" phenomenalists, which I think is out of the question for reasons that go beyond the present discussion. See Rudolph Carnap, "Empiricism, Semantics, and Ontology," in *Meaning and Necessity*, 2nd edition (University of Chicago Press, Chicago, 1956).

22. W. V. Quine, *Word and Object* (MIT Press, Cambridge, Mass., 1960), p. 261.

23. J. L. Austin, *Sense and Sensibilia* (Oxford University Press, London, 1962), p. 8.

24. The notion of sortal-dependence has been introduced to contemporary philosophy by Wiggins's seminal work, but I cannot tell what his attitude is towards quantifier variance. See David Wiggins, *Sameness and Substance* (Harvard University Press, Cambridge, Mass., 1980). I discuss sortal-dependence in *The Concept of Identity* (Oxford University Press, N.Y., 1982), especially chs. 2 and 3, and "Basic Objects: A Reply to Xu", *Mind and Language*, Vol. 12, 3 (1997), 406–412.

25. Lewis, *On the Plurality of Worlds*, p. 3.

26. A variation of Lewis's argument, with convincing arguments that there must be examples of the relevant kind of indeterminateness, is given in Theodore Sider, "Four Dimensionalism", *The Philosophical Review*, Vol. 106, no. 2, 197–231.

27. Lewis, *On the Plurality of Worlds*, pp. 212–213.

28. Ibid, p. 212.

29. But the argument I am about to go through would be unaffected if we accepted instead Williamson's epistemic view of vagueness. Lewis and Williamson agree that, for the quantifier to be vague, it must admit of different "interpretations". The argument is unaffected by whether these interpretations are taken to be different possible "precisifications", as in Lewis, or different guesses (which we can't verify) about the one correct interpretation, as in Williamson. See Timothy Williamson, *Vagueness* (Routledge, London, 1994), especially pp. 164, 237, 257–258.

30. An argument similar to Lewis's, but somewhat more difficult to unravel, stems from the vagueness of identity sentences. Such an argument is given in Sydney Shoemaker, "On What There Are", *Philosophical Topics*, 16 (1988). I try to show why that argument doesn't work, appealing in effect to quantifier variance, in my "The Vagueness of Identity", *Philosophical Topics*, 26 (1999).

31. For the uninitiated, who may possibly think that at least in this example I am tilting at windmills, the example actually expresses the position defended in Peter van Inwagen's extremely influential *Material Beings* (Cornell University Press, Ithaca, N.Y., 1990).

32. *Philosophical Investigations*, I, 122.

33. J. L. Austin, "A Plea for Excuses", in *Philosophical Papers* (Oxford University Press, London, 1961). It goes without saying that we need not be sympathetic to everything that went under the name "ordinary language philosophy."

34. Lewis often presents his methodology as involving this kind of balancing. See, for example, *Philosophical Papers*, vol. I (Oxford University Press, N.Y., 1983), p. x, and *On the Plurality of Worlds*, pp. 134–135.

35. See G. E. Moore, "A Defense of Common Sense", p. 41, and "Four Forms of Scepticism", p. 222, both in *Philosophical Papers* (Collier Books, N.Y., 1962). See also Ned Markosian, "Brutal Composition", *Philosophical Studies* 92 (1998), 211–249.

36. See his "Radical Interpretation", in *Philosophical Papers*, Vol. I.

37. *Philosophical Investigations*, I, 401.

38. Lewis, *On the Plurality of Worlds*, pp. 202–204.

39. Because to say that a shape is intrinsic might mean intuitively that a thing's having a certain shape at a certain time does not depend on how it is related to other things at that time.

40. In *Dividing Reality* I sought to uncover some general constraints that would make it impossible for a natural language to diverge (too much) from the taken-at-face-value semantic structure of English. My conclusion in that book was that no interesting constraints seem to be defensible. Had the sought-after constraints emerged, although they would certainly have allowed some forms of quantifier variance (in particular, the quantifier variance involved in quantifier vagueness, and that involved in sortal-dependence), they may have implied that either Lewish or Inwagish is not a possible language. An argument for the impossibility of Shmenglish would have to move in the opposite direction: to show that the taken-at-face-value semantic structure of English is not a possibility. In responding to an earlier version of my argument from Shmenglish a few years ago, Sider in fact held that Shmenglish is not a possible language (because, very roughly, its quantifier fails to correspond to the world's logical joints). (See, further, the Introduction to Theodore Sider, *Four Dimensionalism: An Ontology of Persistence and Time* [Oxford University Press, forthcoming].) Will that, I wonder, be the deep ontologist's standard response to my question?

Philosophical Issues, 12, Realism and Relativism, 2002

CONCEPTUAL RELATIVITY AND METAPHYSICAL REALISM

Terry Horgan, University of Arizona
Mark Timmons, University of Memphis

Is conceptual relativity a genuine phenomenon? If so, how is it properly understood? And if it does occur, does it undermine metaphysical realism? These are the questions we propose to address. We will argue that conceptual relativity is indeed a genuine phenomenon, albeit an extremely puzzling one. We will offer an account of it. And we will argue that it is entirely compatible with metaphysical realism.

Metaphysical realism is the view that there is a world of objects and properties that is independent of our thought and discourse (including our schemes of concepts) about such a world. Hilary Putnam, a former proponent of metaphysical realism, later gave it up largely because of the alleged phenomenon that he himself has given the label 'conceptual relativity'. One of the key ideas of conceptual relativity is that certain concepts—including such fundamental concepts as object, entity, and existence—have a multiplicity of different and incompatible uses (Putnam 1987, p. 19; 1988, pp. 110–14). According to Putnam, once we recognize the phenomenon of conceptual relativity we must reject metaphysical realism:

> The suggestion ... is that what is (by commonsense standards) the same situation can be described in many different ways, depending on how we use the words. The situation does not itself legislate how words like "object," "entity," and "exist" must be used. What is wrong with the notion of objects existing "independently" of conceptual schemes is that there are no standards for the use of even the logical notions apart from conceptual choices." (Putnam 1988, p. 114)

Putnam's intriguing reasoning in this passage is difficult to evaluate directly, because conceptual relativity is philosophically perplexing and in general is not well understood.[1] In this paper we propose a construal of conceptual relativity that clarifies it considerably and explains how it is possible despite its initial air of paradox. We then draw upon this construal to explain why, contrary to Putnam and others, conceptual relativity does not conflict with metaphysical realism, but in fact comports well with it. Our paper has two main parts.

In part I we dwell on the phenomenon itself. We explain why conceptual relativity is so puzzling—indeed, why it initially appears impossible. We identify three interrelated assumptions lying behind this apparent impossibility—assumptions about concepts, meanings, and affirmatory conflict—and we argue that in order to make sense of conceptual relativity, all three must be rejected. We then set forth an account of relativity-susceptible concepts and meanings that explains how conceptual relativity is possible and why it is actual—an account that eschews the three problematic assumptions.

In part II, we turn to the issue of the compatibility of conceptual relativity and metaphysical realism. Our main task here is to explain how the two can be reconciled. In doing so, we sketch a general account of *truth* that in previous writings we have called "contextual semantics." We argue that the framework provided by contextual semantics smoothly accommodates the phenomenon of conceptual relativity (as explicated in part I), while at the same time allowing this kind of relativity to be combined with metaphysical realism.

I. Understanding Conceptual Relativity

1. Why Conceptual Relativity Seems Impossible

Putnam uses the expression 'conceptual relativity' for a property of intentional notions including truth, reference, and meaning. He says that conceptual relativity "is a property which has only emerged as central in the twentieth century, and its very existence is still most often ignored, if not actually denied" (Putnam 1988, p 110). In fact, there is an air of paradox surrounding the various illustrations of this alleged phenomenon. Consider, for instance, one of Putnam's illustrations of conceptual relativity—the well-known example of Carnap and the Polish logician (Putnam 1987, pp. 18–20).

In this scenario (slightly modified), Carnap and the Polish logician are presented with a number of objects (say, books lying on a table) and each of them is asked how many objects there are on the table. Carnap, employing the ordinary concept of object, reports that there are exactly three objects on the table: $O1$, $O2$, and $O3$. By contrast the Polish logician, who accepts a particular mereology of objects according to which for every two particulars there is an object that is their "mereological sum," counts the objects on the table and reports that there are exactly seven: $O1$, $O2$, $O3$, $O1+O2$, $O1+O3$, $O2+O3$, and $O1+O2+O3$.

This case seems to be one in which we have *conflicting* but *equally correct* judgments about the number of objects on the table. We might express this combination of ideas in terms of two principles:

Principle of affirmatory conflict. There is a genuine conflict in what Carnap and the Polish logician are respectively affirming about how many objects there are: Carnap's claim that there are exactly three objects on the table conflicts with the Polish logician's claim that there are exactly seven.

Principle of mutual correctness. Both Carnap and the Polish logician are correct in their respective claims about how many objects there are on the table, because each of them is making a claim which, relative to a specific way of using the concept of object, is true.[2]

It seems to us that Putnam is pointing to a genuine, and important, phenomenon. In a significant sense, Carnap's way of counting objects and the Polish logician's way are in conflict; they are not just talking past one another. And yet, given the principles for counting that they each are employing, they are both making claims that are correct.

But although the phenomenon in question seems real, on reflection it is also quite puzzling because, initially anyway, these principles appear to be mutually incompatible. Here are two complementary arguments that make the point.[3]

The argument from affirmatory conflict. According to the first principle, there is a genuine conflict between the claims of Carnap and the Polish logician about how many objects there are. Now in order for there to be genuine conflict in this case, Carnap and the Polish logician must be employing the same concept of object and using the associated term with the same meaning. Otherwise, there is no genuine conflict between their respective claims; they are just talking past one another. But if they are employing the same concept of object and so using the term 'object' with the same meaning, then their conflict must consist in the *mutual inconsistency* of their respective claims about how many objects are on the table. But if the two claims are inconsistent, then they cannot both be correct! And this means that the other key ingredient in the phenomenon of conceptual relativity—the principle of mutual correctness—is false. In this way, reflection on one side of the phenomenon of conceptual relativity leads to the denial of the other.

The argument from mutual correctness. We get a similar result if we begin with the principle of mutual correctness, according to which Carnap and the Polish logician, given their uses of the concept of object, are both correct in their respective claims about the number of objects on the table. If each of their claims is correct, then those claims cannot be inconsistent with one another. Furthermore, if the respective claims are not mutually inconsistent—if, that is, when Carnap says there are exactly three objects on the table his claim does not contradict the Polish logician's claim that there are exactly seven—then they must be employing different concepts of object and using the term 'object' with different meanings. But if they are employing different concepts of object and using the term 'object' with different meanings, then their claims are really not in conflict after all! Thus, if Carnap and the Polish logician are both correct in their respective claims, then they are just talking past one another—contrary to the principle of affirmatory conflict. Again, reflection on one of the key ingredients involved in conceptual relativity (this time the principle of mutual correctness) leads, by a series of seemingly plausible steps, to the denial of the other ingredient.

Thus, we arrive at the apparent conclusion that conceptual relativity, understood as involving the two principles in question, is impossible.

2. Questionable Assumptions

As we have said, we do think that conceptual relativity is a genuine phenomenon, and thus should be accounted for. Also, the phenomenon does indeed involve the features described by the principles of affirmatory conflict and mutual correctness. So something must be wrong with the reasoning that leads to the rejection of this phenomenon. When confronted with a philosophical puzzle of this sort, the thing to do is to look for one or more underlying assumptions—ones that, while perhaps common and initially plausible, should be challenged. What are they?

In connection with the identity of concepts and meanings, there is a pair of related assumptions that we question. Both involve semantic standards that govern the correct employment of concepts and words—that is, standards that determine the conditions under which statements employing the words, and judgments employing the concepts those words express, are true. Regarding concepts, the assumption involved is this:

I_1 If the semantic standards governing the correct employment of concept C_1, as employed by person P_1 at time t_1, differ from the semantic standards governing the correct employment of concept C_2, as employed by person P_2 at time t_2, then $C_1 \neq C_2$.

That is, any difference between two persons with respect to the semantic standards governing their respective usage of certain concepts is sufficient to make it the case that they thereby are employing *non-identical* concepts. (Likewise for one person's usage at two different times.) Here is a parallel assumption, with respect to words and their meanings:

I_2 If the semantic standards for the correct employment of word W, as it is used by person P_1 at time t_1, differ from the semantic standards for the correct employment of W, as it is used by person P_2 at time t_2, then the meaning of W as used by P_1 at $t_1 \neq$ the meaning of W as used by P_2 at t_2.

That is, any difference between two persons with respect to the semantic standards governing their respective usage of a certain word is sufficient to make it the case they thereby are employing that word with *non-identical* meanings. (Likewise for one person's usage at two different times.) We dub the view of concepts and meanings captured by I_1 and I_2 the *invariantist* view. The idea is that the semantic standards that govern concepts and words cannot vary from one usage to another, insofar as the *same* concept of word-meaning is employed in both usages: any difference in governing semantic standards reflects a distinct concept or word-meaning. Concepts and word-meanings never preserve their self-identity under changes of the semantic standards that govern them.

But, in addition to these assumptions, the pair of arguments challenging conceptual relativity rests on a certain conception of genuine affirmatory conflict, namely:

> DI   All cases of genuine affirmatory conflict—cases in which what person P_1 affirms at time t_1 conflicts with what person P_2 affirms at time t_2—involve straightforward inconsistency between what P_1 and P_2 are thinking or saying.

Call this the *direct-inconsistency conception* of affirmatory conflict.

If indeed conceptual relativity is a genuine phenomenon—as we contend it is—then these various assumptions will have to be rejected. In order to make sense of conceptual relativity, one needs to explain how the members of the following list of ideas can be mutually compatible:

1. Persons P_1 and P_2 are making conflicting claims. [Principle of affirmatory conflict]
2. So they must be employing the same concept of object and using the term 'object' with the same meaning.
3. But they are also making claims that are mutually correct. [Principle of mutual correctness]
4. So their claims cannot be flatly inconsistent.

The gist of the puzzle is to explain how all four of these claims can be correct. Doing so should also thereby explain why and how it is that although Carnap's statement and the Polish logician's statement do indeed conflict semantically, nevertheless this conflict between them is not a theoretically *weighty* one, but rather is "no big deal"—as they themselves might well both acknowledge.

Executing this explanatory project requires accomplishing three interrelated tasks. First, we must replace the invariantist view of concepts and meanings with what we will call a *variantist* conception. The key idea is that the semantic standards that govern certain concepts can vary from one usage to another even though the same concept is employed on both occasions—and even though the word expressing it has the same meaning on both occasions. Such semantic differences in correct usage are *identity-preserving* differences in concepts and meanings. The task is to explain why and how it is that some concepts and meanings actually do conform to this variantist conception.[4]

Second, we must harness the account of identity-preserving semantic differences in order to explain the principle of mutual correctness. The task is to explain why it is that Carnap and the Polish logician, despite the fact that they are employing a single concept of object and using the term 'object' with a single meaning, are both correct in their respective claims about how many objects are on the table.

Third, we also must harness the account of identity-preserving semantic differences to explain the principle of affirmatory conflict. The task is to explain why it is that the respective claims of Carnap and the Polish logician, despite the fact that they are both correct, nevertheless do conflict with one another in some fairly robust way. Such an explanation must repudiate the third assumption identified above—the direct-inconsistency conception of affirmatory conflict—and must replace it with an alternative conception. This alternative must identify a tension-relation R that obtains between Carnap's claim and the Polish logician's claim, and that exhibits these two features: (i) R is compatible with the mutual correctness of the two claims, and yet (ii) R still has enough bite, qua tension-relation, to count as a genuine form of affirmatory *conflict* (albeit conflict that is, in an important sense, "no big deal").

Accomplishing all three tasks will provide an explanation of how items 1–4 can all be true, and thus how conceptual relativity is possible. Let us now proceed to the first task.

3. The Variantist View of Concepts and Meanings

Entities of various sorts certainly can change in some ways—can alter through time—without thereby losing their identity. Persons, for instance, change as they grow older, and yet they retain their self-identity all the while. They undergo identity-preserving changes, and the differences between a person at one moment in time and that same person at another moment of time are identity-preserving differences.

The claim we want to make, by way of rejecting the invariantist view as expressed in theses I_1 and I_2, is this: whatever exactly concepts and meanings are, they are subject to certain kinds of identity-preserving differences in correct usage. One and the same concept can be used by two persons (or by one person, at different times) in ways that are governed by somewhat different semantic standards, while still being the *same* concept. Likewise, one and the same word can be used in two ways involving somewhat different semantic standards, while still possessing the *same* meaning under both uses. A concept or word as used by one person can differ somewhat in its semantically proper employment from its proper employment as used by another person (or by the same person at a different time), and yet it is the *same* concept or word anyway: the differences are identity-preserving. Adapting a useful philosophical term from Derrida, we will say that an identity-preserving difference in two uses of a given concept, or in the meaning of a given word, is a *différance* in concepts (or in meaning).[5]

Let us consider some examples. Putnam himself has noted the diachronic version of the phenomenon we are calling différance in concepts and meaning—although he does not call it by this name, and he does not link it directly to conceptual relativity (as we will do presently). One of his examples features the concept of momentum in physics:

> In Newtonian physics the term *momentum* was defined as "mass times velocity." (Imagine, if you like, that the term was originally equated with this *definiens* by the decision of a convention of Newtonian physicists.) It quickly became apparent that momentum was a conserved quantity.... But with the acceptance of Einstein's Special Theory of Relativity a difficulty appeared. Einstein...showed that the principle of Special Relativity would be violated if momentum were *exactly* equal to (rest) mass times velocity. What to do?... Can there be a quantity with the properties that (1) it is conserved in elastic collisions, (2) it is closer and closer to "mass times velocity" as the speed becomes small, and (3) its direction is the direction of motion of the particle? Einstein showed that there *is* such a quantity, and he (and everyone else) concluded that that quantity *is what momentum is*. The statement that momentum is *exactly* equal to mass times velocity was revised. *But this is the statement that was originally a "definition"*! And it was reasonable to revise this statement; for why should the statement that momentum is conserved not have at least as great a right to be preserved as the statement "momentum is mass times velocity" when a conflict is discovered?... When the statements in our network of belief have to be modified, we have "trade-offs" to make; and what the best trade-off is in a given context cannot be determined by consulting the traditional "definitions" of terms. (Putnam 1988, pp. 9–10)

According to Putnam, then, the term 'momentum' and its associated concept has undergone, over time, an identity-preserving change. In this example and others like it, the meaning of at least some terms, and the nature of their associated concepts, depends to some extent upon a certain network of background beliefs; when those change sufficiently, the concept and meaning change in certain ways. But the difference between the concept and meaning at an earlier stage, and the concept and meaning at a later stage, is an identity-preserving difference—a différance. As Putnam remarks about this phenomenon:

> If this seems strange, it is because we are not used to thinking of meanings as being historic entities in the sense in which persons or nations are historic entities.... There are practices which help us decide when there is enough continuity through change to justify saying that the same person still exists. In the same way, we treat "momentum" as referring to the same quantity that it always referred to, and there are practices which help us decide that there is enough continuity through change to justify doing this. Meanings have an identity through time but no essence. (Putnam 1988, p. 11)

Turn next to synchronic cases of différance (which will be particularly important for purposes of understanding conceptual relativity). Here a given concept, and the meaning of a term expressing the concept, both have a certain structural feature: viz., possessing one or more implicit semantic aspects or dimensions that are subject to contextual variation across different uses of the term or concept. We will call such an aspect a *contextually variable parameter*; it is what David Lewis (1979/1983) called a component of the "score in the language game." Consider, for example, competing uses of the term 'flat', with respect (e.g.) to whether or not a particular sidewalk is flat. Lewis has this to say, concerning Peter Unger's views about flatness:

> Peter Unger has argued that hardly anything is flat. Take something you claim is flat; he will find something else and get you to agree that it is even flatter. You think that the pavement is flat—but how can you deny that your desk is flatter? But flat is an *absolute* term: it is inconsistent to say that something is flatter than something that is flat. Having agreed that your desk is flatter than the pavement, you must concede that the pavement is not flat after all. Perhaps you now claim that your desk is flat; but doubtless Unger can think of something that you will agree is even flatter than your desk. And so it goes. Some might dispute Unger's premise that "flat" is an absolute term, but ... I think he is right.... The right response to Unger, I suggest, is that he is changing the score on you. When he says that the desk is flatter than the pavement, what he says is acceptable only under raised standards of precision. Under the original standards the bumps on the pavement were too small to be relevant either to the question whether the pavement is flat or to the question whether the pavement is flatter than the desk. (Lewis 1983, pp. 245–46)

We claim, with Lewis, that the semantically correct use of the notion of flatness depends upon certain implicit, contextually operative, standards of precision—standards that can permissibly vary somewhat from one usage to another. The standards of precision that govern a particular use constitute the specific current setting of what may be called the *precision parameter* for flatness. As the passage from Lewis makes clear, this parameter is contextually variable: it can take on different specific settings in particular contexts. This contextual variability is semantically built into the *single* concept flatness, and into the meaning of the term 'flat'. What you mean when you use 'flat' in such a way that the sidewalk counts as flat is somewhat different from what Unger means when he uses 'flat' in such a way that it doesn't; likewise, mutatis mutandis, for the nature of the concept of flatness as employed by you, as distinct from its nature as employed by Unger. But these differences in meaning, and in concept, are *identity-preserving* differences. There is a différance in meaning, and in concept, between yourself and Unger.

In light of these observations we propose to replace the invariantist view of concepts and meanings with what we will call the *variantist* conception, which recognizes the phenomenon of identity-preserving differences. Thus, we replace I₁ with:

V_1 The semantic standards for the correct employment of C_1, as C_1 is employed by person P_1 at time t_1, may differ in certain permissible ways from the semantic standards for the correct employment of concept C_2, as C_2 is employed by person P_2 at time t_2, while $C_1 = C_2$. When this occurs we have differance in concepts.

And a similar principle about the meanings of words replaces I_2:

V_2 The semantic standards for the correct employment of word W, as it is used by person P_1 at time t_1, may differ in certain permissible ways from the semantic standards for the correct employment of W, as it is used by person P_2 at time t_2, and yet the meaning of P_1's word W = the meaning of P_2's word W. When this occurs we have a differance in meanings.

Two potential sources of differance in concepts and meanings have been mentioned in this section. One source, manifested in diachronic cases of differance like Putnam's example of momentum, is the fact that the synchronic nature of a concept or a word-meaning at a particular moment in history depends partly upon certain background beliefs prevalent at that time; concepts and meanings can change through time, when the pertinent background beliefs change in certain ways. A second source of differance, which can be manifested synchronically in cases like competing uses of the term 'flat', is the fact that such terms, and the concepts they express, are semantically governed by implicit, contextually variable, parameters. This second form of differance, we will suggest, is at the heart of conceptual relativity.

4. Mutual Correctness

The next task we face is to harness the synchronic form of differance in order to explain the mutual-correctness aspect of conceptual relativity. Return to the case of Carnap and the Polish logician. Our suggestion is that the concept of object bears a structural similarity to concepts like flat; and likewise for the meanings of the respective terms expressing these concepts. That is, the concept of object is semantically governed by an implicit, contextually variable, parameter—in this case a parameter that affects matters of counting and mereology. We will call it the *mereology parameter*. The idea is that on different occasions of use the setting of this mereology parameter may vary.[6] In the case at hand, Carnap employs the concept of object in a way that is semantically governed by one particular setting of the mereology parameter, while the Polish logician employs the *same* concept in a way that is semantically governed by another, somewhat different, setting of the same mereology parameter. Given the mereological parameter-setting that governs Carnap's usage, he correctly judges that there are exactly three objects on the table. Given the different mereological parameter-setting that governs the Polish logician's usage, she correctly judges that there are exactly seven objects on the table. Each is right, as each respectively is employing the concept of object. Although the concept as employed by Carnap does *differ* from the concept as employed by the Polish logician (since the mereology parameter has different settings in the two cases), it is the *same* concept nonetheless; likewise, mutatis mutandis, for the meaning of the term 'object' as employed by Carnap and by the Polish logician respectively. We have here a difference in concept and in meaning— that is, an identity-preserving difference.

5. Why Content Should Not be Relativized

So far we have completed two of the three tasks that need to be accomplished in order to explain conceptual relativity: articulating a variantist conception of concepts and meanings, and harnessing it to explain the principle of mutual correctness. The third task remains: to develop an account of affirmatory conflict that avoids the idea that all such conflict involves direct inconsistency, and yet identifies a form of semantic tension that is robust enough to deserve the label 'conflict' anyway. In order to see more clearly what must be done in order to accomplish this third task, let us now consider a tempting but mistaken way of elaborating our variantist treatment of relativity-susceptible concepts and terms. This approach will run afoul of the principle of affirmatory conflict. Seeing why a given path leads to a dead end can help reveal the right path.

Consider what we call the *relativized content* view of relativity-susceptible concepts and terms. As applied to the example of Carnap and the Polish logician, it involves three main ingredients. First, it embraces the variantist idea that Carnap and the Polish logician are using the same concept of object—one that allows for a differance in their respective uses of that concept. Second, it also embraces the contention that the source of this differance is the fact that the concept of object is semantically governed, in various different contexts, by specific settings of a contextually variable mereology parameter. Both of these ingredients are taken from the account we ourselves offered above. But now comes a third ingredient: viz., the contention that both Carnap and the Polish logician are making claims whose full content is more than what is explicitly expressed by their words, and is really an implicit relativity claim—a claim to the effect that the explicit content obtains relative to a specific setting of the mereology parameter. If one were to spell it out, making such implicit aspects of content explicit, Carnap would be saying: *There are exactly three objects on the table, relative to such and such mereological principles for 'object'*, while the Polish logician would be saying: *There are exactly seven objects on the table, relative to so and so mereological principles for 'object'*.

The problem, of course, is this: relativizing content in this way is obviously at odds with the phenomenon of conceptual relativity because the statements being expressed, even if they are both correct, do not involve genuine affirmatory conflict at all. Intuitively, this problem is something like a use/ mention conflation. What is actually going on in the Carnap-Polish logician example is that each of these parties is *using* a certain conceptual scheme, a certain way of "carving" the world into objects. But according to the relativized-content view, in effect what each is doing is *mentioning* (implicitly) a certain way of carving, and then asserting that there are thus-and-such many objects relative to that way of carving. Both of these relativity claims are correct, all right, but they do not really conflict in any interesting way at all. Instead, their apparent conflict is entirely a surface phenomenon, one that dissolves when one makes explicit the full content of the two respective relativity claims. Indeed, once the content of the respective relativity claims is made explicit, both Carnap and the Polish logician could perfectly well affirm *both* statements.[7]

But Carnap and the Polish logician are not making relativity claims; implicit reference to a setting of the mereology parameter is not a component of the content of what either of them is saying. Rather, both Carnap and the Polish logician are speaking and judging *categorically*, from within respective semantic stances in which they are employing the notion of object in a way that is semantically governed by a specific parameter-setting. On our view, the content of what Carnap is saying is properly expressed this way: *There are exactly three objects on the table*, while the content of what the Polish logician is saying is properly expressed this way: *There are exactly seven objects on the table*. Both statements are categorical, and thus neither of them is an implicit relativity claim. Although the respective statements are semantically *governed* by different settings of the mereology parameter, and although each statement is correct under the particular parameter-setting that governs it in context, neither statement is implicitly *about* its own governing parameter-setting.

6. Affirmatory Conflict

The relativized content view is an instructive failure, with respect to the task of explaining the kind of affirmatory conflict that Carnap's claim and the Polish logician's bear to one another. The reason why there is no real affirmatory conflict, under this approach, is that it allows for a way of reformulating what each party is supposedly claiming—a way of making each party's respective relativity-claim fully explicit—such that Carnap and the Polish logician each can happily affirm *both* statements (as reformulated) and thus can happily affirm the conjunction of the two statements.

This lesson helps triangulate the kind of affirmatory conflict we seek to understand. A key feature of it should be this: there is no way to formulate the respective claims of person P_1 at time t_1 and person P_2 at time t_2 such that *a single person at a single time* could correctly affirm both statements (as so formulated) and thus could correctly affirm their conjunction. As we will put it, the two statements are not *correctly co-affirmable*.

It is crucial to this kind of affirmatory conflict that the two original statements are not *reformulable* in a way that allows for correct co-affirmability by
one person at one time. Suppose, for instance, that Jones correctly says "I am
over 6 feet tall" and Smith correctly says "I am not over six feet tall." Neither
of them can correctly affirm the conjunctive sentence "I am over 6 feet tall and
I am not over 6 feet tall." However, each of them has a way of reformulating
the other's statement that will make the two statements co-affirmable under
reformulation. (Jones, for instance, can correctly say "I am over 6 feet tall and
Smith is not over 6 feet tall.") So Jones's and Smith's respective claims about
their own heights, both of which employ the indexical term 'I', are not in affirmatory conflict.

Failure of correct co-affirmability is a generic kind of affirmatory conflict.
One species of this genus—a familar way that two statements can fail to be
correctly co-affirmable—is for them to be directly inconsistent with one another. But, given our above account of synchronic dif'erance, this is not the
only way. Another species of the genus arises from the fact that the various
permissible settings for contextually variable semantic parameters are *mutually
exclusionary*, i.e., for a single person P at a single time t, no more than one
parameter-setting for a given concept or word can semantically govern correct
usage, by P at t, of that concept or word. So, suppose that two statements S_1
and S_2 both contain a common word W that is semantically governed by a contextually variable parameter π; suppose also that person P_1 affirms S_1 at time t_1
under a setting α_π of π, and that person P_2 affirms S_2 at time t_2 under a distinct
setting β_π of π. The relevant form of affirmatory conflict, obtaining between
P_1's affirmation of S_1 at t_1 and P_2's affirmation of S_2 at t_2, is this:

(1) There is no circumstance C such that either
    (a) in C, S_1 and S_2 are both true under α_π, or
    (b) in C, S_1 and S_2 are both true under β_π, and
(2) there are no content-preserving translations $T(S_1)$ of S_1 and $T(S_2)$ of
    S_2 such that for some circumstance C, either
    (a) in C, $T(S_1)$ and $T(S_2)$ are both true under α_π, or
    (b) in C, $T(S_1)$ and $T(S_2)$ are both true under β_π, and
(3) there is some circumstance C such that
    (a) in C, S_1 is true under α_π, and
    (b) in C, S_2 is true under β_π.

Clause (1) captures the idea that statements S_1 and S_2, as explicitly formulated,
are not correctly co-affirmable, under either of the relevant parameter-settings
α_π or β_π. This idea has a modal aspect: for each of these two parameter-
settings, there is *no* possible circumstance in which S_1 and S_2 are both true.
Clause (2) captures the idea that this lack of correct co-affirmability is not a
feature that can be eliminated by suitably rephrasing one or both of the statements S_1 and S_2—for instance, by replacing an indexical term by a coreferen-

tial, non-indexical term. Together, clauses (1) and (2) express the genus-level features of affirmatory conflict, as these features apply to S_1 and S_2 under either of the contextually operative settings of the implicit parameter π. Clause (3) differentiates the distinctive species of the genus of affirmatory conflict—a species that is not a matter of S_1 and S_2 being directly inconsistent with one another.[8] The key idea, which also has a modal aspect, is this: unlike cases of direct inconsistency, it is *possible* for person P_1 and person P_2 both to be correct in their respective statements, because these statements are respectively governed by the distinct parameter-settings α_π and β_π of the implicit parameter π. That is, there is some possible circumstance in which person P_1 correctly affirms S_1 (under α_π) at t_1 and person P_2 correctly affirms S_2 (under β_π) at t_2.[9]

The affirmatory conflict at work in cases of conceptual relativity, we suggest, occurs when two claims made by two different persons (or by one person at two different times) exhibit the features just described. The two statements fail to be correctly co-affirmable, and this failure stems from the fact that they are respectively semantically governed by mutually exclusionary settings of some contextually variable semantic parameter. The respective claims of Carnap and the Polish logician fail to be correctly co-affirmable for just that reason; and this feature constitutes their affirmatory conflict with one another.[10]

We can express this kind of affirmatory conflict by coining a philosophical term (again, in the spirit of Derrida); let us say that the respective claims of Carnap and the Polish logician are inconsist*ant*, even though they are not directly inconsistent. The two parties are not just "talking past one another" by using two non-identical concepts and employing the term 'object' with two non-identical meanings, and they also are not just directly contradicting one another either. They are doing something in between, something that emerges as a genuine possibility once we recognize (i) that there can be différance in concepts and meanings, (ii) that the source of synchronic différance is contextually variable semantic parameters, and (iii) that such différance is the basis for conceptual relativity. This in-between relation in their respective claims is one under which both claims are correct despite conflicting with one another in the sense of not being mutually co-affirmable. Although the semantic conflict is genuine, it is also "no big deal" insofar as both parties are speaking and judging correctly under the semantic parameter-settings that govern their respective use of the notion of object. This distinctive semantic-conflict relation is what we are calling inconsist*ance*.

This completes the three tasks that needed accomplishing in order to secure the mutual compatibility of items 1–4 in section I.2, thereby explaining conceptual relativity. To summarize: The first task was to explain why and how it is that some concepts and meanings conform to the variantist conception. We did so by identifying two forms of différance—the diachronic version illustrated by Putnam's example of momentum, and the synchronic version illustrated by Lewis's treatment of the concept of flatness—and by highlighting the respective sources of identity-preserving difference for both kinds of case.

In synchronic cases, the source is implicit, contextually variable, semantic parameters.

The second task was to harness this source of synchronic differànce in order to explain the principle of mutual correctness. This we did by pointing out that although Carnap and the Polish logician are employing a single concept of object, and are using the term 'object' with a single meaning, nevertheless their respective uses are semantically governed by different settings of the implicit mereology-parameter. Each of their respective claims is true under the specific setting of the mereology parameter that governs the claim.

The third task was to harness the source of synchronic differànce in order to explain the principle of affirmatory conflict. This we did by pointing out that the respective settings of the mereology parameter that respectively govern Carnap's statement and the Polish logician's statement are mutually exclusionary, and that there is no single setting of the mereology parameter under which both statements are true at once. Thus, the two statements are not mutually co-affirmable, and this constitutes their affirmatory conflict. Although the two statements are not inconsistent, they are indeed inconsist*ant*.

II. Combining Conceptual Relativity with Metaphysical Realism

We turn now to the question of the relation between conceptual relativity and metaphysical realism. We will draw upon our account in Section I to argue that these two theses are compatible, and in fact comport well with one another. Doing so will require specific attention to the concept of truth.

1. Conceptual Relativity, Direct Correspondence, and the Denial of Metaphysical Realism

Metaphysical realism asserts that there is a mind-independent, discourse-independent, world—a world containing mind-independent, discourse-independent, objects that instantiate mind-independent, discourse-independent, properties and relations. Hereafter, it will be useful to adopt Putnam's capitalization convention in order to speak of this putative world and these putative objects, properties, and relations; this makes unambiguously clear when we mean to be talking about the kinds of entities whose existence the metaphysical irrealist denies. (More below on how to construe the capitalization convention, given what will be said about truth.)

Conceptual relativity is often thought to be incompatible with metaphysical realism. An initially plausible line of reasoning, leading from conceptual relativity to the denial of metaphysical realism, goes as follows. According to conceptual relativity, there are various incompatible ways of "carving" reality—e.g., incompatible forms of mereology, yielding incompatible ways of counting objects, each of which is equally right. But if there is really a WORLD of OBJECTS that instantiate various PROPERTIES and RELATIONS, then it couldn't be that these incompatible ways of "carving" are all correct; for, the only *correct* way of carving would be the one that corresponds to how THE WORLD is *in itself*—that is, the carving that picks out the genuine, mind-independently real, OBJECTS, and that employs predicates expressing the genuine, mind-independently real, PROPERTIES and RELATIONS. Thus, if conceptual relativity obtains, then metaphysical realism is false. So, given that conceptual relativity *does* obtain, metaphysical realism is false.

This line of reasoning assumes the following *direct-correspondence* conception of what truth would have to be, given metaphysical realism.

> DC If metaphysical realism is correct, then *truth* must be a matter of straightforward, direct, *correspondence* between the content of language and thought, on one hand, and how things are with THE WORLD on the other hand.

Under the direct-correspondence conception of truth, an atomic statement 'Fa', for instance, is true iff there exists some OBJECT O and some PROPERTY P such that (i) 'a' denotes O, (ii) 'F' expresses P, and (iii) O INSTANTIATES P. An existential statement '$(\exists x)Fx$' will be true iff there exists some OBJECT O and some PROPERTY P such that (i) 'F' expresses P, and (ii) O INSTANTIATES P. And so forth for logically more complex statements, in accordance with the recursion clauses in a Tarski-style truth characterization.

It has very often been supposed that the direct-correspondence conception of truth is mandatory for metaphysical realism. Indeed, some philosophers (notably Dummett and Putnam) actually build this assumption into their *characterization* of metaphysical realism—something we are not doing here.[11] And once one conjoins the direct-correspondence conception with metaphysical realism, then this package deal does appear incompatible with conceptual relativity. With respect to Carnap and the Polish logician, for example, the package-deal view would entail that they cannot *both* be right in how they count objects, because at most only one of their competing mereology/counting schemes generates the *truth* about such matters—in particular, the truth about how many OBJECTS are on a given table at a given moment.

2. Truth as Indirect Correspondence

But the metaphysical realist need not—and *should* not, we maintain—acquiesce in the direct-correspondence conception of truth. Rather, the realist can—and should—construe truth as correspondence of a more generic kind—a genus that has various species. Direct correspondence is one species but there are also various other kinds of truth-constituting correspondence.

In a number of prior writings, we have articulated and defended a general approach to truth that incorporates this idea; we call it *contextual semantics*.[12] Here we will briefly sketch some central themes of contextual semantics in enough detail to serve our purpose of explaining how conceptual relativity can mesh with metaphysical realism.

One fundamental claim of contextual semantics is this: although truth is correspondence between content (in language or thought) and the WORLD, often our language and thought work in such a way that the relevant kind of correspondence is *indirect* rather than direct—so that that there need not be any OBJECTS that answer to the singular terms or the quantifiers in a given statement, or PROPERTIES that answer to the predicates. Take, for instance, this statement:

Beethoven's fifth symphony has four movements.

Its truth does not require that there be some genuine OBJECT answering to the term 'Beethoven's fifth symphony', and also instantiating a genuine PROPERTY expressed by the predicate 'has four movements'. Rather, the relevant correspondence-relation is less direct than this. Especially germane is the behavior by Beethoven that we would call "composing his fifth symphony." But a considerably wider range of goings-on is relevant too: in particular, Beethoven's earlier behavior in virtue of which his later behavior counts as composing his *fifth* symphony; and also a broad range of human practices (including the use of handwritten or printed scores to guide orchestral performances) in virtue of which such behavior by Beethoven counts as "composing a symphony" in the first place.

Another fundamental claim of contextual semantics, intimately connected to the notion of indirect correspondence, is that truth is *semantically correct affirmability* under contextually operative semantic standards. Likewise, falsity is semantically correct deniability, under such standards. The relevant notion of semantic correctness has nothing to do with matters of etiquette; a statement can be semantically correct, in the relevant sense, even if it would be impolite, impolitic, or otherwise inappropriate to utter it. Semantic correctness is also distinct from epistemic warrant: a statement can be epistemically warranted but semantically incorrect, and can be semantically correct but epistemically unwarranted. (Suppose that Beethoven engaged in behavior correctly describable as "composing his tenth symphony," and that no traces of this fact exist—perhaps because he burned his score and sketchbooks and never mentioned the project to anyone. Then the statement 'Beethoven composed only nine symphonies' is semantically incorrect despite being epistemically warranted.)[13]

Contextual semantics also stresses that semantic standards vary somewhat from one sociolinguistic context to another. In the limit case, the applicable standards require direct referential linkages connecting a statement's basic subsentential constituents to OBJECTS and PROPERTIES. In this limit case, truth (i.e., semantically correct affirmability) is direct correspondence. But the contextually operative standards also can work in such a way that the requisite goings-on in the world need not involve OBJECTS or PROPERTIES answering to the statement's basic subsentential constituents. In such cases, truth is indirect correspondence.

Limit-case semantic standards frequently come into operation in philosophical contexts where ontological issues are under discussion. It is plausible that they also are operative in various scientific contexts, for instance in discussions in physics about the subatomic constituents of matter.[14] But for typical uses of numerous kinds of non-scientific discourse—including discourses in which statements like "Beethoven's fifth symphony has four movements" would naturally occur—it is plausible that the contextually operative semantic standards are not limit-case standards. Thus, for statements in such discourses, truth (i.e., semantically correct affirmability) typically is indirect correspondence.

3. The Compatibility of Metaphysical Realism and Conceptual Relativity

We maintain that contextual semantics is a plausible and theoretically attractive approach to truth; elsewhere we have set forth various arguments in support of it (as well as articulating it more fully).[15] Our present objective is to explain why metaphysical realism and conceptual relativity can be naturally, and simultaneously, accommodated within the framework of contextual semantics. This means, of course, that metaphysical realism and conceptual relativity are entirely compatible with one another.[16]

So consider, first, metaphysical realism—which asserts that there is a WORLD containing OBJECTS instantiating various PROPERTIES and RELATIONS. Contextual semantics comports well with this thesis. For one thing, contextual semantics is perfectly *consistent* with it. Moreover, in contexts where language and thought are governed by limit-case semantic standards, truth is a matter of *direct correspondence* between language/thought content on the one hand, and how things are with these OBJECTS and their PROPERTIES and RELATIONS on the other hand. Under direct-correspondence standards conceptual relativity cannot be operative.

Even under limit-case semantic standards, of course, one must still be employing certain specific concepts in certain specific ways: one must be thinking and judging *with* those specific concepts, and from *within* those context-specific semantic standards. In this mundane sense, one's judgments and assertions are still relative to a specific "conceptual scheme." But it is just a non sequitur to infer from *this* kind of conceptual-scheme relativity that metaphysical realism is false.[17] For, when one is employing concepts under limit-case semantic standards, one purports to be carving THE WORLD at its mind-independently real joints; one's judgments and statements are true iff they directly reflect how things are with OBJECTS, in terms of the PROPERTIES and RELATIONS they instantiate.

Now consider conceptual relativity, as explicated in part I above. Contextual semantics comports well with this thesis too. The key point is this: insofar as the contextually operative semantic standards governing the correct usage of a person's concepts and words only require indirect correspondence rather than direct correspondence, the items to which one's judgments and statements are "ontologically committed" by Quinean standards need not be mind-independently real; they need not be OBJECTS. Thus, for example, different contextually specific semantic standards governing the notion of *object* could involve different, mutually incompatible, mereology parameters—say, Carnap's on one hand, and the Polish logician's on the other. As long as Carnap and the Polish logician are not both employing limit-case, direct-correspondence, semantic standards, there is no reason why they cannot each be employing the notion of object in such a way that under the respectively operative settings of the mereology parameter, each of them is counting objects *correctly*. In short: contextually variable semantic standards often work in such a way that truth—that is, semantic correctness under contextually operative standards—is indirect correspondence rather than direct correspondence; and conceptual relativity is accommodated by the range of different potential forms of indirect correspondence, involving different settings of contextually variable semantic parameters.[18]

Although our principal example of conceptual relativity has been Putnam's case of Carnap and the Polish logician—which on our account involves different settings of an implicit mereology-parameter governing the notion of object—we emphasize that the phenomenon of conceptual relativity extends well beyond matters of counting and part/whole relations. It also covers, for example, entire domains of entities that count as legitimate posits under various kinds of non-limit-case semantic standards. Plausible examples include (inter alia) nations, universities, symphonies, and numbers. Under contextual semantics, there need not be genuine OBJECTS answering to thought and talk that carries Quinean ontological commitment to such entities; and we doubt that there are such OBJECTS. Thus, an ontologically minded philosopher might claim that *nations* do not exist, whereas someone employing nation-talk under more typical contextually operative semantic standards would claim that *of course* nations exist. Both claims could well be correct, we maintain, given the differing contextually-operative semantic standards that govern their respective uses of the nation-notion. Thus, matters of existence and non-existence are subject to conceptual relativity too.[19]

4. Ontology in Light of Conceptual Relativity

Given contextual semantics, numerous entities to which our language and thought carries Quineian "ontological commitments" might turn out to be only mind-dependently, discourse-dependently, real, in this sense: although statements positing such entities are true under various sorts of indirect-correspondence semantic standards that often are contextually operative, such statements are not true under limit-case, direct-correspondence, standards. This means that questions of ontology, about what OBJECTS there are and what PROPERTIES and RELATIONS they instantiate, are methodologically subtle, within the framework of contextual semantics. In inquiring into them, one needs to attend carefully to whether language and thought are, or are not, being employed under limit-case semantic standards—and also to questions about what sorts of items are, or are not, appropriate to posit when one is speaking and judging under *those* standards. In principle, however, there is no clear reason why such matters should not be open to human theoretical investigation— including scientifically informed investigation.[20]

One can, if one so chooses, deliberately undertake serious ontological inquiry—thereby employing discourse governed by limit-case semantic standards—to ask questions about what EXISTS. (The capitalization convention is a device for overtly signaling that one is employing direct-correspondence standards.) In this rarified form of thought and discourse, conceptual relativity no longer holds sway. Thus, if Carnap and the Polish logician both were to deliberately shift into direct-correspondence discourse, and also both were to persist in their respective claims about the number of objects, then their dispute would thereby become a "big deal" ontologically. For, although Carnap and the Polish logician can both be right about how many objects are on the table when at least one of them is speaking and judging under indirect-correspondence semantic standards, nevertheless if they intend their dispute to be a genuine *metaphysical* conflict about how many OBJECTS are on the table, then they cannot both be correct.[21,22]

Notes

1. See Lynch (1998) for an illuminating attempt to make sense of conceptual relativity which, because of space considerations, we are not able to consider in this paper. But see note 7 below for an indication of why we think Lynch's view does not really handle the phenomenon of conceptual relativity.

2. For expository convenience, we have formulated these two principles in a way that makes them specifically about just the one case of Carnap and the Polish logician. But such principles can also be formulated more abstractly, to apply to cases of conceptual relativity in general. Of course, it need not always be the case that each of the persons in affirmatory conflict is actually making a *true* statement (relative to the given person's own way of using relativity-susceptible concepts); for, the affirmed statement might happen to be false even relative to the speaker's own way of using the relevant concepts.

3. See also van Inwagen (this volume), who also argues that conceptual relativity is not really possible.

4. The account we offer will not constitute a full theory of concepts and meanings, by any means. Rather, it potentially could be incorporated into various alternative general theories.

5. It is important to distinguish the phenomenon of différance in concepts from what Putnam (1981, p. 116–19) calls difference in *conception* (even though the distinction is somewhat fuzzy). The latter is a matter of different *beliefs* about a given subject matter, not differences in concepts and in meaning. Différance, on the other hand, does involve differences in concepts and in meaning—albeit identity-preserving ones.

6. Different settings of the mereology parameter do not appear to conform to any simple ordering, however; in this respect the mereology parameter differs from the precision parameter for flatness.

7. These remarks are further supported by reflecting on the attempt to accommodate the phenomenon of conceptual relativity in Lynch (1998), pp. 91–93. Lynch appears to accept a version of what we are calling the relativized content view (although the text is not completely unambiguous about this), and in order to make sense of the principle of affirmatory conflict, he claims that the statements made by Carnap and the Polish logician are in conflict in the sense that *"if these propositions were relative to the same scheme, they would be inconsistent"* (p. 93). But this sort of conflict is merely counterfactual; it does not constitute or explain the *actual* affirmatory conflict that is present in the claims that are actually made by Carnap and the Polish logician. Yet once one embraces a relativized content view about the claims in question, one seems forced to make a move like Lynch's in trying (unsuccessfully) to accommodate the idea that there is genuine affirmatory conflict in the actual claims being made in the Carnap-Polish logician case.

8. Nor are S_1 and S_2 direct *contraries* of one another either—that is, statements that can be mutually false but cannot be mutually true. Being direct contraries is a form of content-conflict which—like being directly contradictory—runs afoul of the principle of mutual correctness.

9. In general, the *actual* circumstance in which these respective affirmations occur need not be one in which both P_1 and P_2 are making correct statements. For, one or both persons might happen to be making a statement that is false even under the parameter-setting that governs the speaker's own usage in context. (In the example of Carnap and the Polish logician, it is built into the case by stipulation that neither party is making this kind of mistake.)

10. Objection:

> Although you say that the respective claims of Carnap and the Polish logician are not co-affirmable, you yourselves affirm the principle of mutual correctness; i.e., you yourselves affirm that Carnap and the Polish logician are both correct in their respective claims. But to affirm that they are both correct is to affirm what each of them is saying! So there is a way of correctly co-affirming their claims after all—which shows that there is no genuine affirmatory conflict between them.

Reply:

> The principle of mutual correctness employs the term 'correct'—and also the word 'true'—in a *relativistic* way: the principle asserts that both Carnap and the Polish logician are making a claim which, *relative to a specific way of using the concept of object*, is true. When one employs the notion of truth in this relativistic way vis-à-vis a statement S, one does not thereby *categorically* affirm that S is true—and hence one does not commit oneself to S itself. Thus, in affirming the principle of mutual correctness one does not thereby co-affirm Carnap's claim and the Polish logician's claim. Cf. note 19 below.

11. In Putnam (1983, p. 272), for instance, metaphysical realism is characterized as a view that assumes the following:

1. a world consisting of a definite totality of discourse-independent objects and properties; and objects
2. 'strong bivalence', i.e., that an object either determinately has or determinately lacks any property P which may significantly be predicated of that object; and
3. the correspondence theory of truth in a strong sense of 'correspondence', i.e., a predicate corresponds to a unique set of objects, and a statement corresponds to a unique state of affairs, involving the properties and objects mentioned in (1), and is true if that state of affairs obtains and false if it does not obtain.

Putnam ascribes to Michael Dummett the same three-part characterization of metaphysical realism. We ourselves are taking metaphysical realism to comprise only the thesis of mind-independent, discourse-independent, OBJECTS, PROPERTIES, and RELATIONS—which Putnam articulates as claim (1) of the package-deal view that he himself calls metaphysical realism. Presently we will reject claim (3), Putnam's formulation of the direct-correspondence conception of truth. We also deny that claim (2) should be built into the very definition of metaphysical realism (although we remain officially neutral about this claim), because metaphysical realists disagree among themselves about whether there are, or can be, *vague* OBJECTS or PROPERTIES—and if so, whether or not they obey the principle of strong bivalence.

12. See Horgan (1986a, 1986b, 1991, 1995a, 1995b, 1996, 1998, 2001), Horgan and Potrč (2000), Horgan and Timmons (1993), and Timmons (1999). Originally Horgan called the view "language-game semantics" and later called it "psychologistic semantics," before Horgan and Timmons decided on the current name. The overall framework includes theses not only about truth and falsity per se, but also about meaning, ontology, thought, and knowledge.

13. Although contextual semantics denies that truth can be construed epistemically— say, as epistemically warranted affirmability, or as some kind of idealization of epistemically warranted affirmability—nevertheless contextual semantics does posit an intimate connection between semantic standards for correct affirmability on one hand, and epistemic standards for warranted affirmability on the other hand. By and large, the epistemic standards we actually employ in assessing the epistemic warrant-status of various statements are appropriate to the contextually operative *semantic* standards governing semantically correct affirmability. This explains why, for example, one need not concern oneself about the ontological status of musical works of art in order to be well warranted in affirming the statement that Beethoven's fifth symphony contains four movements (given the plausible assumption that this statement, as ordinarily employed, is governed by indirect-correspondence semantic standards).

14. Although this is initially plausible, there also are considerations that count against it, having to do with conceptual problems that threaten the possibility of ontological vagueness. See Horgan and Potrč (2000).

15. See the texts cited in note 12.

16. Pendlebury (1986) shows how it is possible to make sense of a realist truthmaking relation that does not presuppose that the object language cuts nature at the joints. This approach, which is similar in spirit to contextual semantics, also appears to lend support to the contention that metaphysical realism is compatible with conceptual relativity.

17. Putnam appears to commit this fallacy in the third sentence of the passage we quoted in the second paragraph of this paper.
18. Even if neither Carnap nor the Polish logician is employing semantic standards requiring direct correspondence to OBJECTS and their PROPERTIES and RELATIONS, one of them might happen to be employing mereological principles that are actually obeyed by OBJECTS themselves. But this could only be so for one of their mereological schemes at most—not for both.
19. The concept of truth is itself subject to conceptual relativity, according to contextual semantics: it too is governed by implicit, contextually variable, semantic parameters. Typically—but not invariably—the contextually operative parameter-settings mesh with those governing first-order discourse in such a way that the claim that statement S is true entails S, and conversely. One important alternative way to employ the truth predicate is a non-categorical, explicitly relativistic usage: one says of statement S that it is true *under* (or, true *relative to*) such-and-such semantic standards (or mode of usage, or conceptual scheme, etc.). The truth predicate is used in this relativistic way in our formulation of the principle of mutual correctness in section I.1, and also in our account of affirmatory conflict in the fourth paragraph of section I.6. Such a non-categorical truth-attribution to a statement S does not entail S.
20. We do acknowledge the worry that perhaps nothing could settle such ontological issues, even in principle—and the fact that this worry potentially threatens metaphysical realism. As is emphasized by Lynch (1998), one need not be a verificationist about meaning to feel the grip of this line of thought. But addressing it is a matter for another occasion.
21. For a discussion that construes their dispute as a genuine metaphysical conflict, and argues that they are both wrong, see van Inwagen (this volume).
22. We thank Elizabeth Giles, Michael Lynch, Michael Pendlebury, John Tienson, and members of an audience at the 2002 Midsouth Philosophy Conference for helpful comments and discussion.

References

Horgan, T. (1986a). "Psychologism, Semantics, and Ontology," *Noûs* 20: 21–31.

Horgan, T. (1986b). "Truth and Ontology," *Philosophical Papers* 15: 1–21.

Horgan, T. (1991). "Metaphysical Realism and Psychologistic Semantics," *Erkenntnis* 34: 297–322.

Horgan, T. (1995a). Critical Study of C. Wright, *Truth and Objectivity, Noûs* 29: 127–138.

Horgan, T. (1995b). "Transvaluationism: A Dionysian Approach to Vagueness," *The Southern Journal of Philosophy* 33: Spindel Conference Supplement, 97–125.

Horgan, T. (1996). "The Perils of Epistemic Reductionism," *Philosophy and Phenomenological Research* 66: 891–97.

Horgan, T. (1998). "Actualism, Quantification, and Compositional Semantics," *Philosophical Perspectives* 12: 503–9.

Horgan, T. (2001). "Contextual Semantics and Metaphysical Realism: Truth as Indirect Correspondence," in M. Lynch, ed., *The Nature of Truth: Classic and Contemporary Perspectives.* Cambridge MA: MIT Press.

Horgan, T. and Potrč, M. (2000). "Blobjectivism and Indirect Correspondence." *Facta Philosophica* 2: 249–70.

Horgan, T. and Timmons, M. (1993). "Metaphysical Naturalism, Semantic Normativity, and Meta-Semantic Irrealism," *Philosophical Issues* 4: 180–203.

Lewis, D. (1979). "Scorekeeping in a Language Game." *Journal of Philosophical Logic* 8: 339–359. Reprinted in his *Philosophical Papers, Volume 1*. New York: Oxford University Press (1983).

Lynch, M. (1998). *Truth in Context: An Essay on Pluralism and Objectivity*. Cambridge MA: MIT Press.

Pendlebury, M. (1986). "Facts as Truthmakers." *The Monist* 69: 177–188.

Putnam, H. (1981). *Reason, Truth and History*. Cambridge UK: Cambridge University Press.

Putnam, H. (1983). "Vagueness and Alternative Logic," in his *Philosophical Papers, Volume 3: Realism and Reason*. Cambridge UK: Cambridge University Press.

Putnam, H. (1987). *The Many Faces of Realism*. La Salle: Open Court.

Putnam, H. (1988). *Representation and Reality*. Cambridge MA: MIT Press.

Timmons, M. (1999). *Morality without Foundations: A Defense of Ethical Contextualism*. Oxford: Oxford University Press.

van Inwagen, P. (this volume). "The Number of Things."

Philosophical Issues, 12, Realism and Relativism, 2002

RESPONSE-DEPENDENCE WITHOUT TEARS

Frank Jackson, Australian National University
Philip Pettit, Princeton University

We believe that it is both unsurprising and untroubling that competence with the semantically basic terms or concepts in our language should be response-dependent. Our aim in this paper is to support that belief by elaborating on the meaning of response-dependence, by presenting a case for the response-dependence of our competence with basic terms, and by neutralising some myths about such response-dependence.

The paper is in six sections. The first gives an introduction to the notion of response-dependence. The second shows why response-dependent terms are subject, as is commonly remarked, to a certain *a priori* biconditional. The third offers a relatively simple argument for the response-dependence of basic terms. And then the remaining sections develop a critique of three assumptions—if you like, three myths—that might otherwise make it difficult to believe in such global response-dependence.

1. Introducing Response-Dependence

Among the terms or concepts that a person uses to characterise the world, we can distinguish between those that are introduced to the subject wholly by definitions that employ words already understood, and those that are not introduced in that way. Those that are not introduced in that way may presuppose a network of other terms, and they may be partly defined by their place in that network. But their introduction—whether this be one by one, or in packages—must directly link the subject with items in the perceived world. Ultimately the mastery of these terms involves ostension: it is accomplished by directing the learner's attention to things that are experientially available. We shall describe the terms as semantically basic.

Speakers may vary among themselves, and each may vary across times, in the matter of which terms or concepts are basic for them in this sense, which defined. For the ordinary person every colour term may be basic, for example, whereas for the colour-blind person one or another term may be defined. And this may be so, although each uses the term in the same way and possesses the same concept: the one person will possess it in the standard, canonical fashion, the other parasitically. But no matter how the speakers of a language vary in this way—and there are certainly limits on the variation possible—it must be true of each that among the terms and concepts they employ, not all are wholly defined in other words; some must be semantically primitive. We shall assume in what follows that with many terms in any language there is a good deal of convergence on which are basic, at least among ordinary users: for ordinary people who are not colour-blind, for example, we shall assume that the colour terms are all basic. But nothing much hangs on this assumption; it serves for convenience only.

It will be granted on all sides that mastery of definitionally introduced terms or concepts involves having certain beliefs: specifically, the beliefs that link the referents of those terms, taken as such, to the referents of others. In that sense mastery of defined terms is belief-dependent. But what about the mastery of basic terms? Is it belief-dependent in the same way? Or can basic terms come to be mastered, basic concepts come to be possessed, without the learner thereby coming to entertain any particular beliefs about the referents of those terms?

Suppose that a certain term in a community's vocabulary is basic, at least for ordinary users. Mastery of such a basic term will be belief-dependent, plausibly, so far as ordinary competence in its use—ordinary possession of the concept associated—requires the speaker to be disposed to form certain beliefs in response to the presence of the referent (or of items that approximate the referent: see section 6). When a term is belief-dependently mastered in this way, then we can also speak of its being response-dependently mastered or of its being response-dependent. We argue in section 3 that not only can basic terms be belief-dependent and, more specifically, response-dependent; the best account of how they are learned ensures their response-dependence. We borrow the term 'response-dependent' from Mark Johnston (1989). While there are sharp differences between his views and ours, there is enough continuity to make it reasonable to adopt his terminology; more on this later.

Let us assume that the term 'red' is semantically basic and that it refers to a perfectly objective property such as the spectral reflectance of certain surfaces. Even supposing that it refers to such a property, our ordinary competence with this term involves the possession of a variety of beliefs in virtue of which it is plausible to describe the term or concept as response-dependent. When we are introduced to the term 'red', we learn that we can generally rely on how things seem in determining whether it applies or not: we can rely on the beliefs that things spontaneously elicit in us. We all quickly find that there are occasional differences across times and persons in regard to applications of the term. And then we are taught that certain obstacles or limitations can warp our responses, leading us to believe that a certain non-red thing is red or a certain red thing not red; we are taught that 'red' designates a property that does not invariably go with appearance, even if it typically does so (see Pettit 1999). We come to believe of anything we encounter that it is red if it seems red and there is no evidence of an obstacle or limitation at work in warping that appearance; and we come to believe that it is not red if it seems non-red and, again, there is no evidence of obstacle or limitation.

We can readily generalise the pattern. Take any basic term or concept, 'T', that is used in common amongst a community of speakers to refer to something, T, where T may be a perfectly objective entity: like a spectral reflectance, it may be the sort of thing that can exist in the absence of the community and in the absence of any thinking creatures. 'T' will be response-dependent just in case an ordinary speaker's competence in the use of the term goes hand in hand with their believing of anything they encounter that it is T if it seems T and there is no evidence of unfavourable influences; and with their believing that it is not T if it seems non-T and there is no evidence of unfavourable influences.

Something's seeming red to the ordinary person will involve a sensation of redness, however sensations are understood. But it is worth noting, of course, that the seemings or appearances that reponse-dependent terms generally require may not involve sensations of this kind; the responses in question, as indeed we shall see in section 5, need not have the character of conscious, sensory representations. They may have no presence for the speaker other than that of a primitive disposition to see this or that item as suitably similar to paradigms of T and to apply the word 'T' to them in expression of the similarity registered.

The obstacles and limitations that may put a person's sensation of redness askew, giving them reason not to authorise it, are fairly obvious. Obstacles are illustrated by colour-glasses and sodium lighting, limitations by colour-blindness. But it is also worth noting that with other terms that are response-dependent in the general way, the obstacles and limitations may be very different. If a term 'T' is partly defined in terms of connections with other terms, be they response-dependent or not—in this respect 'red' looks particularly simple—then ignorance or error about the application of those other terms in a given instance may constitute an important limitation for the subject.

Our account makes response-dependent terms belief-dependent in a characteristic, case-by-case way; competence goes with a set of case-by-case beliefs—a belief about this encountered object, a belief about that encountered object, and so on—together with a disposition to form other such beliefs. But does it entail a more general sort of belief-dependence? Does it entail the general belief, for the response-dependent term, 'T', that among the things encountered by speakers those and only those that seem T under favourable conditions, C, are T and deserve to be called 'T'? Does our account mean that people who master the term are committed to this general principle?

We can agree that our account does commit users of the term to this principle, provided it is clear that those who enjoy ordinary competence with the term may only believe the principle in question in a distinctively tacit or practical manner. They need not have independent terms for the different elements in the principle; they may have no word for 'favourable conditions, C', for example. They may believe the principle only in the sense that they treat it as true, rather than explicitly thinking that it is true, and only in the sense that they treat it as true on a case-by-case basis, not under the aspect of a general truth: they believe it, as used to be said, *in sensu diviso*, not *in sensu composito*. The principle will serve as a rule of reasoning that governs the transitions they make from appearance—something's seeming to be T—to assumption—that something is T—and to move from assumption to the expectation of appearance (Pettit 1998a). To go to a familiar analogy, they will believe it in the way in which non-logicians believe *modus ponens*.

So much for response-dependently mastered basic terms or concepts, and so much for how their response-dependence amounts to a variety of belief-dependence. Someone who thinks that certain basic terms can be response-independent rather than response-dependent will have to say that no connection is necessary between a speaker's using a term with an appropriate semantic value, on the one hand, and the speaker's having any particular beliefs or being disposed to form any particular beliefs on the other. Semantic competence with a basic term is attainable, so it will be claimed, without epistemic commitment. Thus there is no general belief that an ordinary speaker must form, however practical in character, in order to master a basic term and come to possess a basic concept. Indeed, mastering the term need not involve forming any such belief, even one that is idiosyncratic and unshared.

How could a response-independent linkage—if you like, an epistemically uncommitted linkage—get established between someone's use of a term and the semantic value of that term: the property or other entity to which it refers? What will presumably be required, at least under a naturalistic account, is a causal or contextual connection that links the person to the property but without giving them any judgmental dispositions. The connection will fix what the person shall refer to by the term but without necessarily giving rise to any beliefs. It will establish the semantic value of the term. And then it will die. It will have no effects—certainly it need have no effects—that impact on the speaker's disposition to apply the term in other cases.

2. The Response-Dependent Biconditional

When a basic term or concept is response-dependent—when it is mastered in the manner sketched in the last section—that will entitle us to assert a certain *a priori* biconditional. Assume that 'red' is response-dependent in this way, for example. It will then be *a priori* that the English term 'red' applies to something if and only if it is such as to evoke a suitable response—such as to seem red—among ordinary speakers of English under favourable conditions: that is, in the absence of obstacles and limitations. Imagine that the actual world where speakers apply the term 'red' might be now this world, now that, now another, without those differences showing up experientially. No matter which world plays the role of the actual world, and no matter which property is picked out by 'red', English speakers will be guided in their use of the term by whatever it is that seems red to them, under presumptively favourable conditions, in that world. And that is just to say that it is *a priori* that their use of the term 'red' will be designed to track the way things seem under such conditions (Stalnaker 1978).

This *a priori* linkage will be reminiscent of the biconditional employed in Mark Johnston's (1989, 145) original definition of response-dependence and that explains our holding onto his word (see too Johnston 1993, 121–26; Wright 1993, 77–82). But there is an important difference between the biconditional to which we are committed and that which he employs. For us an English term 'T' will be response-dependent just so far as it is *a priori* that *'T' serves to pick out a property (or whatever) in something* if and only if that thing would seem T under certain independent, favourable specifications. For Johnston the term is response-dependent just so far as it is *a priori* that *something is T* if and only if it is such as to seem T under those specifications.

The difference between these biconditionals comes out in the fact that it is possible to be committed to ours without having reason to assert his; ours is a more cautious formulation. Suppose that T is a certain objective property, as redness under our earlier supposition is a certain spectral reflectance. The fact that *'T' serves to pick out a property in something* makes it *a priori* that when conditions are favourable that thing should seem T to relevant speakers; that is what is required, under the approach that attracts us, for the term to get established among those speakers as referring to T. But the fact that the thing is T does not support the same *a priori* connection. For something may be T in a certain world—it may have the property picked out in our usage by 'T'—without its being *a priori* that there are independently specifiable conditions such that observers in those conditions track that property.

The *a priori* implication of '*"T" serves to pick out a property in something*' expresses one of the conditions for the possibility that 'T', a semantically basic term, should get established among speakers of the relevant language as having a certain a referent. 'T' can attract a semantic value of the appropriate kind, so the thought goes, only if there are certain conditions under which people's disposition to use the term is authoritative. But there is no corresponding *a priori* implication attaching to '*something is T*'. Why should it be *a priori* that just because there is a possible world where something has a property that we happen to designate with a semantically basic term—a property that may be as objective as a spectral reflectance—there must be observers specifiable, at that world or some other, who are equipped and positioned to track it?

If anything of the kind is thought to hold, that must be because it is an *a priori* implication of a fact presupposed by our reporting the fact that something is T: viz., that 'T' picks out a property for us. But the object envisaged would have been T, even if we had never gotten around to reporting it, so that it could have been T in the absence of any observers whose disposition to use 'T' is authoritative in favourable conditions.

It may be *a priori*, then, that given the denominability of T—given its accessibility to us as something that we can ascribe or pick out by the English term 'T'—something is T if and only if it is such as to seem T under independent, favourable specifications (Pettit 1998b). It may be *a priori* that something is denominably T, as we can put it, if and only if it is such as to seem T under independent, favourable specifications. But it will not thereby be *a priori*, for any such response-dependent term 'T', that something is T if and only if it is such as to seem T under favourable specifications.[1]

In our usage, to sum up this line of thought, a response-dependent term or concept is one whose ordinary possession-conditions or mastery-conditions involve the disposition to respond in a certain way to the corresponding referent (cf Peacocke 1992). That is why there is an *a priori* connection between 'T''s applying rightly to something in our linguistic community and that thing's being apt to produce the T-response in us under conditions that count for independent reasons as favourable. In Johnston's usage, a response-dependent term or concept is conceived in a different mould. We surmise that he takes the response-dependence of a term or concept to imply that it itself represents the referent as being connected with the relevant response; it more or less explicitly relates the referent to the response (see Pettit 1991, 598). That would explain why there is said to be an *a priori* connection between something's actually being T and that thing's being apt to produce the T-response. More on this in section 4 below.

Arguing for any *a priori* connection between being and seeming, even a connection that supposes denominability, will worry some people. They may think that it compromises the reality of the world putatively addressed or the fallibility of our access to it. But we stress that for that all we have said, neither realism nor fallibilism is in danger. The response-dependent terms and concepts we use can still refer to quite objective properties, as we have mentioned. And our access to those properties remains quite fallible. That a term 'T' behaves response-dependently does not guarantee that there is a corresponding T-property, for observers may not prove to converge on any property of the kind envisaged, under conditions that count independently as favourable. And while such observers, if they do converge, cannot be wrong in their use of the term under favourable conditions—they may of course be wrong in the use of non-basic terms—they cannot ever rule out the possibility that their current conditions are unfavourable; they cannot ever be sure that their conditions are unaffected by a factor that they will later come to see, say in the light of resolving further discrepancies, as perturbing or limiting.[2]

3. A Simple Case for the Response-Dependence of Basic Terms or Concepts

One of us has presented elsewhere an argument from the possibility of rule-following to the response-dependent character of semantically basic terms (Pettit 1990, 1991, 1993). But there is a case for the response-dependent character of basic terms that does not have to presuppose the possibility of rule-following; it constitutes only a first and relatively uncontroversial part of the larger argument. We present that simpler case here.

Suppose that someone is to be initiated in the use of a basic term 'T'. And let us assume that this term is a simple predicate, as some basic terms certainly must be. The term cannot be introduced by definition, being semantically fundamental, and so the speaker must be made aware of its semantic value—must learn to master the term—on the basis of ostension or something like ostension. Those of us who introduce the term must get the person to grasp the property that it denotes and ascribes by presenting exemplars of its application and non-application, ensuring that the circumstances are especially propitious for making the referent-property salient.

There is a familiar difficulty that is going to dog such an ostensive enterprise, however. This is that any set of exemplars, no matter how cunningly constructed, will be finite in extension and will instantiate an infinite variety of properties. They may instantiate the property that we wish our learner to associate with 'T' but they will instantiate much else besides. Let the exemplars be meant as examples of games, for example. The trouble will be that any finite number of games will be instances, not just of the property of being a game, but also of all those other properties—those infinite, unnamed properties—that just happen to coincide with game-ness in the examples on hand.

This difficulty raises a telling question. Assume that our learner succeeds in identifying the desired property as the semantic value of the term 'T'. Assume that things change with this person in such a way that we can now say that 'T' in their mouth—like 'T' in our mouths—is used to ascribe such and such a property. The question raised is this. What can make it the case on the side of the speaker that it is indeed that property, and not this or that other property, co-instantiated in the examples, that they associate with the term: that it is indeed that property, and not one of those others, that impacts upon them?

What has to happen is that that property comes to be privileged among the coinstantiated set by the fact that it is, as we say, salient or striking. It is the property such that the instances present themselves as instances of that property—or at least of a relatively narrow set to which it belongs—and not of any other. The instances will have a distinctive effect, then, on the subject. They will lead the subject to believe that those instances have that property—this belief will show up in the subject's discriminatory and classificatory dispositions—and to use the term in question, 'T', in order to express that belief. The subject will go on to believe that other things are T just so far as other things have that same effect, where he or she finds no reason to think that the effect is the product of some irrelevant influence.

The plausibility of these claims becomes apparent when we ask about what we would say of the person if the instances had a different effect. Suppose that the instances presented are all S, as we put it, as well as being all T. And suppose that they led the subject generally to apply the term 'T', not to things that are T, but to things that are S and only to things that are S. Surely in that case we would take it that the person had—wrongly, as we will see it—associated the term 'T' not with what we describe as T but with what we describe as S.

None of this should be surprising. Belief is a state that is designed to fit the facts: a belief that p would not play its characteristic role in our mental life if it was not suitably responsive, at least under favourable conditions, to such inputs as the perception that p or the perception that not p (Anscombe 1957, Smith 1987). Learning the semantic value of a term like 'T' is learning to use it in order to express how we take things in a certain respect to be. But it is wholly unsurprising, then, that learning its semantic value goes hand in hand with being disposed to apply the term in some circumstances and not in others: with being disposed to apply it in those cases where we take things to conform to the required pattern and not to apply it in those cases where we do not.

To say that the appearance of a suitable extrapolative disposition is necessary for a learner to associate 'T' with the T-property, and not with anything coinstantiated in the ostensive exemplars, is just to embrace a response-dependent account of how the person gets to refer to T. That account postulates precisely the sort of extrapolative disposition required. It maintains that under the impact of the ostensive exemplars the learner will learn what it is for something to seem T and will become disposed to infer being T from seeming T, and seeming T from being T, at least under what are taken to be favourable specifications.

It transpires, then, that a necessary condition for someone to get to refer to a particular property by means of a semantically basic term is that their use of the term should be response-dependent in character. If the term is not response-dependent—specifically, if it is not associated with a guiding belief—then there is no explaining what can make it the case that it refers to the property in question, and not to any old property that happens to be coinstantiated in the exemplars by which it is introduced.

We describe this as a simple case for the response-dependence of semantically basic terms. What makes it simple is that the argument says nothing about how other more complex problems are solved. Those other difficulties are elements in the full set of rule-following problems. One is that even if the extrapolative disposition tracks the appropriate property across the full range of cases accessible to the speaker, or indeed the speaker's community, still there are bound to be a number of abstractly distinguishable properties that are consistent with the operation of that disposition: they will be co-instantiated, not only in the ostensive exemplars, but in every case that comes up for judgment (see Pettit 1993, postscript). And another problem is that even if it is construed as a practical form of belief, instantiating an extrapolative disposition does not amount in itself to trying to be faithful to a rule for the use of the term; more needs to be said if a response-dependent story is to be built up into an account that makes sense of such an intentional, norm-governed enterprise (see Pettit 1993, Ch.2).

The problem which we invoke response-dependence to solve is close to what two sympathisers of response-independence, Michael Devitt and Kim Sterelny (1987, Chs 4 and 5), describe as a 'qua-problem' that faces their approach. The problem is that any exemplars whereby a term is to be learned will be capable of being taken in any of a number of ways: qua instances of the desired property, for sure, but also qua instances of any of an infinite variety of other properties. Without doing anything to resolve all the rule-following problems, we believe that the qua-problem already gives us reason to espouse a response-dependent line on basic terms.

We believe this, in particular, because of believing that the response-independent theory has no satisfactory answer to the question of what makes it the case that the learner associates the desired property, and not a clearly distinct property that is co-instantiated in the exemplars, with the term introduced. Defenders of that line may say that the desired property is the referent of the term because it is that property and not any of the co-instantiated partners that causally or contextually impacts on the speaker. But this is 'Hail Mary' semantics. Under a response-independent account, there is nothing to make it the case that it is one property and not a co-instantiated partner that is responsible for the impact. According to such an account the impact secures reference and then it dies; it leaves no further trace: in particular, it does not leave the trace of a distinctive extrapolative disposition. In the absence of any such trace, there is nothing to make it the case that the term introduced refers to the desired property, and not to something co-instantiated.[3]

So much for the case in favour of taking all semantically basic terms—all terms that involve some direct experiential anchoring—to be response-dependent. We want to show in the sections following that we can hold that basic terms are all response-dependent—response-dependence is in that sense global—without forcing them into a procrustean mould. Response-dependence does not constrain basic terms or concepts in a severe manner; it is consistent with enormous variation.

4. Response-Dependent Concepts Are Not All Response-Relational

It may be tempting to illustrate the category of response-dependent concepts by reference to words like 'nauseating', 'aromatic', and 'comfortable'. For it is manifest that we normally learn to apply such terms in virtue of experiencing nausea, pleasant smells and comfort. And it is unsurprising that there should be an *a priori* connection between something's being nauseating and its being such as to induce nausea, at least when things are normal.

Terms or concepts like 'nauseating' refer, plausibly, to anthropocentric dispositions: to dispositions in things to evoke one or another response in human beings. When we use such a term what we have in mind is a disposition of a kind with fragility or solubility. The fragility of an object is the higher-level role property of having a lower-level, realiser property that makes it shatter under certain impacts (see Jackson, Pargetter, Prior 1982). And equally the nauseating or aromatic or comfortable feature of something can be plausibly cast as its higher-level, role property of having a lower-level, realiser property that produces nausea, or a pleasant smell, or a feeling of comfort.

In a more recent piece than that in which he defines 'response-dependence', Mark Johnston (1993, 103–04) introduces the word 'response-dispositional' to apply, as we understand him, to terms or concepts that refer to such anthropocentric dispositions. But it should be clear that response-dependent terms or concepts, on our account, need not be response-dispositional in this sense. For all that we have said, the response-dependent term or concept need not refer to a higher-level role property—the property of having a property that produces that response—but to the lower-level realiser property: the property that implements the role by actually producing that response.

Consistently with being response-dependent, for example, it should be clear that the concept of redness may be a concept, not of the property of having a property that makes things look red under suitable conditions, but of the property that has that effect. It may be a concept of realiser-redness, not of role-redness. It may be a concept of that very property in surfaces that may be otherwise identified, say, as a spectral reflectance of a certain kind.

In arguing that semantically basic terms and concepts are response-dependently learned, indeed, we explicitly took for granted a story under which they are not response-dispositional. This is how that story goes. People experience a certain response, say the sensation of redness, in the presence of certain things. This response means that they see the things in question as similar: they all look red. They learn to use the term 'red' of things that display that similarity, then, or at least of things that display that similarity in conditions that they have no reason to question: they do not give rise, for example, to discrepancies across times or subjects in the application of the term. So far as they are concerned, then, redness just is that property, as they will think of it, the one that saliently binds those things into a single kind.[4] The term 'red' refers to that common property, under this story, and not to the higher-order property of having a lower-order property that evokes appearances of similarity: not to the disposition to look red. Ordinary people may not even reflect on the fact that red things tend to look red—they may not even have the concept of a sensation of redness—and may not associate redness with the disposition to look red; they will typically think of it as a categorical property. Which categorical property? The most straightforward answer is: the property that realises the disposition (but see McGinn 1996).

We saw in the first section that in his original definition of 'response-dependence' Johnston focussed on terms or concepts that more or less explicitly relate the properties (or whatever) to which they refer to human responses: they represent their referents as items that essentially involve a connection with the responses in question. Response-dispositional concepts are response-relational in this sense: directing us to anthropocentric dispositions, they represent their referents as inherently involving human responses. Thus it should be no surprise to find that, consistently with his original focus, Johnston concentrates on such terms or concepts. It should be no surprise that he defends a stronger biconditional than we do. And it should be no surprise that response-dependent terms or concepts, as we conceive of them, are a distinct category.

We began this section by noting that terms like 'aromatic', 'nauseating' and 'comfortable' are plausibly taken to ascribe higher-order dispositions, so that they are response-dispositional in Johnston's sense. But there is another account of such terms, according to which they refer to realiser properties, not role properties, and are distinguished by the fact that they pick out those realiser properties under the explicit aspect of playing an anthropocentric role or grounding an anthropocentric disposition. On this account to say that a substance is nauseating is to ascribe a non-role property to the substance but to represent that property under the aspect of its producing nausea in humans. Terms like 'nauseating' are still response-relational, on this approach, for they represent the things to which they apply as connected with human responses. Even if 'nauseating' or 'comfortable' does not ascribe an anthropocentric disposition, it does ascribe, and ascribe as such, the property of grounding an anthropocentric disposition.

As response-dependent terms need not be response-relational through referring to anthropocentric dispositions, so they need not be response-relational in this other way either. That a term is response-dependent implies that it picks out a certain referent in virtue of that referent's having a suitable effect on human beings under favourable conditions. But a term might pick out a referent in virtue of its having certain effects without picking it out under the aspect of having those effects. Suppose that the term is a predicate. It may be that the predicate ascribes a certain property in virtue of the responses that that property typically evokes but it need not be that it ascribes the property under the aspect of evoking such responses; it need not be that when we use that term, to put the matter intuitively, we speak in part about the bearer of the property and in part about its connection with us human beings. We may do that when we talk about how aromatic or nauseating something is but we need not do it when we use response-dependent terms in general.

Do we do this when we use the predicate 'red' of things? On some accounts, talking about the redness of things is partly talking about the connections between those things and us sentient creatures; this is the sort of account, though in the response-dispositional key, that Johnston defends. But such accounts may be excessively influenced by an awareness of the scientific facts about colour. We suggest that for ordinary people, to say that something is red is to ascribe a certain salient objective property without any intention, let alone any commonly recognised intention, to comment on the effects that it is liable to have on creatures like us human beings. This is supported by the fact that intuitively there is a contrast in this respect between saying that something is red and saying that it is nauseating.

In conclusion, a query. If response-relational concepts represent their referents as properties giving rise to such and such responses—and this, whether they are response-dispositional or not—can't we think of them as concepts the mastery of which requires, not having such responses, but rather having the concepts of those responses? Can't we think of the concepts as being introduced by a definition that employs the concept of the response—itself no doubt a response-dependent concept—so that 'nauseating', for example, is defined as referring to the disposition to produce nausea in normal people, where we already have a concept of such a state? And doesn't that mean that the concept of the nauseating is not strictly response-dependent in anyone's usage: mastering it does not in itself presuppose the ability to have the response, only the ability to understand the concept of nausea (which may itself, being response-dependent, presuppose the ability to have the response)? For all that has been said, people might understand nausea as a state that comes and goes, often in a wholly random way, and might then learn to use 'nauseating' of those things that are found to produce the state reliably within them.

There is no problem in recognising that a concept that has to be mastered response-dependently by some people, like the concept 'red', will be mastered in a parasitic, theoretical way by others: this, in the way 'red' will be mastered by colour-blind people. But the suggestion now is that response-dispositional concepts, being definable in terms of other concepts—including the no doubt response-dependent concept of the response—do not themselves have to be mastered response-dependently by anyone. They are not semantically basic terms in anyone's usage.

We do not think that this suggestion is very plausible. The most likely story in the sorts of examples given is that we learn to master the concept of the property and the concept of the response—the concept of nausea and the concept of the nauseating—at one and the same time. Certainly this is a real possibility. And so far as that possibility is realised, the mastery of response-dispositional concepts will presuppose in itself the ability to have the responses in question, not just to conceptualise them, so that the concepts will count as response-dependent. Some response-relational concepts may be theoretical in character but we are happy to think that many of them are response-dependent in our sense.

To sum up, then, we concede that response-relational concepts, understood in either of the two ways distinguished, may often be response-dependent in our sense and so that some basic concepts may be response-relational. But we insist that not all response-dependent concepts, as we understand the category, are response-relational. A concept's being response-dependent—a concept's being response-dependently possessed or mastered—is a distinct and indeed more interesting feature.

5. Response-Dependent Concepts are Not All Response-Specific

The example of 'red' has served us quite well up to this point. It illustrates the general category of response-dependent terms or concepts and it shows how they can be response-dependent without being response-relational. But the claim that semantically basic terms or concepts are response-dependent may generate many misgivings so far as a colour term of that kind is presented as the lone example of the category. For the concept of redness is not just response-dependent; it is also, as we shall say, response-specific. And response-dependent terms or concepts need not generally be response-specific in this sense. So, at any rate, we shall argue.

Like any concept, the concept of redness is used to represent things as being of a certain kind or having a certain property. But the kind that it represents things as being need only be associated by those who possess it with the production of the relevant response; it may have little significance for them other than as the kind that makes things look red under favourable specifications. Despite not being response-relational, then, the concept may have a very specific connection to the response in question. It may be the concept of a kind that need have no more effects, according to those who master and employ the term, than its effect in making things look red under favourable conditions. If surface redness is a certain spectral reflectance and if that reflectance is associated with effects other than making things look red under such specifications, then that will come as a discovery, not as an inherently expected sort of result, among those who possess the concept.

The response-specificity of the concept of redness comes out in how we would naturally introduce a congenitally blind person to the concept. We cannot make the property of redness salient to such a blind person in the way that we can make it salient for someone sighted. But we can present it to them as precisely the (let us assume, realiser) property that makes things look red—we will have to provide some background explanation on the nature of colour sensation—in conditions and among observers that count by people's lights as favourable.

Not all putatively basic concepts display this response-specific character. Presumably the concept of something's being straight or flat or regular in shape may be semantically primitive, as may the concept of something's being, relative to certain conditions and impacts, soft or hard. And yet it is clear that we associate the kind that such a concept represents things as being with effects that far outrun the effect of eliciting a certain response in us; it has a wider role than that of affecting human beings (cf Wright 1992). The shape properties in question have effects on how things line up against each other, not just on how they impact on us. And the property of softness or hardness has effects on how things affect other bodies, not just on how they affect ours.

This lack of response-specificity comes out in the fact that were we to try to introduce one of these concepts to someone lacking the capacity for the relevant response, it would be downright misleading to employ the sort of approach that we use with the blind person in introducing a colour concept. We would not try to characterise a response like looking or feeling straight or flat or hard, in the way that we try to characterise colour sensation, and then present the property in question as that which has such an effect on the likes of us, at least under favourable conditions. To do so would be utterly pickwickian. What we would naturally do instead is to describe the effects that bodies, including our bodies, have on one another and then characterise the properties in question as those associated with such and such effects.

How is it possible for response-dependent concepts not to be response-specific? The answer lies in recognising that the responses whereby we are sensitised to certain properties—the responses that mediate our mastery of terms or concepts for those properties—may differ from the colour sensation in a number of important ways. The effects whereby the presence of a suitable property is registered may not be as specific to sentient creatures as colour sensation; think of the effect of a smooth object in rolling comfortably against the skin. Or the effects may involve a practical response on the part of the observer; think of the effect of an object in bending under intentionally applied pressure. Or the effects may be holistically tied up with effects that simultaneously make other properties salient; even colour sensations may display a degree of holism, so far as something's looking red rules out its looking green or yellow. Or, finally, the effects may not be restricted to a single modality of sense; think of the different senses that register shape as distinct from colour.

Such variations from the simple sensation model can make for huge differences in how response-dependent concepts behave. Suppose that the flatness of a body becomes salient to me in the effect, at least under favourable conditions, of offering no resistance to my hand as I move it across the surface. Or suppose that the hardness of an object becomes salient in the parallel effect of resisting my efforts to press my finger into it. In each case the property that becomes prominent, the property that becomes available as something to which I can aspire to refer—something that I can conceptualise—is naturally associated, not just with the type of effect it has on my body, but with the type of effect that it has in general on bodies of any kind. Modulo favourable conditions, flatness is the property associated with the unimpeded movement of objects across a surface and hardness is the property associated with the impenetrability of an object by other objects.

It is not surprising that these terms or concepts should pick out properties of these kinds. Not only may I freely move my hand across a flat surface, and fail to insert my finger into a hard object. What is also available to me is the discovery that I can freely move an object held in my hand across a flat surface and that I can fail to insert an object held in my hand into something that is hard. Thus I may directly experience, as it were, the effects of the properties, not just on my body, but also on other bodies. The properties may become salient to me in the effects of bodies on bodies that I experience through manipulation.

These effects, it should be noticed, may enable me to identify a number of different properties at once, representing those properties as necessarily connected in various ways. The concave shape of one object, and the convex shape of another, may show up in the fact that the first fits into the second. The greater size of one shape, and the lesser size of another, may show up in the fact that the second can be placed within the first. At the limit, it may not be possible to register the effect that makes one property salient without registering, or having the capacity to register, the effect that gives salience to another; and it may not be possible to have the one property satisfied without the other being simultaneously satisfied. This holism means that there is room for the discovery of more and more interrelated effects whereby different shape properties can be identified; it may begin to make sense of how we can discover, *a priori*, different geometrical ways of specifying various shapes.

Apart from this practical, potentially holistic aspect of the responses associated with the concepts of flatness and hardness, there is another feature that may help to make intelligible the contrast with colour concepts. This is that flatness, and to a certain extent hardness, is a property associated for me not only with tactile responses, but also with visual ones. I can feel or see that a surface is flat and so the response in which the property becomes salient to me as a potential term of reference may be a complex one. This being so, it is unsurprising if the property is represented as being capable of effects beyond the single effect that may be associated with colour. If it is capable of effects in both tactile and visual dimensions, then that alone is a reason why it has to be represented as a property with a wider causal potential than that which may be assigned to colours.

6. Response-Dependent Concepts are Not All Response-Opaque

Under the account of response-dependence given up to now, it would be natural to assume that the following holds. There is a response on the part of speakers that involves things seeming T—we may suppose that T-ness is a ground-level, realiser property. And that response serves to direct speakers to what is T—it makes the property of T-ness salient—under suitably favourable specifications. What is T-ness, then, on this account? It is the property that would make things seem T under those idealised conditions; it is the instantiated realiser of that idealised role. (The instantiated realiser may be the realiser in whatever world, actual or counterfactual, is under discussion; or, regardless of what world is under discussion, it may be the realiser in the actual world: that is, the term 'T' may be used in a rigidified way. But henceforth we can neglect that complication.)

If the realiser property to which a response-dependent term refers is always the instantiated realiser of an idealised role then, despite the fact that we will not normally take the property under the aspect of playing such a role, a curious result follows (Smith and Stoljar 1998, Pettit 1998b). The property that is picked out by the term may be different, as the relevant instantiating world differs. If we use the term 'red' in characterisation of this world, then it will pick out the particular spectral reflectance here in this world that makes or would make things look red under favourable specifications. But were a different world to be actual, in particular a world in which a different spectral reflectance played that role, then the term in our mouths would pick out that different property. Thus for all that we know just by mastering the use of the term 'red', the property picked out may be any of a variety of candidates. To put the matter in a phrase, the property of redness to which our responses—our seemings—direct us is opaque to those responses.

Response-opacity is avoided, of course, if the property to which our responses direct us in such a case is the higher-order disposition. The higher-order property of being such as to make things look red remains the same, even as the relevant instantiating world is envisaged as changing; what shifts and what eludes us is the nature of the property grounding that disposition: this does remain opaque, so that opacity is postponed rather than really avoided (Pettit 1998b). What we want to argue in this section, however, is that response-dependent concepts, even if they refer to realiser properties, need not be response-opaque. Response-opacity is genuinely avoidable, then: it is a feature of some respondent-dependent terms, but not necessarily of all.

Where a concept directs us to the instantiated realiser of the idealised, response-dependent role, then such opacity will certainly materialise. Our semantic competence with a predicate will enable us to know what property we ascribe in the sense of knowing that we ascribe the property that is salient here or there or wherever; the property, in effect, that plays a role in virtue of which our attention is engaged. But it will not enable us to know which of a variety of candidates is indeed salient here or there, which of a variety of candidates plays the role. We will be in the same position that we are in with defined terms when we know that in using a term like 'mass' we are ascribing whatever property plays the mass-role in physical theory—whatever property connects suitably with force and acceleration and so on—but do not know which of a variety of possible candidates is instantiated in that role. We cannot rule out the possibility that intrinsically different properties might play that role, though we may not be able of course to give an account of the difference between them.

The reason response-dependence does not entail response-opacity is that a response-dependent concept need not refer, as in the case imagined, to the instantiated realiser of an idealised role. It may refer instead to the idealised realiser of an idealised role. It may be what we can describe as an idealised concept. What an idealised response-dependent predicate is going to pick out, then, is not the instantiated property that plays the relevant idealised role but the idealised property that plays that role. It will pick out whatever property, instantiated or not, that will play the role under suitably favourable specifications.

Why would idealisation avoid response-opacity? If we use an idealised predicate 'S' to characterise the world and if 'S' picks out the idealised property that would play a certain idealised role, then no matter which world is actual we will be picking out the same property. Whether the world that is actual be this or that or yet another, the property picked out will be the same idealised realiser of the idealised role. Even if the user of the term is an isolated brain in a vat, indeed, the term will still pick out that property.

But it is one thing to see that idealisation would ensure that response-dependent terms or concepts are not response-opaque. It is quite another thing to show that there are such terms or concepts in active employment. If a term is idealised in the relevant way, then there are two features we may expect it to display. First, we should be willing to think that even if the property or whatever is not instantiated in a world under discussion, still the property picked out in false ascriptions is well defined; directing us to an idealised realiser, the response-dependent role picks out a determinate property even if there is no actual realiser to be found. And second, we should see an intuitive contrast between the abstract sort of property or whatever picked out by an idealised term and the concrete type of property to which an unidealised counterpart would direct us. The idealised term refers to the realiser in certain idealised conditions and, since those conditions may cover a variety of possible ways things can be, such a realiser is bound to be a disjunction of many different properties and, consequently, a property that abstracts from all such further variations; it is bound to contrast in this way with the concrete, instantiated sort of property— the property about which much more can in principle be learned empirically— that answers to an unidealised term.

Using these expectations as a heuristic, the predicates that assign geometrical properties stand out as likely examples of idealised terms, in particular of idealised, response-dependent terms. We are thinking of predicates like 'straight' and 'parallel', 'smooth' and 'flat' and 'regular' and so on. With such terms we are readily prepared to admit that none of the things in the actual universe, certainly none of the things with which we are familiar, may actually instantiate the corresponding properties: no edges may be straight, no pairs of edges parallel, and so on. And with such terms we do spontaneously see the properties to which they refer as being abstract rather than concrete. With the property to which 'red' directs us there are all sorts of empirical questions as to its physical nature, and so on, that naturally teem. With the property to which 'straight' or 'flat' directs us, there are not; we do not think of the property as one about which there is more to be empirically learned over and beyond what we learn in mastering the term or concept.

Given this hypothesis about geometrical terms, it should be no surprise that we intuitively think that the properties in question are not opaque to the responses in which they manifest themselves to us. There is little sense to the worry that we cannot know which property is the property of straightness or flatness or parallelhood that we pick out in our use of corresponding terms. It is sensible to allow that we may not know which property is picked out by 'red'—that is, which realiser property is picked out—but it would border on nonsense to entertain a similar thought with the geometrical terms and properties.

But how can a term like 'straight' be response-dependent and yet have an idealised, abstract referent? The response-dependent term is always associated with the occurrence of an effect on human beings under independent, favourable specifications. Such specifications, as in the case of redness, involve ruling out obstructive factors of the kind that give rise to discrepancies across time and place: sodium lighting, rotating objects, coloured glasses, and the like. But favourable specifications may also involve the availability of, say, as much information as possible on a matter on which it is always possible to get more and more information. And with such specifications—with specifications that things are ideal, as we may put it, not just normal—we may have to admit that they cannot be fully satisfied in the sort of world that is actual; they refer us to wholly idealised conditions. Where a response-dependent term is guaranteed to go with the relevant response only in idealised conditions, it becomes feasible to think of the semantic value of the term, not as the instantiated property that fulfils that idealised role, but as the idealised property that does so: the property that would do so in idealised conditions. This, we believe, is what happens with a term like 'straight'.

Is this edge straight, we ask. You say, yes; I say, no. Suppose that I can produce better information in the sense of being able, with the help of technology, to give you access to the edge at a greater level of tactile or visual resolution. In that case the discrepancy will naturally be resolved in favour of my response. The edge may be straight-for-practical-purposes—it may be approximately straight—but it is not straight in the strict sense of the term. Extrapolating from this case, we must admit that for any actual-world edge it is always possible to envisage more information such that it would lead us to say that the edge is not strictly straight. The property of straightness that we identify on the basis of our visual and/or tactile responses is one that will show up for sure only under conditions of information that are not satisfiable in the actual or in any plausible world. And so we are naturally led to admit that the property of straightness is idealised in character. Although we manage to make semantic contact with it—although it has the status of a property that we lock onto immediately—it is identified without any presupposition of instantiation.

A second example—one of a predicate, plausibly, that is holistically linked with 'is straight'—may help to sheet home the possibility. Are these presumptively straight edges parallel? You say, yes; I say, no. Suppose I can extend them further than you—extend them, by our shared lights—and that the information revealed shows that they are approaching each other. In that case the difference between us will be resolved in favour of me. The edges may be more or less parallel but they are not parallel, strictly speaking. Extrapolating from this case we can see that for any actual-world pair of edges it is always possible to envisage more information of the relevant kind being available such that it shows that they are not after all parallel: nearly parallel, perhaps, but not quite. The property that we identify on the basis of extending pairs of edges, or imagining them extended, and finding them still apart is one that may never actually be instantiated. It is, as we took straightness to be, a wholly idealised property. It links up *a priori* with how things would present themselves—how edges would behave on being extended—only under wholly idealised specifications: only with how they would present themselves when infinitely extended.

We conceive of straightness or parallelhood, then, as the abstract property that would play the required role in idealised circumstances, not as the instantiated, concrete property that does so. And we do so prudently. For the way in which our use of the term is guided shows that by our own lights the property might not be suitably instantiated. Thus to let the term track the putatively instantiated property, not the idealised one, would be to run the risk of having it fail to ascribe anything.

Under this account, it should be noted, we still identify the property of being straight or parallel so far as we are capable of having certain responses; that is what makes the corresponding terms response-dependent. But the actual responses that we experience may be, for all that our conceptualisation entails, responses just to things that approximate the property rather than instantiating it. We do not conceive of the property that we ascribe, now here, now there, as that instantiated property that connects with such and such responses under such and such conditions. We think of it as that which would connect with the types of responses involved under idealised specifications that we can never hope to satisfiy. We think of it as a property that remains available to be ascribed— ascribed falsely—even if it is not suitably instantiated.

Conclusion

The point of these last three sections has been to show that the response-dependence that semantically basic terms must display, by the argument of earlier sections, is not so hard to live with as might have been expected. Response-dependent terms need not be response-relational. They need not be response-specific. And, as we have just seen, they need not be response-opaque: they may not be instantiation-bound in such a way that users do not necessarily know which realiser-properties the terms can be used to ascribe. It may be compulsory to admit the response-dependence of semantically basic terms; but the cost of doing so need not be as great as some have supposed.

Another way of putting the conclusion of these last three sections is this. The response-dependence of a term or concept means that it comes into use by virtue of a happy contingency: the fact that human beings are disposed to respond in certain ways to the things around them. Accepting response-dependence, then, involves accepting that the terms or concepts in question are infected by a certain anthropocentricity. But that anthropocentricity, we can see from the last three sections, comes in different degrees or grades. Response-relational concepts are more anthropocentric than those that are not relational, response-specific concepts are more anthropocentric than those that are not specific, and response-opaque concepts are more anthropocentric than those that are not opaque. Accepting the response-dependence of semantically basic terms may force us to acknowledge a certain anthropocentricity in the way we form concepts but it need not involve the full-blown version that might trouble those of us who aspire to embrace various realist and objectivist positions.[5]

NOTES

1. Entering the qualification makes for an important correction of the claim about *a priori* linkage in Pettit (1991), (1993) and elsewhere, as noted in Pettit (1998c). Only when the correction is made, for example, do we see the contrast discussed below between terms like 'red' and 'comic' on the one hand and terms like 'straight' and 'square' on the other. In the earlier formulations, there is already a divide between Pettit's approach and Johnston's (1991, 609–11), but from the present perspective the divide is not wide enough.

2. We are grateful to Richard Holton for pressing us on these matters. See Pettit (1999) for a fuller treatment of fallibility.

3. We have been discussing the qua-problem, and arguing for response-dependence, with regard to predicate terms. But it is worth noticing that the same problem arises with terms of all kinds, including terms for relations, functions and particulars. And so it suggests that all semantically basic terms, whether predicative or not, will be response-dependent in character. The point may be resisted with proper names, in view of the causal or baptismal theory mooted by Kripke (1980): according to this theory the referent of a proper name can be fixed, and fixed without any epistemic trace in the learner, by the causal origin of the name-use. We cannot present a proper critique of the approach here (see Jackson 1998). But we note that with basic names, as with other basic terms, there is a problem of the same kind as the qua-problem and that its resolution points us towards a response-dependent line. The problem with the semantically basic name is whether the individual presented as bearer of the name is to be taken under this or that kind: qua instance of the-biological-entity-that-has-had-such-and-such-actual-causal-contact with me; qua instance of the-continuous-object-enjoying-such-contact, whether or not that object is human or even animate; qua instance of the-perhaps-quite-discontinuous-thing-at-the-origin-of-such-contact, in which case the bearer could even be a hologram; and so on.

4. This is to say that they will think of 'red' as rigidified; it will refer to the actual property that makes things look red, not to whatever property in any possible world we are imagining that would make things look red there. See Haukioja 2001. The story may be varied, however, so as to allow for a non-rigidified reference.

5. We benefitted from many useful comments received when this paper was presented at a conference in the University of Sydney, organised by Stephen Buckle and Huw

Price, and at a colloquium in the Graduate Center, City University of New York. We are particularly grateful for written comments received from Richard Holton, our commentator at the Sydney conference, and Jussi Haukioja.

References

Anscombe, G. E. M. 1957. *Intention*, 2nd ed., Oxford: Blackwell.
Haukioja, Jussi. 2001. The Modal Status of Basic Equations, *Philosophical Studies*, 104: 105–22.
Jackson, Frank, Robert Pargetter and E. W. Prior. 1982. Three Theses about Dispositions, *American Philosophical Quarterly*, 19: 251–57.
Jackson, Frank. 1998. Reference and Description Revisited, *Philosophical Perspectives*, 12: 201–218.
Johnston, Mark. 1989. Dispositional Theories of Value. *Proceedings of the Aristotelian Society*, Suppl. Vol. 63: 139–74.
Johnston, Mark. 1993. Objectivity Refigured: Pragmatism with Verificationism, in *Reality, Representation and Projection*, edited by J. Haldane and C. Wright. Oxford: Oxford University Press.
Kripke, Saul. 1980. *Naming and Necessity*, Cambridge, Mass.: Harvard University Press.
McGinn, Colin. 1996. Another Look at Color, *Journal of Philosophy*, 93: 537–53.
Peacocke, Christopher. 1992. *A Study of Concepts*, Cambridge, Mass.: MIT Press.
Pettit, Philip. 1990. The Reality of Rule-Following, *Mind*, 99: 1–21.
Pettit, Philip. 1991. Realism and Response-dependence, *Mind*, 100: 587–626.
Pettit, Philip. 1993. *The Common Mind: An Essay on Psychology, Society and Politics*, paperback edition, with new Postscript, 1996. New York: Oxford University Press.
Pettit, Philip. 1998a. Philosophical Theory and Practical Belief, *Australasian Journal of Philosophy*, 76: 15–33.
Pettit, Philip. 1998b. Noumenalism and Response-dependence, *Monist*, 81: 12–132.
Pettit, Philip. 1998c. Terms, Things and Response-dependence, *European Review of Philosophy*, 3: 61–72.
Pettit, Philip. 1999. A Theory of Normal and Ideal Conditions, *Philosophical Studies*, 96: 21–44.
Smith, Michael. 1987. The Humean Theory of Desire, *Mind*, 96: 36–61.
Smith, Michael and Stoljar, Daniel. 1998. Global Response-dependence and Noumenal Realism, *Monist*, 81: 85–111.
Stalnaker, Robert. 1978. Assertion, in P. Cole (ed.), *Syntax and Semantics*, Vol. 9, New York: Academic Press.
Wright, Crispin. 1992. *Truth and Objectivity*, Cambridge, Mass: Harvard University Press.
Wright, Crispin. 1993. Realism: The Contemporary Debate—Whither Now? in *Reality, Representation and Projection*, edited by J. Haldane and Crispin Wright. Oxford: Oxford University Press.

Philosophical Issues, 12, Realism and Relativism, 2002

IS THERE A TRUE METAPHYSICS OF MATERIAL OBJECTS?

Alan Sidelle
University of Wisconsin-Madison

The work that has been done in the metaphysics of material objects over the past twenty or so years is full of creativity guided by the hand of rigor. In what follows, I have no desire to disparage it. Nonetheless, at the end of the day, I think the best interpretation of these good works is as developing and showing how one or more scheme of description—one 'package' account of what there is, how things change and trace through time (and possible worlds) and how our 'ordinary' views on these matters fit in—can (or can't) be coherently worked out. More simply, I will argue that there is no fact of the matter about which package is true—each is metaphysically as good as the others, and the world is incapable of discriminating among them. How best to articulate this position will be considered in the final section of this paper.

In Section I, I will discuss the most prominent views in the area, illustrating what I mean by a 'package', and claiming that for each view, there is an acceptable package that meets standard objections and all *clear* requirements. I hope this rehearsal of views and packages will provide some intuitive force to the idea that these packages don't really make different claims about the world, but just provide different ways of describing the material contents of space-time (including property instantiations and causal relations). Thus, the differences between the views look more semantic than factual. In Section II, I will argue that there is nothing in the world that could make for the truth of one of these views as opposed to the others,[1] although each provides an acceptable way of describing the world. Finally, I will consider some objections to and questions raised by my proposal.[2]

I. The Views

1. Background

Much recent work in this area has been guided by puzzles that aim to show that not all of our ordinary views about what there is, and how things persist through change, can be true together with strongly held theoretical views. One central such view I call 'The No Coincidence Thesis' (NC): There cannot be two material objects wholly located in the same place at the same time (some prefer: No two objects can wholly consist, at a time, of just the same parts). This principle conflicts with our everyday judgments that there are both ordinary objects—sweaters, trees and cows—and 'constituting' objects—pieces of yarn and wood, maybe aggregates of cells or quarks—combined with our views about how these things move through time, which, more theoretically, underlie our views about the persistence conditions for these sorts of things. Since the 'macro' objects can go from existence while the constituting objects persist, and more generally, since the histories traced by each can differ, an object and its 'constituting' object cannot, in general, be identified, so we are committed to coinciding objects (Wiggins (1968)). NC also plays a role in Van Inwagen's (1981) modern version of the ancient Dion/Theon puzzle; he shows that this principle is inconsistent with our belief in arbitrary undetached parts, combined with the view that objects can lose parts (plus an intuitive judgment that undetached parts persist if all their parts persist arranged in just the same way). Whether the Doctrine of Arbitrary Undetached Parts is one of our 'ordinary views' isn't as important as the fact that many find it very intuitive, and commonsense seems committed to it in our judgments of persistence when things break—the broken bits count as objects, but don't seem to have just come into existence. All recent theories of the nature of material objects and/or change at least try to handle these puzzles somehow, and many, if not most, are motivated by their purported ability to provide solutions.[3] So, one desideratum for an acceptable theory is to either avoid coincident entities, or explain how to make sense of its possibility.

Another theoretical idea often invoked in criticism of ordinary (and other) views is a proscription against *arbitrary distinctions*. Arbitrariness, or its appearance, can show up in judgments about which portions of the world do, and which do not, contain objects, and in judgments about how things persist through change—what changes are 'substantial', and how things move through time. For instance, we commonly think cells arranged in certain ways constitute cows, but that no object is constituted by this paper and my eye. But one may wonder whether there is any difference here which can, in an appropriate way, substantiate such a distinction, especially when science reveals how much space there is between small particles making up cows. What of our judgment that something ceases to exist when a cow dies, but not when a hoof is clipped, or it catches cold? In each case, it seems that something persists, but some properties change. Or why does a car become larger when bumpers are attached, but not when a trailer is?[4]

The point is not that these questions have no answers, but that the failure, or absence, of obvious answers is often presented as grounds for rejecting a theory—so, conversely, a positive desideratum for a theory is to avoid arbitrariness, and to have explanations for those distinctions that might be challenged as being so.

Now, as theories attempt to avoid arbitrariness and coincidence, they wind up rejecting or revising some, or many, of our ordinary views about what there is and how things persist—for instance, Mereological Essentialism meets both desiderata by denying that anything ever genuinely persists through any change in parts, so we needn't distinguish the persistence conditions for trees and bits of wood, nor between parts an object can and can't lose. But this, of course, runs quite against the bulk of our ordinary reidentifications of objects. This is standardly offered as an objection, and all sides agree that the Mereological Essentialist—and more generally, the critic of common sense—must somehow accommodate our ordinary views. One must at least rationalize them, if not actually make them come out true.

Thus, an acceptable theory needs to avoid inconsistency with (1) ordinary judgments/intuitions, about what there is and how things persist, and (2) theoretical judgments/principles, most notably NC and No Arbitrary Distinctions, though there could be others. And a theory should avoid simple internal incoherence. Correspondingly, the correlative types of consistency are positive desiderata. With these puzzles, challenges and desiderata in view, we can now survey the major views currently taken seriously, and see how they can attempt to motivate themselves and handle challenges. To keep things manageable, I will often give a feel rather than track things down fully, but I hope to make it clear enough that each view can make itself 'adequate' to the above requirements, and I will then argue that beyond this, there are no truth-makers to distinguish among the positions.

Typically, a view has a 'leading idea' which is either itself strongly intuitive, or else is intuitive or promising in light of the puzzles and one or more of our desiderata. Each such idea, however, on its own, runs up against some of these desiderata, and so a proponent needs to build on, or add to, the leading idea to somehow accommodate the difficulties.

In general, conflicts with our ordinary views are handled by some combination of (a) ascription of mistake to us, with some explanation of our confusion (e.g. the universalist may say we have practical reason to 'privilege' certain objects, which may lead us to overlook other sorts), and (b) a scheme of paraphrase or redescription such that our ordinary judgments, so understood, can be allowed as either true, or at least 'appropriate' and tracking *some* genuine feature of the world. Conflicts with our theoretical principles are met either by challenging the principle (this is done, for instance, by those who appeal to 'brute facts' to combat arbitrariness), or trying to show that *properly understood*, the principle does not conflict with the main idea (for instance, Wiggins' proposal that NC should really only be No Coincidence of objects of the same kind).[5] In each case, to use Quine's figure, the leading idea can meet our desiderata by 'making accommodations elsewhere in the system,' thus generating a package view.

2. The Views

A. *'Commonsense'/Coincidence.* Let's begin with what I think of as the 'commonsense' or 'ordinary' view, as represented by Wiggins. The 'leading idea' here is given simply by our ordinary judgments about what there is, what there isn't, and how things trace through time. In Wiggins (1968), he argues that these judgments combine to commit us to coinciding entities, but he then attempts to make this acceptable by suggesting that (a) the coincident entities can be distinguished by sort, (b) we can still say that the tree just is the wood—in the sense of being wholly constituted by it, and (c) we can still accept the claim that no two objects *of the same sort* can coincide—implicitly suggesting that the intuitive pull of NC really resides in the truth of this more restricted doctrine. However, to many, this seems a misdiagnosis, for it is equally mysterious how such objects *can* differ in sort. Whatever might make some *tree* sortally a tree—have the identity conditions for trees—will also be true of the *wood* co-located with the tree. So, appeals to difference in sort, or identity conditions, or modal properties, are as problematic—and seemingly, for just the same reasons—as the original claim that there are, or could be, two objects.[6]

Now, the defender of coincidence may point out that this argument presupposes that kind membership, and/or identity conditions, supervene on other, non-modal and 'less problematic' properties, and in a very particular way. This allows two moves. One may simply deny that these properties are so supervenient; alternatively, one may suggest that while they *are* supervenient, we have to be clearer about supervenience. Usually, the supervenience of F on G is understood as roughly:

(x)(y)(if x and y agree with respect to their G properties, they agree with respect to F),

thus implying that there can be no difference in F without a difference in G. Since the tree and wood don't differ in their non-modal, current actual properties, they can't differ in sort or identity conditions. However, the core idea behind the supervenience of identity conditions—the main idea behind wanting to deny their 'brutality'—is roughly that, if matter gets arranged in exactly the same way, by the same processes, etc., in two situations, then if you have, say, a tree in one case, you have one in the other. But here, we've focused on *two situations* not differing: there is a tree in each. It is less clear that we want or need to insist that the wood *in the same* situation needs to realize all the same non-actual properties the tree does. So long as there is *a* tree, the two situations don't differ by a 'brute fact', and in some sense, the presence of an object of some particular sort, with these identity conditions, is not something 'above and beyond' the obtaining of the less problematic properties. Along these lines, then, it may be urged that all supervenience really requires is that whenever these G properties co-occur, there is *an* F.[7]

Theory	'Leading Idea'	Need to Deal With:	Ways of Dealing
Commonsense	Normal judgments of what there is, persistence are correct	Coincidence	Modified supervenience, brute fact
		Arbitrariness (what there is/isn't, what changes are substantial)	Causal relations, brute facts
Persistence Views:			
Mereological Essentialism (ME)	Handles puzzles about change; 'An object is its parts'	Ordinary views about change; possibly arbitrary?	Series, sets, paraphrase; temporal counterpart theory
Hyper-Essentialism 'Intrinsic' Essentialism	Leibniz's law (LL); puzzles LL, but for 'real' properties; puzzles	Ordinary views, distinctions Ordinary views; explain intrinsic/extrinsic distinction	Same Same; intuitive, various options
Four-Dimensionalism	Time relevantly like space; Apparent coincidence is identity of parts (sometimes LL; vagueness)	Apparent ordinary views; Lumpl/Goliath; Spatiotemporal essentialism	Paraphrase and bullet biting; Counterpart theory
Burke (Sortal Dominance)	Avoid coincidence by denying apparent persistence conditions of 'under object'—"when wood is a tree, it isn't 'just' wood"	When and why does G dominate F?	Various options ('F implies more properties')

View		Are 'under objects' and arbitrary parts actually saved?	Yes—revision is only partial
Persistence Universalism	Arbitrariness of alteration/corruption distinction	Ordinary persistence judgments	Emphasize partiality of revision
Ontological Views: Universalism (Ontological)	Arbitrariness of distinctions (but worries about Nihilism)	Ordinary distinctions; coincidence	Rediscribe/paraphrase; (triviality)
		Ordinary distinctions; commitment to ME	Redescribe/paraphrase Same as ME
Nihilism	Distinctions arbitrary, suspicion of modality/identity conditions/boundaries	Ordinary claims; no values of variables for redescription	Paraphrase; blame the medium
'Just Simples'	Complexity root of all problems	Arbitrariness; ordinary claims	Deny arbitrariness; paraphrase
Van Inwagen (There are simples and living organisms)	Cogito commits us to humans, non-arbitrariness to other living things; nothing comes to be when sand forts made; no coincidence	Ordinary commitment to artifacts, the inanimate and arbitrary parts.	Paraphrase
		Arbitrary to allow organisms?	Deny arbitrariness?
		Commitment to simples?	Bite or deny commitment

It doesn't much matter whether this is viewed as a reinterpretation of supervenience, or its denial and replacement by an alternate 'determination' relation; either way, it goes *some* way towards meeting the counterargument against Wiggins. Of course, it does not make things utterly unmysterious—it trades the 'brute fact' that something is sortally an F, or has such-and-such persistence conditions, for the 'brute fact' that despite both realizing the same G properties, the tree, but not the wood instantiates these identity conditions (while only the wood instantiates *those* conditions). But there is no *incoherence* here, and it does say *something*.

I don't want to say that I am *happy* with this; it still violates deep theoretical ideas. But it will seem enough, I think, to those who are deeply enough committed to our other views that lead to coincidence, and so who think one merely needs to show that the view is not incoherent. For our purposes, what matters is that the commonsense view has a reply, by offering a total, coherent story within which its leading idea fits, and which, to the satisfaction of some, at least, addresses the objection.

The other approaches, except for Persistence Universalism, try to avoid coincidence. Consequently, they need to deny one or another ordinary view about what there is, or how things persist. To avoid coincidence, one must make out that in all cases where coincidence threatens, either (a) one (or both) of the objects does not exist, or (b) they are identical. (Though four-dimensionalism may not seem *best* captured by (b), claiming instead that the objects are not wholly located in the same place.) As far as 'leading ideas' go, the first sort of approaches may be thought of as 'ontological'—revising some view about what there *is* (here I place Van Inwagen, Ontological Universalism and Nihilism), while the latter may be thought of as revising some view about how things *persist*, since these are what seem to preclude identity, and so, force coincidence, in these cases (here, I put Mereological Essentialism (and other 'strong' essentialisms—see note 10), four-dimensionalism, and Burke's sortal dominance view). Of course, on investigation, views of either sort may wind up needing to make changes of the other kind as well—four-dimensionalism and the strong essentialisms may delete ordinary objects from their ontology, and Ontological Universalism may need to embrace a strong essentialist view about persistence. But each *starts* with one sort of idea.

B. Views about Persistence. One view of the 'change our views about persistence' sort that is always around, though rarely explicitly endorsed, is Mereological Essentialism (ME).[8] This is the view that an object cannot gain or lose parts.[9] ME rejects the ordinary judgments about persistence that give rise to the puzzles of coincidence—a tree *cannot* survive the loss of a branch any more than its constituting wood can, nor can a statue or organism survive the loss of a leg. Strictly, by only providing a necessary condition for persistence, coincidence may still be possible—x and y might differ over what *non*-mereological changes they can undergo or what rearrangements of smaller parts, if any, they can tolerate (like a sweater and a piece of yarn). Thus, most friends of ME either embrace persistence of parts as a sufficient condition as well, or add some further necessary condition (such as that the parts remain appropriately related—this, I think, is Chisholm's view). ME also avoids Sorites puzzles, and the arbitrariness that seems to infect any other theory's attempts to say just how much mereological change an object can undergo.[10]

Despite these advantages, ME is, as I say, rarely championed, and this is for one main reason: It is incompatible with everyday and obvious judgments of persistence. On versions requiring some sort of continued 'unity' or arrangement of parts, things that seem to persist do not—the tree in my yard was not there five minutes ago, much less two hundred years—and versions that take the survival of parts to alone suffice would have the tree, and everything else, be millions of years old, and imply that the locations of these things at other times is never what it seems—though the tree existed ten years ago, it was not (wholly) located in my yard.

Mereological Essentialists (and the others—note 10) may and do make two general sorts of moves in reply, though they aren't always distinguished and it may not be that important to do so.[11] One is to simply *accept* the implications, and try to explain why they *seem* wrong (as in Chisholm's echoing of Butler's distinction between 'strict and literal' and 'loose and popular' identity); the other is to deny the implications by denying the existence of the seemingly mereologically incontinent objects. Either way, they need to give *some* reasonable interpretation of our ordinary judgments, and either way, it is pretty clear how it will go—our ordinary use of 'car', etc., traces *series* of objects, related to each other in various ways, such as sharing parts and causal relations. On the first interpretation, our ordinary claims are all *false*, because we apply 'car C' to numerically distinct objects; on the second, our judgments may be *true*, but that is because 'car' applies to *series*, rather than single, objects. (There are, of course, variations upon this strategy.) Notice that insofar as others have accounts of how cars and cows 'genuinely' persist, ME can ride piggy-back upon such accounts and simply reinterpret: what the opponent sees as persistence conditions, ME sees as the conditions guiding ordinary judgments or 'unifying' series.

One may not like this—one may think it doesn't *really* square ME with our normal views, and that it 'strictly and literally' is tantamount to denying that cars and cows exist.[12] But it does square with all the *hard* facts, and it is handy with the puzzles. If we cross the three sorts of strong essentialism with universal and more restrictive views about when one has an object, we get six possible views, all with something to recommend them and some champions, and all needing—and able to use—some reconstruction strategy, to make sense of our ordinary judgments.

Another approach, in some ways like the above, is Four-Dimensionalism (sometimes called the Temporal Parts view). This view sees time as a fourth dimension along which material objects extend, and along which an object may be arbitrarily divided into parts. Many people claim to find this intuitive, while opponents think all that is intuitive is that the *career* of an object is so extended and divisible. Be that as it may, Four-Dimensionalism allows us to treat cases of apparent coincidence as we treat cases of objects sharing spatial parts. Just as two highways may share a common stretch, or Siamese twins may share a hand, so a tree and its wood may share a *temporal* part. In none of these cases are there actually two things wholly located in the same place at the same time: what is wholly located, in the relevant spot, is just *one* thing, which is a part of both (and more) objects. Consequently, each object *is partly* located at that place and time—but only partly. Some Four-dimensionalists also claim motivation and support, as our strong Essentialists do, through worries about how objects can really persist through change: Four-dimensionalists explain that different temporal parts bear the contrary properties. And Four-dimensionalists also tend to be Universalists about when temporal parts compose a single object, and so can say that there is a single four-dimensional object with precise boundaries for each vague possible boundary a three-dimensionalist might try to arbitrarily select as demarcating the coming or ceasing to exist of a three-dimensional object.[13]

It is often claimed that Four-Dimensionalism goes strongly against our ordinary views, that we are intuitively Three-Dimensionalists. I am not holding just part of a paper—I'm holding the whole thing! I find this hard to assess. It is also claimed that Four-Dimensionalism is incompatible with change: change requires a common subject to be at one time F and at another time not-F, while on Four-Dimensionalism, one temporal part is F while a *different* one is not-F. But of course, the Four-Dimensionalist will reply that these are temporal parts of the same Four-Dimensional object, so there *is* a common subject. And if one charges that change requires the common subject to be the 'primary' or 'direct' bearer of the properties, one may deny this or even challenge its sense. There are, though, a couple of more serious problems. One is that examples of apparent coincidence are not restricted to cases where the objects differ historically—most famously, Allan Gibbard's "Lumpl/Goliath" case. Here, one cannot say the objects are only *partly* co-located, because neither object has any *other* temporal parts. But then, coincidence is not entirely avoided, or else there are other ways of avoiding it. A related problem, due to van Inwagen (1981, section VI), is that on pain of coincidence, Four-Dimensionalism seems committed to a temporal, or maybe even a spatiotemporal, boundary essentialism: an object cannot have existed any longer or shorter than it actually exists—for if it had, it would have coincided with another object which is a temporal part of it (in the case of shorter existence), or of which it—or something for all the world exactly like it—would be a temporal part (in the case of longer existence). This is particularly important insofar as the Four-dimensionalist hopes—or hoped—to claim superiority to competitors in handling coincidence, since it could also preserve our views about objects' ability to survive change, the existence of arbitrary undetached parts, *and* our ordinary ontology. But ordinary objects aren't obviously saved—anyway, not intact—if their spatiotemporal boundaries are so modally intractable. Surely, the Colossus at Rhodes might have lasted longer than it did—so if the four-dimensional hunk of rock with which it shared its entire career could not, the Colossus is not identical to it. Thus, to avoid coincidence, the Four-dimensionalist must revise our ordinary modal views, or deny that the Colossus exists.

The Four-Dimensionalist has various options here; most combine some amount of bullet-biting with some amount of paraphrasing. Heller, for example, gives up ordinary objects—there is neither the statue nor the piece of clay nor the Colossus at Rhodes: there are just Four-Dimensional hunks of matter with essential spatiotemporal boundaries, and since ordinary objects are not these, there just aren't such (Heller (1990), especially Chapter Two). This, of course, requires some accounting of our ordinary claims, and these are as easily rendered as for ME, in paraphrases. Another option is to adopt a sortally-relative Counterpart Theory for modal discourse.[14] Since the Counterpart relation is sortally relative, it would not simply be true that Lumpl, but not Goliath, would have survived smooshing, or that the Colossus, but not the Four-dimensional lump, might have lasted longer. Rather, Lumpl—and Goliath—have lump counterparts that are not statues, and the name 'Lumpl', but not 'Goliath', invokes the lump counterpart relation in modal contexts; ditto for the Colossus. This allows contingent identity statements, and for pairs of identicals, in the relevant sense, to differ in their modal properties—so one could claim that Lumpl *is* Goliath, and the Colossus *is* the four-dimensional lump, but that statue-counterparts needn't be lump-counterparts, and vice-versa, and they might endure for different lengths of time.

I shan't rehearse the familiar back-and-forth about Counterpart theory; as at least a paraphrase strategy, it doesn't seem obviously worse than that required by any of the other views, and at worst, there is always the retreat to the more simple denial and more ordinary paraphrase.

Perhaps the most creative 'persistence altering' view is Burke's 'Sortal Dominance' view (Burke, 1994a and b). Burke, like the others, starts with a denial of coincidence. But in diagnosing apparent cases of coincidence, he sees the mistake not—as in more obvious approaches—in our judgments about the persistence of the 'superobject'—the tree or sweater—rather, he finds it in persistence judgments of the constituting objects—the wood or yarn. After all, if we *start* with the idea that in one location, only one set of identity conditions can be instantiated, why should the yarn win out over the sweater? If we are confident that the sweater, or statue, or tree, comes into existence at a certain time, then so must the yarn, bronze or wood that is located there. An interesting point Burke notes to help this seem more palatable is the plausibility of the claim that when a piece of bronze (wood, yarn) is formed as a statue (tree, sweater), it is not 'just' a piece of bronze: it is a *statue*—when asked 'what is it?', 'statue' ('tree', 'sweater') seems the right answer. Now, if the piece of bronze we had at t1 was just a piece of bronze, while that at t2 is a *statue*, is it so strange to claim that, as things of different sorts, they have different identity conditions, and so cannot really be the same? The denial of this apparent identity is no more bizarre than the answer 'this is a statue' (tree, sweater). Similarly for arbitrary undetached parts—a 'torso'—the part of a body apart from its left foot—is 'just' a torso when it is a part, but when a body loses its foot, we have a torso which is an organism. Burke thus tries to hold onto our 'commonsense' ontology along with No Coincidence, by what can seem a relatively small change in some of our judgments of identity through time.

One question for Burke is: when and why does one sortal dominate another? There are various options; Burke suggests that one sortal dominates another when it 'implies more properties'—'tree', for instance, implies everything 'wood' does, plus further functional and formal features. As this stands though, it can only be clearly applied when one sortal implies another. 'Statue' doesn't imply anything about specific materials—so does 'statue' imply more properties than 'piece of clay' or 'bronze'? But there may be other options, and one might leave it intuitive—asked what this piece of clay is, 'Statue' *is* a better answer than 'piece of clay'. An account would be nice, but does the view *require* one? The same might be said about 'Why?' One might want to know why the fact that F implies more properties than G makes it determine the object's identity conditions—but at this level of analysis, it isn't clear *any* view can tell us *why* meeting its conditions makes for objecthood or persistence: the theory merely needs to get it right.[15]

A potentially more damaging objection asks whether, given what Burke says about the persistence of torsos, lumps and pieces of yarn, he can really claim to have *saved* them, and especially, whether there is any motivation for saving them *in this way* which wouldn't be better served by just denying their existence, like Van Inwagen. After all, perhaps the main argument for believing in arbitrary undetached parts is that they can *become* detached, and when they do, it seems clear that they have not just came into existence. But according to Burke, a fair number of these parts *cannot* become detached: a torso that ceases to be attached to a foot ceases to be—it is replaced by another torso which is an organism. Worse, this 'new' torso is made of just the same matter arranged just the same way through a causally continuous path. Is denying that this suffices for torso—or lump, yarn or aggregate—identity compatible with acknowledging their existence at all (at least, short of hyper-essentialism)? A related objection asks whether, if a torso becomes detached from a foot, and the resulting torso is reattached, isn't the third torso identical to the first?[16]

While this is serious, Burke may respond in various ways. First, he may emphasize that he only changes our views about persistence *in certain cases*—namely, when an object comes to satisfy another sortal. And this is rare. Relatively few of an object's arbitrary undetached parts can be an object of the higher sort. And of those that *can*, most *never will* become detached, so we needn't change our views about *their* persistence. Similarly for most lumps and aggregates. So this may stave off the charge of motivational incoherence. The problems of reidentification call for different treatment, but there are again various options. One can allow for gappy existence, or explain the *appearance* of identity in terms of the common components. Again, one may not like this, but we can *understand* it, and it can claim some amount of independent motivation from our ordinary answers to Aristotelian 'What is it?' questions.

One last view in this category that is, I think, never explicitly discussed but worth mentioning may be called 'Persistence Universalism'. On this view, for any materially occupied path through time, there is an object whose career that path traces.[17] This is rather like liberal four-dimensionalism, but in a three-dimensional framework—what we have at t1 and t2 are not parts of an extended object, but the numerically same object. It is 'Universalism' in that *all* possible candidates for persistence conditions are acknowledged to be the conditions of persistence for *some* object. In this, it claims to avoid the arbitrariness of more restrictive views about persistence, as do liberal versions of four-dimensionalism.[18] This, presumably, would be the chief motivation for the view.[19] The view certainly appears to conflict with commonsense—but only in allowing identities and persistence where commonsense denies them (that is, it agrees with commonsense where commonsense *finds* identities). However, one might maintain that commonsense doesn't so much deny them as ignore them, and that when we *appear* to make a denial, we are only denying that some *particular* object—like this *car*, or *Tony*—would be present in a certain possible future location—not that there is *no* object which is both present here, and would be (is) present there.[20] This, though, does bring out another seemingly serious problem—the view is committed to massive coincidence of objects. Even if the *car* is not identical to the (t2) paint chip (say), there is some object wholly located where the car is, which *is* so identical. So we have vastly many objects co-located at any place and time—not just the usually problematic two. On the other hand, the extent of coincidence, I think, makes this an interesting view, because it makes coincidence so *trivial*. That is, since wherever you have an object, every possible criterion of identity/method of tracing is instantiated, there is no special problem saying why, for each one, it *is* instantiated, and coincidence follows trivially. There may remain the problem of explaining how the car has the persistence conditions it does, while the other objects there do not, but given this view, the denial of the supervenience of identity conditions is natural and straightforward, and may be urged as the price we have to pay for not being arbitrary. So, while coincidence is not avoided, the view offers a novel account of its acceptability.[21]

C. Ontological Views. Having spent this much time on the above views, I hope the basic picture of the sort of objections—particularly from commonsense—and the sorts of package-building replies that may be offered, is apparent enough that it can be easily applied to the remaining views. Thus, I shall be rather briefer with them, hitting only significant highlights.

There are two extreme views about what there is which are fairly familiar— Universalism and Nihilism. According to Universalism, wherever you have some matter, you have an object which that matter composes, while according to Nihilism, there are no objects—there's just the matter.[22] These views share their fundamental 'leading idea', that any distinctions between (materially filled) portions of the world which do, and which do not, contain objects would be ultimately arbitrary—so they both treat all such regions alike. Universalism is then more impressed with the seemingly obvious fact that there are objects, while Nihilism urges that there is a problem with how the conditions distinctive of objects—identity conditions—can be supported by the world at all. Even if we have a simple, what determines whether a change in property at that location constitutes an accidental or a substantial change?[23] And while certain sorts of arbitrariness are avoided by the extreme essentialist views, like Hyperessentialism, what makes 'objects never survive change' a better answer than 'they always do'? Since the world is not up to determining which changes are accidental and which substantial, the Nihilist urges denying the presupposition of such questions, by denying the existence of objects altogether.[24]

Universalism here—like Persistence Universalism—may seem to score poorly on commonsense, but as suggested earlier, it isn't clear that commonsense so much denies the bulk of scattered objects, as it ignores them. I haven't found many people deeply committed (prior to certain arguments like the one to follow) to denying that there is something composed of my fish and my daughter's left pinky. At any rate, to the extent that we do make such distinctions, the Universalist will just redescribe our distinction between objects and non-objects as distinctions between objects of different sorts, and will do so not only for commonsense, but for whatever distinctions other views which fall between Universalism and Nihilism have to offer. Nihilism will offer the same sorts of redescriptions, except (a) it will not be able to claim with any plausibility that the view doesn't conflict with commonsense, and (b) the distinctions will not be between objects of different sorts, but non-objects of different sorts—different distributions of matter and properties. Nihilism here is actually threatened with incoherence in a way none of our other views are, which could potentially rule it out as a live option. For it is not completely clear that we can understand the distinctions it wants to and must acknowledge without being committed to objects of some sort or another. For instance, if one attempts to redescribe what we ordinarily would describe as one car surviving being painted, and to distinguish this from, say, a car being destroyed by pulverization, the nihilist will want to talk about car-shaped portions of matter, at different times, and causal relations and properties thereof—but what about these portions? How are they not objects? The Nihilist seems committed to denying that these portions are literally the same before and after the changes: otherwise, we would have the sort of persistence he purports to find so problematic; but if he does so deny, he looks just like a mereological or hyperessentialist, who doesn't deny objects, but only their persistence. And if he offers no paraphrase, one may wonder whether he can truly claim to have a theory about the real world at all—or anyway, one compatible with the 'palpable phenomena'.

I don't think the Nihilist's position is really so hopeless; I have elsewhere (Sidelle (1998) section VI) suggested a number of options available to him, citing, in part, the 'feature-placing' language proposed by Hawthorne and Cortens (1995), and the idea that each apparent objectual expression in a paraphrase can be seen as just a place holder. If this is right, the Nihilist can continue to speak with the vulgar, and acknowledge all facts about the distribution of matter through space and time, while denying 'in his heart' that there really are objects.

The Universalist's further problem arises when he turns to persistence. Van Inwagen's (1981) argument against arbitrary undetached parts applies equally against Universalism (since Universalism entails the existence of arbitrary undetached parts): it seems to show that on pain of coincident entities—which Universalists by and large wish to avoid—the Universalist must adopt one of the strong essentialist views we've discussed, denying, at least, that objects can gain or lose parts. Otherwise, they would 'run into' the larger, or smaller, objects which also, according to the Universalist, exist. Van Inwagen, and others, take this as reason to reject Universalism—but the Universalist himself can make all the moves we earlier saw were available to the mereological and other strong essentialists. Van Cleve (1986), indeed, starts with Universalism in an argument for Mereological Essentialism, thus presenting the package as a whole.

Another option for the Universalist is to adopt a Burkeish, sortal dominance view of persistence. Such a package amplifies the questions already posed for Burke's view, since *whenever* a 'normal' object undergoes mereological change, some aggregate will cease to exist—i.e. the one that would otherwise be located where the object now is. But perhaps this is just a difference of degree, and isn't much more objectionable than what we've already seen.

Finally, between Universalism and Nihilism come more restrictive ontologies. Obviously, there are many options here. The most obvious ones—those close to commonsense—lead to coinciding entities unless they are combined with a revisionary view about persistence. Thus, these packages would be either like Wiggins', or one of those discussed in the above section on persistence. What this leaves among well-known and reasonably motivated views are those that allow one or more of: simples, masses (lumps) and organisms.

Views that allow simples differ, I think, from the rest we've been discussing insofar as it seems a genuine scientific question whether matter has smallest parts. That aside, it is plain what looks good about simples—not being complex, they seem to avoid troublesome puzzles. On the other hand, those concerned about arbitrariness—Universalists and Nihilists—may want to know what is so special about simples that allows them to have genuine persistence conditions of a sort nothing else in the world has. And what are they? Which properties of a simple can be lost, while the simple persists? Unless one property, or set of properties, can be singled out, there is a threat of coinciding entities here—the simple for which 'being a quark' (say)—and only that—is essential, and that for which having spin up is essential. And plainly, avoiding coincidence must be done in a way that doesn't give us arbitrariness.[25] Of course, anyone who thinks the truth is somewhere between Universalism and Nihilism will think *something* counts as sufficiently non-arbitrary; one common answer appeals to causal powers—here, those most central to any particular simple.

In addition, a view will really be intermediate only if it does not allow aggregates—otherwise, it will amount to Universalism. If it *only* allows simples, it will be like other views which deny the existence of most common-sense objects, and will presumably try to accommodate our ordinary judgments via some paraphrase strategy. The same goes for masses—if masses can be scattered, then mass theory is a Universalist view; if they must be, in some way, unified, it will need to say what sort of unity is object-making; again, some appeal to causal relations among parts can be expected, and if done well, this will resonate with some, while raising the question 'What's so special—from the metaphysical, object-making perspective—about causality?' from Universalists and Nihilists. Further, as Zimmermann (1995) has argued, mass theory cannot be combined with ordinary objects without encumbering coincidence (again, short of a modified theory of persistence).

This brings us finally to organisms, the most visible non-ordinary, non-Universalist champion of which is van Inwagen, who also allows simples.[26] There isn't a simple leading idea behind van Inwagen's position, but perhaps we can summarize it like this. Of course there are simples. However, not every collection of simples is an object—this Universalism, besides being counterintuitive, generates either coinciding entities (van Inwagen's objection is to objects sharing all their parts) or Mereological Essentialism, both of which are unacceptable. However, the Cogito—combined with obvious scientific facts—ensures that at least one non-simple exists: me (van Inwagen has a different favored first complex object). But there is no non-arbitrary reason for allowing myself but not other living organisms—thus, living organisms exist. On the other hand, artifacts and other inanimate objects are not 'sufficiently like' living organisms—or better, the simples 'arranged chairishly' and 'rockly' are not related sufficiently like the way those constituting organisms are. They are, really, rather more like aggregates. So there are no such other things.

If van Inwagen really has established that there are organisms, then Nihilism is out. But of course, many have wondered about what the Cogito really establishes: why does thought have to have a subject? Why can't there just be some stuff arranged so that thought occurs there, just as conductivity may so occur? Nihilism aside, the move from the Cogito to the claim that I (or van Inwagen, anyway) am (is) an organism has been questioned. Why isn't the subject of thought a certain aggregate? The appeal to identity through time, which van Inwagen uses to argue that he is not an aggregate, while *independently* plausible, is not supported by the Cogito, which is a synchronic matter. It is of course true that the matter underwriting the thought 'I think' has a certain biological arrangement—but it has lots of features. Another more restrictive move from this starting point would restrict the ontology to *thinking* things, or conscious things—after all, they have more in common, in arrangement of parts, with van Inwagen, than non-thinking animate organisms, and in particular, more in common that has something to do with the purported need to acknowledge the existence of the first complex item. I suppose these questions all come under the general rubric of 'arbitrariness'—and we can expect van Inwagen to deny that his way of extending from himself is arbitrary. And he will be able to point to an interesting feature—constituting a life—that all and only his preferred candidates for object-constituting simples have. But both the broader and narrower intermediate proposals share interesting features as well.

Van Inwagen's negative views have probably attracted more attention than his positive ones, and his response to them is especially important for us—indeed, we've more or less presupposed it throughout. van Inwagen, more than any other 'revisionary' ontologist, has developed a proposal about how to paraphrase ordinary claims without commitment to the objects one wishes to eschew from one's ontology. van Inwagen develops it mostly in connection with his rejection of artifacts: when, as we would say, I am sitting on a chair, van Inwagen would have it that I am sitting on simples arranged chairishly. Particularly noteworthy, and praiseworthy, is van Inwagen's discussion of transtemporal statements. There has been a fair bit of discussion of whether van Inwagen is right to claim that our ordinary claims should be understood in terms of his paraphrases, so that his view can truly be said to be compatible with ordinary claims like 'There are three chairs in the room' [27]—but even if this fails, his paraphrases can give us what is genuinely true in our ordinary, false assertions. And all that is really required is that our ordinary views be *accommodated*—handled, rationalized—not that they come out true. van Inwagen's work here is particularly worth noting because it provides resources for all of the revisionary views we've been discussing. As we've seen, all the views require some revision, and van Inwagen's work here makes it clear that acceptable paraphrases will be available. And as we noted earlier, those unhappy with his *particular* proposals can hardly deny that whatever their 'right' view is, it can supply a basis for a van Inwagenesque paraphrase to ride piggy-back upon. Thus, the desideratum of 'accommodating ordinary views' can be made part of the package of any of the views we've been discussing. On the other hand, in all these cases, it can hardly be denied that the ontologies are *revisionary*, and that the answers they give to 'how is your favored ontology not arbitrary?' are hardly candidates for logical truths.

II. (Contra Realism)

Now, I have to admit to being *unhappy* with many of the packages, but there is a minimum constraint they all meet. Their leading ideas are well-motivated, they have *something* to say to each desideratum, we can *understand* them (some charges of incomprehensibility notwithstanding), and crucially, any distribution of matter in space-time can be coherently described by them. This is why each is defensible at least to the satisfaction of its proponents—who, in each case, consist of at least some intelligent philosophers. What I submit is that, among these packages—and perhaps others—there can be no fact of the matter as to which *truly* describes the material ontology and persistence of things in the world. They can only be understood as different ways of articulating, extending and making coherent the combination of our ordinary judgments and theoretical ideas. But short of showing that really, all but one are incoherent, I don't see what in the world can *make* one true; or equivalently, while the theories plainly *differ*, I don't see how *that with respect to which they differ* can be understood as a factual matter.

What can I mean in questioning whether these views differ factually? According to Mereological Essentialism, no dog has ever survived the loss of a tail, while on most other views, this has happened plenty. According to van Inwagen, there really aren't cars; on most other views, there are. According to Burke, this piece of yarn did not exist yesterday, when my sweater had not yet been unraveled; on most other views, it did. According to Wiggins and Persistence Universalism, the tree and its wood are two material objects, occupying the same space in my yard; according to four-dimensionalism, they aren't entirely there, according to Burke and Mereological Essentialism, they are identical, while according to van Inwagen and Nihilism, one or both don't exist. According to van Inwagen and commonsense, certain causal relations among things are needed for them to compose an object; according to Universalism and Nihilism, this cannot be the difference between the presence and absence of an object. What more can you want?

But I hope, after our lengthy discussion of the views and their resources, it is clear why I am not moved. What we describe as a dog's losing its tail, ME describes as one dog-shaped sum replacing another slightly larger one; what we call a car, van Inwagen calls some car-arranged simples. What we distinguish as 'a collection of objects,' Universalists call 'a spatially dispersed object'. What Wiggins calls the persistence of a piece of yarn and destruction of a sweater, Burke calls the coming to be of 'just' a piece of yarn. One may, of course, insist that at most, one of each pair is true—but it is not hard, I think, to see them as just different descriptions of the same situation, the same spatiotemporal distribution of matter (properties and causal relations). What could *make* one of them true? What would it *be* for there *really* to be the same dog after tail-amputation—or really *not* the same dog?

One way to consider the matter is to ask: what story about the world are these theories telling us? Are these 'facts of persistence' or 'objecthood', etc., *extra* facts, beyond the arrangements of matter in various ways, with certain properties and in certain causal relations, to which all parties are agreed? Or is it enough that we simply do, in fact, use words like 'object' and 'same' to mark distinctions which are independently recognizable and of no further significance? For example, some might say that the question: "What is it about the difference between spatiotemporally continuous S-paths and other paths that makes only the first paths traced by single objects?"—a question some press to urge the arbitrariness of our ordinary judgments—asks too much. That may simply *be* the distinction we mark with the expressions 'same/different object' (used transtemporally). Call this 'the semantic account'. On this approach, what would make one of the views true is not the correct postulation of 'extra facts' beyond what we all agree upon, but rather, the proper description *of* this agreed upon stuff *in English*. We all acknowledge A at t1 and B at t2, differing in respect of part P—the question is whether the rules of English permit, or require, or rule out, the claim that A is B. Is the difference between objects having different parts that which we mark by 'not the same thing'? (A sophisticated version might hold that while not 'directly' what we mean, this is how we must interpret the expression, given other things we want to hold on to.) On this view, there is nothing 'metaphysical', so to speak, determining the truth of the views—our metaphysical vocabulary simply marks non-metaphysical distinctions, and does so, roughly, via linguistic rules.

The semantic approach is easily comprehensible—but on such a view, I submit, none of the theories can claim victory over the others. Each package represents a total reconciliation of our otherwise inconsistent cluster of particular judgments and theoretical views, each with some important ties to our usage and 'deep convictions'. The fact that each view is *comprehendible* shows that it is not 'simply' false in virtue of meaning, and by the same token, that none are *simply* true, on the semantic approach. At best, one view might offer the 'best' reconciliation.

I suppose it is clear that this is how I view things, and is, at bottom, why I think there is no fact of the matter. It is also why I think that even if there were a fact of the matter, it would be a matter of convention.

In contrast, one might think there *are* further facts, and that such further facts are what could make one of the theories true. For example, in addition to the difference in parts between A at t1 and B at t2, there is the *further*, non-semantic fact that this constitutes A's non-identity to B. That you cannot have two things in the same place at the same time would be another further fact, not made true by our rules of description, but instead, by 'the nature of things'. Call this, in contrast to the semantic approach, 'the metaphysical approach'. It is, I submit, the view of anyone who thinks there can be a genuine fact of the matter as between our views. When I earlier said I didn't see how one of the views could be true, that might be read as: "I see how one of the views might in principle be true on semantic grounds—but none of them is—and I don't understand a more metaphysical interpretation".

To some extent, the suspicion I've expressed about non-semantic facts discriminating among the views comes from the intuitive force of seeing the pairs of descriptions offered in the second paragraph of this section as just offering different descriptions of the same facts. But perhaps I've focused too much on particular judgments, while overlooking our theoretical constraints—for example, No Coincidence. Wiggins' and our ordinary descriptions here, *if* they were true, would imply that there could be coincidence and complete sharing of parts. Since this is *not* possible, some of our ordinary descriptions are false. But how much factual content is there to NC? Is *it* more than a possible constraint upon descriptions? Admittedly, the question of how two such things could differ in sort, or persistence conditions, has force—but sufficient prior commitment to our persistence judgments will make it seem adequate to note that when matter is so-and-so arranged, there is an instantiation of such-and-such identity conditions, and more than one such arrangement can be instantiated at a particular location. Still—isn't just one of these *right*? Either there *can*, or *cannot* be two such objects! But—I hope I'm not alone here—I find it very hard to get a handle on this, unless considered in terms of particular cases, and then we are back to our questions about whether there is a factual difference between more specific, less theoretical, pairs of descriptions. I admit not *liking* coincidence, and preferring views that avoid it (all else equal). But pressed on what the difference could be between coincidence being possible or not, I am at a loss, except as we go round and round about what other descriptions of cases we can give consistently with either acceptance or rejection. (Similar remarks apply to other contested theoretical constraints.)

My position here, I think, is an application of Carnap's (1950) distinction between internal and external questions, and his rejection of external questions as only apparently factual. Within each view, one can answer questions like "Was this tree in my yard yesterday?" and even questions like "In virtue of what is this the tree that was in my yard yesterday?" Of course, the views will often give different answers. And one can say *of* each view what it implies, in each case. But when one asks "But is there *really* an object that was in my yard both yesterday and today, with different parts?" no answer can be sensibly given (beyond repetition). "Really", and other such terms, just don't have the content to generate an answer at a level 'above' those given within each theory—or as Carnap might call them, 'linguistic frameworks'.

Put another way, each theory attempts to address questions like "In virtue of what is object Z still around?" or "Under what conditions do we have an object?" When we see the diversity of answers, we are moved to ask another set of questions: *Why* does the presence of a,b,c make for constitution, or persistence, or substantial change? These questions can have *semantic* answers—'that's what 'constitution' means'—but if we want *metaphysical* answers, these will be hard to come by. One might object that these are questions which cannot *have* any answers: if this is what persistence is, that is what it is. And sometimes, such answers are fine. But when faced with competing theories, each of which is *understandable* and can be used to coherently describe any possible situation, this simple answer is unsatisfactory.

Here's something of an argument, or at least, something which may make the metaphysical option, and consequently, the view that the views differ factually, seem even more mysterious than I hope it already seems. If we suppose the theories differ factually, and that the deep facts about objecthood and identity are what determine their truth-values, then it seems we should be able to make sense of any of these views, so far as they are coherent, being the correct description of these facts, and of the more manifest facts the correct description of which depends upon this. So far, so good. But now let us ask: Can the truth here be contingent? Or must it be necessary? There is reason to think it must be necessary—but on the 'factual difference' view, this is hard to sustain.

Certainly, no advocate of any of the views proposes their view as just a contingent truth—those who think it impossible for two objects to coincide don't think this just happens to be true in *our* world—it is supposed to be the metaphysical truth about material objects. Those who think objects can't survive the loss of a part don't think they *might* have been able to, but it turns out they can't *here*. And so on. This is as it should be. These views are all themselves modal, and it is hard to interpret the modalities as anything other than the strongest sorts of necessity and correspondingly weakest sorts of possibility. The weakest possibilities, that is, count against the views.[28] So, if one of the views is true, it is necessarily true and if false, necessarily false.

But I suggest that insofar as we have any grasp at all on factual differences between the views, we cannot think of one as necessarily true and the rest necessarily false. The factual differences between the views would consist in the 'extra' truths that, say, such-and-such a relation between parts was (or wasn't) necessary, or sufficient, for objecthood—or that when any A and B were exactly co-located, they'd have (or might not) the same conditions of persistence and transworld identity. Insofar as we can make sense of one 'package' of superfacts obtaining, we can make sense of *any* of them obtaining, just as, if laws of nature are something supra-Humean, we can equally make sense of any of a host of such laws being the 'real ones' governing motion and change. And this, I think, makes it impossible to see any of them as actually necessary in the widest sense.[29]

Of course, one may object that the necessity here is *metaphysical*, not logical, so we cannot take the equal *conceivability* of each view to establish their equal *possibility* in any but an epistemic sense. If, as a matter of fact, objecthood *is* the obtaining of such and such relations, or persistence *is* continuity of form, then all the other views just give necessarily false descriptions of the one true way things are and can be. But now we are piling mystery on mystery. I had enough trouble understanding how there is any factual difference at all— now I'm being told that of these supposedly factual differences, only one is really possible? Only one of these 'extra sets of facts' really *can* obtain? At this point, I have lost my frail grip on there being a factual difference between the views, insofar as only one of these 'extras' is so much as possible. This feeling is further encouraged, I think, insofar as so-called 'metaphysical necessities' really always cover up some genuine possibility, but require it to be differently described. The 'necessity' of water's being H_2O doesn't rule out the other cases we might have thought of as non-water H_2O or non-H_2O water—it only keeps them from *counting* as non-water, or water, respectively. There is still a robust sense, then, in which the possibilities—H_2O that behaves very unwaterly, and non-H_2O that is like water in all other relevant respects—are still acknowledged.[30] As Kripke saw and insisted, handling these apparent possibilities is crucial for the plausibility of the corresponding necessity claim. But in the current case, what possibilities can be acknowledged for the other views? None— and I think this is indicative of the fact that the *only* handle we have on the supposed factual differences between the views is *given by the very descriptions themselves*. That is why no 'redescription' of the possibilities they postulate is left. I, of course, have no brief for metaphysical necessity in the first place, but even granting its sensibility in other cases, I contend we have no handle on it at all here. And so, I think we do *not*, in fact, have any genuine handle on factual differences between these views, *even if* we try to take the 'metaphysical' route seriously.

At this point, one might draw back and reconsider the possibility that the true view is only true contingently, just as the laws of nature, whatever they are, are true contingently—but I don't see that our handle on the differences between the views is anything like sufficient to undermine our conviction that whatever is true here—if anything at all—it is so as a matter of necessity.

III.

That ends my basic brief for taking the differences between these views to be non-factual, and so, along with no semantic resolution, for thinking there is no fact of the matter as to which view is correct. The views, instead, represent different coherent ways of describing the world in terms of objects at a time and across times, which take seriously our actual particular usage and general principles. I will conclude with a couple of questions that should be asked about this view.

One important question—or set of questions—is whether my supposed meta-perspective on these disputes is not in fact a commitment to some substantive position. For instance, the major ground for my position is that I cannot understand the 'superfacts' upon which differences between these views would have to depend. But is that not to say, then, that all the views are really *false*, except, perhaps, Nihilism?

I don't think so. The theories would be false if they were committed to such facts, but I do not see that they are. The theories themselves only make claims about objects, how they persist, and the like. The metaphysical interpretation of the theories, whereby comes the commitment to these superfacts, is no more a part of them than is Platonism in the practice of mathematics. No doubt, it may be accepted by many *advocates* of the theories, but that doesn't make them part of the theories themselves. And so, my position does not entail that the theories are all false—at least, not for this reason.[31]

But perhaps it is incompatible with *some* of the views. In particular, my argument, or 'intuition' if you prefer, might seem incompatible with the appeal to brute facts I described some of the theories as having recourse to. I treated such appeals, in a way, as trump cards—something upon which one may look with disdain, but against which one is powerless to argue. But am I not really saying that I cannot understand such appeals? If so, I cannot really think it is okay for commonsense to claim it is a brute fact that the sweater is sortally a sweater, and not a piece of yarn, while the co-located piece of yarn is not, sortally, a sweater. Similarly, I cannot think challenges of arbitrariness can be met by brute appeals: these simply do, and those—apparently relevantly similar—do not, constitute an object, or a substantial change.[32] Am I not committed to claiming that these claims really are not understandable, and so, it *is* a fact that they are false, and the metaphysical requirements of No Coincidence and No Arbitrariness *are* factual?

But, in accordance with my above remark, I think there is a difference in the sense in which the particular theories discussed may appeal to brute facts, and that in which *all* the theories, interpreted metaphysically, postulate brute facts. They all attempt to say what makes for objecthood, or persistence, or what accounts for certain distinctions. Insofar as one advances any view in contrast to the others, and doesn't think it is *just* the correct description in English—as the semantic view would have it—one must be taking seriously the differences between the theories. *Insofar as one is taking this seriously, everyone* is accepting brute facts—even the nihilist must think there *are* necessary conditions for objecthood, which are just never (and perhaps cannot be) met. So the sort of rejection of brute facts I am suggesting—insofar as that is what I am suggesting—is, I think, neutral among the theories. *Within* particular theories, on the other hand, the appeal to brute facts does not concern the *interpretation* of the view. Rather, it is, in effect, the assertion that a certain fact has no further explanation. And I think our ordinary and theoretical judgments, taken together, allow this sort of move—especially if it is needed to hold onto the set of our ordinary judgments of persistence, as discussed earlier. If yarn is yarn, and a sweater is a sweater, and so have different identity conditions despite their common location, the having of the identity conditions of a sweater, and not of a piece of yarn, can only be, in some sense, a brute fact about the sweater. But so long as we are playing this game, this is something we can, I believe, understand. And certainly, interpreted *semantically*, there is no puzzle how apparently arbitrary distinctions may nonetheless mark distinctions between concepts we apply. Thus, to be Carnapian about it, I'd like to say that certain positions—certain descriptions—may be acceptable *within* a framework for describing the world in terms of objects, even if they include appeals to brute facts—but that the sort of appeal to such facts needed to metaphysically *interpret* a framework, for it to be 'the true framework,' is something of which we simply have no understanding (beyond the semantic).

Finally, there is a cluster of interrelated questions about the evaluation of the various theories. On the one hand, our view is partly motivated by the idea that in some way, the theories differ only verbally, and so, in some sense, 'say the same thing'. This would then seem to push towards saying that they do not really contradict each other, and so, to a semantic interpretation which would accord with this. On the other hand, it seems very hard to maintain that the claims of the theories do *not* contradict each other, or that when someone says 'I used to think objects could survive changes in parts, but now I don't,' he is not truly expressing a change in view. Further, if the theories and claims *do* contradict each other, does this not mean that at least one of each pair is false, contrary to my earlier claims that none of the theories is false?

One obvious approach would claim that advocates of each theory speak in their own idiolects, with their theories providing varying definitions for 'object', 'same object', 'was located at L at t', and so on, so that in fact there was but a verbal dispute among the views, and the claims—both theoretical ('objects can/can't lose parts') and particular (that is/isn't the tree that was in my yard yesterday) did not contradict each other. The views, however, could be said to 'say the same thing' in that for any complete distribution of matter through space-time, each view could give a complete description—including paraphrases—which was true in the language of that theory, and made true by the complete world. Further, there is a straightforward mapping between chunks of the theories—claims and paraphrases—which would have exactly the same truth-conditions.

While this approach is elegant, I find it in important ways unsatisfactory. Start by noting that we *see* ourselves as contradicting each other in these claims—so at the least, the claim that we are really all speaking different languages is a revisionary one. Of course, that is hardly final—many seemingly real disputes are *not* genuine, and the apparently contrary claims involve either the same words with different meanings, or words that are relativized or relational with the disputants in relevantly different contexts. But it is important to note that when it doesn't *seem* so, the claim of nonunivocality needs special defense, and the proposed definitions must be defended as only implicit. And here, the usual signs of 'implicit definition' seem lacking. For example, one can usually imagine oneself being persuaded, by argument, to adopt the contrary view. That means the opposing claims don't seem *self-contradictory*— just false (even if necessarily so). Further, we provide *arguments* for our views, and typically feel compelled to *respond* to arguments against our views. Another relevant point is that many of us don't *have* fixed views—even when, at the moment, we find one side's claims more compelling.

A deeper point is that even if we *attempt* to stipulate meanings here, this can be expected to be unstable. Someone will always come along and say: 'Fine. Your 'objects' can survive loss of parts. But then, 'object' for you does not—or may not—represent the important ontological category—let's talk about *schmobjects*. I say your objects are not schmobjects'. Insofar as the challenge can be understood and taken up, and everyone so challenged can be expected to defend their views about 'schmobjects' in just the way they had defended their claims about *objects*, it is hard not to see the resulting discussion as simply the earlier discussion about *objects*—which it could not be, if 'objects' (etc.) had had its meaning successfully stipulated.

I think the reason for this is that the categories in question—object, persistence, part, past and future predications—are so general and fundamental. There is *some sort of core meaning* to each of these terms—given, more or less, by the formal or functional role each plays in our overall descriptions of the world—that, I think, all parties agree to, and at that level, there is neither factual nor verbal disagreement. For example, objects are the suitable values of first-order variables. They are subjects of properties. They are that which persists, if anything does. But this core meaning only provides necessary conditions. It is, of itself, neutral between the more substantive specifications which is what makes it possible to sensibly disagree with other views, and also, to think that even if one tried to 'define' one of the views into analytic truth, there would remain some question, e.g. "But are these *really* the values of first-order variables" or "Does persistence *really* occur under these conditions?" Now, if what I've argued is correct, these questions don't have any answers—don't, as Carnap would say, have any answers understood *externally*. But because of the role of these concepts, they will always sensibly admit a variety of specifications, and this, I think, is what keeps us from being able to say, with all the plausibility we could hope, that any of these specifications can be treated as the meaning of the term, even in a speaker's own idiolect. But it is *also* true that in *no* acceptable specification can one simultaneously say, for example, nothing persists through the loss of a part, and some things do—and this, I think, is the respect in which the different theories contradict each other. They cannot simultaneously be specifications of a univocal term, 'object', and as I say, there is pressure to *treat* the term as univocal.

So tentatively, here's what I'd like to say. We should treat this as other cases of indeterminacy, where certain parameters of a term have been specified, but others are left open.[33] The view that the positions don't each define their own senses of the key terms seems clear because there is agreement on the core, formal meaning of the terms, and everyone can *understand* the views of the opposition *as about a common subject matter*—namely, that determined by the core meaning. *Nonetheless, insofar* as we are considering the possibility of one of the views being *true*, this can only be in virtue of treating the more substantive portion of the view as given in the term's full meaning. But no one can actually be seen as *adopting* such a meaning, and all of the views are *acceptable* specifications, insofar as they fit adequately with our ordinary and theoretical judgments: this is why, from the semantic perspective, there is no fact of the matter among them. But what about our initial question: Do the views contradict each other? My inclination is to say 'Yes.' I think this is because while the assertions are each indeterminate, the common use suffices for them to be *univocal*: no one *wants* his use to be 'constrained' by the definitions of his own idiolect. Thus, I think, on any acceptable understanding, my 'This dog was in my yard yesterday' and your 'This dog was not in my yard yesterday' cannot both be true together. Thus, they contradict each other. If there are powerful reasons for denying that indeterminate claims can be genuinely contradictory, I suspect we can find a 'quasi-contradiction' relation which answers to our purposes. But a full discussion of the best way to think about and articulate indeterminacy is, unfortunately, something we cannot undertake here.[34]

Notes

1. Let me enter one caveat at the start, which I will ignore hereafter. I can understand there being a factual difference between three- and four-dimensional ontologies if both the following are true: (a) four-dimensionalism requires eternalism about time, while three-dimensionalism entails presentism (Merricks (1995)) (or simply allows presentism, and presentism is true) and (b) there is a factual difference between eternalism and presentism (of a sort, say, that physics could bear upon). I find these both doubtful, but here is not the place to discuss it. However, even if this is a factual difference, there remains, within each camp, the full range of total packages—does the four-dimensionalist require spatial continuity? Temporal continuity? Causal relations? How will he deal with apparent full-term coincidence, as in the Lumpl/Goliath case? So, while four- dimensionalism is usually represented as simply one of the candidate views, on a par with, say, commonsense or reductionism, it really represents but one parameter of disagreement, needing as much filling out to make an appropriate full package as 'three-dimensionalism *per se*', and so, will allow for the same variety of views which I maintain cannot be discriminated among. So, a factual difference here would only mildly affect my claims.
2. My proposal may recall Carnap's ideas about frameworks and external questions, Quine's Ontological Relativity and his liberality about holding onto views by 'making adjustments elsewhere in the system', and perhaps even Goodman's views about 'worlds'. Perhaps this will make it seem less plausible, or original; however that may be, the current controversy hasn't been much presented in this light, so I hope there is value in this investigation even if it is not wholly original in conception. (Since this was written, I have become aware of some efforts in this direction—see Goggins (1999) and Yablo (1998)—so perhaps this is an idea whose time has come.)
3. For a good selection and bibliography, see Rea (1997a).
4. This last question was first asked, to my knowledge, by Eli Hirsch (1982), 86–90.
5. Wiggins (1968), 93.
6. See Burke (1992).
7. Rea suggests this move in (1997b). Zimmermann suggests it in passing in (1995), 88–90.
8. But see Chisholm (1973, 1976, Appendix B), and Van Cleve (1986).
9. More carefully (and tediously): for any time at which the object exists, there is some complete decomposition into parts such that the object has always had exactly those parts—this allows changes in more complex parts by rearrangement of constituent parts, but without explicit commitment to simples. Those not worried about such commitment could just say that an object must always have the same ultimate, simple parts.

10. Some people also claim to find ME intuitively obvious (E.g. Chisholm (1976, Appendix B). I suspect that typically, those who find it so really find obvious one of two more extreme essentialist positions. The first, sometimes called 'Hyperessentialism', holds that an object cannot persist through change *period*, and is almost always advocated because it is thought to follow from Leibniz' law. The second view only disallows change in *intrinsic* or 'genuine' properties, although, contrary to Hyperessentialism, it permits 'Cambridge change', such as coming to be the tallest person in the room due to the only taller person's leaving. As both these views entail ME, it is 'obvious' if they are. But it would be misleading to advocate ME *as such*—one should instead forward one of these other views.

11. See Chisholm's articles again.

12. I argue this in Sidelle (1998), section III.

13. Sider (1997) argues along these lines.

14. Van Inwagen suggests—but does not (to put things mildly) endorse—this, in his (1990a).

15. Rea (2000) offers similar and further criticisms in presenting his own sortal-dominance view.

16. See Carter (1997).

17. We might distinguish a wholly universal view from ones requiring temporal, or spatiotemporal, continuity. The latter might be called 'Persistence permissivism'.

18. The 'permissive' versions (note 17) look less arbitrary than non-universalistic views, but as they make distinctions the extreme universalist view does not, they need some motivation for their particular choice.

19. Unwin (1984) seems to offer a view of this sort.

20. I offer a similar defense of permissive views against our ordinary judgments in Sidelle (1992), especially section V.

21. Perhaps ultimately, the 'acceptability' of coincidence offered here doesn't differ from that already offered to the commonsense view, but its being offered in a more 'set-theoretic' framework may make it seem less mysterious. The question 'Why doesn't having actual properties p1...pn suffice to make Goliath a lump, if they are all Lumpl's properties, and Lumpl *is* a lump?' may have less bite if we are already committed to all methods of tracing being instantiated.

22. Universalism is sometimes formulated as the view that whenever you have some objects, there is a further object they compose. As it stands, however, a Nihilist could accept this as well, and the obvious claim which would distinguish them—that there are simples—doesn't seem something to saddle Universalists with at the outset. Hence, the current formulation.

23. For further discussion, see Sidelle (1998). sec. V.

24. Perhaps Nihilism is better contrasted with *Persistence* Universalism, since worries about persistence conditions motivate its denial of objects. However, since it is most straightforwardly presented as a view about what there is(n't), I include it under Ontological views. The main grounds for preferring Nihilism to Persistence Universalism—which also avoids arbitrariness here—is the avoidance of coincidence.

25. I raise this objection in my (1998), sec. V.

26. For his fullest presentation, see van Inwagen (1990b).

27. See, for instance, Hawthorne and Michael (1996), and Rosenberg (1993).

28. Furthermore, insofar as these matters were thought to be contingent, how could anyone hope to tell which was the right view? The evidence would be just the same in any possible world.

29. In the case of laws, however, I think this is an unobjectionable result—laws of nature, whether Humean or not, need *not* be really necessary in the widest sense. See Sidelle (forthcoming).

30. I argue for this in Sidelle (1989), chapter 3.

31. Trenton Merricks, in comments on this paper, disagrees, maintaining that the metaphysical interpretation *is* built into the views of (serious) practicing metaphysicians. While I think this is false (does one retract acceptance, say, of a psychological theory of personal identity, if one thinks ultimately, this is grounded in the meanings of the words 'person' and 'same'?), my points would not be materially affected if we distinguished the THEORY—which involves the metaphysical interpretation— from the theory—which does not, though perhaps is *accompanied* by it: I would then have to say the former is false, but that my discussion concerns the latter.

32. See Markosian (1996).

33. Here's an imperfect example—Dr. Seuss books often have a number of pictures of strange characters on a page, variously arranged, and a list of names in the text. There may be more characters than names. Now, suppose the doctor didn't have in mind any particular name to go with any particular character, and suppose also that no 'obvious' mapping is clear (e.g. start at the left, move right and then down to the left again, assigning names until they are gone). In some such cases, I think, the 'core' facts are that these names each apply to one of the characters, but it is not determinate to which. (It may help further to imagine Seuss at one point considering each of two mappings—neither of them at all 'natural', but then deciding against either.) At any rate, I hope this illustrates how indeterminacy is not vagueness, and that the pressures there may be for epistemic accounts of vagueness don't obviously apply to this sort of indeterminacy.

34. Many thanks to audiences at Arizona State University's conference on Convention and Logic, and Syracuse University's Mighty Midwest Metaphysical Mayhem, for helpful comments, skepticism and encouragement. Special thanks to Ted Everett, Martha Gibson, Trenton Merricks, Antonio Rauti and Dennis Stampe.

References

Burke, Michael (1992) "Copper Statues and Pieces of Copper: A Challenge to the Standard View," *Analysis* 52 : 12–17

Burke, Michael (1994a) "Dion and Theon: An Essentialist Solution to an Ancient Puzzle," *Journal of Philosophy* 91: 129–139

Burke, Michael (1994b) "Preserving the Principle of One Object to a Place: A Novel Account of the Relations among Objects, Sorts, Sortals and Persistence Conditions," *Philosophy and Phenomenological Research* 54: 591–624

Carnap, Rudolf (1950) "Empiricism, Semantics and Ontology," reprinted in Rudolf Carnap, *Meaning and Necessity* (Chicago: University of Chicago Press, 1956)

Carter, William R. (1997) "Dion's Left Foot and the Price of Burkean Economy," *Philosophy and Phenomenological Research* 57: 371–379

Chisholm, Roderick (1973) "Parts as Essential to their Wholes," *Review of Metaphysics* 26: 581–603

Chisholm, Roderick (1976) *Person and Object* (LaSalle: Open Court)

Goggins, P. (1999) "How Not to Have an Ontology of Physical Objects," *Philosophical Studies* 94: 295–308

Hawthorne, John O'Leary and Andrew Cortens (1995) "Towards Ontological Nihilism," *Philosophical Studies* 54: 143–165

Hawthorne, John O'Leary and Michaelis Michael (1996) "Compatibilist Semantics in Metaphysics: A Case Study," *Australasian Journal of Philosophy* 74: 117–134

Heller, Mark (1990) *The Ontology of Physical Objects: Four Dimensional Hunks of Matter* (Cambridge: Cambridge University Press, 1990)

Hirsch, Eli (1982) *The Concept of Identity* (New York: Oxford University Press)

Markosian, Ned (1996) "Brutal Composition," *Philosophical Studies* 92: 211–249

Merricks, Trenton (1995) "On the Incompatibility of Enduring and Perduring Entities," *Mind* 104: 523–531

Rea, Michael (ed.) (1997a) *Material Constitution* (Lanham, MD: Rowman and Littlefield)

Rea, Michael (1997b) "Supervenience and Co-location," *American Philosophical Quarterly* 34: 367–373

Rea, Michael (2000) "Constitution and Kind Membership," *Philosophical Studies* 97: 169–193

Rosenberg, Jay (1993) "Comments on Peter Van Inwagen's *Material Beings*," *Philosophy and Phenomenological Research* 53: 701–708.

Sidelle, Alan (1989) *Necessity, Essence and Individuation* (Ithaca: Cornell University Press)

Sidelle, Alan (1992) "Rigidity, Ontology and Semantic Structure," *Journal of Philosophy* 89: 410–430

Sidelle, Alan (1998) "A Sweater Unraveled: Following One Thread of Thought for Avoiding Coincident Entities," *Noûs* 32: 423–448.

Sidelle, Alan (forthcoming) "On the Metaphysical Contingency of Laws of Nature," in John O'Leary Hawthorne and Tamar Gendler (eds.), *Conceivability, Imagination and Possibility* (Oxford: Oxford University Press)

Sider, Ted (1997) "Four-Dimensionalism," *The Philosophical Review* 106: 197–231

Unwin, Nicolas (1984), "Substance, Essence and Conceptualism," *Ratio* 26: 41–53

Van Cleve, James (1986) "Mereological Essentialism, Mereological Conjunctivism, and Identity Through Time," French, Uehling and Wettstein (eds.) *Midwest Studies in Philosophy* XI (Minneapolis: University of Minnesota Press): 141–156

van Inwagen, Peter (1981) "The Doctrine of Arbitrary Undetached Parts," *Pacific Philosophical Quarterly* 62: 123–137

van Inwagen, Peter (1990a) "Four Dimensional Objects," *Noûs* 24: 245–255

van Inwagen, Peter (1990b) *Material Beings* (Ithaca: Cornell University Press)

Wiggins, David (1968) "On Being in the Same Place at the Same Time," *Philosophical Review* 77: 90–95

Yablo, Stephen (1998) "Does Ontology Rest on a Mistake?" *Proceedings of the Aristotelian Society, Supplement* 72: 229–261

Zimmermann, Dean (1995) "Theories of Masses and Problems of Constitution," *Philosophical Review* 104: 53–110

Philosophical Issues, 12, Realism and Relativism, 2002

KNOWLEDGE OF THE WORLD[1]

Galen Strawson
University of Reading

1 The Problem

Can we apprehend the nature of *reality*? Can we apprehend the nature of *concrete*[2] reality? Can we apprehend the nature of concrete reality *as it is in itself*?[3] Can we apprehend the nature of *non-mental* concrete reality as it is in itself? This is my central question.[4]

Some say Yes, some say No. Against Kant and a great crew of empiricists, positivists, anti-realists, and hopeless post-modernists, I think there is no insuperable difficulty in the answer Yes—no difficulty *of principle* in the idea that finite beings like ourselves may be able to apprehend or form a correct representation of the nature of reality as it is in itself, at least in certain respects. To this extent I am with Descartes and Locke.[5]

Put slightly differently, the question is this. Could any account or representation of the nature of reality render or represent it as it is in itself in any respect? There is certainly difficulty in this idea, but one of the most important things about the difficulty is what it is not. It is not that there is any deep difficulty in this claim:

[1] Something is real—reality, no less—and this reality has some intrinsic or ultimate nature.

Of course something is real, and of course it has some nature. And whatever nature it has just is its intrinsic or ultimate nature. There is nothing wrong with using these words, even when they add little or nothing.

Nor is there any deep difficulty in the supposition that

[2] There may be features of reality that are completely inaccessible and unintelligible to us.

Barest common sense—not to mention a minimum degree of modesty—requires us to grant the truth of [2].[6]

If there is a difficulty it is not with [1] or [2]. It is a difficulty with the claim that

[3] There could be an *account* or *representation* or *apprehension* of the nature of reality available to finite beings that captured the nature of reality as it is in itself, at least in some respect.

[1], the fact that there is a certain way things are, does not entail [3] that it is possible to represent how things are, in themselves—not so long as we are concerned with finite beings like ourselves.

In this paper I will concentrate on [3], but I will first make a couple of points about [1]. [2] is a topic for another time, but it should not need to be a topic at all.

2 Naturalizing the Noumenal: 'As It is in Itself'

[1], the supposition that reality is in fact a certain way, whatever we can manage to know or say about it, is obviously true. Some have denied it; every position has its defenders; the closet mysticism of some quantum theorists and other anti-realist extremists should not be underestimated. But not all positions are worth arguing against. [1] is obvious. Nothing can exist or be real without being a certain way at any given time.[7] If this is metaphysics, thank heavens for metaphysics. To be is to be somehow or other.

Suppose our best models of the behaviour of things like photons credit them with properties that seem incompatible to us—for example wave-like properties and particle-like properties. This does not threaten the truth of [1]. What we learn is just that this is how photons affect us, given their intrinsic nature, and ours. It does not provide any reason to think that photons do not have some intrinsic nature at any given time. Whatever claim anyone makes about the nature of reality—including the claim that it has apparently incompatible properties—just is a claim about the way it is. This remark applies as much to the Everett 'many-worlds' theory of reality as it does to any other.

Some think that what we learn from quantum theory is precisely that there is, objectively, no particular way that an electron or a photon is, at a given time. They confuse an epistemological point about undecidability with a metaphysical claim about the nature of things. The problem is not just that such a claim is unverifiable, the problem is that it is incoherent. For whatever the electron's or photon's weirdness (its weirdness-to-us, that is, for nothing is intrinsically weird), its being thus weird just is the way it is.

So we may *naturalize the noumenon*: we may talk without reservation of reality as it is in itself. Such talk involves no odd metaphysics. Its propriety derives entirely and sufficiently from the thought that if a thing exists, it is a certain way.

Some may still think the phrase 'as it is in itself' disreputable. But anyone who still doubts its honesty should consider the account of it just given. For we all agree that something (reality, no less) exists, and all that is added here is that if something exists, then it is a certain way. And the way it is just is—of course—how it is in itself. The notion of how things are in themselves is an entirely innocent and indispensable notion in any remotely sensible philosophy, as Kant was well aware.

It may be thought that there is a special problem with the idea that conscious mental reality is always a certain way for any given conscious being— Louis, for example—at any given moment. But there is no special problem; the case is the same. For whatever happens mentally, with Louis, at any given time, things will just be a certain way, mentally, with Louis, at that time. It may well be that no one can give a definitive account of how things are mentally with Louis; not even—sometimes least of all—Louis. But this epistemological point is irrelevant to the ontological-metaphysical point that things are a certain determinate way, mentally, for Louis, at any given time.

Understood in this way the phrase 'as it is in itself' contributes nothing except emphasis. Nevertheless it is often extremely helpful, and I will use it freely.[8]

3 Conscious Experience

—'It's obvious that the answer to your opening question is Yes. It's obvious that an account or at least an apprehension of the nature of reality available to finite beings with a specific sensory-intellectual constitution can constitute or contain a correct representation or apprehension of the nature of reality as it is in itself, in certain respects. For conscious experience is itself part of concrete reality. More particularly, the phenomenon of conscious experience's having a certain *experiential-qualitative* character for whoever or whatever has the experience—call this phenomenon E—is a richly featured part of reality, as much part of concrete reality as anything else, including anything that may be held to 'realize' E and yet be in some way other than or ontologically over and above E. E is accordingly something that must be included in any full account of the general nature of reality, and we can indeed be said to know it as it is in itself, at least in certain respects, simply because our having it as we do is our knowing it: the having is the knowing. Consider pain. It may have non-experiential being, in some sense, in addition to having experiential qualitative being, and there may be respects in which we are not able to grasp the nature of that non-experiential being (considered as it is in itself). But we know the nature of part of concrete reality (considered as it is in itself) just in feeling the pain as we do, whatever else is or is not going on. One's own conscious experience is a part of reality for which the gap between reality and its apprehension does not open up, when one considers the question of one's acquaintance with it.'

I think this claim about conscious experience is correct, although it needs some defence, and although recent philosophical fashion may make it hard for some to see. Nothing in what follows depends on accepting it, however, and I am going to put the case of conscious experience aside. Having assumed that there is such a thing as *non-mental* concrete reality, I am going to continue to restrict my attention to the question of whether one can have any grasp or knowledge of the nature of non-mental concrete reality.[9]

4 A Paradox?

In setting out the main argument I will use '*R*' to denote either some particular part of (concrete non-mental) reality, considered as it is in itself, or (concrete non-mental) reality in general, considered as it is in itself. 'As it is in itself' adds nothing, strictly speaking, as already remarked, but is often useful as a reminder of what is at issue.[10]

It seems intensely plausible—to begin—that

[I] One can form a representation of *R*, and a fortiori a correct representation of *R*, only if one is affected by it.

One must be in some sort of *contact* with *R*.[11] And this contact or affection-relation must involve some sort of mental change.[12]

In spite of the plausibility of [I], it is arguable that one can form a correct representation of *R*, only if one is *not* affected by it, or rather—less paradoxically—that

[II] One can attain a correct representation of the nature of *R* only if the representation one forms of *R* does not essentially involve elements whose representational content depends essentially on the particular way in which one is affected by *R*.[13]

And here a standard (Kantian) presumption is that the content of one's representation of *R* does always essentially involve elements whose content depends essentially on the particular way in which one is affected by *R*; so that if [II] is right, correct representation of the nature of *R* is not—is never—possible.

In the next section I will give an argument for [II]. First, though, it is worth asking whether the putative correct-representation-engendering affection or contact must be sensory, at least in part.

The notions of affection and contact are highly general. One can be in contact with something X via a written or spoken description. This involves sensory experience of sounds or shapes, but it does not involve sensory experience of X itself. Direct alteration of one's neuronal connections by neuroscientists in contact with X who operate with a view to inducing correct beliefs about X may also constitute a form of contact with X that suffices to furnish one with a representation of X without one's having any sensory experience of X.[14] And there may be other, stranger possibilities. Nevertheless I will take it in what follows that any putative correct-representation-engendering contact with **R** will always involve sensory affection by **R**, directly or indirectly.

I will also take it that the notion of non-conceptual sensory content—merely or purely phenomenal sensory content—is in good order for purposes of philosophical analysis of the nature of experience. This, like nearly everything in philosophy, has been doubted, but it is widely accepted.[15]

5 An Argument

Recast in terms of sensory affection, [II] becomes

[II] One can attain a correct representation of the nature of **R** only if the content of one's representation of **R** does not essentially involve elements whose content depends essentially on the particular way in which one is sensorily affected by **R**.[16]

The argument for [II] runs as follows:

[II.1] If an experiencing being B is sensorily affected by **R**, then how B is sensorily affected by **R** is necessarily a function not only of how **R** is, but also of how B is.

[II.2] It is always possible that there should be two experiencing beings B and C who differ in their natures in such a way that they differ significantly or dramatically in the way they are sensorily affected by **R**, even when they are functioning normally given the kinds of being they are.

[II.3] Suppose that there are two such beings B and C. One cannot say that B-type beings are right or correct in the way they are sensorily affected, while C-type beings are wrong or incorrect, given that both are functioning normally given the kinds of being they are. There is, plainly, no such thing as the correct way of being sensorily affected by **R**—the single universally correct way. Instead one can talk only of how B-type beings are (normally) sensorily affected by **R**, how C-type beings are sensorily affected by **R**, and so on. One cannot even say that one way of being sensorily affected is closer to being correct than another. Nor can one speak of roughly the correct way of being sensorily affected.

So [?]

[II.4] If a representation one forms of **R** essentially involves elements whose content depends essentially on the particular way in which one is sensorily affected by **R**, it cannot constitute a correct representation of the nature of **R**.

It cannot be a correct representation of any feature of the nature of reality as it is in itself.

Does [II.4] really follow from [II.1]–[II.3]? I will consider this question shortly. First, though, note that many would continue the argument by accepting [II.4], asserting its antecedent as applied to finite beings, and detaching the corresponding consequent as follows:

[II.5] All representations of *R* available to finite beings do essentially involve elements whose content depends essentially on the particular way in which those beings are sensorily affected by *R*.

This would then allow them to conclude

[II.6] Finite beings cannot attain to any correct representation of the nature of *R*—of concrete, non-mental reality-as-it-is-in-itself.

Does [II.4] follow from [II.1]–[II.3]? It is not at all obvious that it does, and the first thing that requires comment is the phrase 'essentially involves'. It allows for the possibility that some elements of a representation may be inessential, and it may be objected that this is not a real possibility: 'Every representation essentially involves whatever elements it involves, for the trivial reason that it is the particular representation it is in virtue of the particular elements it involves.'

This is true but irrelevant. The issue is whether the content of a representational element can be essential or inessential to a representation in one specific respect: in respect of the representation's correctness—where its correctness is a matter of its representing some feature of a thing's nature considered as it is in itself. Consider a simple case: if in the normal course of things you wish to form a representation of a cube, and form a visual representation of a red cube, the red element in the representation is inessential. Blue would have done just as well, and a person blind from birth may form a representation of a cube that is not visual at all.

The phrase 'depends essentially' also requires comment. To say that the content of a representational element—call it 'C'—depends essentially on a particular way of being sensorily affected is to say that C cannot be made available by anything else. Access to C not only depends on having been sensorily affected in some way or other; it also depends on having been sensorily affected in some particular way—in some particular sense modality or modalities.

It seems clear that this dependence can be essential only if C either is itself, or essentially involves, an instance of a particular type of sensory content.[17]

A colour-involving representation is an obvious candidate for being a representation with content that depends essentially on a particular—visual—way of being sensorily affected.[18] And a representation of triangularity is, I take it, an example of a representation with content that does not depend essentially on a particular way of being sensorily affected. It may be that no finite creature can have a notion of triangularity without having had some sensory experience or other, but it seems that the sensory experience may be either visual or tactile or echolocatory or.... If so, the representation of triangularity does not depend essentially on any particular one of these ways of being sensorily affected.

Suppose this is granted. The question then re-arises: Do [II.1]–[II.3] entail [II.4]?

Well, let R be the triangularity of some particular object (I assume—hereby—that triangularity may be and at any rate could be a feature of reality as it is in itself).[19] And now suppose [II.4] is false. Suppose

[a] a being B has formed a correct representation V[20] of R

and

[b] V's being correct in this respect essentially involves V's containing a certain representational element E;

suppose, in other words, that E cannot be altered or replaced by any other representational element without V ceasing to be correct in the respect in question.[21] Suppose further that

[c] the ability to have E-type representations depends essentially on the ability to have a particular type of sensory experience;

that is, one cannot have E-type representations unless one can have such sensory experience.

Suppositions [a]–[c] amount to the claim that [II.4] is false. That is, they amount to the claim that V can be a correct representation of R although it essentially involves elements that depend essentially on a particular way of being sensorily affected. So the question is this: is the joint truth of [a]–[c] ruled out by [II.1]–[II.3]?

No. The first thing to say, perhaps, is that the argument equivocates on the word 'correct'.[22] It is certainly true that there is no single correct way of being sensorily affected, given the way that the word 'correct' is used in [II.1]–[II.3]. Given this use there are as many 'correct' ways of being affected by R as there are species whose normal members are differently affected by R. But it doesn't follow that no way of being sensorily affected is intrinsically better than any other, so far as the attempt to form a correct representation of R is concerned. Nor do [II.1]–[II.3] actually rule out the possibility directly rejected by [II.4]—the possibility that one particular way of being sensorily affected may in fact be essential to forming a correct representation of the nature of R.

I will take these two points in turn. As for the first, it seems plausible that some ways of being sensorily affected are intrinsically more useful or reality-revealing than others. Suppose B and C are placed in front of a triangle and that both are sensorily affected by light reflected from it. Suppose B has the same basic visual experience that you have when you look at a triangle of that sort, and that C has the sort of experience you have when you hear G-flat played on a clarinet. It seems intrinsically more useful to have B-type experience than C-type experience, given the shape-content of the B-type experience, if one is trying to find out how things are.

—'The usefulness of any sensory input, and the extent to which it is reality-revealing, depend entirely on what one makes of it and can do with it. The B-type being might apprehend its visual intake as a baby does, while the C-type being might automatically infer complex spatial information from differences in the volume, pitch, and timbre of the sound it hears.'

True, but this reply won't deal with every case. Consider D, who is like C in responding to light waves with auditory experience, but whose hearing is so primitive that the sounds it hears differ only in pitch, never in loudness or timbre. In this case, it seems, D's way of being sensorily affected by reality is intrinsically less informative than C's or B's. And if this is right, we can make sense of the comparative claim that one way of being sensorily affected may be intrinsically better than another, so far as the attempt to form a correct representation of the nature of *R* is concerned.

As for the second point: it is true that [II.1]–[II.3] do not entail [II.4], but [II.4] is none the less correct. It is correct in denying that any one particular way of being sensorily affected could be essential to forming a correct representation of the nature of *R* (some feature of concrete, non-mental reality as it is in itself). How could some way 1 of being sensorily affected be essential to forming a correct representation of *R* in such a way that no other way 2 would do *however the representational elements that derived from way 2 were interpreted by the subject*? The answer seems clear. This could not be: any way 2 of being sensorily affected that systematically had the same degree of structural complexity as some supposedly essential way 1 could deliver experience that could possibly be interpreted by its subject in such a way as to yield the same information as the information yielded by the experience delivered by way 1. Quite generally, it cannot be the sensory content as such that matters when we consider representations that purport to represent (non-mental) reality as it is in itself. It must be how it is interpreted that matters.

6 Intellectual Intuition

The argument set out in the last section requires some further comment. First, though, I want to say something about Kant's notion of 'intellectual intuition'. This is sometimes dismissed as a foolish obscurity, but it is of great interest in the present context, for it is, precisely, an attempt to characterize a kind of knowledge-of-*R*-engendering or knowledge-of-*R*-involving contact or, more neutrally, relation with *R* (i.e. some feature of concrete, non-mental reality as it is in itself) which does not involve being sensorily affected by *R*. Kant's characterization of intellectual intuition seems to be motivated precisely by an awareness of the force of the thought that if one's potentially knowledge-of-*R*-involving relation to *R* essentially involves one's being sensorily affected by *R* then there is an immoveable sense in which one can only ever hope to attain to knowledge of an *appearance* of *R*, and hence (so the thought goes) never to knowledge of *R*.[23]

Descartes rejects this idea. He argues in his Second Meditation that one can attain to correct representation of the essential nature of *R* (for example a lump of wax) even if one starts from an essentially-sensation-involving contact with it. But Kant insists that if one's potentially knowledge-of-*R*-involving relation to *R* essentially involves one's being sensorily affected by *R* then one's representation of *R* will inevitably be sensation-dependent in such a way that one can only ever hope to attain to knowledge of an appearance of *R*, never to knowledge (correct representation) of *R* as it is in itself.

In fact, Kant's thought seems more general than this. It seems that one can drop the qualification 'sensorily' to give

if one's potentially knowledge-of-*R*-involving relation to *R* essentially involves one's being *affected* by *R* in any way at all then there is an immoveable sense in which one can only ever hope to attain to knowledge of an *appearance* of *R*, and hence never to knowledge of *R* (as it is in itself).

The point of intellectual intuition is precisely that it does away with affection. As a possible example, Kant offers the knowledge-involving relation that a divine creator would stand in to its works—call them '*R*'—in being their creator or originator.[24] If the relation holds, *R* is somehow fully specified and grasped in its creator's intellect, and therefore completely known, without the knowledge resulting in any way from *R*'s being a thing that 'stands over against' the subject as something which affects it in some particular way. There is no indirectness or mediatedness of apprehension of a kind that seems to be necessarily involved in any sensation-involving experience or sensation-dependent representation of *R*. Nor is there any sort of partiality of perspective of the kind that is necessarily involved in any sensation-involving experience of *R*, and that might also be thought to threaten the possibility of knowledge or correct representation of the nature of *R*. Equipped with intellectual intuition, one may be supposed to attain directly to the 'absolute conception of reality', in Bernard Williams's phrase, or to the view 'from nowhere', in Nagel's and Merleau-Ponty's phrase—the view from no particular perspective.[25] Kant concedes that we 'cannot comprehend even the possibility' of such intellectual intuition, in the sense of having a positive conception of what it might be like, but insists that the idea is free from contradiction.[26]

Partiality of perspective that stems from the fact that finite beings always occupy a particular place in space-time doesn't raise a deep problem for the idea that they might attain some general theoretical correct representation of the nature of *R* (at least in certain respects), for one can readily generalize away from specificities of spatiotemporal location. It is the particularities of perspective imposed on us by our most basic sensory-intellectual equipment—by the fundamental conceptual categories and sensory modalities that we happen to have—that are presumed to pose the problem. We are, for example, inescapably committed to a spatio-temporal way of experiencing things, but it is conceivable, according to Kant and a number of present-day thinkers, that reality as it is in itself is not spatial—or not in anything remotely like the way we suppose—and not temporal either—or not in anything remotely like the way we suppose.

Kant does not think that finite rational creatures differ in their most fundamental conceptual equipment (the pure concepts of the understanding), although he allows that they may differ in their fundamental forms of sensibility.[27] Nor does he think that our fundamental conceptual equipment, considered quite independently of our sensory equipment, constrains or puts limits on our thought in such a way that it is itself a potential bar to the representation of reality as it is in itself. The trouble is rather that the fundamental conceptual equipment cannot be understood considered independently of the forms of sensibility, in the case of finite creatures like ourselves. Its operation in us—its very existence in us as a set of categories—is primordially conditioned by the spatio-temporal form of our sensibility.[28] This is why we can only ever attain to knowledge of how *R* appears to us, not to knowledge or correct representation of *R* as it is in itself.

There are many complications here. Note, for example, that in Kant's scheme differences of *sensory modality* are superficial as compared with differences of *forms of sensibility*. Thus the spatial form of sensibility doesn't have to involve the sensory modality of vision; it may involve only touch, or echolocation, or who knows what else. Forms of sensibility offer a higher-order classification of types of sensory modalities, and creatures with entirely different sensory modalities can clearly share the same fundamental forms of sensibility.

In the light of this, it might be said that although one does not have to have touch or vision or echolocation in order to form a representation of a triangle one must at least have a spatial form of sensibility. But many difficult questions arise here—especially if we consider the possibility that space may be quite radically different from what we suppose it to be—and although these questions are of great interest I will not pursue them here. The purpose of this brief section is to suggest that in introducing the idea of intellectual intuition Kant is trying precisely to characterize what knowledge or correct representation of the nature of *R* (of reality as it is in itself) would have to be like. It seems that a necessary condition of such knowledge or correct representation, for any being B, is this:

knowledge of **R** has to flow from B's being in *relation* with **R** without B's being *affected* by **R** in such a way that B can only be said to have access to an *appearance* of **R**.[29]

7 Sensation and Correct Representation

Can we (or any finite beings) fulfil this Kantian necessary condition? I don't see why not. I see no difficulty of principle in the idea that we may be able to be in cognitive relation with **R**—with reality as it is in itself or some feature of it—without being affected by it in such a way that we can only be said to have access to an appearance of it.

In §5 I stressed the point that there can be no such thing as the right way of being sensorily affected by **R**. B-type beings may be in a far better position to elaborate a practically useful theoretical account of **R** than C-type beings, given the differences in their characteristic ways of being affected by reality, and this may be so even if B-type and C-type are equal with respect to intellectual capacities (assuming that their intellectual capacities can be compared independently of their sensory equipment). But still there is and can be no such thing as the right way of being sensorily affected by **R**, either in general or when it comes to the question of whether one can form a correct representation of **R**. Nor is any one way of being sensorily affected by **R** closer to being right than any other; one might as well claim that the decimal system is closer to being the right way of representing the nature of numbers than the binary system.[30]

Let '**R**' now denote some particular feature of reality considered as it is in itself, and consider the following restatement of [II.4]:

> [II.4.1] If specification of the positively descriptive content of any account or representation V of **R** available to finite beings necessarily involves reference to features of how the beings are sensorily affected by **R**, in such a way that the content of V is not fully graspable by beings who do not or cannot have experience with those sensory-affection features, then there can be no such thing as a correct positively descriptive account or representation of **R**, so far as any finite being is concerned.

As with [II.4], so with [II.4.1]: some philosophers may accept [II.4.1] and its antecedent and detach the consequent, concluding that there can be no such thing as a (or the) correct positively descriptive account of **R**, so far as any finite being is concerned. Their conclusion is not just the unremarkable conclusion that one could never know for sure that one had attained a correct representation of the nature of **R**. It is the conclusion that it is demonstrably impossible for a finite, essentially sensory being to attain to such a representation.

[II.4.1] raises a number of questions. The most important of them, I think, is whether one can deny its antecedent. Perhaps the descriptive (not merely referential) content of a finite being's representation of the nature of **R** can be radically independent of its sensory experience in certain vital respects, even if its sensory experience is genetically speaking indispensable to its achieving any representation of the nature of **R** at all.

Let me stress the point that my concern is with descriptive and not merely referential content. It is with content that is reality-representing in some way that goes essentially beyond being reality-representing in being reality-denoting. This concern is captured, in effect, in the phrase 'know the nature of', but it is worth drawing attention to it.

8 Empiricism?

Can one reasonably deny the antecedent of [II.4.1]? Consider the following Cartesian-sounding claim:

[II.4.2] If we are going to be able to give good sense to the notion of a being B's achieving a correct representation of **R**, then we have to suppose that B's representation of the nature of **R** is intellectually abstract in some way: there must be some fundamental respect in which B can be correctly said to abstract, in its mode of representation of **R**, from all features of how it is sensorily affected by **R**.[31]

Is this a help? I think it is. We are to consider the suggestion that a being can form an intellectual conception of **R**, partly as a result of being sensorily affected by **R**, in such a way that its conception of **R** is in some strong sense independent of the particular quality of the (sensory) affection which is, for it, a condition of the possibility of its formation of the conception.

'As a result of' is intentionally imprecise. An old question arises: what is the relation between the (non-referential) content of the sensory affection and the (non-referential) content of the intellectual conception? Is there some straightforward sense in which the content of the sensory affection is the source or 'original'—even more vaguely, the inspiration—of the content of the intellectual conception? Or is the sensory affection best thought of as a kind of trigger for (the unfurling of) the intellectual conception, rather than as a source of the content of the intellectual conception?

Empiricists maintain, with varying degrees of ingenuity, that the content of our conceptions of the nature of reality is ultimately derived from, and is therefore ultimately reducible to, the sensory content of our experience. 'Rationalists' deny this, and there is certainly something staggeringly implausible about the classical empiricist programme.[32] I think the theory of evolution may be able to effect a full reconciliation between rationalism and a kind of empiricism, but that is a topic for another time.[33] My present concern is with the idea that the (non-referential) content of concepts of certain features of (non-mental) reality may in some way radically transcend any origins that they may have in the sensory content of our experience. A concept, I take it, is a thought-element, a thought-content element, a thing that plays a role in a mental economy. I prefer the term 'thought-element' to 'concept', because of all the disparate accretions on the latter, but I will stick to 'concept' for the purposes of this paper.

From here on I feel I am not fully in control of this topic—as will become evident. I hope that what I have to say may be useful in spite of this.

9 I-Concepts and S-Concepts

The central thought was expressed in [II.4.1] and it can be rephrased as a partial definition of a *sensory-element-transcendent* concept or *intellectual* concept or *I-concept* for short:

> If a concept C is an I-concept, specification of the content of C does not involve any essential reference to any particular type of sensory content S in such a way that the content of C is fully graspable only by beings who have experience of or acquaintance or familiarity with S.[34]

This may be shortened to

> If C is an I-concept, specification of the content of C does not involve reference to any particular type of sensory content.

A concept is an essentially *sensory-element-involving* or *S-concept* just in case it is not an I-concept: just in case specification of its content does essentially involve reference to some particular type of sensory content. I take it that the distinction is exhaustive as well as exclusive, and that the converse of the partial definition is obvious, so that one can advance to the stronger claim that a concept is an I-concept *if and only if* specification of its content does not involve reference to any particular type of sensory content. This allows room for the idea that one must have experience of or acquaintance with some sensory content or other in order to have any given I-concept, although it does not endorse it.

How does the distinction between I-concepts and S-concepts divide up the realm of concepts? One suggestion is that there are no I-concepts, strictly speaking. This is what empiricists—or at least 'concept-empiricists'—are supposed to suppose. A slightly less extreme suggestion is that there are no I-concepts when one considers concepts of straightforwardly physical properties of reality, rather than considering intuitively more abstract concepts like JUSTICE, BEAUTY, IMPLICATION, HERE, and $\sqrt{-1}$.[35]

But perhaps this is the wrong way round. Perhaps there are no S-concepts—or very few. Concepts, after all, are concepts. They are paradigmatically intellectual phenomena, not sensory phenomena. Perhaps the only

S-concepts are concepts like COLOUR (or RED), TASTE (or SWEET), and so on; or, more narrowly, concepts like RED-AS-SEEN (SWEETNESS-AS-TASTED); or, more narrowly still, RED-AS-SEEN-BY-B-AT-*t* (and so on). Perhaps even DOG, WATER, and TRAIN are I-concepts, as well as MOTHER, PRESIDENT, and APARTHEID. Perhaps this is so even though 'S-concept' certainly does not stand for 'purely' sensory concept (whatever that might mean) but only for 'essentially-sensory-element-involving' concept. A creature's sensory-intellectual constitution may be such that it has to have sensory experience of a certain kind in order to acquire use of a certain concept, as already remarked, and we may assume, at least for the purposes of argument, that this is true of all of us and all our concepts,[36] but it doesn't follow that all our concepts are S-concepts. Sensory experience may be an essential part of what triggers or fosters the acquisition of a concept without being a source of its content in such a way that specifying its content involves reference to any part of the sensory content of the triggering experience; and this may be so even when the triggering or activating or fostering relation between the content of the experience and the content of the concept is non-accidental or non-brute in the way that we intuitively suppose it to be, whether we are considering DOG or TRIANGLE or CAUSE.

This notion of non-accidentality promises (threatens) to be of enormous importance (and difficulty) in any general account of concept acquisition, and it is extremely hard to know what it amounts to. It seems that accidentality can be fairly clearly characterized: there is no logical difficulty in the idea that a creature might be so constituted that a certain experience—a stroboscope flashing 47 times a second—was a mere or brute ON switch for a concept—DODECAGON—in such a way that no intelligible contentual relation held between the two.[37] To this extent, we can give a clear negative characterization of non-accidentality. But it is far less clear how to go on to a positive account—one which would, crucially, allow us to say something about differing *degrees* of non-accidentality.[38]

Well, this is not my present concern. I am considering the possibility of knowledge or correct representation of (concrete, non-mental) reality as it is in itself, and I am simply going to assume that sensory experience can be an contributory factor in our coming to possess concepts without *ipso facto* being a source of their content in such a way that full specification of their content will always involve reference to the sensory content of some experience or experiences. I am simply going to assume, in other words, that we have I-concepts, and acquire them in the course of our experience, this being so even if 'experience' is understood to be something that is always and essentially sensation-involving. It seems clear that this is how things go even in the case of intuitively more abstract concepts like USEFULNESS or IMPLICATION or JUSTICE, for example.[39] But my current interest is not in I-concepts of this sort. I am interested in the considerably less obvious idea that basic concepts of concrete physical reality like SHAPE (TRIANGULARITY), EXTENSION, POSITION, MOTION, HARDNESS or SOLIDITY—may also be I-concepts.

I will call such basic concepts of physical reality *P-concepts*. My question is whether such P-concepts can be I-concepts, considered specifically as things that have descriptive and not merely referential content. And—to narrow things further—I am principally concerned with P-concepts that feature in ordinary thought, rather than with those that are taken as basic in physics. I want to consider the idea that everyday P-concepts like SHAPE or TRIANGLE are I-concepts, for it is P-concepts like these, with their observational air, that are most likely to be thought to be S-concepts.

The *point* of considering the proposal that P-concepts are I-concepts is the same as before: to try to remove an obstacle (radical empiricist, positivist, Kantian, anti-realist, post-modernist, whatever) to the idea that we may be able to grasp something about the nature of (concrete) reality as it is in itself. The question is whether the descriptive (not merely referential) content of the concepts can be supposed to correctly represent reality as it is in itself in any respect.

I will begin with some loosening-up comments about a patently more abstract I-concept, and about some putative S-concepts.

10 An I-Concept

We come to be able to deploy USEFULNESS on the basis of our experience, but very different forms of experience—Martian, pre-Christian Abyssinian, 20th-century Japanese—can lead to its acquisition. The content of USEFULNESS is, surely, independent of the experiential details of its many individual acquisitions, and *a fortiori* of the sensory-experiential details of these acquisitions. Hence its specification does not involve essential reference to any particular type of sensory affection. It is an I-concept.

It may be said that this is mere assertion. 'Perhaps each individual's concept of usefulness is somehow constitutively saturated with features—including sensory features, however vague their presence—of the experiences which led to its acquisition (yours involved Swiss Army penknives, mine involved wheels); not to mention features of the experiences in which it has subsequently been active.'

On this view, each person's concept of usefulness is likely to be different from everyone else's, in greater or lesser degree, both within and across cultures. But there is no reason to believe this; it has no phenomenological or behavioural support, and Wittgensteinian arguments that equate concept-possession with language mastery move heavily against it, especially when we consider members of a single language-community who have acquired the concept in very different ways. Wittgensteinian arguments are doubtful things, and I will question an application of this one in the next section, but the idea that cultural differences may lead to significantly different concepts of usefulness, rather than to different views about what is useful, although axiomatic in some academic circles, does not I believe survive unprejudiced reflection.[40]

11 S-Concepts

Among the prime candidates for being S-concepts are concepts like RED, which raise famous and highly instructive difficulties.

Some think that colour properties are essentially *phenomenal* properties, i.e. properties whose whole and essential nature can be fully revealed in sensory experience given only the qualitative [experiential] character that that experience has. Others think colour properties are not phenomenal properties, and are best thought of as powers or dispositional properties of objects. On this familiar view, for an object to be red is for it to be disposed to cause certain sorts of experiences in creatures like ourselves in certain conditions. Members of a third group agree with members of the second group that colours are not phenomenal properties, but think that 'red' is best thought of as a name for whatever 'categorical' properties—for example molecular-structure properties—underlie the dispositional properties just mentioned.

The second and third views are not worth distinguishing for present purposes. The important disagreement is over whether or not colour properties are phenomenal properties. I take it that they are—I favour the first view. I think that colour concepts like RED are *essentially* concepts of properties whose whole and essential nature can be fully revealed in sensory experience, given only the qualitative experiential character that that experience has, and that the same goes for colour words like 'red', *mutatis mutandis*.

This view is certainly correct according to common sense, but it is little more than a terminological decision in philosophy, for the philosophical discussion of colour has taken on a life of its own. And it is far from being unproblematic. Consider the word 'red'. If we take it that it is essentially a word for a phenomenal property, then the problem is that it does not seem that it can name any *particular* phenomenal quality. For it seems very plausible—it is an old idea, which I take it to be correct—that creatures who have mastery of the word 'red', and who apply the word on the basis of experience that they take to be experience of red, and who fully agree in language on what things are red, may none the less have radically qualitatively different sensory experiences when they look at things they agree to be red.[41] But then it is hard to resist the conclusion that 'red' cannot be supposed to name any one particular phenomenal quality. But if this is so, and if shared mastery of the word 'red' amounts to shared possession of the concept RED (as Wittgensteinians suppose), it seems clear that specification of the content of RED does not require reference to any particular type of sensory content—e.g. *phenomenal red* as you think you know it now. In which case RED is an I-concept. The argument quickly generalizes to all other concepts of phenomenal qualities, with the striking consequence that they are all I-concepts.

The argument is too quick, whatever you think of the conclusion. Consider the following four positions. First, P1, the extreme behaviourist view that a creature—for example a robot or 'zombie'—can possess RED even if it is incapable of any sort of conscious experience at all (it has sensors that detect and distinguish the light-reflection properties of objects, and is able to acquire colour vocabulary on that basis).

Less extreme is P2, the view that mastery of colour concepts must be tied to experience of *some* type of sensory content, but that the sensory content in question needn't be *visual* content as we know it. It may it may be some form of auditory experience; it may involve some sort of exquisitely refined echoic content, or it may be something unimaginable by us.

Note that I am assuming that the general qualitative character of experience we agree to call 'visual' is fundamentally the same for all of us even if we differ strikingly in respect of the colour quality of the experiences we have when exposed to identical light stimuli. I am assuming, in other words, that 'visual' names a particular *general qualitative type* of sensory content. It does not merely name a particular *functional type* of sensory content which can be roughly characterized as follows: sensory content that results from a creature's sense organs receiving light reflected or emitted from objects in such a way that the creature is in a position to master colour vocabulary directly on that basis.

It follows from P1 that RED is an I-concept, and also from P2, given the present account of I-concepts. A third view is a restriction of the second: P3 states that mastery of colour concepts is essentially linked to specifically *visual* sensory content as just (qualitatively rather than functionally) defined. According to P3 you and I may both fully possess RED even though your red-experience is qualitatively the same as my green-experience and *vice versa*. What matters is that we both have genuinely visual sensory content (in the qualitative-type sense just sketched), master colour vocabulary on that basis, and take colour properties to be directly revealed in visual sensory content.

A fourth view, P4, dismisses all these complications and insists that RED is indeed the concept of one particular phenomenal quality—you know, phenomenal red, call it *RED!* According to P4, RED is a red-blooded S-concept: specification of its content involves essential reference to one particular—highly specific—type of sensory content, *RED!*, and RED is fully graspable only by a being who is acquainted with that type of sensory content.

I don't, however, think one can ignore all the old complications, as P4 suggests. Even untutored thought tends to wonder whether we all experience colour in the same way. P4 may seem attractive, but it really is too simple. And P1 can be rejected outright. I favour P3, in spite of its paradoxical air—it says that RED is the concept of a phenomenal property whose whole and essential nature can be directly revealed in visual sensory content *even though it is not the concept of any one particular phenomenal property*—on the grounds that it effects the best compromise between common sense and adequate acknowledgement of the philosophical complications.

—'But if you accept P3, you cannot say that P2 is indefensible. For P2 differs from P3 only in that it relativizes the notion of visual experience in the way P3 relativizes the notion of red-experience.'

—True. I think P2 is defensible. I favour P3, but P2 is an interesting position. It can't be disproved.

Does P3 treat RED as an I-concept or an S-concept? It treats RED as an S-concept, for it states that specification of the content of RED does involve essential reference to a particular type of sensory content—visual content understood to be a particular general qualitative type of sensory content, not merely a particular functional type—in such a way that it is fully graspable only by beings who are acquainted with that type of sensory content. P3 does not, however, treat RED as what one might call a *first-level* S-concept, in the way that P4 proposes to do: it does not require reference to *RED!*, phenomenal redness as naively conceived (it takes it that there is no such single thing as phenomenal redness naively conceived). Instead it treats RED as a *second-level* S concept. By which I mean only that there is no essential reference to the phenomenal character of phenomenal redness as naively conceived in the specification of its content. Instead there is essential reference to the phenomenal character of specifically visual experience.[42] It is true that this reference to the phenomenal character of specifically visual experience doesn't distinguish red from blue, or indeed RED from BLUE, but this is just as it should be, on the present view.

Some may think P3 strained, so it is worth pointing out that it respects the intuition behind P4 as far as possible. It makes the smallest change to P4 that is compatible with allowing that two people can both have the concept RED even if the colour-experience one of them has on looking at a ripe tomato is qualitatively the same as the colour-experience that the other has on looking at well-watered grass. If Nida-Rümelin is right, this difference in colour-experience is actually found among human beings whom we firmly believe to possess the concept RED. But the change to P4 would be necessary even if this were not so.[43]

On my view, then, RED may be supposed to be an S-concept, and the argument for this view generalizes to all other concepts of sensory qualities.[44] They are not, however, S-concepts as naively conceived. They are second-level S-concepts, and there are no first-level S concepts—no concepts specification of whose content requires reference to particular phenomenal qualities naively conceived (that's concepts for you). As for DOG, SUBWAY, and so on, they are clearly I-concepts, on this view: you do not need to have experience in any particular sensory modality in order to possess them, even if you must have experience in some sensory modality or other to possess them, and indeed to possess any concepts at all.[45]

Two final comments on colour. First, we are driven to this conclusion by the colour-spectrum inversion thought experiment, and although the use of the thought-experiment is valid and cannot be ignored, it is open to someone to say that if all human beings who are capable of the same sorts of colour discriminations do *in fact* have the same sort of colour-experience when looking at ripe tomatoes, then RED—the human concept—can after all be taken to be a first-level S-concept. I think that this suggestion is worth recording, although it faces very serious (I believe overwhelming) difficulties.[46]

The second and connected comment is this. There is pressure to say that the—*the*—concept RED cannot be the concept of any particular phenomenal quality only if one assumes that we all share a common, single *concept* of red as well as a common, single *word* for red. Many, Wittgensteinians and others, take it as axiomatic that a common word entails a common concept, but it is not clear why one should agree with this. Perhaps the concept-name 'RED', as used here, is deceptive in so far as it affects to be the name of a single shared concept. Perhaps the best thing to say is that each of us has a private concept of red that essentially incorporates a particular sensory-phenomenal colour-element in its content, and that it is on this basis that we participate successfully in a common linguistic practice involving a single word 'red'.[47]

On this view, words are one thing, concepts are another. The word 'red' is not tied to any one single concept, *the* concept RED, for there is no such thing. Instead, 'red' is the common, public linguistic correlate of a whole group of simple S concepts, X'S RED, Y'S RED, and so on, which are indeed all first-level S concepts.

Does it matter which side one takes in this debate, in the case of colour concepts? I'm not sure that it does. Perhaps one can take both sides. I have opted for position P3 above, according to which colour concepts are taken to be shared second-level S-concepts, but I have no strong objection to the privatized version of P4 just described, according to which they are taken to be private first-level S-concepts.

12 Are P-Concepts I-Concepts?

Back now to the central question of this paper: Is it possible for finite creatures like ourselves to grasp or correctly represent the nature of (concrete non-mental) reality as it is in itself? Or, to put it in the more particular form that it assumed at the end of §9:

> Are P-concepts—SHAPE (TRIANGULAR), SIZE, EXTENSION, MOTION, SOLIDITY, POSITION—I-concepts? Could they be?

The first issue that arises, given the preceding section, is whether a privatizing move of the sort considered in the case of RED can be extended, not only to DOG or indeed USEFULNESS, but also to P-concepts like SHAPE, in such a way as to reintroduce the possibility of arguing that they are S-concepts after all, each with its local, private, person-relative content (Swiss army knives for your concept of usefulness but not for mine, tactile elements for the congenitally blind person's concept of shape, visual elements for the non-tactile and asomatosensory person's concept of shape, and so on).

The privatizing move can be made with P-concepts as with concepts like RED, but not, I think, with any theoretical peacefulness. Consider SHAPE. It seems so clear that different creatures can come to have the concept of shape we possess—*the* concept of shape, for there is only one—here I explicitly reject the privatizing move—on the basis of very different sensory experiences; so that superintelligent bats (for example) could on the basis of their echolocation experiences acquire and subsequently deploy exactly the same concept of shape as we acquire and deploy on the basis of visual and tactile experiences. In fact, it suffices to note that exactly the same concept of shape can plausibly be supposed to be fully masterable by two different creatures B and C on the basis of sensory experiences in entirely different sensory modalities familiar to us— sight and touch—in order to illustrate the sense in which the concept of shape floats free of the sensory elements in the different possible bases of its acquisition and subsequent deployment. One has to endorse a rather crude form of meaning-empiricism or concept-empiricism to suppose that B and C do not— cannot—have the same concept, as they do geometry together. A concept, after all, is not a faint copy or transform of a sensory experience; it is a concept.

I choose to concentrate on concepts like SHAPE, and on more particular concepts of shape like TRIANGULAR, because the claim that P-concepts are I-concepts may seem considerably harder to believe in their case than in the case of ELECTRICITY, say, or SOLIDITY. In the case of ELECTRICITY it is perhaps relatively easy to see that its content is not somehow made up of particular sensory elements (one might as well suppose that its content, or some part of its content, can be given in the sensory content of an experience of an electric shock).[48] In the case of SOLIDITY it is at first harder to see this, but it is something that one should learn as an undergraduate in philosophy.[49] In the case of TRIANGULAR it seems more counterintuitive (in spite of the fact that TRIANGULAR is a member of one of the few classes of concepts that seem to be open to exhaustive verbal definition), for TRIANGULAR is the concept of a property that we tend to think of as (capable of) being directly and fully presented to us in sensory experience.

A general obstacle to allowing that concepts like TRIANGULAR are I-concepts is that sensory content can sometimes seem to be quite generally pervasive of the content of thought, especially when one has been raised (as so many of us have) on empiricist fare. One may later come to doubt this idea, but it can still seem very hard to deny in the case of the concepts like TRIANGULAR. And yet it seems that the antidote is simple, once one has rejected the privatizing move described above: all one has to do, as remarked, is to consider the point that congenitally blind and congenitally non-tactile and asomatosensory beings may both have the—*the*—concept TRIANGULAR. The same argument can be adapted to work for MOTION, EXTENSION, and so on. Even if we suppose that all processes of conscious thought in human beings do in some way inevitably involve or implicate occurrent sensory content (this seems to be clearly false, in fact, but let us grant it for the sake of argument) nothing follows about the content of *concepts*, for we are given no reason to think that these occurrent sensory contents are an essential part of what makes these processes entertainings of specific conceptual contents,[50] and the view that congenitally blind and congenitally unfeeling human beings and superintelligent non-human echolocators may all have the concept SHAPE (EXTENSION, and so on) remains as compelling as ever.

13 Concepts without Intuitions?

I assumed earlier that sensory experience is necessary for the *acquisition* of any concept in the case of finite beings like ourselves.[51] From which it follows that sensory experience is necessary for the acquisition of all P-concepts even if P-concepts are I-concepts.[52] But this, so far, is quite a weak claim. As it stands, it allows that one might continue to possess an acquired concept while losing any sort of capacity for sensory experience, and a natural stronger suggestion is that possession of I-concepts (including all P-concepts, on the present account) may require contemporaneous possession of capacities for certain sorts of sensory experience.

Is this true? Well, it too has weaker and stronger forms. We can increase its plausibility by taking the limiting case of possession of a capacity for a certain sort of sensory experience to be possession of a capacity for a certain sort of sensory imagining. This allows one to say, plausibly, that one can possess the concepts SHAPE and TRIANGULAR even if one has lost (or perhaps never had) sight and tactile-somatosensory feeling, so long as one retains a capacity to imagine seen or felt shape. But now suppose that one has also lost the capacity to imagine seen or felt shape. Can one still possess the concept?

I don't know. My inclination is to say No; but even if this is right it doesn't follow that sensory content derived from visual or tactile experience is constitutive of the content of our shape concepts in such a way that these concepts are not I-concepts. One can answer No while still holding that SHAPE, TRIANGULAR, MOTION, EXTENSION, and so on are all-out I-concepts, P-concepts whose content radically, and in some way entirely, transcends the content of our sensory experience. An account of the conditions of *possession* of such a concept must be sharply distinguished from an account of the *content* of the concept.

All these things being so, it is not only possible that we may fully share P-concepts with other beings who have radically different sensory equipment. It is also possible, crucially for the present argument, that some at least of our P-concepts may feature in a (the) correct representation of *R* in spite of all the particularities of the specifically human idiom of reality representation; and that this is so even though the P-concepts are being considered specifically in respect of their descriptive content and not merely in so far as they have referential content.

Neither of these possibilities is available on the view according to which the (descriptive or more than merely referential) content of our concepts is not ultimately independent of our sensory experience. The first is obviously unavailable: if our P-concepts really are essentially informed by our sensory peculiarities, then we can't fully share them with creatures that have radically different sensory equipment. The second is unavailable given the truth of [II.4.1], endorsed on p. 156: given that no representation can correctly represent any feature of *R* if its representation of that feature essentially involves sensory elements. If, however, the claim that our P-concepts are I-concepts is correct, it undercuts [II.5], which led from [II.1]–[II.4], which are true, to [II.6], the claim that no account or apprehension of *R*, on the part of a finite sensory-intellectual creature, can ever be supposed to constitute a correct representation of (any feature of) *R*.

14 A Speculation

I have argued that there is no reason in principle why we cannot attain to a correct and descriptively substantive representation of certain aspects of the nature of *R*—reality as it is in itself. (Those who think this obvious may feel I am wasting their time, but many others take it to be obviously or provably false.) I want now to consider a simple Kantian speculation that does not undercut the preceding argument in any way, but may be thought to throw a dampener on it. First, though, and briefly, it should be noted that one reason why the qualification about descriptive content is important is that the possibility of grasp or correct representation of aspects of *R* seems otherwise too easily secured. For it is widely accepted that even if we are in fact quite profoundly wrong or ignorant about certain features of the nature of mercury and electrons (say), we can none the less refer to these things and talk about them, if indeed they exist, and on this view statements like 'atoms of mercury contain electrons' may qualify as representations—possibly fully correct representations—of *R* even though formulated by us in our human terms and even if we have a hugely imperfect grasp of the nature of what we are talking about. In general, as soon as one grants that such natural-kind concepts can reach out referentially to *R* (reality as it is in itself) despite the limits and particularities of our sensory-intellectual apparatus, vast tracts of the claims of science and common sense—for example the view that *cats like cream*, and that *some human beings like gold*—are irresistible candidates for being correct representations of *R*: our concepts of natural kinds give us a magic-bullet referential link to *R*. And yet it seems that for all this, our more-than-merely referential grasp of how things are may still be fabulously wrong. It may be fabulously wrong given fundamental error in our general concepts of matter and spacetime, say, for this will translate into fundamental error in our concepts CAT and CREAM—in so far as these concepts are being considered [a] in respect of their descriptive content, and [b] as candidates for representing reality as it is in itself.

This brings me to the Kantian speculation: perhaps R is indeed far, far stranger than we suppose. Perhaps an appropriate analogy for the overall experiential relation in which we and other very different beings of types B and C stand to R is provided by the case of three physical creatures who have exactly the same patterns of electrical impulses transmitted to their brains (these impulses play the role of the concrete non-mental reality that affects us), but react to them in very different ways. In the first the impulses produce colour experience, in the second they produce auditory experience, in the third they produce smell experience. Perhaps the differences between our overall (not merely sensory) sensory-intellectual apprehension of reality and those of the B-type and C-type beings are as great as the differences between these three modes of sensory experience. Perhaps we are entities constituted of some unintelligible substance receiving the same input from one common thing, but experiencing things in inconceivably different and utterly incommensurable ways.

If this analogy is in fact appropriate to our actual situation, then, in spite of the apparent sophistication of our theories of reality, the nature of R is as inaccessible for us and the B-type and C-type beings as any conception of the nature of electrical impulse is for beings whose only possible mental states are just uninterpreted colour experiences or sound experiences or smell and taste experiences.

We cannot know that the analogy is not appropriate. And so it seems that even if we can and do in fact grasp—know—something about the nature of R, we can never know that we do.

Well, this conclusion is correct (whether or not it is warranted by the considerations that deliver it): acknowledgement of the irrefutability of scepticism, so far as claims to knowledge of the ultimate nature of (non-conscious features of) things are concerned, is an essential part of a realist attitude to the world, and indeed of any defensible philosophical attitude to the world. Many philosophers have taken it that it is a prerequisite of a good philosophical theory that it should provide an answer to scepticism, but this is the reverse of the truth. Realism itself is inescapable, at least in the form summarized in [1] and [2] at the beginning of this paper, and with realism comes the irrefutability of scepticism. Any theory which on its own terms provides an answer to scepticism—scepticism with respect to knowledge claims about the ultimate nature of reality—is ipso facto refuted.[53]

15 What Can We Know?

I have argued that there is no difficulty of principle in the idea that finite sensory-intellectual creatures like ourselves can have descriptively substantive (rather than merely referential) knowledge of R, the nature of reality as it is in itself. But how much do we actually have?

I don't know, but I will indicate two areas—to do with numbers and space—where I think we may be cottoning on, at least in certain respects, to R.

Consider Eddington's description of the achievements of physical theory:

> *Something unknown is doing we don't know what*—that is what our theory amounts to. It does not sound a particularly illuminating theory. I have read something like it elsewhere—
>
> > ...the slithy toves
> > Did gyre and gimble in the wabe.
>
> There is the same suggestion of activity. There is the same indefiniteness as to the nature of the activity and of what it is that it is doing. And yet from so unpromising a beginning we really do get somewhere. We bring into order a host of apparently unrelated phenomena; we make predictions, and our predictions come off. The reason—the sole reason—for this progress is that our description is not limited to unknown agents, executing unknown activities, but *numbers* are scattered freely in the description. To contemplate electrons circulating in the atom carries us no further; but by contemplating eight circulating electrons in one atom and seven circulating atoms in another we begin to realise the difference between oxygen and nitrogen. Eight slithy toves gyre and gimble in the oxygen wabe; seven in nitrogen... .[54]

I think this is an essentially correct account of how things stand in physics, but it does not have the consequence that we know nothing about the nature of reality as it is in itself. Up to this point I have omitted NUMBER from the list of P-concepts, but it must now be added back in, accompanied by the crucial claim that number knowledge, mathematical knowledge, is *genuinely descriptive of the nature of reality*, not merely referentially substantive (however that particular mereness might be supposed to work).

This claim may give some people pause, but I think it is evident on reflection. I think there are eight oranges in front of me. And I think I may well be getting something right about *R*, no less, in taking it that there are eight things in the offing[55]—however wrong I am about the nature of space, time and matter and, therefore, oranges (and the offing). And I cannot here be supposed to be *merely referring* to things, in using the term 'eight', without giving any descriptively substantive account of *how things are*. Perhaps there is some beautiful sense in which Parmenides is right that All is One, but my bet is that this is not so and that eightness—number in general—is a real and ultimate property of things, and that we possess a great deal of mathematically expressible, descriptively substantive knowledge of *R*. A lot of us think we know that gravitational attraction between two objects x and y decreases as a function of the square of the distance between them, and if we are right, then, again, we have some very substantial and not merely referential, descriptive knowledge of an aspect of the nature of reality as it is in itself, even if the referring expressions 'gravitational attraction', 'x', 'y', and even 'distance' pick out entities that we are, given our grasp of the nature of space, time, and matter, in some ways hopelessly wrong about.

This claim to knowledge of *R* may seem rather thin, even if it is allowed. It may be asked whether we have any non-mathematical knowledge of the nature of concrete, non-mental reality as it is in itself? I am inclined to believe that we do, for I think we may also possess some non-referentially substantive knowledge of the nature of space—of the spatial properties of *R*—even if we can never know that we do.[56] And perhaps also of time, as Eddington attractively suggests, although intuition fails me here.[57] These, though, are questions for another occasion.[58]

This may still seem rather exiguous; sceptics about the possibility of knowledge of *R* may even feel that their essential point has been conceded. But this is certainly not true if their point is the point of principle—the claim that it is in principle impossible for finite beings to know the nature of *R*. And if anything else about the conclusion makes them feel more in accord with this paper, so much the better.[59]

Notes

1. When I cite a work I give the original publication date, while the page reference is to the edition listed in the bibliography.
2. Some hold that there is *abstract* reality (for example mathematical reality) as well as *concrete* reality (the universe) but in this paper I will take 'reality' to refer only to concrete reality.
3. I defend the much maligned phrase 'as it is in itself' in the next section.
4. It is close to the old question 'Can we know the nature of the *mind-independent, external* world?', but the words in italics cause unnecessary problems and I will not use them.
5. But unlike Descartes I simply assume, here, that there is such a thing as non-mental concrete reality. (If there is some sense in which all reality is mental, 'non-mental' may be replaced by 'non-human-mental'.)
6. A number of 'anti-realist' philosophers reject [2], sometimes on the extraordinary ground that it is incoherent (the idea, roughly, is that no phrase like 'features of reality' can really succeed in denoting anything that is proposed to be completely inaccessible and unintelligible to us).

   It is of course metaphysically possible, even on a fully realist view, that reality is dependent on or interdependent with human minds in such a way that there are in fact no features of reality that are completely inaccessible and unintelligible to us, but I am going to assume that this is not so in fact.
7. If one is worried about the concept—or reality—of time, one can drop the last four words.
8. 'As it is in itself' can also be used to distinguish the 'intrinsic' properties of a thing from its 'relational' properties, and it is worth noting that the existence of the universe involves the instantiation of relational properties just as surely as it involves the instantiation of intrinsic properties, and that there is a way instantiations of relational properties are in themselves just as surely as there is a way instantiations of intrinsic properties are in themselves.

9. Strictly speaking it might be better to make the cut between *experiential* concrete reality and *non-experiential* concrete reality rather than between mental and non-mental reality (for there may be non-experiential reality that is none the less part of mental reality; see Strawson 1994: ch 6). But I will ignore this detail here.

10. '*R*' can always be expanded to '*R* as it is in itself'.

11. Scientists in a hydrogen-and-oxygen stocked but waterless world may postulate the existence of water and correctly predict its properties, on the terms of their science, without ever having been in any contact with it; but they have been in contact with the constituents of water, and are merely contemplating different arrangements of them. They may work out the nature of zinc in a zincless universe, having a good command of the periodic table; but zinc is not part of concrete reality in their universe, and, once again, they have been in contact with the constituents of zinc.

12. I will be concerned only with cognitive or sensory change.

13. The two occurrences of 'essentially' make this a little heavy, and I will eliminate one of them in due course.

14. Why should alterations in neuronal connections brought about in this way be inferior to alterations in neuronal connections brought about by hearing someone speak, when it comes to acquiring a representation of *R*?

15. I am not going to say anything about the curious current debate between those who think that all content is conceptual content and those who think that there is non-conceptual content as well as conceptual content.

16. '*R*' functions both as a name for a type of feature and also as a name for particular tokens of that type, as required.

17. Note that sensory experience induced by brain tinkering involves sensory affection on the present understanding of the term, as does the auditory and visual experience of a 'brain in a vat' without eyes or ears, or a creature in whom such experiences arise with no external cause at all. It is the qualitative-experiential content of the experience that matters, not the process by which it comes to exist. It may take place wholly in the imagination.

18. What does 'visual' cover? I consider some complications in §11.

19. I choose to discuss TRIANGULAR rather than SQUARE because I am not sure what consequences the theory of relativity has for the view that squareness is an objective property of anything, and take it that triangularity (or pyramidicity) may be an objective or non-frame-relative property even if squareness (or cubicity) is not. This is merely to advertise my ignorance, but it may be helpful to somebody.

20. 'V' for *Vorstellung*.

21. Change of colour would not matter in the present case.

22. To see this it may help to replace 'sensorily' by 'intellectually' in [II.1]–[II.4]; [II.1]–[II.3] stay true and [II.4] loses all plausibility.

23. It is natural to use 'knowledge' rather than 'correct representation' in this section on intellectual intuition although I am not in general concerned with questions of justification. I take it that knowledge entails correct representation in the cases in question—even if not all knowledge of how things are requires representation of how they are.

24. See Kant 1781/7: B72, A248–256/B307–312. Kant's views form part of a long tradition of discussion of the nature of an omniscient being's knowledge (there is an interesting discussion of Aquinas's approach to this problem in Stump & Kretz-

mann 1996). It is arguable that the model of a creator's relation to its own works is less interesting as a model of intellectual intuition than 'pure' omniscience.

25. 'The house itself...is the house seen from nowhere. But what do these words mean? Is not to see always to see from somewhere?' (Merleau-Ponty 1962: 67). See also Nagel 1986: ch. 2, Williams 1978: 65–68, 245–249.

26. Kant 1781/7: B307, A254/B310; he takes the same line about human freedom.

27. A27/B43, B72.

28. This is the lesson of the 'Schematism'. Kant certainly does not think that one cannot meaningfully apply the categories to reality as it is in itself (as many have supposed). He thinks only that one cannot do this in such a way as to acquire *knowledge* of any sort. See e.g. B166 n: 'in our *thinking* the categories are not limited by the conditions of our sensible intuition, but have an unbounded realm'.

29. 'Nothing which emerges from any affecting relation can count as knowledge or awareness of the affecting thing as it is in itself. Therefore there can be no knowledge or awareness of things which exist independently of that knowledge or awareness and of which that knowledge or awareness is consequently an effect. More exactly, there can be no knowledge of such things as they are in themselves, but only as they appear—only of their appearances' (Strawson 1966: 238–239; see also 249–256, 264–265). Note that the claim is not limited to sensory affection. No product of any affection relation can produce knowledge, on this view.

30. It helps in this connection to think not just of the possibility of creatures having greater or lesser discriminatory sensitivity in respect of a given sensory modality, but also of the possibility of differences of the kind imagined in the 'colour-spectrum inversion' thought experiments, and also of the possibility of creatures possessing entirely different sensory modalities. See for example Kant 1781/7: B43, B72; Hume 1748: 20. For discussion of the colour-spectrum case see for example Locke 1690: II. xxxii. 14–15, Shoemaker 1982, Nida-Rümelin 1996.

31. This is, in effect, the contrapositive of [II.4.1].

32. 'Everybody's a Rationalist in the long run' (Fodor 1981: 315). For his development of this view, see Fodor 1996. See also McGinn (1983: 126).

33. For the basic idea see Strawson 1989b: 247–250. See also William James's profound thoughts on this matter (1890: 2. 617–640).

34. I intend 'acquaintance' and 'familiarity' to cover characters like Davidson's Swamp-
· man (the basic thought-experiment is a very old one), who coagulates freakishly into existence from slime, qualitatively identical to the adult Davidson. The Swampman begins, we may imagine, in dreamless sleep, lying next to Davidson, also in dreamless sleep. At this point he has had no *experience* at all, and yet there is a clear sense in which he has just as much familiarity with sensory content as Davidson himself, as they lie side by side. Another way of putting the point is by saying that there could be creatures whose knowledge of or acquaintance with sensory phenomena—the knowledge or acquaintance one has when one has had sensory experience—was wholly innate.

35. I use small capitals for names of concepts.

36. 'There can be no doubt that all our knowledge begins with experience... . But although all our knowledge begins with experience, it does not follow that it all arises out of experience' Kant (1781/7: B1).

37. The present notion of accidentality only concerns the relation between the content of the concept and the content of the triggering experience; the strobo-

scope-DODECAGON connection could of course be non-accidental, evolutionarily speaking.

38. A form of experience can be both non-accidental and inessential, relative to the acquisition of a concept: both the congenitally blind being and the congenitally non-tactile and asomatosensory being can acquire the concept TRIANGLE. On the general question of non-accidentality approached from an informationalist position, see Fodor 1998: ch. 6, and, again, the great William James (1890: 2.617–640).

39. Clearly concepts like these can be acquired only from experience that already has conceptual content as well as sensory content, but this is not an objection to the present point.

40. Suppose we have two expressions, 'useful' and 'beautiful', where a New Guinea language has only one. It doesn't follow that we don't have the same concept of usefulness, rather than (say) different views about what is useful. It doesn't even follow that we have different views about what is useful: the most accurate thing to say about the New Guinea language may well be that there are two words which are homonyms (it would be a simple mistake about language use and understanding to think that there will necessarily be some sort of semantic seepage from one to the other). And even if it were granted that we had different concepts, the fundamental point would remain: there would be no reason to think that specification of the content of the concepts involved any essential reference to sensory elements.

41. See e.g. Locke 1690: II. xxxii. 14–15.

42. I count black, white and grey among the colours, and take it that all visual experience is essentially colour experience (thanks here to Brian McLaughlin).

43. Nida-Rümelin (1996) estimates that 14 out of every 10,000 males may differ from other people in this way.

44. Pain raises a curious issue. See Strawson 1994: 247–250.

45. Might SENSATION, EXPERIENCE, and CONSCIOUSNESS count as third-level S-concepts, on this account? They certainly seem to be concepts that one cannot fully grasp unless one is acquainted with sensation, experience, and consciousness—and not simply because one cannot be said to grasp any concept at all unless one has knowledge of these things—and one can perhaps express matters as follows:

Levels	Types of affection	Sub-types
1	Visual	colour-experience, visual shape-experience...
2	Sensory	Visual, auditory, gustatory (defined as qualitative types not functional types)
3	Experiential affection in general	Sensory, emotional, propositional, intellectual-intuition-involving (?)

Adding level 3 allows one to integrate the thought that SENSATION is an S-concept into the existing scheme of things; it presupposes—reasonably, I think—that the idea of non-sensory experiential affection is intelligible. A further question is how this scheme might cope with Kantian forms of sensibility; but I will leave it here.

46. See e.g. Strawson 1994: 246–247. I have drawn on Strawson 1989a throughout this section.

47. Back to the 'beetle in the box'—and not in a way that Wittgenstein (1953: §293) would clearly have to reject. Note that there are also certain constraints on possession of colour concepts that flow from the similarity and difference relations between different colours (see McLaughlin forthcoming).

48. See Evans 1980: 270.

49. Hume makes the point that our concept of solidity is sensory-element-transcending in the *Treatise* (1739: 229–231). Reid makes it in a very accessible manner in §V.2 of his *Inquiry* (1764: 61–64). See also Mackie (1976: 24–26).

50. This point connects to a familiar Rylean and Wittgensteinian thesis.

51. The assumption is made for the sake of argument. It begs no questions because it can only make things more difficult for me.

52. I take it that this is compatible with all these very deep respects in which our predisposition to acquire P-concepts is innate (see e.g. Spelke 1994).

53. The claim about the correctness and necessity of scepticism has a reverse side: it is arguable that Kant's principal mistake in *The Critique of Pure Reason* is to suppose that we can know for sure that we cannot attain to 'something like the truth' about the ultimate nature of reality (the 'noumenal').

54. 1928: 291.

55. According to one objectively valid principle of counting things. Another principle of counting might pick up on the number of fermions and bosons constituting the oranges.

56. Russell disagrees, at least at one point in his career (see e.g. Russell 1927a, 1927b), as does Lockwood (1989).

57. 'I do not see how the essence of "becoming" can be much different from what it appears to us to be' (1928: 95).

58. I consider the question of knowledge of the nature of space directly in Strawson 2002.

59. This paper is a revision and expansion of chapter 7 and appendix B in Strawson 1989b. I am especially grateful to Lucy Allais and Mark Greenberg for their comments, and to Quassim Cassam, Brian McLaughlin and Ernie Sosa. I also learnt from audiences at London, Oxford, and NYU (where different assumptions about what concepts are led—in 1997—to a complete breakdown of communication).

References

Eddington, A. 1928. *The Nature of The Physical World*. New York: Macmillan.

Evans, G. 1980. 'Things Without the Mind.' In *Philosophical Subjects*, edited by Z. van Straaten. Oxford: Clarendon Press.

Fodor, J. 1981. 'The Present Status of the Innateness Controversy.' In *RePresentations*. Brighton: Harvester.

Fodor, J. 1998. *Concepts*. Oxford: Oxford University Press.

Hume, D. 1748/1975. *Enquiries Concerning Human Understanding*, edited by L. A. Selby-Bigge. Oxford: Oxford University Press.

Kant, I. 1781–7/1996. *Critique of Pure Reason*, translated by W. S. Pluhar. Indianapolis: Hackett.

Locke, J. 1690/1975. *An Essay Concerning Human Understanding*, edited by P. Nidditch. Oxford: Clarendon Press.

Mackie, J. 1976. *Problems from Locke*. Oxford: Clarendon Press.

McGinn, C. 1983. *The Subjective View*. Oxford: Clarendon Press.

McLaughlin, B. (forthcoming), 'Color, Consciousness, and Color Consciousness,' in *Consciousness: New Essays*, edited by Q. Smith (Oxford: Oxford University Press).

Merleau-Ponty, M. 1945/1962. *The Phenomenology of Perception*, translated by Colin Smith. London: Routledge and Kegan Paul.

Nagel, T. 1986. *The View from Nowhere*. New York: Oxford University Press,

Nida-Rümelin, M. 1996. 'Pseudonormal Vision. An Actual Case of Qualia Inversion?' *Philosophical Studies* **82**: 145–157.

Quine. W. V. 1969. 'Epistemology Naturalized.' In *Ontological Relativity and Other Essays*. New York: Columbia University Press

Reid, T. 1764/1970. *Inquiry into the Human Mind*, edited by T. Duggan. Chicago: University of Chicago Press.

Russell, B. 1927a/1992a. *The Analysis of Matter*. London: Routledge.

Russell, B. 1927b/1992b. *An Outline of Philosophy*. London: Routledge.

Shoemaker, S. 1982/1984. 'The inverted spectrum.' In *Identity, Cause, and Mind*. Cambridge: Cambridge University Press.

Spelke, E. 1994. 'Initial knowledge: six suggestions,' *Cognition* **50**: 431–455.

Strawson, G. 1989a. 'Red and "Red"'. *Synthese* **78/2**: 193–232.

Strawson, G. 1989b. *The Secret Connexion*. Oxford: Clarendon Press.

Strawson, G. 1994. *Mental Reality*. Cambridge, MA: MIT Press.

Strawson, G. 2002. 'Real materialism.' In *Chomsky and His Critics*, edited by L. Antony and N. Hornstein. Oxford: Blackwell.

Stump, E. and Kretzmann, N. 1996. 'God's Knowledge.' In *The Rationality of Belief and the Plurality of Faith*, edited by T. D. Senor (Ithaca, NY: Cornell).

Williams, B. 1978. *Descartes: The Project of Pure Enquiry*. Harmondsworth: Penguin.

Wittgenstein L. 1953. *Philosophical Investigations*, translated by G. E. M. Anscombe. Oxford: Blackwell.

THE NUMBER OF THINGS

Peter van Inwagen
University of Notre Dame

1. I wish to attack a certain idea—roughly speaking, the idea that it is non-sensical to speak of the number of objects. I begin with two long quotations that express this view, or variants on it. The first is from Wittgenstein's *Tractatus*[1], the second from Putnam's *The Many Faces of Realism*[2].

> 4.1271 Every variable is the sign of a formal concept.
>
> For every variable represents a constant form that all its values possess, and this can be regarded as a formal property of those values.
> 4.1272 Thus the variable name '*x*' is the proper sign for the pseudo-concept *object*.
>
> Wherever the word 'object' ('thing', etc.) is correctly used, it is expressed in conceptual notation by a variable name.
>
> For example, in the proposition, 'There are two objects which ...', it is expressed by '($\exists x, y$)...'.
>
> Wherever it is used in a different way, that is as a proper concept-word, non-sensical pseudo-propositions are the result.
>
> So one cannot say, for example, 'There are objects', as one might say, 'There are books'. And it is just as impossible to say, 'There are 100 objects', or, 'There are $\aleph_0$ objects'.
>
> And it is nonsensical to speak of the *total number of objects*.[3]

Conceptual relativity sounds like 'relativism', but has none of the 'there is no truth to be found ... "true" is just a name for what a bunch of people can agree on' implications of 'relativism'. A simple example will illustrate what I mean. Consider 'a world with three individuals' (Carnap often used examples like this when we were doing inductive logic together in the early nineteen-fifties), **x1, x2, x3**. How many *objects* are there in this world?

Well, I *said* "consider a world with just three individuals", didn't I? So mustn't there be three objects? Can there be non-abstract entities which are not 'individuals'?

One possible answer is 'no'. We can identify 'individual', 'object', 'particular', etc., and find no absurdity in a world with just three objects which are independent, unrelated 'logical atoms'. But there are perfectly good logical doctrines which lead to different results.

Suppose, for example, that like some Polish logicians, I believe that for every two particulars there is an object which is their sum. (This is the basic assumption of 'mereology', the calculus of parts and wholes invented by Lezniewski.) If I ignore, for the moment, the so-called 'null object', then I will find that the world of 'three individuals' (as Carnap might have had it, at least when he was doing inductive logic) actually contains *seven* objects:

World 1	World 2
x1, x2, x3	x1, x2, x3, x1+x2, x1+x3, x2+x3, x1+x2+x3
(A world à la Carnap)	('Same' world à la Polish logician)

Some Polish logicians would also say that there is a 'null object' which they count as a part of every object. If we accepted this suggestion, and added this individual (call it **O**), then we would say that Carnap's world contains *eight* objects.

Now, the classic metaphysical realist way of dealing with such problems is well-known. It is to say that there is a single world (think of this as a piece of dough) which we can slice into pieces in different ways. But this 'cookie cutter' metaphor founders on the question, 'What are the parts of this dough?' If the answer is that **O**, x1, x2, x3, x1+x2, x1+x3, x2+x3, x1+x2+x3 are all the different 'pieces', then we have not a *neutral* description, but rather a *partisan* description— just the description of the Warsaw logician! And it is no accident that metaphysical realism cannot really recognize the phenomenon of conceptual relativity—for that phenomenon turns on the fact that *the logical primitives themselves, and in particular the notions of object and existence, have a multitude of different uses rather than one absolute 'meaning'.*

In these passages, Wittgenstein and Putnam defend similar conclusions—perhaps the same conclusion, although whether their conclusions are strictly the same is a nice question. Their arguments, however, are certainly different.

I will first make some remarks that pertain to their common conclusion—if their conclusions are the same—or apply equally to their two similar conclusions.

(1) Suppose that one accepts the following two theses about sets. First, that the words 'set' and 'member' express, respectively, a unique attribute and a unique relation that everyone familiar with the language of set theory grasps, and that every sentence in the language of set theory, in consequence, expresses a determinate proposition—in the case of the simpler sentences, a proposition that everyone familiar with the language of set theory grasps. Secondly, that all the sentences in the language of set theory that are theorems of Zermelo-Fraenkel set theory express true propositions. One is then, as we may say, a "set-theoretical realist," and, if numbers and sets are objects, the set-theoretical realist will regard it as nonsensical to speak of the total number of objects—or, if not nonsensical at any rate demonstrably incoherent, since it is a theorem of Zermelo-Fraenkel set theory that for every number there is a set containing a greater number of objects than that number. (We could state this theorem informally in these words: There are too many objects for them to be numbered.)

Whether these theses and their consequences are true or not, the sense in which they entail that there is no such thing as the number of objects is not the sense either Wittgenstein or Putnam intended to give to these words. As to Wittgenstein, he would certainly not have accepted anything remotely resembling set-theoretical realism. He would, moreover, have argued that 'There are more than 100 objects' was nonsensical for the same reason that 'There are 100 objects' was nonsensical—and the set-theoretical realist will certainly want to say that the former sentence expresses a truth. As to Putnam, his point obviously does not depend on an appeal to facts, if there are facts, about sets or any other abstract objects. His argument contains no premise that contradicts the strictest nominalism.[4] I will therefore assume in the sequel that if there is no such thing as the total number of objects, this is true for some reason other than that there are too many of them to be numbered.

(2) Suppose (as I have argued is at least possible[5]) there is such a thing as vague identity. That is, suppose that the following is possible: for some x and for some y, it is indeterminate whether $x = y$. If there were such a thing as vague identity, there would be no such thing as the total number of objects—at any rate, no number would be such that it was definitely the number of objects. Here is a simple case:

$\exists x \, \exists y$ (it is indeterminate whether $x = y$ and $\forall z$ (it is indeterminate whether $z = x$ or it is indeterminate whether $z = y$ or it is determinately true that $z = x$ or it is determinately true that $z = y$)).

If we are asked what the number of objects is in any of the rather sparsely populated universes in which this sentence is true, we can say the following and no more than the following: it is indeterminate whether the number of objects is 1; it is indeterminate whether the number of objects is 2; for every other number (including 0), it is determinately true that that number is not the number of objects.

This point, however, is unrelated to the arguments of Wittgenstein and Putnam. In the sequel, I will assume that when we raise the question whether there is such a thing as the total number of objects, we are asking this question about a universe in which identity is not vague. (Wittgenstein, as we shall see, denies that there is any such relation as identity. This is consistent with my assumption, for identity is vague only if there is such a relation as identity.)

(3) Suppose that "identity is always relative to a sortal term." Suppose, that is, that there is no such thing as identity *simpliciter*, but only a two-or-more-membered class of symmetrical and transitive relations each of which is expressible by a sentence of the form 'x is the same N as y', where 'N' represents the place of a sortal term (or at least that this is true of each member of the class that is expressible in English). And suppose that there are sortals

M and N such that "For some x and y, x is the same M as y and x is not the same N as y" is true.[6] If this is the case, then there is no such thing as counting or numbering *simpliciter*; there is only counting or numbering by Ns. Suppose for example, that there are two such relations, "is the same being as" and "is the same person as". Suppose that there exist an x, a y, and a z such that none of x, y, and z is the same person as the others, each of x, y, and z is the same person as itself [i. e., each is a person], and each of x, y, and z is the same being as the others; suppose, too, that everything has this feature: it is the same being as one of x, y, and z and it is the same person as one of x, y, and z.[7] In a universe whose population is given by this description, there is no answer to the question, 'How many objects are there?' The best one could do in reply to the question would be to say something like, "Well, how do you want me to count them? Counting objects by beings, there is exactly one. Counting objects by persons, there are exactly three." (There was no need to appeal to Trinitarian theology to make this point. The point could have been made in terms of 'is the same gold statue as' and 'is the same piece of gold as'— provided one was willing to say that x might be the same piece of gold as y but not the same gold statue as y.)

This point, again, is unrelated to the arguments of Wittgenstein and Putnam. In the sequel, I will assume that when we raise the question whether there is such a thing as the total number of objects, we are assuming that there is no case in which x is the same M as y but not the same N; I will assume that statements of the form 'x is the same M as y' are to be understood as the corresponding statements of the form 'x is M and $x = y$' where '$=$' represents the classical identity-relation: the relation whose logical properties are given by these two conditions: it is reflexive; it forces indiscernibility—that is, if x is identical with y, then whatever is true of x is true of y. Again, my assumption is consistent with Wittgenstein's thesis that there is no such relation as identity—that is to say, his assumption that the identity-sign is meaningless. If the only way to understand the expression 'x is the same M as y' is as a stylistic variant on 'x is M and $x = y$', and if the identity-sign is meaningless, all that follows is that 'x is the same M as y' is meaningless.

So: we will assume that if there is no such thing as the number of objects, this is not because there are too many objects for them to be counted, and we will assume that identity is neither vague nor "relative to a sortal term." Given these assumptions, is there some reason to suppose that it is nonsensical to speak of the total number of objects? Let us first examine Wittgenstein's argument for this conclusion.

2. I divide Wittgenstein's argument into two parts, the first ending with 'it is expressed by "$(\exists x, y)$ ...".', and the second comprising the remainder of the passage I have quoted. Although I am not entirely sure I understand everything Wittgenstein says in the first part of the argument, it seems plausible to me to suppose that he is saying something very much like this:

'Object' is simply an unrestricted count-noun, a count-noun of maximal generality. An object is anything that can be the value of a variable, that is, anything that we can talk about using pronouns, that is *anything*. These two points—that 'object' is an unrestricted count-noun and that an "object" is anything that can be the value of a variable can be combined in the following observation: the word 'object' is so used that any substitution-instances of the following pair of formulae are equivalent:

$$\forall x \ (x \text{ is an object} \rightarrow Fx) \qquad \forall x \ Fx;$$

and of the following pair:

$$\exists x \ (x \text{ is an object} \ \& \ Fx) \qquad \exists x \ Fx.$$

Thus, the word 'object' is a mere stylistic convenience: anything we can say using this word we can say without using it; it can be dispensed with in favor of variables—or pronouns.

If this is (more or less) what Wittgenstein is saying in the first part of the argument, then I (more or less) agree with him. But what is said in the second part of the argument does not seem to follow from what is said in the first—nor does it seem to be true.[8] *Why* can one not say that there are objects?[9] Why not say it this way: '$\exists x \ x = x$'? And why can one not say 'There are at least two objects' like this:

$$\exists x \ \exists y \sim x = y,$$

or say 'There are exactly two objects' like this:

$$\exists x \ \exists y \ (\sim x = y. \ \& \ \forall z \ (z = x \vee z = y))?$$

(If we had sufficient patience and sufficient paper, we could say 'There are at least 100 objects' and 'There are exactly 100 objects' in similar fashion.) The identity-sign would seem to express what Wittgenstein calls a formal concept, and, it would seem, it can be combined with quantifiers and variables (which express the formal concept "object") to say how many objects there are.

Wittgenstein's reply to this objection lies in his account of the identity-sign in 5.53–5.532, which in effect says that '=' means nothing and must be banished from a "correct conceptual notation." (Russell in his Introduction to the *Tractatus* (p. xvii) sees very clearly the connection between what Wittgenstein says about the total number of objects and what he says about the symbol '=.)

Let us examine what Wittgenstein says in 5.53–5.532. Proposition 5.53, on which the rest of the passage is a commentary, is

Identity of object I express by identity of sign, and not by using a sign for identity. Difference of objects I express by difference of signs.

Now consider someone who has mastered the treatment of identity in any standard logic text of the present day, and who is reading the *Tractatus* for the first time. This reader will probably want to protest that it is simply wrong to suppose that "difference of objects" *can* be expressed by "difference of signs"—or that statements apparently asserting the difference of objects can be translated into statements in which what had apparently been expressed by the negation of an identity-statement was to be expressed by using different signs. If we examine 5.532, which reads in part

> ... I do not write '$\exists x \, \exists y \, (Fxy \, \& \, x = y)$', but '$\exists x \, Fxx$'; and not '$\exists x \, \exists y \, (Fxy \, \& \, \sim x = y)$', but '$\exists x \, \exists y \, Fxy$'.

(I have replaced Wittgenstein's *Principia* notation with current logical notation), we shall see what troubles our imaginary reader: although the first two formulae are logically equivalent, the second two are not. But this reaction on the part of the imaginary reader is premature, as the remainder of 5.532 shows. Wittgenstein is not proposing to replace a formula with a formula that is not logically equivalent to it; he is rather proposing an alternative logical notation. In the proposed "Tractarian notation," '$\exists x \, \exists y \, Fxy$' does not mean what it means in standard notation, but rather what '$\exists x \, \exists y \, (Fxy \, \& \, \sim x = y)$' means in standard notation. What is expressed by '$\exists x \, \exists y \, Fxy$' in standard notation is expressed in Tractarian notation by

$$\exists x \, Fxx. \vee \exists x \, \exists y \, Fxy.^{10}$$

Wittgenstein says no more than this about how Tractarian notation is to work, but it is not hard to extend the line of thought hinted at in 5.532.

What is expressed in standard notation by '$\exists x \, \exists y \, \exists z \, Fxyz$' will be expressed in Tractarian notation by

$$\exists x \, Fxxx. \vee \exists x \, \exists y \, Fxyy. \vee \exists x \, \exists y \, Fxyx. \vee \exists x \, \exists y \, Fxxy. \vee \exists x \, \exists y \, \exists z \, Fxyz.$$

And what is expressed in Tractarian notation by '$\exists x \, \exists y \, \exists z \, Fxyz$' is expressed in standard notation by

$$\exists x \, \exists y \, \exists z \, (Fxyz \, \& \, \sim x = y \, \& \, \sim x = z \, \& \, \sim y = z).$$

The difference between standard and Tractarian notation has been usefully described by Hintikka in these words: the variables of standard notation are "inclusive"; the variables of Tractarian notation are "exclusive."[11]

Using exclusive variables, the sentence 'There are at least two chairs' may be rendered as

$$\exists x \, \exists y \, (x \text{ is a chair } \& \, y \text{ is a chair}),$$

and 'There are at most two chairs' as

$\sim \exists x\ \exists y\ \exists z$ (x is a chair & y is a chair & z is a chair).

'There are exactly two chairs' is then represented by the conjunction of these two formulae. The situation is similar with the universal quantifier. The Tractarian formula '$\forall x\ Fxx.$ & $\forall x\ \forall y\ Fxy$' replaces the standard '$\forall x\ \forall y\ Fxy$', and the Tractarian '$\forall x\ \forall y\ Fxy$' is equivalent to the ordinary '$\forall x\ \forall y\ (\sim x = y. \rightarrow Fxy)$'.

How far can this technique be extended? Consider the standard language of first-order logic, with the identity sign, but with no terms but variables. Can all closed sentences in this language be translated into Tractarian notation? Well, certainly not all. Not

(1) $\forall x\ x = x$,

or

(2) $\forall x\ \exists y\ (Fx\ \&\ x = y)$.

But it would seem that all standard formulae that do not contain an "unpredicated" occurrence of a variable can be translated into Tractarian notation. (An occurrence of a variable is unpredicated if it occurs beside an occurrence of '$=$' and no occurrence of the same variable is one of the string of occurrences of variables following a predicate-letter within the scope of the quantifier that binds it. The second and third occurrences of 'x' in (1) are thus unpredicated; the second occurrence of 'y' in (2) is unpredicated. But the third occurrence of 'x' in (2) is "predicated" because another occurrence of 'x' follows the predicate-letter 'F', and that occurrence falls within the scope of the quantifier that binds the third occurrence of 'x'.) The reader is referred to the article by Hintikka cited in note 11 for a systematic statement of rules for translating formulae in standard notation into Tractarian notation. Hintikka also gives systematic rules for translating formulae in Tractarian notation into standard notation. If a standard formula is translated into Tractarian notation by the first set of rules, and the resulting Tractarian formula translated into standard notation by the second set of rules, the result will not in general be the original standard formula; but it will always be provably equivalent to the original standard formula.

What is the philosophical meaning of this result? Let us call those formulae in standard notation that cannot be translated into Tractarian notation—like (1) and (2) above—"untranslatable." The standard formulae that I offered above as ways of saying 'There are objects' [$\exists x\ x = x$], and 'There are exactly two objects' [$\exists x\ \exists y\ (\sim x = y.\ \&\ \forall z\ (z = x \vee z = y))$] are untranslatable; each contains—in fact, quantifier phrases aside, contains only—unpredicated occurrences of variables.[12] But why should this trouble those who believe that untranslatable formulae are meaningful? The fact that something cannot be translated into a particular notation does not necessarily mean that it is nonsense; it may mean only that that notation is deficient in expressive power. Wittgenstein does not argue that untranslatable formulae are meaningless simply because they cannot be translated into Tractarian notation. The general form of his argument is rather this: the identity-sign is strictly meaningless; therefore the statements in which it occurs can be meaningful only if it is a mere notational convenience, eliminable in principle. But why does Wittgenstein think the identity-sign is strictly meaningless? First, because the *Principia* definition of identity (an identity-of-indiscernibles definition: $x = y$ if and only if everything that is true of x is true of y and everything that is true of y is true of x) is inadequate, owing to the fact that it is at least *possible* for there to be two distinct things that share all their attributes (like Kant's two raindrops). Secondly,

> 5.5303 Roughly speaking, to say of *two* things that they are identical is nonsense, and to say of *one* thing that it is identical with itself is to say nothing at all.

As to the first point, it could be debated at great length whether there could be two things that were indiscernible. I will not, however, enter into this debate. Let us suppose that Wittgenstein is right on this point. It can hardly be true that a sign that has no explicit definition must for that reason be meaningless, or all signs would be meaningless. (Just as—as Wittgenstein said later in his career—explanations come to an end somewhere, so explicit definitions come to an end somewhere.) Why can we not simply define '=' as shorthand for 'is identical with'—perhaps coupled with an informal discussion of "numerical" versus "descriptive" identity? Or one might define identity as a universally reflexive relation that forces indiscerniblity. Admittedly, for all anyone can say, there might be two relations that satisfied this definition; but the following is provable: if '$=_1$' expresses one of these relations, and '$=_2$' the other, then

$$\forall x \ \forall y \ (x =_1 y \leftrightarrow x =_2 y).$$

(The fact that there might be two such relations leads *me* to regard this definition as unacceptable. The definition does not, or at least may not, tell us what relation identity *is*. I am willing to accept the definition of '=' as 'is identical with'—a phrase we, as speakers of English, understand—and to say that "a universally reflexive relation that forces indiscerniblity" embodies a correct theory of the logically valid inferences that can be made using 'is identical with'.) As to the argument of 5.5303, I think it suffices to point out that we do other things with 'is identical with' than say things like 'Tully is identical with Cicero and Tully and Cicero are two things' or 'Tully is identical with Tully'. I will not rest my case on the supposed informativeness of 'Tully is identical with Cicero', for Wittgenstein—at least this seems to me to be what he should say—will reply that the only informative proposition that this sentence could express is the proposition that something is called both 'Tully' and 'Cicero', and I do not wish to enter into the questions this reply would raise. I will point out instead that when one makes assertions using complex closed sentences that contain expressions like '$z = x$' and '$\sim y = z$', what one thereby does fits neither of the following descriptions: 'saying of two things that they are identical'; 'saying of one thing that it is identical with itself'. Whether or not sentences like '$\exists x\ \exists y\ (\sim x = y.\ \&\ \forall z\ (z = x \lor z = y))$' are meaningful, it is evident that the person who uses them can neither be said to be asserting of two things that they are identical nor be said to be asserting of something that it is identical with itself.

A parenthetical remark: I am convinced that Tractarian notation can be explained only in terms of standard notation—that the concept of an exclusive variable can be grasped only by someone who has a prior and independent grasp of the concept of numerical non-identity. But any way I can think of to argue for this conclusion would be called (and probably rightly) circular, so I shall not press this point.

It seems doubtful that Wittgenstein's contention that '$=$' is strictly meaningless is right. But let concede, for the sake of the argument, that '$=$' is meaningless. What follows? It does not follow that one cannot say that there are objects or cannot say how many objects there are—although it does of course follow that one cannot employ '$=$' in any essential way in making these assertions. Some other device will be needed. No such device can be found within the language of pure logic, for the only formulae of pure logic that can (on anyone's account) be used to make assertions contain the identity-sign: this two-place predicate is the only predicate that belongs to the language of logic, and one cannot make assertions without using predicates. To assert the existence of and to count "objects," we need an open sentence that everything satisfies. All such sentences that the language of pure logic affords—in fact, all sentences of any kind that the language of pure logic affords—contain '$=$'. But the language of "impure" logic, which comprises sentences in which quantifiers bind variables that occur in expressions containing words belonging to some natural language, affords an unlimited supply of open sentences that are satisfied by everything. And there is no rule that restricts us to the language of pure logic. Here is a proposal for representing the assertion 'There are objects' in which the formal concept "object" is expressed by means of variables:

$$\exists x\ (x \text{ is a chair} \lor \sim x \text{ is a chair}).$$

What objections can be brought against this proposal? Well, there is an aesthetic objection: the choice of the predicate 'is a chair' is entirely arbitrary, and thus the definition can hardly be put forward as a paradigm of elegance. But aesthetical deficiencies really do not bulk much larger in judging philosophical theses than they do in judging plans for rescuing a child trapped in a well: the only really important question in either case is: Will it work?

It is possible that someone will object to this proposal on the ground that 'is a chair' is a vague predicate, and that the vagueness of 'x is a chair' is inherited by 'x is a chair $\vee \sim x$ is a chair' (it may be that something that is a borderline-case of "chair" does not determinately satisfy 'x is a chair $\vee \sim x$ is a chair'; determinately to satisfy this predicate, it might be argued, is determinately to satisfy one or the other of its disjuncts). And vagueness causes problems for counting. We need not examine the merits of this objection, however, for there are predicates that are determinately satisfied by everything, whether or not 'x is a chair $\vee \sim x$ is a chair' is one of them. Here is one: 'x is evenly divisible by 3 $\vee \sim x$ is evenly divisible by 3'. (I take it that '$\sim$ Frederick the Great is evenly divisible by 3' expresses a truth. Frederick certainly does not belong to the extension of 'x is evenly divisible by 3'.) Since this "out" is available, I will assume in what follows that 'x is a chair $\vee \sim x$ is a chair' is determinately satisfied by everything. Having this predicate at our disposal, we can say, for example, 'There are exactly two objects' using only language that meets all Wittgenstein's requirements. Using Tractarian notation (that is, exclusive variables) we render 'There are at least two objects' as follows:

$\exists x \, \exists y$ (x is a chair $\vee \sim x$ is a chair. & .y is a chair $\vee \sim y$ is a chair).

And we render 'There are at most two objects' as

$\sim \exists x \, \exists y \, \exists z$ (x is a chair $\vee \sim x$ is a chair. & .y is a chair $\vee \sim y$ is a chair. & .z is a chair $\vee \sim z$ is a chair).

'There are exactly two objects' is, of course rendered as the conjunction of these two sentences.

"To say, 'Frederick the Great is a chair $\vee \sim$ Frederick the Great is a chair' is to say nothing at all." (*Cf.*, "... to say of *one* thing that is identical with itself is to say nothing at all." See 5.513.) Well, it's certainly to say nothing at all controversial. ("So tell your Papa where the Yak can be got,/And if he is awfully rich,/He will buy you the creature—/Or else he will not./I cannot be positive which."—Hilaire Belloc.) But it is not to say nothing at all in the sense in which to utter any of the following sentences would be to say nothing at all:

It is now five o'clock on the sun

Boggle the main franistan

Das Nichts nichtet

Turn right, and the entrance is diagonally opposite, by the next street.[13]

Instances of the law of the excluded middle frequently appear as (obviously meaningful) lines in mathematical proofs—e.g., 'The number N is either prime or it is not prime; In the latter case, it is not the greatest prime; In the former, it is also (as we have seen) composite, which is a contradiction; Therefore, there is no greatest prime.'. I conclude that there is no merit in this objection.

We can, therefore, if we have world enough and time, write a sentence that expresses any of the propositions in the following infinite sequence:

There are no objects

There is exactly one object

There are exactly two objects

There are exactly three objects

.

.

.

Each of these sentences is meaningful and has a truth-value (given that identity is neither vague nor relative to a sortal term). At most one of them is true. If one of them *is* true, it gives the number of objects. If none of them is true, then there are infinitely many objects. In the latter case, if we allow ourselves the apparatus of transfinite numbers (if we allow ourselves, say, the language of Zermelo-Fraenkel set theory) we can say, for any number x, that the number of objects is x; we say: There is a set of objects such that x is the number of that set's members, and no number greater than x is the number of the members of any set of objects. And any such statement will be meaningful and will have a truth-value, since every set has a cardinal number and every cardinal number is either the cardinal number of a given set or it isn't. (If we do not allow ourselves the apparatus of transfinite numbers, and if all the sentences in our sequence are false, then admittedly we can't say what the number of objects is. But we can say that they are *numberless*: that for any number x, there are at least $x+1$ objects. And this will be a statement that is true without qualification. But, if Wittgenstein is right, this statement is as meaningless as 'There are exactly 100 objects'.) Now if "object" is, as we have been supposing, a formal concept—so that sets and numbers are by definition objects—all sentences of the form 'x is the number of objects' will be false, owing to the fact that no distinction can be made between sets of objects and sets *tout court* (which do not form a set and hence have no number). But suppose we restrict the question of the number of objects to "individual" or "non-abstract" objects, as Putnam does. Then it would seem that the number of "objects" must be 0 or 1 or 2 or ... or infinite. If it is infinite (and if, as it seems reasonable to suppose, there are not too many *individuals* for them to be numbered), and if we allow ourselves the apparatus of transfinite numbers, then *some* number must be the number of objects—at least assuming that we can refer without paradox to the set of all things that satisfy 'x is an individual or non-abstract object'.[14] After all, every set has a cardinality. But if Putnam's argument is right, this conclusion must be wrong. Let us examine his argument.

3. What can Putnam mean when he says that "the logical primitives themselves, and in particular the notions of object and existence, have a multitude of different uses rather than one absolute 'meaning'."? This sentence presupposes the truth of several theses. One of them is that the notion of an object is a "logical primitive." What does this mean? Not, obviously, that some symbol used in formal logic is a logical primitive in the sense that, say, '~' is, and, moreover, bears the same relation to the English word 'object' that '~' bears to 'it is not the case that'. Perhaps the best way to understand the idea that the notion of an object is a logical primitive—I should think the only way to understand this idea—is to equate it with Wittgenstein's idea that "object" is a formal concept: that anything one can say using the word 'object' one can say without using it; it can be dispensed with in favor of variables—which is to say, in favor of third-person-singular pronouns. But then what can it mean to say that 'object' has "a multitude of different uses rather than one absolute 'meaning'."? Have variables "a multitude of different uses rather than one absolute 'meaning'."? Have third-person-singular pronouns?

We might understand the thesis that variables have a multitude of different uses rather than one absolute meaning as the familiar thesis that variables are essentially "sorted," that each "logical category" requires its own style of variable. But different styles of variable are a mere notational convenience. If we like, we can use, say, bold-face variables for, say, sets, and ordinary italic variables for other objects, but this is only a labor-saving device. It allows us to write

$$\exists \mathbf{x}\ \exists \mathbf{y} \sim \exists z\ (\mathbf{y} \in \mathbf{x}\ \&\ \sim z \in \mathbf{x})$$

in place of

$$\exists x\ \exists y \sim \exists z\ (x \text{ is a set } \&\ y \text{ is a set } \&\ \sim z \text{ is a set. } \&\ y \in x\ \&\ \sim z \in x).$$

And "unsorted" variables are what we must start with, for a variable is in essence a third-person-singular pronoun, and there is only one-third-person-singular pronoun, and it has only one meaning. We do not have one third-person-singular pronoun for talk about objects in one logical category and another for talk about objects in another, and we do not use 'it' with one sense when we are talking about artifacts and with another when we are talking about numbers or laws or amounts of money or trade routes. If these things were not so, the following sentences would be nonsense:

Everything has this property: if it's not a proper class, then it's a member of some set

No matter what "logical category" a thing belongs to, it can't have contradictory properties

If something belongs to the extension of a predicate, it can do so only as the result of a linguistic convention.

And these sentences are quite plainly *not* nonsense. It is therefore hard to see what Putnam can mean by saying that 'object' has a multitude of different uses. (He is certainly not saying that the word 'object' is used in more and less restricted ways—that in many contexts we use 'object' as an abbreviation for '... object' or 'object that is F'. He is not saying that the "world à la Carnap" and the "world à la Polish logician" really have the same inhabitants, and that Carnap and the Polish logician are merely using two sets of linguistic conventions, conventions according to which Carnap restricts the range of his variables to three of the inhabitants of the seven- or eight-membered world and the Polish logician does not restrict the range of his variables.)

If this argument is correct, a parallel argument would seem to apply to what Putnam says about 'existence'. If existence is a "logical primitive" (that is, if the words 'exist' and 'existence' can be dispensed with in favor of '∃') it cannot have "a multitude of different uses." If it did, number-words like 'three' and 'six' and 'forty-three' would have a multitude of different uses. It is evident, however, that Carnap and the Polish logician do not mean different things by 'three' when Carnap says 'There are exactly three objects' and the logician says, 'There are more than three objects'. It is not possible to suppose that Carnap and the Polish logician mean different things by the formula

$$\exists x\, \exists y\, \exists z\, (\sim x = y.\ \&\ \sim x = z.\ \&\ \sim y = z.\ \&\ \forall w\, (w = x \lor w = y \lor w = z)).$$

If Carnap and the Polish logician differ about whether this formula is true in some world, this cannot be because they mean different things by this formula—or mean different things by 'three'. They cannot mean different things by this formula because there is only one thing for this formula *to* mean. (Well, one could give it "different meanings" in a sense: one could place various restrictions on the range of its variables. But, again, this cannot be what Putnam is talking about when he says that "existence has a multitude of different uses rather than one absolute 'meaning'.")

It is therefore not at all clear what Putnam's conclusion is. But perhaps we can understand his conclusion if we examine his argument. (It is usually a good strategy to examine an argument when you do not understand its conclusion.) The argument has to do with counting things. But what sort of thing, or what sorts of things, are being counted in Putnam's argument? I will begin my attempt to find an answer to this question by listing the count-nouns that Putnam uses in connection with counting:

—individual

—object

—(non-abstract) entity [used only once, in connection with the suggestion that there might be objects that were not individuals]

—particular

—logical atom [used only once, and in scare-quotes]

—part [used only once, in connection with the "cookie cutter" metaphor: 'What are the parts of the dough?'].

The most important of these count-nouns would seem to be 'individual', 'object', and 'particular'. Apparently, the relation between these three terms is more or less as follows:

We are discussing only non-abstract things—"particulars." Among the particulars, perhaps co-extensive with them, are "individuals." But it may be that there are "objects" that are particulars but not individuals. 'Object' is the most general of the three count-nouns: everything is an object; particulars are non-abstract objects. But since we are not discussing abstract objects, since we have excluded them from our universe of discourse, 'object' and 'particular' in effect coincide. We can, therefore, let the word 'particular' drop out of the discussion, and simply ask whether there are objects that are not individuals.

I am afraid I have no sense of what the distinction between an individual and a (non-abstract) object that is not an individual is supposed to be. When we try to see what Putnam is getting at in attempting to distinguish individuals and objects that are not individuals, we find only one clue: it seems that if x and y are individuals, then $x + y$ is an object that is not an individual. But I do not find that this clue leads me anywhere. Let me try to explain why. I will begin by discussing the symbol '+'. This symbol is a "term-maker": it takes two terms and makes a term. What does this term-maker mean? It is not normally (in developments of "mereology") taken as a primitive. It is normally defined in terms of some other mereological predicate—say, 'overlaps' or 'is a part of' ('part' being used in the "inclusive" sense in which everything is a part of itself). Let us take 'is a part of' as primitive. Using this predicate, we first define 'x overlaps y' or 'x and y have a common part' in the obvious way. We may then write

$$F \, x + y =_{df}$$

$\exists ! z$ (Fz and x is a part of z and y is a part of z and $\forall w$ (if w is a part of z, then w overlaps x or w overlaps y)).

This definition can be generalized. We can define a more general operator, an operator on sets, 'the sum of' or 'the sum of the members of'. The operators

'+' and 'the sum of' are related in the obvious way: the sum of $\{x1, x2\}$ = $x1 + x2$, and the sum of $\{x1, x2, x3\}$ = $x1 + x2 + x3$. (And the sum of $\{x1$, the sum of $\{x2, x3\}\}$ = $x1 + (x2 + x3)$—which, as Putnam's notation suggests is just $x1 + x2 + x3$; in mereology, as in arithmetic, when using '+' we can move or remove brackets as we will.)[15]

The operators '+' and 'the sum of' are used by "the Polish logician" in connection with a theory called 'mereology'. Putnam calls mereology a "logical doctrine" and "the calculus of parts and wholes invented by Lezniewski." But that is like calling Zermelo-Fraenkel set theory a logical doctrine and "the calculus of sets and members invented by Zermelo and Fraenkel." Mereology is in no sense a part of logic and it is certainly misleading to call something that makes such intransigent existential claims a "calculus." As set theory is a theory about members and sets (that is, a theory about the membership relation), so mereology is a theory about parts and wholes (that is, a theory about the parthood relation). And mereology is a *particular* theory about parts and wholes. Different theories of parts and wholes are possible, theories that differ from one another far more than competing versions of set theory differ from one another. Competing versions of set theory differ about rather esoteric matters. Any two versions of set theory agree that if x and y are two individuals, then the set $\{x, y\}$ exists. Competing theories of parts and wholes disagree about such fundamental matters as whether, if x and y exist, $x + y$ exists. Consider, for example, the theory of parts and wholes I have called Nihilism,[16] whose sole axiom is 'Nothing has any proper parts'[17] or 'Parthood is coextensive with identity'. A second theory of parts and wholes that is inconsistent with mereology can be obtained by stipulating that any set has *at least* one mereological sum (and thereby leaving open the possibility that some sets have two or more mereological sums); by stipulating, that is, that for any such set, there will be *at least* one object that has all that set's members as parts and all of whose parts overlap some member of that set (see note 15). We could call this theory "Pluralism." Pluralism will be congenial to those philosophers who maintain that a gold statue can be distinct from the lump of gold from which it is made. For if the statue and the lump are distinct objects, then they are distinct mereological sums of the same gold atoms: the statue has certain gold atoms as parts and every part of the statue overlaps at least one of those atoms; the lump has those same gold atoms as parts and every part of the lump overlaps at least one of them.

When we consider Nihilism and Pluralism—the former denies the numerically distinct objects x and y a mereological sum and the latter allows them to have *two* mereological sums—, we can see why I have used the words "competing theories of parts and wholes" rather than the words "competing versions of mereology." Mereology with and without the null individual can sensibly be called competing versions of one theory. Nihilism, Pluralism, and any version of mereology are competing theories, full stop. To emphasize the fact that mereology is a particular theory about parts and wholes, one of many competing theories, I will in the sequel spell 'mereology' with a capital 'M'. Mereology has two axioms: that parthood is transitive and that any non-empty set has a (unique) mereological sum.[18] (Perhaps it should be mentioned that some advocates both of Mereology and Pluralism may want to regard the quantifier "any set" as restricted in some way, since they may think that there are objects whose nature unfits them for being parts—they may want to say, for example, that only individuals, or only concrete objects, or only material objects, can be parts. To accommodate such possible scruples, we could understand "any set" as "any set all of whose members are ontologically suited to being parts of something." This reading would not affect any of the points at issue in this discussion.)

Now that we know what is meant by Mereology, let us examine "the world à la Carnap" and "the world à la Polish logician." The former is supposed to contain three individuals. Putnam's language ('independent', 'unrelated') pretty clearly suggests that these three individuals are not supposed to overlap mereologically—they are not supposed to have any parts in common. (And not only is this suggested by his language, it must be his intent. If, say, $x1$ were $x2 + x3$, then Putnam's Carnap and the Polish logician would agree about the number of objects: they would both say that there were three; the Polish logician will count seven or eight objects only if $x1$ and $x2$ and $x3$ do not overlap one another.) Putnam's language ("logical atoms") also suggests that $x1$ and $x2$ and $x3$ have no proper parts, that they are mereological simples. (And not only is this suggested by his language, it must be his intent. If any of them did have proper parts, these proper parts would themselves be individuals—or so I would suppose, but I'm feeling my way about in the dark here—, and, assuming "no overlap," there would be *more* than three individuals in the world à la Carnap.) Let us suppose, therefore that the world à la Carnap contains exactly three simples. These would be "Carnap"'s "three individuals." It is a theorem of Mereology that if a world contains exactly three simples, it also contains exactly four composite objects (non-simples, objects with proper parts) and contains nothing else. (From now on I will ignore the null individual, owing simply to fact that I can make no sense whatever of the idea of a null individual.) Are composite objects, objects with proper parts, not individuals? Are the mereological sums of individuals not themselves individuals? Why on earth not? If Putnam's Carnap says that a world that contains exactly three simples contains exactly three objects or exactly three individuals full stop, then he must reject Mereology—he must contend that Mereology is a false theory. And the "Polish logician" must hold that the description 'a world that contains three simples and nothing else' is an impossible description. (Of course, the friends of Mereology will be perfectly happy with the description 'a world that contains three individuals and nothing else'; this description would be satisfied by a world that contained exactly two simples, $x1$ and $x2$; this world would have exactly one other inhabitant, $x1 + x2$. And if $x1$ and $x2$ are individuals, no doubt $x1 + x2$ will also be an individual. How not?) It makes perfect sense to ask, Who (if either) is right, "Carnap" or "the Polish logician"? It makes perfect sense to ask, "Could there be a world that contained nothing but three simples?" If Mereology is a true theory about the part-whole relation, the answer is No. If Mereology is a false theory about the part-whole relation, the answer may well be Yes.

Since Mereology is a theory, we are free to reject it—in the absence of compelling reasons for accepting it or at least for regarding it as plausible. As it happens, *I* reject it. (I regard it, in fact, as wholly implausible.) At least: I reject it if 'is a part of' in the statement of the theory means what 'is a part of' means in English. (And I do not know what else it could mean.) Mereology makes assertions about what there is, and I do not accept these assertions. Take, for example, my dog Sonia and my cat Moriarty. If Mereology is a true theory, then there is such a thing as the sum of Sonia and Moriarty. What properties does this object have? The theory itself tells us only that it has Sonia and Moriarty as parts and that each of its parts overlaps either Sonia or Moriarty—and that it has such other properties as may be logically derivable from these. But I know some things about Sonia and Moriarty, and I know some things about parthood (e.g., that if a point in space falls inside a part of a thing all of whose parts are extended in space, then it falls inside that thing; that if $x = y + z$ and y and z do not overlap, then the mass of x is equal to the sum of the masses of y and z). It follows from Mereology and these things I know that there exists a scattered object[19] that weighs about twenty-five pounds and has two maximally connected parts[20] each of which is now asleep, is about forty feet from the other, and is covered with fur. I do not believe there is any such thing, since I do not believe anything has these properties. Just as those who believe that I have no immaterial soul believe this because they think that nothing has the set of properties a thing would have to have to be my soul, so I think that nothing is the sum of Sonia and Moriarty because I think that nothing has the set of properties a thing would have to have to be that sum. And why should one think there was any such thing? After all, that there is a theory that says there is something with certain properties is, taken by itself, a rather unimpressive reason for believing that there is something that has those properties. I can, if I like, put forward a theory ("soul theory") that says that every mental property is instantiated only by something that also has the property immateriality, but if you think that nothing has both the property *is thinking about Vienna* and the property immateriality, you are unlikely to believe my theory. And I don't believe Mereology—any more than I believe Nihilism. Although I don't deny that some sets of material objects have sums, I don't think a very high proportion of them do. For most sets of, say, atoms, I don't think that there is anything that has the set of properties that the sum of that set of atoms would have to have. Putnam's Polish logician and I disagree not only about simple, imaginary worlds, but about the real world. We mean the same thing by 'mereological sum', since we mean the same thing by 'is a part of', which is no technical term but a term of ordinary English. (Or very close to it. Perhaps the English phrase 'is a part of' means what 'is a proper part of' means in the language of Mereology.) The "Polish logician" and I simply disagree about what mereological sums there are; like the atheist and the theist, the dualist and the materialist, and the nominalist and the platonist, we disagree about what there is. The "Polish logician" and I use the definite description 'Sonia + Moriarty' in the same sense; he thinks something has the right properties to be the denotation of this phrase and I don't.

I cannot, therefore, grant that "Carnap"'s and the "Polish logician"'s descriptions are equally good or equivalent descriptions of the population of a world—not, at least, if Carnap's description is 'a world that contains three mereological simples and nothing else'. I cannot grant that they *could* be equally good or equivalent descriptions of the population of a world, for they are straightforwardly incompatible, as incompatible as 'a world that contains immaterial souls' and 'a world that contains only material things'. Putnam's argument, therefore, is, as I have understood it, incoherent. It is, of course, possible that I have *not* understood it. There are two ways in which this might have happened. One of them is that there is something there to be understood and I have failed to understand it.[21]

Notes

1. Ludwig Wittgenstein, *Tractatus Logico-Philosophicus: The German text of Ludwig Wittgenstein's Logisch-Philosophische Abhandlung, with a new Translation by D. F. Pears & B. F. McGuinness, and with the Introduction by Bertrand Russell, F.R.S.* (London: Routledge & Kegan Paul, second impression, 1963). In citations, I will use Wittgenstein's "proposition numbers," rather than page numbers.
2. Hilary Putnam, *The Many Faces of Realism: the Paul Carus Lectures* (La Salle, Illinois: Open Court, 1987). The quoted passage occurs on pp. 17–19.
3. Proposition 4.1272 does not end at this point.
See also 4.128 and 5.453. Proposition 4.128 reads

   > Logical forms are *without* number.
   > Hence, there are no privileged numbers in logic, and hence there is no possibility of philosophical monism or dualism, etc.

   By 'monism' and 'dualism', Wittgenstein of course means the thesis that there is one object (as Spinoza held) and the thesis that there are two objects (a thesis that perhaps no one has held)—not the thesis that there is one *kind* of object (as materialists and idealists hold) and the thesis that there are two *kinds* of object (as Descartes held).
4. It might be that there were more nominalistically acceptable objects than could be numbered. This could not happen if all nominalistically acceptable objects were spatio-temporal objects and were within the same space-time. But suppose there were more space-times than could be numbered (a supposition consistent with David Lewis's modal ontology). Then there could be more objects extended in space and time—there could, in fact, be more tables—than could be numbered. In the sequel I shall simply assume that if it is impossible to number the nominalistically acceptable objects, this is not because there are too many of them. (And we assume that there are no non-existent objects of any sort: I should think that if there *were* non-existent tables and elephants and neutron stars, it would be entirely plausible to suppose that there were too many of them to be numbered.)
5. *Material Beings* (Ithaca, N.Y.: Cornell University Press, 1990), §18.

6. (I use bold-face double-quotes for "Quine corners" or "quasi-quotation-marks.") This assumption requires us to assume that the following two theses do not hold:

   "For all x and for all y, if x is the same M as y and F...x... , then F...y..."

   "For all x and for all y, if x is the same N as y and F...x... , then F...y...",

   where 'F...x...' is a sentence in which 'y' does not occur and 'F...y...' is the result of replacing some or all of the free occurrences of 'x' in 'F...x...' with 'y'. Roughly speaking: if the analogue of the principle of the indiscernibility of identicals held for all "relative identities," one could not have a case in which relative identities did not "coincide."

7. I did not have to use English phrases like 'the others' and 'one of' to say this; all that is required to say it is the apparatus of quantifier logic, the usual sentential connectives, and the predicates '1 is the same being as 2' and '1 is the same person as 2'.

8. Carnap seems to assert that the second part of the argument does not follow from the first—see *The Logical Syntax of Language* (London: Routledge & Kegan Paul, 1937), p. 295—but I am not sure I understand Carnap's point.

9. Wittgenstein says that one cannot say ' "There are objects', as one might say, 'There are books'." I have no idea what the words 'as one might say' ['*wie man etwa sagt*'] could mean, so I will ignore them.

10. In standard notation, '∃x ∃y Fxy' is, of course, equivalent to

   $$\exists x\, Fxx. \lor \exists x\, \exists y\, (Fxy\ \&\ \sim x = y).$$

11. Jaakko Hintikka, "Identity, Variables, and Impredicative Definitions," *The Journal of Symbolic Logic*, 21 (1956), pp. 225–245.

12.

   5.534 And now we see that in a correct conceptual notation pseudo-propositions like '$a = a$', '$a = b\ \&\ b = c. \to a = c$', '$\forall x\ x = x$', '$\exists x\ x = a$', etc. cannot even be written down.

   (As before, I have replaced Wittgenstein's *Principia* notation with current logical notation.)

13. Suppose that the second of these sentences is uttered by someone as a parody of nautical terminology. The fourth is from Stephen Potter's *Lifemanship*. It is recommended for inclusion in a letter giving instructions to a visiting team on how to find the home team's playing field. It has, according to Potter, the following annoying virtue: the fact that it is meaningless will not become evident to the visiting team till they have exhausted themselves in the attempt to find the home team's playing field.

14. And assuming that 'individual' is meaningful and does not admit of borderline cases. There may well be problems about the meaning of 'individual'—but if there are, Putnam's argument does not appeal to them. (Is 'individual' perhaps ambiguous? If

so, pick one of its possible senses and concentrate on that one. If Putnam is right, there can be no meaning to the question 'How many objects are there in a world containing three individuals?' when the word 'individual' is used in that sense.) And if the word 'individual' is meaningful, it's hard to see how there could be borderline cases of individuals; at any rate, Putnam's argument does not have as a premise that 'individual' is vague.

15. The more general definition is:

$$F(\text{the sum of } S) =_{df}$$

$$\exists! z \ (Fz \text{ and every member of } S \text{ is a part of } z \text{ and every part of } z \text{ overlaps some member of } S).$$

It should be noted that we do not *have* to suppose that the word 'sum' can occur only within a definite description. If we wished, we could read the predicate 'every member of S is a part of z and every part of z overlaps some member of S' as 'z is a sum of S'. That would allow us to say that the members of a set had *more than one* mereological sum.

16. *Material Beings*, §8.

17. A proper part of an object is a part of that object other than the whole object—for in the formal theory of parts and wholes, it is convenient to regard every object as being by definition a part of itself.

18. As Putnam has said, some versions of mereology recognize a "null individual," the sum of the empty set. In those versions, the second axiom is that every set has a sum.

19. That is an object that is not "all in one piece": a spatial object having at least two parts that are such that every path through space that joins those two parts passes outside that object.

20. A connected object is an object that is not a scattered object: an object that is "all in one piece." A maximally connected object is a connected object that is not a proper part of a connected object. A maximally connected part of an object x is a connected part of x that is not a proper part of any connected part of x. If there are cats and (undetached) cats' tails, then a cat's tail is a connected part of the cat, but not a *maximally* connected part, since there are connected parts of the cat—the cat itself if no other—of which it is a part. If a dog and a cat (spatially separated in the ordinary way; not surgically joined or anything special like that) have a mereological sum, then the cat is a maximally connected part of that sum, since there is no *connected* part of the sum that has the cat as a proper part. (Couldn't we simply define a maximally connected part of x as a part of x that is a maximally connected object? No: if a cat's head and tail have a sum, the tail is a maximally connected part of the sum, but is not a maximally connected object.)

21. In "Truth and Convention: On Davidson's Refutation of Conceptual Relativism," *Dialectica* 41 (1987), pp. 69–77, Putnam imagines some criticisms of the lessons he draws from the confrontation between "Carnap" and "the Polish Logician," and these criticisms bear at least some resemblance to my criticisms. The criticisms are put into the mouth of a "Professor Antipode," a figure of fun. (Professor Antipode, like most figures of fun, is not very intelligent.) I believe that the resemblance is

superficial. However this may be, I do not understand Putnam's reply to Professor Antipode. The reader must judge: either I am obtuse in the extreme, or (inclusive) the words of Putnam's reply to Professor Antipode, like the words of his original argument, cease even to seem to mean anything when they are subjected to careful analysis.

In *Representation and Reality* (Cambridge, Mass.: MIT Press, 1988), p. 110 ff, Putnam makes a point that could be applied to the confrontation between Carnap and the Polish Logician in this way: the whole dispute is really about which things to apply the word 'object' to, and that dispute is to be settled by establishing a convention. (He goes on to attempt to "deconstruct" the fact/convention distinction. I am sorry to be boring about this, but I am afraid I shall have to say once more that I do not understand the words this attempt comprises. I am aware that "I don't understand" is used by many philosophers as a substitute for argument, but I really *don't* understand what he says.) I have in effect replied to this argument (leaving aside the attempted deconstruction of the fact/convention distinction, which I am not in a position to say anything about) in *Material Beings*, pp. 6–12. The essence of my argument was this: if a thing doesn't exist, it isn't *there* for you to establish a convention to the effect that it shall be called an 'object' (or anything else); if it does exist, the term 'object' applies to it, since the term applies to everything.

Philosophical Issues, 12, Realism and Relativism, 2002

ON LOGICAL RELATIVITY

Achille C. Varzi
Columbia University

One logic or many? I say—many. Or rather, I say there is one logic for each way of specifying the class of all possible circumstances, or models, i.e., all ways of interpreting a given language. But because there is no unique way of doing this, I say there is no unique logic except in a relative sense. Indeed, given any two competing logical theories T_1 and T_2 (in the same language) one could always consider their common core, T, and settle on *that* theory. So, given any language L, one could settle on the minimal logic T_0 corresponding to the common core shared by all competitors. That would be a way of resisting relativism, as long as one is willing to redraw the bounds of logic accordingly. However, such a minimal theory T_0 may be empty if the syntax of L contains no special ingredients the interpretation of which is independent of the specification of the relevant L-models. And generally—I argue—this is indeed the case.

1. From Pluralism to Relativism

The view that I hold stems from the familiar semantic conception of logic, according to which

   (1) A valid argument is one whose conclusion is true in every model in which all its premises are true.

As J. C. Beall and Greg Restall have recently argued,[1] this definition is by itself relativistic insofar as the notion of 'model' may be cashed out in different ways. Take models to be worlds (or world-like structures) and (1) yields some sort of classical logic. Take models to be situation-theoretic set-ups (possibly incomplete and/or inconsistent) and (1) results in some sort of relevant logic. Thus, the question "Is this argument valid?" does not admit of a unique answer because there is more than one sense in which an argument can be valid, and to the extent that these senses are equally good one would be entitled to hold a relativistic position.

This sort of consideration could leave one unmoved. Ambiguity is no evidence for relativism if disambiguation stamps out all disagreement. In fact, Beall and Restall prefer to speak of 'pluralism' rather than 'relativism', and I think their pluralism is best interpreted as the moderate claim that there are several equally good, non-equivalent ways of *reading* (1), i.e., several equally good senses of construing the relevant notion of a model, regardless of whether these senses leave room for internal disagreement. The view that I intend to outline, and that provides evidence for a more recalcitrant brand of relativism, is stronger. I hold that there exist ways of reading (1) that do leave room for internal disagreement. They leave room for disagreement because they are compatible with different ways of characterizing that portion of the language that is responsible for the required nexus between the premises and the conclusion of a valid argument—different ways of characterizing the "logical vocabulary". And these ways of reading (1) need not be idiosyncratic. They can be as ordinary as one likes, provided that we do away with a number of misleading traits that we are accustomed to associate with our favorite notion of a model.

Ultimately, of course, even this sort of disagreement could be construed as a form of ambiguity: it is still ambiguity on the relevant notion of a model. Suppose we disagree on whether the identity predicate should be treated as a logical constant. You say that it should be so treated, and therefore you exclude from the range of admissible models anything that doesn't do justice to the intended interpretation of this predicate. I say that the identity predicate should not be treated as a logical constant, and therefore regard as admissible even models that reflect a different interpretation. Here 'model' could be construed in the ordinary fashion, assuming the language to be some familiar sort of first-order language. So our disagreement concerns the exact composition of the class of first-order models: You say it should only include certain models; I say it should not. And surely we could blame it on semantic ambiguity. We could say that we are not using the same notion of a first-order model after all. In this sense our disagreement would be just as innocuous as any other divergence that trades on ambiguity. However, this is only one way of looking at the impasse. Surely we could also insist that we possess exactly the same concept and yet we disagree on its extension: You say the extension only includes certain models and I say it includes many more. In this sense, our disagreement would not just be a sign of ambiguity. It would be genuine and irreducible, and enough to make a difference when it comes to the logic of arguments involving the identity predicate.

This sort of disagreement concerning the status of identity is familiar from logic textbooks. Is identity the only case in point? I don't think so. On the contrary, I think the same sort of disagreement may apply across the board and affect the status of any portion of the relevant vocabulary. Tarski once suggested that *every* term can in principle be treated as a logical term or as a non-logical term, as the case may be,[2] so the relativism ensuing from this view may be termed *Tarskian Relativism*. Indeed, once Tarskian relativism is admitted a different sort of logical relativism must be admitted as well, according to which different ways of specifying the semantics of a fixed logical vocabulary are also possible. You and I may agree that identity is a logical constant but you may think that it stands for a transitive relation whereas I may not.[3] Again, this amounts to a genuine disagreement concerning the range of admissible models. And, again, I see no reason to restrict the possibility of such disagreement to a few cases: given any way of drawing the boundary around the logical vocabulary, we may in principle disagree on the exact interpretation of any portion of that vocabulary. Quine famously argued against this view by stigmatizing deviance: "Change of logic, change of subject".[4] On the other hand, Carnap's "principle of tolerance" famously implied that everyone is at liberty to build his or her own logical theory, even when this means casting the ship of logic off from the *terra firma* of classical forms.[5] So we may label this view *Carnapian Relativism*. It is the relativism that comes with the claim that the meaning of the logical vocabulary is up for grabs, which is not the same as the claim that the choice of the vocabulary is itself up for grabs. My contention in the following is that both varieties of relativism, even in their most extreme forms, are defensible.

2. Logical and Extra-logical

Let us begin with Tarskian Relativism. What are the reasons for maintaining that the distinction between the logical and the extra-logical is up for grabs? Broadly speaking, my reasons stem from the consideration that all bits of language get their meaning fixed in the same way, namely, by choosing some class of models as the only admissible ones. One notable difference, of course, is that in one case (the logical terms) the relevant class of admissible models is normally thought of as constituting the class of *all* possible models, whereas in the other case the chosen models are just meant to characterize a certain way of understanding the terms in question—a preferred way among many possible others. In this sense, logic is a uniquely ambitious theory. It aims to be the theory included in every other theory; its models want to include the models of every other. Yet this notable difference—I argue—does not rest on any intrinsic peculiarity of the logical terms. One can draw the line between the logical and the extra-logical vocabulary in many ways, and depending on how one draws the line one can think of the models that fix the meaning of the logical terms as constituting the class of all models. Alternatively, one can specify the class of all possible models in many different ways, and depending on how one specifies that class one can think of the terms whose meaning is invariant across the board (in some sense to be clarified) as constituting the logical vocabulary. Logic is ambitious, but precisely for that reason the competition can be tough.

Here is how Tarski put it in his 1936 paper, "On the Concept of Logical Consequence":

> The division of all terms of the language discussed into logical and extra-logical ...is certainly not quite arbitrary. If, for example, we were to include among the extra-logical signs the implication sign, or the universal quantifier, then our definition of the concept of consequence would lead to results which obviously contradict ordinary usage. On the other hand no objective grounds are known to me which permit us to draw a sharp boundary between the two groups of terms. It seems to be possible to include among logical terms some which are usually regarded by logicians as extra-logical without running into consequences which stand in sharp contrast to ordinary usage.[6]

As I mentioned, Tarski even went as far as saying that

> In the extreme case we could regard all terms of the language as logical. The concept of *formal* consequence would then coincide with that of *material* consequence.[7]

This last statement is actually a non-sequitur, unless treating all terms as logical is taken to imply drastic restrictions on the cardinality of the admissible models. (Ordinarily, a statement of the form 'There are exactly m things' is a material consequence of a statement of the form 'There are exactly n things' ($n \neq m$) if, and only if, the number of objects in the domain of quantification is either different from n or equal to m.[8]) But never mind that. The relevant claim is that all (or any) terms of the language could in principle be regarded "as logical"—and I agree with that.

Now, what are the objections to this view? A lot has been said in this regard,[9] but I think the main complaints boil down to three, and none of them is compelling. Two objections can be stated and replied to easily; the third requires a detailed response, and the bulk of the sequel will be devoted to it.

The first objection comes with the intuition that a logical term is semantically invariant—that it is a logical *constant*. Take a first-order language L whose vocabulary includes an extra-logical constant, say, the binary predicate 'parallel to'. As an extra-logical term, this predicate is characterized by a strong semantic variability: its extension in an L-model can be any binary relation whatsoever, any set of ordered pairs. Indeed, all things being equal, 'parallel to' is an extra-logical predicate precisely insofar as the class of its possible extensions coincides with that of any other extra-logical binary predicate. Can we make it into a logical term just by stipulating instead that its extension be kept constant in all L-models? Hardly so. The only way to make the stipulation would involve drastic restrictions on the variability of a model's domain. For example, if R is the extension in question, we would have to rule out as inadmissible all models whose domain contains fewer elements than the field of R, and this is hardly a way of doing justice to the intended meaning of 'parallel to'. So, at least cardinalitywise, the interpretation of 'parallel to' must vary from model to model.

This objection, however, proves little. After all, the same consideration would affect the status of some typical logical constants. The interpretation of 'identical with', for instance, depends just as much on the domain of discourse, or on its cardinality, so strictly speaking it cannot be kept constant in all models. Semantically, what distinguishes a logical constant is not the fact that its interpretation is invariant from model to model, for sometimes its does vary. So the fact that the interpretation of 'parallel to' *must* vary can hardly be a reason for not including it into the logical vocabulary.

A second line of objection stems from the intuition that logicality requires *generality* (as opposed to semantic invariability). True—one could argue—the intended interpretation of a predicate such as 'identical with' may vary from model to model. Nonetheless it can always be identified with the identity relation defined on the model's domain. Its intended interpretation works fine in every domain, for all (pairs of) objects in the domain. As Quine put it, identity knows no preferences, it treats all objects impartially.[10] By contrast, the intended interpretation of a predicate such as 'parallel to' only makes limited sense in certain domains. (What is this predicate supposed to mean in a domain of entities that cannot be compared with regard to direction—say: properties?) So, again, treating 'parallel to' as a logical term would seem to involve drastic restrictions on the composition of a model's domain, and this would suffice to cash out a significant difference between this predicate and a logical predicate such as 'identical with'.

This objection, I think, is also inadequate. For if treating certain bits of language as logical constants amounts to identifying a certain class of models with the class of *all* possible models, then the sort of restriction at issue, though drastic, would have to be expected. Models in which the parallel-to relation makes no sense would simply have to be dismissed if 'parallel to' were treated as a logical constant. On pain of begging the question, it is hard to see how the necessary condition of generality can be violated, in this case as in many others. Moreover, as a sufficient condition generality is dubious, too. For there are other theories besides logic that seem to fit the bill. Formal ontology, for instance, understood in the spirit of Husserl's "pure theory of the objects as such",[11] is arguably a theory of equal generality and its primitive notions (such as 'part of' or 'depends on') would seem to apply across the board.

One could press the objection here. One could argue that the difference between 'identical with' and 'parallel to' (or 'part of') is that the meaning of the former can be captured by a rule that does not require distinguishing the identity of objects in a given universe, whereas the meaning of the latter does require that. This, in turn, could be explained in terms of invariance under permutations: no matter how one picks a model, the extension of 'identical with' is not affected by any permutation of the universe (i.e., any one-one transformation of the universe onto itself), as all things are sure to remain self-identical no matter how one manipulates them. By contrast, a rule for 'parallel to' (or 'part of') could be so affected. Ergo, only 'identical with' is a logical term—or so one could argue.

This way of pressing the objection has a respectable pedigree. Tarski himself considered the invariance criterion in a joint article with Adolf Lindenbaum, "On the Limitations of the Means of Expression of Deductive Theories"[12] (where it is shown that every notion definable in the simple theory of types is invariant under all permutations of any given domain) and eventually articulated it extensively in his 1966 lecture, "What are Logical Notions?".[13] The same idea was taken up by Mostowski and Lindström in their papers on generalized quantifiers[14] (where the invariance property was explicitly employed to license a genuine extension of standard first-order logic) and recently refined and defended by Gila Sher.[15] Indeed, the invariance criterion is nowadays widely accepted as an extensionally adequate criterion, i.e., as a tool for correctly identifying the traditional set of logical constants and some of its most natural extensions. (It is precisely in this sense that Tarski was interested in the criterion, in spite of the fundamentalist skepticism of his 1936 paper.) However, the criterion is ultimately inadequate—in fact, question-begging—if our concern is what distinguishes logical from extra-logical terms *in its most general form*, without reference to any particular logical theory. For what is it that would allow us to say whether the interpretation of a given term is *always* invariant under all permutations of the given domain, if not a preconceived understanding of what is logically admissible? Take again the case of predicates. The problem is not only that we could interpret 'identical with' as a relation other than identity, for that would still be compatible with the identity relation itself enjoying a special status regardless of how we choose to designate it. Nor is the problem that *many* predicates could turn out to designate the same identity relation (consider 'x is identical with y iff y is either white or not white'). Rather, the problem is that the special status of the identity relation is itself dependent on a conception of the range of admissible models. If models with self-different objects were admitted (as someone might urge), then identity would not comply with the invariance criterion. Conversely, if all admissible models had their domain defined by a set of parallel lines (for instance), or by a set of lines no pair of which are parallel, then the parallel-to relation *would* comply with the criterion and the predicate 'parallel to' could therefore be treated as a logical constant.

From a general semantic standpoint, then, I am inclined to resist the objection. Generality is hardly a better criterion for logicality than constancy of meaning. Are there any other options? One last, important option would seem to be the flat refusal of the liberal semantic standpoint that we have been presupposing. My reasons for maintaining that the distinction between the logical and the extra-logical is up for grabs stem from the thought that all bits of language get their meaning fixed in the same way, namely, by choosing some class of models as the only admissible ones. However, one could object that only the meaning of the extra-logical terms is fixed that way. Indeed, according to the usual way of spelling out a semantics for a given language (most notably inspired by Tarski's own characterization of the semantics for first-order languages), the logical constants are interpreted *outside* the system of models. Their meaning is not captured by the basic semantic interface relating a language with its models. Rather, it is imposed upon it *ab initio*. It is characterized only indirectly through the recursive definition of truth (or satisfaction). In Sher's words

> The meaning of a logical constant is not given by the definitions of particular models but is part of the same metatheoretical machinery used to define the entire network of models.... The meaning of logical constants is given by *rules external to the system*.[16]

To this line of objection I reply that the customary way of spelling out semantics is indeed significant, but also misleading. If we are not going to consider other ways of interpreting certain symbols, then of course there is no need to do otherwise. So, if the meaning of the logical terms is to be kept constant (in some relevant sense) throughout the class of all models, then of course it is convenient to pull them out of the model-theoretic machinery and not worry about them every time we specify a model. But does this have any significance apart from pragmatic convenience? Does this provide any ground for a principled distinction between logical and extra-logical terms? I think not. In principle, one could certainly proceed otherwise. Provided that one works with a semantic apparatus that is sufficiently general and unbiased to support alternative practices, one could treat any given term outside the system of models or inside it, as the case may be. This is sometimes a genuine option with regard to the identity predicate, whose meaning is sometimes fixed *not* by a recursive clause of the form

(2) '*a* is identical with *b*' is true iff $Val(a)$ is identical with $Val(b)$

(where *Val* is a function assigning semantic values) but rather by a stipulation about the interpretation of the predicate itself, namely a stipulation to the effect that 'identical with' picks out the identity relation. This stipulation, as we have seen, amounts to a constraint on the class of the admissible models. But if this option is available for the identity predicate, then it is equally available when it comes to other predicates that we might want to treat as logical constants. If we are ready to regard a semantic rule such as (2) as a sign of logicality for 'identical with', then there is no reason not to regard the analogous rule for 'parallel to',

(3) '*a* is parallel to *b*' is true iff $Val(a)$ is parallel to $Val(b)$,

as a sign of logicality as well. And if we do so, what prevents us from doing the same with all other predicate and relation terms?

This reply, of course, only works to the extent that it can be fully general-ized. I am saying that one could treat any given term outside the system of models or inside it, as the case may be, provided that a semantic apparatus is available that is sufficiently general and unbiased to support such practices. In the case of binary predicates the familiar Tarskian apparatus seems to be fine. But it remains to be shown that the same sort of flexibility is available in every case, with regard to expressions of any syntactic category, including for exam-ple the familiar connectives and quantifiers. If only some bits of language would resist the treatment that I am advocating, then the boundary between the logi-cal and the extra-logical would not be up for grabs and the prospects for a relativistic account of logic would be undermined. Thus, in order for the reply to be successful we have to delve deeper into the relevant "metatheoretical ma-chinery" and provide evidence to the contrary. This is why I said that the third objection calls for a detailed response, and to these details I now turn.

3. The Paradigm of Functional Application

If our aim is generality we cannot just confine ourselves to first-order lan-guages, as I implicitly did so far. And of course we cannot just confine our-selves to classical Tarskian models, i.e., interpretation structures defined by a non-empty domain of discourse along with a series of individuals, subsets, and relations based on this domain. These are the customary structures used in model theory but they are not general enough for our purposes. The semantic frame-work that we need consider must be much broader as regards both the notion of a language and the notion of a model.

Now, I reckon that the best suggestion in this sense is still the general theory of types, or better the theory of types as filtered through the theory of catego-rial grammars. This is known to be utterly overgenerating from the linguist's standpoint, but it is also a theory that covers virtually every case of logical interest. So let us take a closer look.

Simply put, the guiding idea is that a language typically involves expres-sions of various types, which can be classified into two sorts: individual (or primitive) types, and functional (or derived) types. Intuitively, the individual types correspond to those categories of expressions whose syntactic status is not analyzed in terms of other categories: sentences, proper names, and presum-ably not many others. By contrast, functional types are defined in terms of sim-pler types in a way that fixes the combinatorial properties of the corresponding categories: for each pair of types t and t', primitive or functional, a new de-rived type t'/t can be formed, corresponding to the category of those functors that combine with expressions of type t' to produce expressions of type t. Thus, for instance, if S is the type of sentences and N the type of names, then S/S will be the type of connectives, N/S the type of predicates, and so on. (More gen-erally, one could consider n-adic types of the form $t_1 \ldots t_n/t'$ for each $n > 0$, corresponding to those categories of n-place functors that build expressions of type t' out of expressions of type $t_1,..., t_n$, in that order. However, such types can be ignored without loss of generality, as they can always be represented by monadic types of the form $t_1 /(t_2 /(.../(t_n/t')...)).$[17])

Suppose, then, that we have fixed upon a sufficiently large set T of types. For instance, we may take an infinite stock of individual types S, N, $\tau_0,..., \tau_n,...$ and close it under the slash operation $/$. Then we can define languages and models of variable complexity in a uniform way. On the one hand, a language's expressions can be specified by recursion on the basis of some type assignment to its symbols: for each type t, the corresponding category of expressions will comprise all t-typed symbols (if any) plus all those expressions that can be obtained by applying some structural operation (e.g., juxtaposition) to pairs of expressions of type t'/t and t' (respectively) for some t'. In other words, a language is essentially a triple consisting of (i) a sequence s of symbols of various types, (ii) a structural operation g for building compound expressions, and (iii) the resulting T-termed system of (possibly empty) categories of expressions, E, one category for each type $t \in T$. Specifically, $E = (E_t: t \in T)$ would be the system defined by:

(4) If s_i is a symbol of type t, then $s_i \in E_t$.
   If $x \in E_{t'/t}$ and $y \in E_{t'}$, then $g(x,y) \in E_t$.

(Some refinements would be in order to rule out certain linguistically implausible structures, but we need not go into such minutiae here.[18]) On the other hand, the notion of a model can be characterized in a perfectly symmetric way. A model must act as a semantic lexicon: it must determine what kind of things may be assigned to the basic components of the given language as their semantic counterparts, and it must do so within the limits set by the relevant type distinctions. Thus, a model for a language $L = (s, g, E)$ is essentially a triple $M = (d, h, I)$ such that (i) d is a sequence of typed denotations, one for each symbol in s; (ii) h is a structural operation subject to the same type restrictions as g, and (iii) I is a T-termed system of domains, one for each category of expressions in E. More precisely, $I = (I_t: t \in T)$ is a sequence of domains satisfying the obvious counterpart of (4):

(5) If s_i is a symbol of type t, then $d_i \in I_t$
   If $x \in I_{t'/t}$ and $y \in I_{t'}$, then $h(x,y) \in I_t$.

Granted, in actual cases a lot depends on the exact make-up of d, h, and I, but from the present perspective the virtue of this definition is precisely that it allows for the greatest flexibility. For instance, typically one would require every functorial domain $I_{t'/t}$ to be a set of functions $f: I_{t'} \rightarrow I_t$, so that h could truly be identified with the corresponding operation of functional application (i.e., $h(x,y)$ would always yield $x(y)$). Models that satisfy such further requirements—call them *stratified models*—are nice because they give direct expression to the paradigm of functional application. But such requirements are nonetheless optional.

So, broadly speaking languages and models are *homomorphic* structures. A language is literally *mirrored* in its models.[19] And this means that the semantic bridge between languages and models—the notion of a valuation—is straightforward. For a model $M = (d, h, I)$ is always sure to provide all the information that is required in order to evaluate every expression of the corresponding language $L = (s, g, E)$: the denotation function d assigns a value to each basic expression and the structural operation h says how to compute the value of a compound expression given the values of its components. In other words, the valuation of a language L on a model M is the unique homomorphism between L and M induced by d, i.e., that function $Val: \cup E \rightarrow \cup I$ such that, in general:

(6) $Val(s_i) = d_i$.
     $Val(g(x, y)) = h(Val(x), Val(y))$.

Broadly speaking, then, it is a general semantic framework of this sort that I think should be considered when it comes to assessing the claims of Section 2. And surely enough, a framework of this sort is compatible with most natural readings of (1). If every model of a given language were admitted, that language would not have any logical terms, i.e., any terms whose meaning is kept fixed in the relevant sense, and nothing guarantees that the notion of logical validity defined in (1) be non-empty. As soon as we rule out some models, though, some expressions get a fixed interpretation and logical validities begin to accrue. The question which may lead to serious disagreement (as opposed to mere ambiguity) is precisely the question of which models should be ruled out as inadmissible. (It is understood that the selection must somehow be exhaustive. The model class defining a logic should not just consist of an arbitrary bunch of widely disparate and ill-assorted models. But this is true of all good theories. In this sense, a logic is just as good a theory as any other, albeit a very important and arguably more fundamental one.)

By way of illustration, let us see how this way of describing languages and models subsumes the familiar semantics of logic textbooks, though in a much more abstract setting. Take a typical propositional language: this can be defined as a language $L = (s, g, E)$ whose symbols are either sentence variables (of type S) or connectives (of type S/S or, more generally, $S/(S/(.../(S/S)...)))$. What exactly such symbols are, and how exactly they combine with one another by means of g to yield compound expressions, we need not specify unless we expressly wish to do so. Rather let us say what a classical model is. It is not just any model M for L. We must additionally require, first, that I_S—the domain corresponding to the category of sentences E_S—is a two-valued set, say the set $2 = \{0, 1\}$ (with 0 representing falsehood and 1 representing truth). Second, and most importantly in view of the third objection of Section 2, relative to such models we need not define the meaning of connectives *via* the recursive definition of truth. Just as connectives are characterized syntactically as symbols that combine with sentences to yield sentences, their denotations are characterized semantically as operations that combine truth-values to yield truth-values. In particular, if L includes connectives for negation '$\sim$' (of type S/S), conjunction, '$\wedge$' (of type $S/(S/S)$), etc., then M would have to satisfy the additional requirement that the denotations of these symbols combine in a way akin to the Boolean operations of complementation, meet, etc.:

(7) If $s_i = \sim$, then $d_i(x) = 1-x$ for all $x \in 2$,
    If $s_i = \wedge$, then $d_i(x)(y) = x \cap y$ for all $x, y \in 2$,

etc. (I am assuming for simplicity that M is stratified and that numbers are sets, so that $0 = \varnothing$ and $1 = \{\varnothing\}$.) It is easy to see that relative to models satisfying these specific conditions, the resulting valuation (homomorphism) would yield the usual results, i.e., the semantic conditions of classical bivalent propositional logic:

(8) $Val(\sim\phi) = 1$ iff $Val(\phi) = 0$.
    $Val(\phi \wedge \psi) = 1$ iff $Val(\phi) = Val(\psi) = 1$.

So, in particular, the notion of validity defined in (1) would yield exactly the valid arguments of classical propositional logic. From this point of view, we are just doing standard semantics. But note the level of abstraction (and the consequent degree of generality). Here not only the domain of individuals, but every domain of every category is specified by the model; not only the "extra-logical" terms but all symbols, including the connectives, are interpreted *inside the models*. And this is exactly what is needed to provide a reply to the third objection of Section 2. This is the sort of treatment that provides support to the claim that the boundary between the logical and the extra-logical is up for grabs—hence support for what I have called Tarskian Relativism—in spite of certain customary practices that suggest otherwise. We can regard any symbols of the language as logical because there is no external constraint on the interpretation of any symbol.

It should also be obvious how this picture supports relativism of the Carnapian variety, at least with reference to propositional logic. We can consider models with a different set of truth-values and corresponding conditions on the interpretation of connectives and obtain, say, Kleene's three-valued logic, or Post's, or Lukasiewicz's. In fact, by the same pattern one can give a semantic account conforming to a plurality of non-classical propositional logics: all that matters is that the desired domains of interpretation and the denotation of each connective be specified accordingly, by setting the relevant constraints on the admissible models. The general format need not change.

4. Extensions

We are not done, though. Truth-functional connectives are easy to handle. But can the picture be generalized? Can we deal with every bit of logic terminology in the same fashion?

I think we can. First of all, note that we can in a similar way account for the semantics of *intensional* languages, say languages with modalities. The semantic analysis of such languages is sometimes viewed as inducing a significant departure from that of purely extensional languages, for the meaning of a modal connective is taken to depend on factors that cannot possibly be captured by a standard model. Thus, a Kripke-style semantics for a modal language is conceptually more convoluted than pure Boolean semantics (though of course the underlying connection can be made to emerge). By contrast, in a framework like the one we are considering the treatment is perfectly uniform: to account for the relevant factors one only has to refer to the appropriate class of models, requiring for instance that the basic domains of interpretation associated with the primitive types be not just sets of flat, unanalysed entities, but sets of functions ranging over those entities and taking as arguments items from an appropriate set of intensional features. Thus, if L is a propositional language with modalities, a suitable model for L could be a model M where the domain corresponding to the category of sentences is not the set 2 of truth-values, but the set 2^W of all functions mapping some set W of "possible worlds" into 2. The interpretation of '$\sim$', '$\wedge$', and the other extensional connectives is not disturbed by this shift from truth-values to truth-valued functions, for we can require that their denotations be constant functions yielding the standard Boolean operations relative to every world in W. But the shift becomes relevant as we turn to the modal connectives, say the necessity connective '$\square$'. For the intensional character of such a connective can be accounted for precisely by requiring its denotation to be a function whose value for a given argument at a given world (relative to h) depends on the value of the argument at different worlds—a function whose value at that world is true iff its argument is true at every world. For example, assuming for simplicity that M is stratified, the relevant clauses would look like this:

(9) If $s_i = \sim$, then $d_i(x)(w) = 1 - x(w)$ for all $x \in 2^W$ and $w \in W$
   If $s_i = \wedge$, then $d_i(x)(y)(w) = x(w) \cap y(w)$ for all $x, y \in 2^W$ and $w \in W$
   If $s_i = \square$, then $d_i(x)(w) = \cap\{x(w'): w' \in W\}$ for all $x \in 2^W$ and $w \in W$

And these are clauses that result in a restriction of the class of admissible models. Models satisfying these clauses, we could say, determine the *logic* of '$\sim$', '$\wedge$', and '$\square$'.

I think at this point it should be clear how the issue of Tarskian Relativism becomes emergent. *To define a logic we need not work out a specific semantic apparatus.* We need not work out the logic before the semantics. All we need to do is to provide a category for the symbols that we want to study (eventually along with a suitable structural operation) and then specify which, among the indefinitely many structures that give a homomorphic interpretation of the language, are to count as "admissible" models. Clearly, this paves the way to Tarskian Relativism (though we could also speak of Leśniewskian Relativism, or perhaps Ajdukiewiczian Relativism, since the theory of categorial grammars that licenses this line of reasoning goes back to the work of Ajdukiewicz and Leśniewski[20]). And it paves the way to Carnapian Relativism, too. For, as we have seen, there is more than one way of selecting the models that fix the meaning of a given logical term, and each way will deliver a different logical theory.

It is still worth stressing that this perspective is supported only to the extent that the same account can be extended to a significant plurality of logics: not only propositional logics or kindred systems whose algebraic structure is easily exploited, but also systems of greater complexity. In this regard, the crucial point is that the entire framework is based on a strong principle of "functional application": For every model of any language, the value of the result of applying a functor x to an argument y is always the result of applying the value of x to the value of y. We saw that there is no other bridge between a language and its models except this simple exploitation of their structural homomorphism, and it is in this sense that no logic is imposed on the semantics *from the outside*. However, there may still be room for skepticism. The claim that no logic is imposed from the outside is unproblematic if we consider such functors as connectives or predicates. These are intrinsically applicative operators, and they lend themselves naturally to the kind of modeling illustrated above. In this regard, the standard practice of specifying the meaning of connectives through the recursive definition of truth is really just a different way of doing the same thing. But can this be generalized to all other operators as well? Is functional application combined with some type assignment all we need to set up the space of all possible interpretation structures?

One need not look far to see linguistic structures that seem to run afoul of the functor/argument scheme. A familiar example is provided by languages with variable-binding operators such as the quantifiers (either standard or generalized). Ajdukiewicz himself concluded his seminal paper on "Syntactic Connexion" with some remarks to the effect that such operators are not (and cannot be treated as) genuine functors, and consequently that languages involving them require at least an additional "circumflex" operation (essentially a form of λ-abstraction). In fact, he went as far as conjecturing that this could be the only necessary departure from the paradigm of a pure categorial grammar:

> Should … it be decided to smuggle the circumflex operator in, we would permit ourselves the suggestion that this subterfuge might well pay, for it is possible that all other operators … might be replaced by the circumflex operator and by corresponding functors.[21]

This is indeed an interesting anticipation of the ideas behind Church's λ-calculus;[22] but of course the advantage of restricting all operators to one kind does not diminish the theoretical importance of the departure from the pure functor/argument paradigm. More generally, starting from the Sixties various authors have argued that pure categorial grammars are essentially equivalent to context-free phrase-structure grammars, hence subject to the same severe limitations.[23] Others have argued that there is a strong connection between the principles of λ-abstraction and those transformation-like rules that seem so necessary to bring out the relations between different levels of linguistic analysis, e.g., between deep logical structure and surface realizations. For instance, Cresswell conjectured that all "semantically significant" transformational derivations can be seen as sequences of λ-conversions.[24] Also Montague grammars are typically seen in this light.[25] As a result, the question of whether a simple abstract model-theoretic apparatus like the one outlined above meets the requirement of generality is commonly accorded a negative answer. In particular, λ-equipped languages are seen as a necessary extension of pure categorial languages. And since such languages are commonly given a mixed Tarskian-categorial semantics (in the sense that the intended meaning of the λ-operator is fixed during a recursive definition of the value of an expression rather than specified directly by the models, in analogy to the way quantifiers are dealt with in a standard Tarskian definition of truth for first-order languages), it would seem that *some* logic must explicitly be imposed on the semantic machinery from the outside, unless we confine ourselves to very simple and expressively poor languages. Thus Tarskian Relativism would fall prey of the third objection of Section 2 after all, in spite of its apparent success in a number of special cases.

I reply that this is a hasty conclusion.[26] Syntactically, there is no real difficulty in squeezing variable-binders into the functor/argument scheme. For instance, a quantifier can be treated as a symbol of type $N/(S/S)$, i.e., as a "mixed" functor taking names and sentences into sentences. Even better, we can simply treat it as a kind of "structured" connective of type S/S, consisting of a quantifier-marker (e.g.,'∀') together with a corresponding bound variable. This is not uncommon even in standard logic textbooks.[27] We would then have, for instance, a universal quantifier '∀x', a universal quantifier '∀y', and so on, one for each variable: symbols are atomic relative to the syntactic operation g, but may still be internally structured. Let us follow this second alternative. Formally this means that an elementary language is simply a language $L = (s, g, E)$ with symbols of type $t/(t/(.../(t/t')...))$ for $t, t' \in \{S, N\}$—i.e., sentence and name symbols (of type S and N respectively), connectives (of type $S/(S/(.../(S/S)...)))$, predicates (of type $N/(N/(.../(N/S)...)))$, and so on. Where Q is any quantifier-marker, e.g., the usual sign for universal quantification ∀, we may then assume that the name symbols of L include a denumerable subset V so that the string Qv is a monadic connective for each $v \in V$, to be thought of as the Q-quantifier binding v.

So the syntax is straightforward. The difficulty is semantic, and it is conceptually tied to the above-mentioned fact that such symbols cannot be regarded as logical terms simply by keeping their denotation constant from model to model, for their intended meaning *depends* on the models' make-up. In particular, it is obvious that quantifiers cannot be reduced to operations on truth-values, like ordinary truth-functional connectives. However we need not do that. Truth-values are the extensions of sentences, if we like; but quantifiers introduce an *intensional* element—they make the value of a sentence depend on factors other than just the truth-values of its component parts. And we just saw that this type of dependence can easily be captured within a categorial framework. With a modal connective the intensional shift is from truth-values to truth-valued functions defined on possible worlds. With a quantifier the shift is due to a different combination of factors, namely the various values that can be assigned to the corresponding bound variables. But the shift is conceptually analogous. We may accordingly define a model for a language with quantifiers simply by requiring that the domains of interpretation consist of functions defined on the set of such value-assignments. More precisely, where U is any non-empty set, we obtain a model $M = (d, h, I)$ for a first-order language $L = (s, g, E)$ by setting $I_S = 2^{U^V}$ and $I_N = U^{U^V}$. Then it is easy to spell out the rest of the semantics. If M is stratified, for example, the interpretation conditions of classical logic are as follows:

(10) If $s_i \notin V$, then d_i is constant, i.e., $d_i(a) = d_i(b)$ for all $a, b \in U^V$.
  If $s_i \in V$, then d_i is i-variable, i.e., $d_i(a) = a(s_i)$ for all $a \in U^V$.
  If $s_i = \sim$, then $d_i(x)(a) = 1 - x(a)$ for all $x \in I_S$ and $a \in U^V$.
  If $s_i = \wedge$, then $d_i(x)(y)(a) = x(a) \cap y(a)$ for all $x, y \in I_S$ and $a \in U^V$.
  If $s_i = \forall v$, then $d_i(x)(a) = \cap \{x(a[^v_u]): u \in U\}$ for all $x \in I_S$ and $a \in U^V$.

(In the last clause, $a[^v_u]$ is the function that is exactly like a except that its value at v is u.[28])

Of course, if we have both quantifiers and modalities, we need both possible worlds and value-assignments. The generalization is obvious. Moreover, the same treatment can be applied to provide an account of any type of variable binding operator, including the λ-operator. Variable-binders are intensional operators, and intensional operators admit of a natural (albeit perhaps not obvious) treatment within the functor/argument scheme.[29] The details are in the appendix. So here is my conclusion. In spite of the appearances, and in spite of Ajdukiewicz's own misgivings, the basic machinery outlined above does allow us to treat the semantics of every bit of language in the same fashion, as something to be handled *within* the system of models rather than via rules *outside* it. And in this sense the third objection of Section 2 is fully discarded.

5. Generalizations

This concludes the technical point, which, together with the discussion in Section 2, should establish the claim that the distinction between logical and extra-logical terms is ultimately ungrounded, hence the claims leading to what I have called Tarskian Relativism. It also establishes the claim leading to Carnapian Relativism. For as we have seen, once the first sort of relativism is accepted, the second follows. Much of this should come as no surprise if one is already familiar with other ways of dealing with these matters in a uniform way. Algebraic models, for instance, provide an analogous way of looking at things "from above", as it were, before deciding which logic to choose. And the generalization of Boolean algebras to cylindric algebras is somewhat similar to the generalization outlined above when it comes to treating quantifiers and other variable-binders by means of pure functorial models. The approach that I have chosen is but one available option. (This is again a sign of the pluralism implicit in (1).)

One question could still be asked at this point: Is this general semantic outlook general enough to support a *fully* relativist position with regard to logic? Note that the argument given so far is not an argument to establish relativism on independent grounds. The direction of the argument is from semantics to logic, and much therefore depends on how one sees (1) to begin with—a starting point that I have not even questioned here. All the same, this general outlook immediately loads opposite views with a threat of inconsistency or circularity. In *The Concept of Logical Consequence*,[30] for instance, John Etchemendy has argued against the adequacy of a semantic account of logical properties on the grounds that such an account converts logical issues into substantive matters. For example, on a semantic account, a finitist would have to rule out models with infinite universes. Thus a finitist would be committed to the existence of some n such that the sentence "there exist fewer than n objects" is a logical truth, whereas a non-finitist would not. But a finitist and a non-finitist may well disagree on the philosophy of mathematics while perfectly agreeing on logic. *Ergo* the semantic account is inadequate.

There is no doubt that this conclusion is opposite to the one defended here. Yet the argument can be resisted. In fact, from the present perspective the argument appears to beg the question. For to assume that the discrepancy between the finitist and the non-finitist is not logical is to assume what is being contested. As Manuel García-Carpintero has observed:

> The finitist must disagree with our semantics. And it is far from clear that *this* is not a logical disagreement. When defenders of finitism actually provide an alternative semantics for quantifiers, it does involve logical disagreement.[31]

The general semantic outlook offered above does not provide a definite proof of this view. It does, however, supply the background and the formal machinery required to support it.

So much for my bias towards a semantic account. This is enough to justify a form of semantic "conventionalism" according to which the demarcation of logic is ultimately a matter of conventions, and this in turns is enough to justify both forms of Tarskian and Carnapian Relativism. However there is also a stronger form of semantic conventionalism, and consequently of logical relativism, that we can now formulate. According to this stronger form, not only are the logical *symbols* of a language on a par with the other symbols; not only are the *theses* of a logical theory on a par with the theses of any other theory; according to this form of relativism no *principle* whatsoever escapes this account, not even the principles of the metalanguage. In other words: no specific logical fact would be fulfilled by the class of all the models admitted by a given language, which means that the relativism stance would be completely free from metalogical interferences. Does our general semantic perspective support this form of relativism, too? Is semantics really logic-free, or does it still involve hidden logical assumptions?

Here I have essentially two remarks to offer. First, there is no doubt that we can still *define* semantic properties in such a way as to make them invariant across models. In fact, although the notion of validity defined in (1) depends heavily on how one draws the boundary between logical and extra-logical terms, it doesn't depend exclusively on that. There are arguments that turn out to be valid even if they do not contain any logical terms whatsoever. An obvious case in point is an argument whose conclusion is included among the premises. More generally, consider the following extension of (1), which allows for arguments with multiple conclusions:

(11) A set of sentences Γ entails a set of sentences Σ (i.e., the argument from Γ to Σ is valid) if and only if some member of Σ is true in every model in which all members of Γ are true.

Then it is easy to see that the so-called classical "structural" rules of classical logic correspond without exception to valid argument forms ('$\models$' for 'entails'):

(12) $\Sigma \models \Sigma$ (Reflexivity)
      $\Gamma \cup \{\phi\} \models \{\phi\} \cup \Sigma$ (Reiteration)
      If $\Sigma \models \Gamma$ and $\Gamma \models \Delta$ then $\Sigma \models \Delta$ (Transitivity)
      If $\Gamma \models \Sigma$ then $\Gamma \cup \{\phi\} \models \Sigma$ and $\Gamma \models \{\phi\} \cup \Sigma$ (Thinning)
      If $\Gamma \cup \{\phi\} \models \Sigma$ and $\Gamma \models \{\phi\} \cup \Sigma$ then $\Gamma \models \Sigma$ (Cut)

These argument forms are independent of the particular language at issue and they are valid irrespective of any particular stipulation concerning the class of admissible models: their validity just follows from (11). Obviously, one could revise (11) so as to get different results, but that is not the point. The point is that it is *possible* to define notions some properties of which hold regardless of which class of models we consider, including the class of all models (for a given language).

Now, this speaks against a fully relativist position. After all, *some* logic does show up in the metalanguage. On the other hand, one can easily explain this and similar facts in terms of metalinguistic conventions. The reason why the argument forms in (12) hold for any choice of models is that these argument forms reflect certain facts that we are presupposing in the very definition of logical validity. On a different interpretation of, say, the universal quantifier 'all', or of the notion of 'set' used in the definition (metalanguage), the picture might look quite different. This does not by itself justify a fully relativist position. However, it suggests that the position can be coherently maintained provided only that a relativism of the Tarskian or Carnapian sort is reiterated at each level of the metalinguistic hierarchy. (Again, I don't mean this to be just an issue of ambiguity. I mean to say that there may be genuine disagreement on the extension of such notions.)

The second remark is more critical and relates to the question of semantic generality. As I see it, there is no doubt that a full-blown relativism calls for further generalizations of the basic "metatheoretical machinery". A framework like the one outlined here embeds the requirement that every model be homomorphic to the corresponding language. This—as we saw—allows a uniform syntactic and semantic analysis. But it also reflects the assumption (typical of a Tarskian semantics) that a model must be made of well-defined, sharp-cut entities, neatly linked to one another and to the language's expressions in a univocal way. One could find this to be a serious limitation in the scope of a semantic theory. There is no *a priori* semantic reason to rule out the possibility that (our model-theoretic representation of) what we talk about may involve "gaps" and/or "gluts" of various sorts. As a matter of fact, even if we assume that the purpose of a language's expressions is to always pick out a definite semantic value, there is no a priori reason to suppose that the underlying conditions will be always *completely* fulfilled. Ordinary language sentences typically involve expressions whose intended reference is only partially defined, or vaguely defined, or not defined at all, and we may want to allow for such phenomena even in a formally reconstructed language. Conversely, even if we assume that every expression is meant to have a unique congruous semantic value, there is in fact no guarantee that the underlying conditions can be always *consistently* fulfilled. We all know, for instance, that a sentence may turn out to be self-referential in unfavourable circumstances, leading to such troubles as the liar paradox. For these reasons, a more general semantic framework, where models with interpretational gaps and/or gluts are admitted, is arguably desirable. In any case, such a generalization appears to be a necessary prerequisite from the perspective of a full-blown relativistic position, for the exclusion of incompleteness and/or inconsistency is surely a way of restricting the range of admissible models.

Without going into too many details, let me say that this question has both a positive and a negative answer. The positive answer is that the semantic framework outlined above can be generalized rather easily to cover such deviant cases. One can allow for models in which certain categories of expressions fail to be instantiated, or in which some symbols may lack a unique denotation (i.e., fail to denote or have more than one denotation), or in which the result of applying the structural operation may not always yield a definite semantic value (i.e., may be indeterminate or overdeterminate for certain arguments). Formally all of this involves allowing a model's basic components d and h to be partial relations rather than total functions, and this will introduce some complexities. Since there exists no homomorphism between a language and an incomplete model, and since there can be more than one homomorphism if the model is inconsistent, the semantic bridge between a language and its models is no longer a straightforward business. Nevertheless it can be defined, and it can be defined without renouncing to the conceptual uniformity of the initial framework. This is the positive answer.

The negative answer is that this can be done, not in one, but in several non-equivalent ways. For instance, personally I favor a supervaluationary approach.[32] Roughly, this says that the value of an expression on an incomplete and/or inconsistent model M is a function of the values that the expression takes on the complete and consistent "sharpenings" of M. Since the sharpenings are models that are homomorphic to the language, we can just apply there the straightforward algorithm in (6) and then compute the function that gives the valuation for M. The problem is that there are *many* candidate functions that could do the job, and depending on which we choose we obtain different semantics.[33] Moreover, other approaches are possible, too. For instance, there exist generalizations of Montague semantics in which the link between a language and its incomplete models is given by a sort of "paramorphic" valuation function that approximates, in some intuitive way, the behavior of the missing homomorphism.[34] The account can readily be imported from the original Montagovian framework into a purely categorial framework like the one considered here, and it can easily be extended to cover inconsistent models as well. But it is a different account from the supervaluationary one, and it yields considerably different semantics. Evidently this is in contrast with the radically relativist view: an abundance of generalizations is just as bad as a total lack, for it leaves open the question of how to account for the resulting variety of metalogical theories.

The same applies to other generalizations that could be considered, and which at this point I shall only mention. For instance, can we relax the type restrictions on the behavior of the structural relations? Can we generalize the notion of a model by admitting self-applicative domains? Can we allow for dynamic models, i.e., models where the value of an expression can change depending on whether we evaluate it before or after other expressions? All of these are questions that seem to introduce serious complications in the account favored here. The account requires a logic-free semantics, but the bounds of semantics don't seem to be arbitrary.

So here my conclusions will be cautious. Perhaps a radical model-theoretic relativism is really a hybrid, belonging to that category of philosophical positions that can only be consistently maintained *up to a certain point*. At the same time, one could regard the request for a logic-free semantics as a plea for a general semantic framework—a framework wherein each of a variety of semantic policies can be accommodated—and in this sense a radical relativism would be perfectly consistent: the same criteria would just apply to a semantic theory as they apply to a logical theory. In other words, a radically relativist position could be regarded as a form of Tarskian Relativism concerning semantics itself rather than logic, or, if you prefer, as a form of meta-relativism. One could then reiterate the account to accommodate stronger and stronger forms of relativism, corresponding to higher and higher levels of analysis. This move into the territory of metalanguage might appear suspicious and is surely debatable. Nonetheless it seems inescapable. My suspicion is that it might actually prove decisive, at least for a proper assessment of logical relativism from the semantic standpoint considered here.

Appendix [35]

Every mode of variable binding can be reduced to functional abstraction. So in the end (and in general terms) the question examined in Section 4 is whether abstraction can be interpreted as a form of application, using models whose domains of interpretation depend on a suitable package of intensional features and value-assignments.

Some forms of abstraction are immediately captured by the treatment illustrated in the main text. For instance, we can enrich an elementary language L with an abstractor λv for each variable $v \in V$, to be treated as a functor of type $S/(N/S)$. The ordinary interpretation of this functor is reflected in the reading "is something v such that". And it is easy to verify that within the proposed framework, this reading translates into the following direct condition on the admissible models for L:

(13) If $s_i = \lambda v$, then $d_i(x)(y)(a) = x(a[^v_{y(a)}])$ for all $x \in I_S$, $y \in I_N$ and $a \in U^V$.

At least, this is the appropriate condition on the assumption that all relevant models are stratified in the sense explained above, i.e., such that every functorial domain $I_{t'/t}$ is a set of functions $f: I_{t'} \to I_t$ and $h(x,y)$ always coincides with $x(y)$.

In the general case, where we have abstractors acting on variables of any type in expressions of any type, the account is not so straightforward. In fact it is clear that we cannot go very far if we stick to stratified models, for the presence of functor variables prevents us from defining adequate intensional models where each functorial domain is a set of functions of the right sort. However, we need not do that. We only need consider models whose domains are built *upon* sets of functions—and that can be done in the appropriate way to obtain the desired result. This is a rather natural generalization, familiar from intensional logics and Montague grammars. Here are the details.

To allow for generalized abstractors, we consider a full categorial language L comprising a non-empty set S_t of symbols for all $t \in T$. Each S_t includes a subset V_t of variables so that the string $\lambda v t'$ is a symbol of type $t'/(t/t')$ for all $t' \in T$ and all $v \in V_t$. Now let $\langle U_t : t \in T \rangle$ be a system of sets so that $U_S = 2$ and $U_{t'/t} = U_t^{U_{t'}}$ for all $t, t' \in T$ and define A to be the Cartesian product $\Pi \langle U_t^{V_t} : t \in T \rangle$. To obtain an adequate model M we simply require that $I_t = U_t^A$ for all $t \in T$. We can then make sure that each $\lambda v t'$ be interpreted as a v-binding abstractor by requiring M to also satisfy the following general condition:

(14) If $s_i = \lambda v t'$, then $h(h(d_i, x), y)(a) = x(a[{}^t_{a_t[{}^v_{y(a)}]}])$ for all $x \in I_{t'}$, all $y \in I_{\tau(v)}$ and all $a \in A$

where $\tau(v)$ is the type of v. Along with the obvious conditions on the interpretation of constant and variable symbols, it can be verified that this clause conforms to the usual principles of the classical λ-calculus.[36]

Notes

1. In Beall and Restall (2000).
2. In Tarski (1936).
3. In fact I do agree that identity is transitive. But there are philosophers who have denied it—e.g., Garrett (1985).
4. Quine (1970), Ch. 6.
5. See Carnap (1934).
6. Tarski (1936), pp. 418–419.
7. Ibid. p. 419.
8. On this point see Sher (1991), p. 46f.
9. See Gómez-Torrente (2002) for a critical overview of the literature.
10. Quine (1970), p. 62.
11. See Husserl (1900/01). Investigation III.
12. Lindenbaum and Tarski (1934/35).
13. Tarski (1986).
14. See Mostowski (1957) and Lindström (1966).
15. See especially Sher (1991) and (1999). Actually, Sher's account includes the invariance criterion but is not exhausted by it. This allows her to meet certain formal objections that can be advanced against the criterion, such as those put forward by McCarthy (1981).
16. Sher (1991), p. 49.
17. The point is due to Schönfinkel (1924) and reflects the set-theoretic isomorphism between $A^{B_1 \times B_2 \times \ldots B_n}$ and $(\ldots((A^{B_1})^{B_2})\ldots)^{B_n}$.
18. For example, it is understood that both s and g need be one-one to avoid ambiguities: combined with the requirement that g be well-grounded on s (i.e., that g and s have disjoint ranges), this will secure that each expression be uniquely defined as either a symbol or a compound of the form $g(x, y)$. Moreover, we may want to require that all functional expressions cancel to individual expressions (in the sense that $E_{t'/t} \neq \varnothing$ always implies that $E_{t'} \neq \varnothing$, hence $E_t \neq \varnothing$), or that g be the operation of concatenation (so that $g(x, y)$ is always the string xy). For a full treatment I refer to Varzi (1999), Ch. 1.
19. At least, things are ideally so. I shall come back shortly to the possibility that such mirroring fails to yield a full homomorphism.
20. See Leśniewski (1929) and Ajdukiewicz (1935).
21. Ajdukiewicz (1935), p. 231.
22. Church (1941).
23. Compare Bar-Hillel et al. (1960).

24. Compare Cresswell (1977), pp. 266–67.
25. See Montague (1970). Still another example is Henkin's (1975) formulation of the (simple) theory of types, which embodies abstraction and equality as the sole primitive notions.
26. The facts and arguments that follow are articulated in greater detail elsewhere. See especially Varzi (1993) and (1995).
27. See e.g. Enderton (1972).
28. It is understood that the values of functional application should not depend on value-assignments unless the arguments do, i.e., one should have $x(y)(a_i) = x(y)(a_j)$ whenever $x(a_i) = x(a_j)$ and $y(a_i) = y(a_j)$. Also, such values should behave coherently, so that $x_i(y)(a) = x_j(y)(a)$ if $x_i(a) = x_j(a)$, and $x(y_i)(a) = x(y_y)(a)$ if $y_i(a) = y_y(a)$.
29. To my knowledge, the intensional character of variable-binders was first pointed out in Lewis (1970), though the 1986 Postscript marks a change of view recommending to treat variable-binding *outside* the categorial framework, in the spirit of Cresswell (1973).
30. Etchemendy (1990).
31. García-Carpintero (1993), p. 121.
32. Along the lines of Varzi (1999).
33. I have examined some possible accounts in Varzi (1997), (2000).
34. See e.g. Muskens (1995).
35. This appendix draws on Varzi (1993), §4.
36. An old ancestor of this paper was first presented at the Symposium on *Meaning* held in Karlovy Vary, in the Czech Republic (September 9, 1993), and appears with the title "Model-Theoretic Conventionalism" in the proceedings of the symposium (James Hill and Petr Koťátko, eds.) Later versions have been presented at a *Logic Colloquium* in the Department of Philosophy of SUNY Buffalo (March 5, 1998) and at the section on "Logical Pluralism" held at the *Australasian Association of Philosophy Conference* (Hobart, Australia, July 4, 2001). I am thankful to all audiences for useful comments and discussion.

References

Ajdukiewicz, K. (1935) "Die syntaktische Konnexität", *Studia Philosophica* 1: 1–27; Eng. trans. by H. Weber: "Syntactic Connexion", in S. McCall (ed.), *Polish Logic 1920–1939*, Oxford: Clarendon Press, 1967, pp. 207–231.

Bar-Hillel, Y., Gaifman C., and Shamir E. (1960) "On Categorial and Phrase-Structure Grammars", *The Bulletin of the Research Council of Israel* 3: 1–16.

Beall, J. C., and Restall, G. (2000) "Logical Pluralism", *Australasian Journal of Philosophy* 78: 475–493.

Carnap, R. (1934) *Logische Syntax der Sprache*, Vienna, Springer-Verlag; expanded Eng. trans. as *The Logical Syntax of Language*, London: Routledge and Kegan Paul, 1937.

Church, A. (1941) *The Calculi of Lambda Conversion*, Princeton: Princeton University Press.

Cresswell, M. J. (1973) *Logics and Languages*, London: Methuen.

Cresswell, M. J. (1977) "Categorial Languages", *Studia Logica* 36: 257–269.

Enderton, H. B. (1972) *A Mathematical Introduction to Logic*, Orlando (FL): Academic Press.

Etchemendy, J. (1990) *The Concept of Logical Consequence*, Cambridge: Harvard University Press.

García-Carpintero, M. (1993) "The Grounds for the Model-Theoretic Account of the Logical Properties", *Notre Dame Journal of Formal Logic* 34: 107–131.

Garrett, B. J. (1985) "Noonan, 'Best Candidate' Theories, and the Ship of Theseus", *Analysis* 45: 12–15.

Gómez-Torrente, M. (2002) "The Problem of Logical Constants", *Bulletin of Symbolic Logic* 8: 1–37.

Henkin, L. (1975) "Identity as a Logical Primitive", *Philosophia* 5: 31–45.

Husserl, E. (1900/01) *Logische Untersuchungen. Zweiter Band. Untersuchungen zur Phänomenologie und Theorie der Erkenntnis*, Halle: Niemeyer (2nd ed. 1913); Eng. trans. by J. N. Findlay, *Logical Investigations, Volume Two*, London: Routledge & Kegan Paul, 1970.

Leśniewski, S. (1929) "Grundzüge eines neuen Systems der Grundlagen der Mathematik", *Fundamenta Mathematicae* 14: 1–81; Eng. trans. by M. P. O'Neil: "Fundamentals of a New System of the Foundations of Mathematics", in S. Leśniewski, *Collected Works* (ed. by S. J. Surma, J. T. Srzednicki, D. I. Barnett, and V. F. Rickey), Dordrecht: Kluwer Academic Publishers, 1992, Vol. 1, pp. 129–173.

Lewis, D. K. (1970) "General Semantics", *Synthese* 22: 18–67.

Lewis, D. K. (1986) "Postscript to 'General Semantics'", in D. K. Lewis, *Philosophical Papers. Volume 2*, Oxford: Oxford University Press, pp. 230–232.

Lindenbaum, A., and Tarski, A. (1934/35) "Über die Beschränktheit der Ausdrucksmittel deduktiver Theorien", *Ergebnisse eines mathematischen Kolloquiums* 7: 15–22; Eng. trans. by J. H. Woodger: "On the Limitations of the Means of Expression of Deductive Theories", in A. Tarski, *Logics, Semantics, Metamathematics, Papers from 1923 to 1938*, Oxford: Clarendon Press, 1956 (2nd edition ed. by J. Corcoran, Indianapolis: Hackett, 1983), pp. 384–392.

Lindström, P. (1966) "First Order Predicate Logic with Generalized Quantifiers", *Theoria* 32: 186–195.

McCarthy, T. (1981) "The Idea of a Logical Constant", *Journal of Philosophy* 78: 499–523.

Montague, R. (1970) "Universal Grammar", *Theoria* 36: 373–398.

Mostowski, A. (1957) "On a Generalization of Quantifiers", *Fundamenta Mathematicae* 44: 12–36.

Muskens, R. (1995) *Meaning and Partiality*, Stanford (CA): CSLI Publications.

Quine, W. V. O. (1970) *Philosophy of Logic*, Englewood Cliffs (NJ): Prentice-Hall.

Schönfinkel, M. (1924) "Über die Bausteine der mathematischen Logik", *Mathematische Annalen* 92: 305–316; Eng. trans. by S. Bauer-Mengelberg: "On the Building Blocks of Mathematical Logic", in J. van Heijenoort (ed.), *From Frege to Gödel: A Sourcebook in Mathematical Logic, 1879–1931*, Cambridge (MA): Harvard University Press, 1967, pp. 355–366.

Sher, G. (1991) *The Bounds of Logic. A Generalized Viewpoint*, Cambridge (MA): MIT Press/Bradford Books.

Sher, G. (1999) "Is Logic a Theory of the Obvious?", in A. C. Varzi (ed.), *The Scope of Logic*, Stanford (CA): CSLI Publications, pp. 207–238.

Tarski, A. (1936) "O pojciu wynikania logiczneg", *Przegląd Filozoficzny* 39: 58–68; Eng. trans. by J. H. Woodger: "On the Concept of Logical Consequence", in A. Tarski, *Logics, Semantics, Metamathematics, Papers from 1923 to 1938*, Oxford: Clarendon Press, 1956 (2nd edition ed. by J. Corcoran, Indianapolis: Hackett, 1983), pp. 409–420.

Tarski, A. (1986) "What Are Logical Notions?", text of a 1966 lecture ed. by J. Corcoran, *History and Philosophy of Logic* 7: 143–154.

Varzi, A. C. (1993) "Do We Need Functional Abstraction?", in J. Czermak (ed.), *Philosophy of Mathematics. Proceedings of the 15th International Wittgenstein Symposium, Part 1*, Vienna: Hölder-Pichler-Tempsky, pp. 407–415.

Varzi, A. C. (1995) "Variable-Binders as Functors", in J. Woleński and V. F. Sinesi (eds.), *The Heritage of Kazimierz Ajdukiewicz*, Amsterdam and Atlanta (GA): Rodopi, pp. 303–319.

Varzi, A. C. (1997) "Inconsistency Without Contradiction", *Notre Dame Journal of Formal Logic* 38: 621–639.

Varzi, A. C. (1999) *An Essay in Universal Semantics*, Dordrecht: Kluwer Academic Publishers.

Varzi, A. C. (2000) "Supervaluationism and Paraconsistency", in D. Batens, C. Mortensen, G. Priest, and J.-P. Van Bendegem (eds.), *Frontiers in Paraconsistent Logic*, Baldock: Research Studies Press, pp. 279–297.

ABSTRACT OBJECTS: A CASE STUDY

Stephen Yablo
Massachusetts Institute of Technology

1. Necessity

Not a whole lot is essential to me: my identity, my kind, my origins, consequences of these, and that is pretty much it. Of my intrinsic properties, it seems arguable that none are essential, or at least none specific enough to distinguish me from others of my kind. And, without getting into the question of whether existence is a property, it is certainly no part of my essence to exist.

I have by contrast *huge* numbers of accidental properties, both intrinsic and extrinsic. Almost any property one would ordinarily think of is a property I could have existed without.

So, if you are looking for an example of a thing whose "essence" (properties had essentially) is dwarfed by its "accense" (properties had accidentally), you couldn't do much better than me. Of course, you couldn't easily do much *worse* than me, either. Accense dwarfs essence for just about any old object you care to mention: mountain, donkey, cell phone, or what have you.

Any old *concrete* object, I mean. Abstract objects, especially *pure* abstracta like 11 and the empty set, are a different story. I do not know what the intrinsic properties of the empty set are, but odds are that they are mostly essential. Pure sets are not the kind of thing we expect to go through intrinsic change between one world and another. Likewise integers, reals, functions on these, and so on.[1]

The pattern repeats itself when we turn to relational properties. My relations to other concrete objects are almost all accidental. But the number 11's relations to other abstract objects (especially other numbers) would seem to be essential.

The most striking differences have to do with existence. Concrete objects (with the possible exception of "the world," on one construal of that phrase) are one and all contingent. But the null set and the number 11 are thought to exist in every possible world. This is *prima facie* surprising, for one normally supposes that existence is inversely related to essence: the bigger x's essence, the "harder" it is for x to exist, and so the fewer worlds it inhabits. And yet here is a class of objects extremely well endowed in the essence department, and missing from not even a single world.

You would have to be in a coma not to wonder what is going on here. Why is it that so much about abstract objects is essential to them? What is it about numbers *et al.* that makes it so hard for them not to exist? And shouldn't objects that turn up under all possible conditions have impoverished essences as a result?

It may be that I have overstated the phenomenon. Not everyone agrees that numbers even exist, so it is certainly not agreed that they exist necessarily. There would be more agreement if we changed the hypothesis to: numbers exist necessarily provided they *can* exist, that is, unless they're impossible.[2] And still more if we made it: numbers exist necessarily provided they *do* exist. But these are nuances and details. I think it is fair to say that *everyone*, even those who opt in the end for a different view, has trouble with the idea that 11 could go missing.

So our questions are in order, construed as questions about how things intuitively seem. Why should a numberless world seem impossible (allowing that the appearance may be only *prima facie*)? Why should it seem impossible for numbers to have had different intrinsic properties, or different relational properties *vis-à-vis* other abstract objects? Why should numbers seem so modally inflexible?

2. Apriority

A second *prima facie* difference between the concrete and abstract realms is epistemological. Our knowledge of concreta is aposteriori. But our knowledge of numbers, at least, has often been considered apriori. That $3+5=8$ is a fact that we *could* know on the basis of experience—of counting, say, or of being told that $3+5=8$. But the same is true of most things we know apriori. It is enough for apriority that experience does not *have* to figure in our justification. And this seems true of many arithmetical claims. One can determine that $3+5=8$ just by thinking about the matter.

Like the felt necessity of arithmetic, its felt apriority is puzzling and in need of explanation. It is a thesis of arithmetic that there are these things called numbers. And it is hard to see how one could be in a position to know apriori that things like that really existed.

It helps to remember the two main existence-proofs philosophers have attempted. The ontological argument tries to deduce God's existence from God's definition, or the concept of God. The knock against this has been the same ever since Kant; from the conditions a thing would have to satisfy to be X, nothing existential follows, unless you have reason to think that the conditions are in fact satisfied. Then there is Descartes's cogito. This could hardly be expected to give us much guidance about how to argue apriori for numbers. Also, the argument is not obviously apriori. You need to know that you think, and that knowledge seems based on your experience of self.[3]

I said that the ontological argument and the cogito were the two best-known existence-proofs in philosophy. Running close behind is Frege's attempted derivation of numbers themselves. If the Fregean line is right, then numbers are guaranteed by logic together with definitions. Shouldn't that be enough to make their existence apriori? Perhaps, if the logic involved were ontology-free. But Frege's logic affirms the existence of all kinds of higher-type objects.[4] (Frege would not have wanted to *call* them objects because they are not saturated; but there is little comfort in that.) The Fregean argument cannot defeat doubts about apriori existence, because it presupposes they *have* been defeated in presupposing the apriority of Fregean logic.

A different strategy for obtaining apriori knowledge of numbers goes via the "consistency-truth principle": in mathematics, a consistent theory is a true theory. If we can know apriori that theory T is consistent, and that the consistency-truth principle holds, we have apriori warrant for thinking T is true, its existential claims included.

There are a lot of things one could question in this strategy. Where do we get our knowledge of the consistency-truth principle? You may say that it follows from the fact that consistent theories have (intended) models, and that truth is judged relative to those models. But that argument assumes the truth of model theory. And apriori knowledge of model theory does not seem easier to get than apriori knowledge of arithmetic.

Even if we do somehow know the consistency-truth principle apriori, a problem remains. Not all consistent theories are on a par. Peano Arithmetic, one feels, is *true*, and other theories of the numbers (AP) are true only to the extent that they agree with PA. It doesn't help to say that PA is true of its portion of mathematical reality, while AP is true of its. That if anything only reinforces the problem, because it makes AP just as true in its own way as PA. It begins to look as though arithmetical truth can be apriori only if we downgrade the kind of truth involved. A statement is not true/false absolutely but only relative to a certain type of theory or model.

3. Absoluteness

I take it as a given that mathematical truth doesn't *feel* relative in this way. It feels as though 3+5 is just plain 8. It feels as though the power set of a set is just plain bigger than the set itself.

It could be argued that the notion of truth at work here is still at bottom a relativistic one: it is truth according to *standard math*, where a theory is standard if the mathematical community accepts and uses it.[5]

But truth-according-to-accepted-theories is a far cry from what we want, and act like we have. For now the question becomes, why is this theory standard and not that? The answer cannot be that the theory is *true*, in a way that logically coherent alternatives are not true, because there is no truth on this view but truth-according-to-accepted-theories; to explain acceptance in terms of acceptance-relative truth would be to explain it in terms of itself. I assume then that PA's acceptance will have to be traced to its greater utility or naturalness given our projects and cognitive dispositions. But this has problematic results. Why is it that $3+5=8$? Because we wound up *passing* on the coherent alternative theory according to which $3+5$ is not 8—and for reasons having nothing to do with truth. Neither theory is truer than the other. That, as already stated, is not at all how it feels.

Another problem is sociological. 3 plus 5 was seen to be 8 long before anyone had formulated a theory of arithmetic. How many people even today know that arithmetic is something that mathematicians have a theory of? Saul and Gloria (my non-academic parents) are not thinking that $3+5=8$ is true-relative-to-the-standard-theory, because they have no idea that such a theory exists, and if apprised of it would most likely think that the theory was standard because it was true. Are they just confused? If so, then someone should pull the scales from their eyes. Someone should make them realize that the truth about numbers and sets is (like the truth about what's polite or what's stylish) relative to an unacknowledged standard, a standard that is in relevant respects quite arbitrary. I would not want to attempt it, and not only because I don't like my parents angry at me. If they would balk at the notion that there's no more to be said for standard mathematics than for a successful code of etiquette, I suspect they're probably right.

Admittedly, there are *parts* of mathematics, especially of set theory, where a relative notion of truth seems not out of place. Perhaps the most we can say about the continuum hypothesis is that in some nice-looking models it is true, while in others it is false. I admit then that the intuition of absolute truth may not extend to all cases. But even in set theory it extends pretty far. A set theory denying, say, Infinity, or Power Set, strikes us as *wrong*, even if we have yet to put our finger on where the wrongness is coming from.

Could the explanation be as simple as this? If a model doesn't satisfy Power Set, or Infinity, then we don't see it as modeling "the sets." That Infinity holds in all models of "the sets" is a trivial consequence of that linguistic determination. It's not as if there is a shortage of models which include only *finite* set-like objects. It's just that these objects are at best the pseudo-sets, and that makes them irrelevant to the correctness of Infinity taken as a description of the sets. Infinity is "true" because models that threaten to falsify it are shown the door; they are not part of the theory's intended subject matter.

Call this the *debunking* explanation of why it seems wrong to deny the standard axioms. I do not say that the debunking explanation is out of the question; it may be that ZF serves in effect as a reference-fixer for "set." But again, that is not how it feels. If someone wants to argue that Infinity is wrong—that the hereditarily finite sets are the only ones there are—our response isn't "save your breath! deny Infinity and you're changing the subject." Our response is:

"that sounds unlikely, but let's hear the argument." No doubt we will end up thinking that the Infinity-denier is wrong. The point is that what he is wrong about is *the sets*. It *has* to be, for if he is not talking about the sets, then we are not really in disagreement.

Suppose though the debunkers are right that ZF is true because it sets the standard for what counts as a set. This still doesn't quite explain our sense that ZF is correct. Why should we be so obsessed with the *sets* as opposed to the pseudo-sets defined by theory FZ? To the extent that ZF and "sets" are a pair, curiosity about why ZF seems so right is a lot like curiosity about why the sets seem so right. It doesn't matter how the questions individuate, as long as they're both in order. And so far nothing has been said to cast doubt on this. So again, why do ZF and the sets seem so right?

4. Abstractness and Necessity

Three puzzles, then: one about necessity, one about apriority, one about absoluteness. It will be easiest to start with necessity; the other two puzzles will be brought in shortly.

The necessity puzzle has to do both with essential properties and necessary existence. About the latter it may be speculated that there is something about *abstractness* that prevents a thing from popping in and out of existence as we travel from world to world.[6] It is, as Hale and Wright put it,[7] hard to think what conditions favorable for the emergence of numbers would be, and hard to think of conditions unfavorable for their emergence. It is by contrast easy to think of conditions favorable for the emergence of Mt. McKinley. The reason, one imagines, is that numbers are abstract and Mt. McKinley is not.

But, granted that numbers do not wait for conditions to be right, how does that bear on their necessity? Explanations come to an end somewhere, and when they are gone we are left with the brute facts. Why shouldn't the existence/nonexistence of numbers be a brute fact? Traditionally existence has been the paradigm of a phenomenon not always admitting of further explanation. Granted that numbers are not contingent *on* anything, one still wants to know why they should not be contingent full stop.[8]

A second possible explanation is that it is part of the *concept* of an abstract object (a "pure" abstract object, anyway) to exist necessarily if at all. An object that appeared in this world but not others would by that alone not be abstract.

Suppose that is right; an otherwise qualified object that does not persist through all worlds does not make the cut. One might still be curious about these contingent would-be abstracta. What sort of object are we talking about here? The obvious thought is that they are *exactly like real abstracta* except in the matter of necessary existence. But the obvious thought is strange, and so let us ask explicitly: Could there be shmabstract objects that are just like their abstract cousins except in failing to persist into every world?

Fiddling with an object's persistence conditions is generally considered harmless. If I want to introduce, or call attention to, a kind of entity that is just like a person except in its transworld career—it is missing (e.g.) from worlds where the corresponding person was born in Latvia—then there would seem to be nothing to stop me. If we can have shmersons alongside persons, why not shmumbers along with numbers?

You may think that there is a principled answer to this: a principled reason why abstracta cannot be "refined" so as to exist in not quite so many worlds. If so, though, then you hold the view that we started with: there is something about *abstractness* that precludes contingency. What is it? Earlier we looked at the idea that where pure abstracta like numbers are concerned, there could be no possible basis for selection of one world over another. But why should that bother us? Why should the choice of worlds not be arbitrary, with a different number-refinement for each arbitrary choice? This is only one suggestion, of course, but as far as I am aware, the route from abstractness to necessity has never been convincingly sketched.

Suppose then that abstract objects *can* be refined. There is nothing *wrong* with shmabstract objects, on this view, it is just that they should not be confused with *abstract* objects. Another set of questions now comes to the fore. Why do we attach so much importance to a concept—abstractness—that rules out contingent existence, as opposed to another—shmabstractness—that differs from the first only in being open to contingent existence? Does the salience of numbers as against shmumbers reflect no more than a random preference for one concept over another? One would like to think that more was involved.

5. Conservativeness and Necessity

So far we have been looking at "straight" explanations of arithmetical necessity: explanations that accept the phenomenon as genuine and try to say why it arises. Attention now shifts to non-straight or "subversive" explanations. Hartry Field does not think there are any numbers. So he is certainly not going to try to *validate* our intuition of necessary existence. He might however be able to *explain the intuition away,* by reinterpreting it as an intuition not of necessity but something related. He does in fact make a suggestion along these lines. Field calls a theory *conservative* if

> it is consistent with every internally consistent theory that is 'purely about the physical world' (Field 1989, 240).

Conservative theories are theories compatible with any story that might be told about how things go physically, as long as that story is consistent in itself. (I am going to skate lightly over the controversy over how best to understand "consistent" and "compatible" here. The details are not important for what follows.)

Now, one obvious way for a mathematical theory to be conservative is for it to be *necessary*. A theory that cannot help but be true is *automatically* compatible with every internally consistent physical theory.

But, although necessity guarantees conservativeness, there can be conservativeness without it. A necessary theory demands nothing; every world has what it takes to make the theory true. A conservative theory makes no demands on the *physical* world. If the theory is false, it is false not for physical reasons but because the world fails to comply in some other way. T is conservative iff for each world in which T is false, there's another, physically just like the first, in which T is true. The theory is false then only due to the absence of non-physical objects like numbers.

You might think of the foregoing as a kind of necessity. A conservative theory T is "quasi-necessary" in the sense that *necessarily, T is satisfiable in the obtaining physical circumstances*. Here again is Field:

> mathematical realists ...have held that good mathematical theories are not only true but necessarily true; and a clear part of the content of this (the only clear part, I think) is that mathematics is conservative....Conservativeness might loosely be thought of as 'necessary truth without the truth.' ...I think that the only clear difference between a conservative theory and a necessarily true one is that the conservative theory need not be true....Perhaps many realists would be content to say that all they meant when they called mathematical claims necessarily true was that they were true and that the totality of them constituted a conservative theory (Field 1989, 242).

From this it seems a small step to the suggestion that the only distinctively *modal* intuition we have about mathematical objects is that the theory of those objects is conservative. So construed, the modal intuition is quite correct. And it is correct in a way that sits well with our feeling that existence is never "automatic"—that nothing has such a strong grip on reality as to be incapable of not showing up.

Is our intuition of the necessity of "$3+5=8$" just a (confused) intuition of quasi-necessity, that is, conservativeness?

I think it is very unlikely. Yes, every world has a physical duplicate with numbers. But one could equally go in the opposite direction: every world has a physical duplicate without them. If the permanent possibility of adding the numbers in makes for an intuition of necessity, then the permanent possibility of taking them out should make us want to call numbers impossible. And the second intuition is largely lacking. A premise that is symmetrical as regards mathematical existence cannot explain why numbers seem necessary as opposed to impossible.

A second reason why necessity is not well-modeled by conservativeness is this. Arithmetical statements strike us as *individually* necessary. We say, "this has *got* to be true," not "this considered in the context of such and such a larger theory has got to be true." But the latter is what we *should* say if our intuition is really of conservativeness. For conservativeness is a property of particular statements only seen as exemplars of a surrounding theory. A statement that is conservative in the context of one theory might change stripes in the context of another. (Imagine for instance that it is inconsistent with the other.) Nothing like that happens with necessity.

A third problem grows out of the discussion above of consistency as sufficient for truth. Suppose that two theories contradict each other. Then intuitively, they cannot both be necessary; indeed if one is necessary then the other is impossible. But theories that contradict each other *can* both be conservative.

Someone might reply that if contradictory means *syntactically* contradictory, then contradictory theories can so be necessary. All we have to do is think of them as describing different domains (different portions of the set-theoretic universe, perhaps).

That is true in a technical sense. But the phenomenon to be explained— our intuition of necessity—occurs in a context where contradictory theories are, the technical point notwithstanding experienced as incompatible. If I affirm Infinity and you deny it, we take ourselves to be disagreeing. But both of us are saying something conservative over physics.

When two statements contradict each other, they cannot both be necessarily true. Unless, of course, the truth is *relativized*: to the background theory, a certain type of model, a certain portion of mathematical reality. This takes us out of the frying pan and into another frying pan just as hot. Once we relativize, standard mathematics ceases to be *right* (full stop). And as already discussed, a lot of it *feels* right (full stop). Once again, then, our problems about apriority and necessity are pushing us toward a no less problematic relativism.

6. Figuralism

The conservativeness gambit has many virtues, not least its short way with abstract ontology. At the same time there are grounds for complaint. One would have liked an approach that made arithmetic "necessary" without making it in a correlative sense "impossible." And one would have liked an approach less friendly to relativism.

The best thing, of course, would be if we could hold onto the advantages of the Field proposal without giving up on "real" necessity, and without giving up on the intuition of absolute truth or correctness. Is this possible? I think it just may be. I can indicate the intended direction by hazarding (what may strike you as) some extremely weird analogies:

(A) *"7 is less than 11"*
"the frying pan is not as hot as the fire"
"a molehill is smaller than a mountain"
"pinpricks of conscience register less than pangs of conscience"

(B) *"7 is prime"*
"the back burner is where things are left to simmer"
"the average star has a rational number of planets"
"the real estate bug doesn't sting, it bites"

(C) *"primes over two are not even but odd"*
"butterflies in the stomach do not sit quietly but flutter about"
"pounds of flesh are not given but taken"
"the chips on people's shoulders never migrate to the knee"

(D) *"the number of Fs is large iff there are many Fs"*
"your marital status changes iff you get married or ..."
"your identity is secret iff no one knows who you are"
"your prospects improve iff it becomes likelier that you will succeed"

(E) *"the Fs outnumber the Gs iff #{x|Fx} > #{x|Gx}."*
"you are more resolute ...iff you have greater resolve"
"these are more available...iff their market penetration is greater"
"he is more audacious...iff he has more gall"

(F) *"the # of Fs =the # of Gs iff there are as many Fs as Gs"*
"your whereabouts = our whereabouts iff you are where we are"
"our greatest regret = yours iff we most regret that...and so do you"
"our level of material well-being = yours iff we are equally well off"

Here are some ways in which these statements appear to be analogous. (I will focus for the time being on necessity.)

All of the statements seem, I hope, true. But their truth does not depend on what may be going on in the realm of concrete objects and their contingent properties and relations. There is no way, we feel, that 7 could fail to be less than 11. Someone who disagrees is not understanding the sentence as we do. There is no way that molehills could fail to be smaller than mountains, even if we discover a race of mutant giant moles. Someone who thinks molehills could be bigger is confused about how these expressions work.

Second, all of the statements employ *a distinctive vocabulary*—"number," "butterflies," "{x|Fx}," "market penetration"—a vocabulary that can also be used to talk about concrete objects and their contingent properties. One says "the number of local affiliates is growing," "her marital status is constantly changing," and so on.

Third, its suitability for making contingent claims about concrete reality is the vocabulary's *reason for being.* Our interest in stomach-butterflies does not stem from curiosity about the aerodynamics of fluttering. All that matters to us is whether people *have* butterflies in the stomach on particular occasions. Our interest in 11 has less to do with its relations to 7 than with whether, say, the eggs in a carton have 11 as their number, and what that means about the carton's relation to other cartons whose eggs have a different number.

Fourth, the vocabulary's utility for this purpose *does not depend* on conceiving of its referential-looking elements as genuinely standing for anything. It doesn't depend on conceiving its referential-looking elements any other way, either. Those if any who take stomach-butterflies, greatest regrets, and numbers dead seriously derive the exact same expressive benefit from them as those who think the first group insane. And both groups derive the exact same expressive benefit as the silent majority who have never given the matter the slightest thought.

7. Necessity as Back-Propagated

I said that all of the statements strike us as necessary, but I did not offer an explanation of why. With regard to the non-mathematical statements, an explanation is quickly forthcoming.

Stomach-butterflies and the rest are *representational aids*. They are "things" that we advert to not (not at first, anyway) out of any interest in what they are like in themselves, but because of the help they give us in describing other things. Their importance lies in the way they boost the language's expressive power.

By making as if to assert that I have butterflies in my stomach, I really assert something about how I feel—something that it is difficult or inconvenient or perhaps just *boring* to put literally. The *real content* of my utterance is the real-world condition that makes it sayable that S. The real content of my utterance is that reality has feature BLAH: the feature by which it fulfills its part of the S bargain.

The reason it seems contingent that her marital status has changed is that, at the level of real content, it *is* contingent: she could have called the whole thing off. The reason it seems necessary that our prospects have improved iff it has become likelier that we will succeed is that, at the level of real content, it *is* necessary, as the two sides say the very same thing.

How does the world have to be to hold up its end of the "the number of apostles is even" bargain? How does the world have to be to make it sayable that the number of apostles is even, supposing for argument's sake that there are numbers? There have to be evenly many apostles. So, the real content of "the number of apostles is even" is that there are evenly many apostles.

That there are evenly many apostles is a hypothesis that need not have been true, and that it takes experience to confirm. At the level of real content, then, "the number of apostles is even" is epistemically and metaphysically contingent. But there might be *other* number-involving sentences whose real contents are necessary. To the extent that it is their real contents we hear these sentences as expressing, it will be natural for us to think of the sentences as necessarily true.

This explains how number-involving sentences, e.g., "the number of Fs = the number of Gs iff the Fs and Gs are equinumerous" can feel necessary, at the same time as we have trouble seeing how they *could* be necessary. Our two reactions are to different contents. The sentence feels necessary because at the level of real content it is tautologous: the Fs and Gs are equinumerous iff they are equinumerous. And tautologies really are necessary.

The reason we have trouble crediting our first response is that the sentence's literal content—that there is this object, a number, that behaves like so—is to the effect that something exists. And it is baffling how anything could cling to existence that tightly.

Why do the two contents get mooshed together in this way? A sentence's *conventional* content—what it is generally understood to say—can be hard to tell apart from its *literal* content. It takes work to remember that the literal meaning of "he's not the brightest guy in town" leaves it open that he's the second brightest. It takes work to remember that (literally) pouring your heart out to your beloved would involve considerable mess and a lengthy hospital stay, not to mention the effect on your beloved. Since there is no reason for us to do this work, it is not generally realized what the literal content in fact is.

Consider now "7 < 11." To most (!) people, most of the time, it means that seven somethings are fewer than eleven somethings. But the literal content is quite different. The literal content makes play with entities 7 and 11 that measure pluralities size-wise, and encode by their internal relations facts about supernumerosity. Of course, the plurality-measures 7 and 11 are no more on the speaker's mind than blood is on the mind of someone offering to pour their heart out. "7 < 11" is rarely used to describe numbers as such, and so one forgets that the literal content is about nothing else.

The literal contents of pure-mathematical statements are quickly recovered, once we set our minds to it. The real contents remain to be specified. I do not actually think that the real contents are always the same, so there is a considerable amount of exaggeration in what follows. But that having been said, the claim will be that arithmetic is, at the level of real content, a body of logical truths—specifically, logical truths about cardinality—while set theory consists, at the level of real content, of logical truths of a combinatorial nature.

8. Arithmetic

Numbers enable us to make claims which have as their real contents things we really believe, and would otherwise have trouble putting into words.

One can imagine introducing number-talk for this purpose in various ways, but the simplest is probably this. Imagine that we start out speaking a first-order language with variables ranging over concreta. Numerical quantifiers "$\exists_n x\ Fx$" are defined in the usual recursive way.[9] Now we adopt the following rule (*S* means that it is to be supposed or imagined that S):

(N) if $\exists_n x\ Fx$, then *there is a thing n = the number of Fs*.

Since (N)'s antecedent states the real-world condition under which we're to make as if the Fs have a number, F should be a predicate of concrete objects. But the reasons for assigning numbers to concrete pluralities apply just as much to pluralities of numbers (and pluralities of both together). So (N) needs to be strengthened to

(N) if $*\exists_n x\ Fx*$ then *there is a thing n = the number of Fs*.

This time F is a predicate of concreta and/or numbers. Because the rule works recursively in the manner of Frege, it gets us "all" the numbers even if there are only finitely many concreta. 0 is the number of non-self-identical things, and $k+1$ is the number of numbers $\leq k$.

Making as if there are numbers is a bit of a chore; why bother? Numbers are there to expedite cardinality-talk. Saying "#Fs $= 5$" instead of "$\exists_5 x\ Fx$" puts the numeral in a quantifiable position. And we know the expressive advantages that quantification brings. Suppose you want to get it across to your neighbor that there are more sheep in the field than cows. Pre-(N) this takes (or would take) an infinite disjunction: there are no cows and one sheep or there are no cows and two sheep or there is one cow and there are two sheep, and etc. Post-(N) we can say simply that the number of sheep, whatever it may be, exceeds the number of cows. The real content of "#sheep $>$ #cows" is the infinite disjunction, expressed now in finite compass.[10]

This gives a sense of the real contents of *applied* arithmetical statements are; statements of *pure* arithmetic are another matter.

Take first quantifierless addition statements. What does the concrete world have to be like for it to be the case that, assuming numbers, $3+5=8$? Assuming numbers is assuming that there is a number k numbering the Fs iff there are k Fs. But that is not all. One assumes that if no Fs are Gs, then the number of Fs and the number of Gs have a sum = the number of things that are either F or G. All of that granted, the real-world condition that makes it OK to suppose that $3+5 = 8$ is that

$$\exists_3 x\ Fx\ \&\ \exists_5 y\ Gy\ \&\ \forall x\ \neg(Fx\&\ Gx) \rightarrow \exists_8 z\ (Fz \vee Gz).$$

This is a logical truth. Consider next quantifierless multiplication statements. What does the concrete world have to be like for it to be the case that, assuming numbers, $3 \times 5 = 15$? Well, it is part of the number story that if $n =$ the number of F_1s $=$ the number of F_2s $= \ldots$ the number of F_ms, and there is no overlap between the F_is, then m and n have a product $m \times n =$ the number of things that are F_1 or F_2 or $\ldots .F_m$. With that understood, the real-world condition that entitles us to suppose that $3 \times 5 = 15$ is

$$(\exists_3 x\ F_1 x\ \&\ \ldots\&\ \exists_3 x\ F_5 x\ \&\ \neg\exists x\ (F_1 x\ \&\ F_2 x)\ \&\ldots)\rightarrow$$
$$\exists_{15} x\ (F_1 x \vee \ldots\vee F_5 x).$$

Once again, this is a logical truth. Negated addition and multiplication statements are handled similarly; the real content of $3+5 \neq 9$, for example, is that

$$\exists_3 x \ Fx \ \& \ \exists_5 y \ Gy \ \& \ \forall x \ \neg(Fx \& \ Gx) \rightarrow \neg\exists_9 z \ (Fz \lor Gz).$$

Of course, most arithmetical statements, and all of the "interesting" ones, have quantifiers. Can logically true real contents be found for them?

They can, if we help ourselves to a few assumptions. First, the real content of a universal (existential) generalization over numbers is given by the countable conjunction (disjunction) of the real contents of its instances. Second, conjunctions all of whose conjuncts are logically true are logically true. Third, disjunctions any of whose disjuncts are logically true are logically true. From these it follows that

The real content of any arithmetical truth is a logical truth.

Atomic and negated-atomic truths have already been discussed.[11] These give us all arithmetical truths (up to logical equivalence) when closed under four operations: (1) conjunctions of truths are true; (2) disjunctions with truths are true; (3) universal generalizations with only true instances are true; (4) existential generalizations with any true instances are true. It is not hard to check that each of the four operations preserves the property of being logically true at the level of real content. We can illustrate with case (4). Suppose that $\exists x \phi(x)$ has a true instance $\phi(n)$. By hypothesis of induction, $\phi(n)$ is logically true at the level of real content. But the real content of $\exists x \phi(x)$ is a disjunction with the real content of $\phi(n)$ as a disjunct. So the real content of $\exists x \phi(x)$ is logically true as well.

9. Set Theory

Sets are nice for the same reason as numbers. They make possible sentences whose real contents we believe, but would otherwise have trouble putting into words. One can imagine introducing set-talk for this purpose in various ways, but the simplest is probably this. "In the beginning" we speak a first-order language with quantifiers ranging over concreta. The quantifiers can be singular or plural; one can say "there is a rock such that it..." and also "there are some rocks such that they ...." Now we adopt the following rule:

(S) if there are some things $a, b, c...$, then *there is a set $\{a, b, c,...\}$*.

Since the antecedent here states the real-world condition under which we're to make as if $a, b, c,...$ form a set, $a, b, c,...$ are limited to concrete objects. But the reasons for collecting concreta into sets apply just as much to the abstract objects introduced via (S). So (S) is strengthened to

(S) if* there are some things $a, b, c...$*, then *there is a set $\{a, b, c,...\}$*.

This rule, like (N) in the last section, works recursively. On the first go-round we get sets of concreta. On the second go-round we get sets containing concreta and/or sets of concreta. On the third we get sets containing concreta, sets of them, and sets of *them*. And so on through all the finite ranks. Assuming that there are only finitely many concreta, our output so far is the *hereditarily finite* sets: the sets that in addition to being themselves finite have finite sets as their members, and so on until we reach the concrete objects that started us off.

What now? If we think of (S) as being applied at regular intervals, say once a minute, then it will take all of eternity to obtain the sets that are hereditarily finite. No time will be left to obtain anything else, for example, the first infinite number ω.

The answer to this is that we are not supposed to think of (S) as applied at regular intervals; we are not supposed to think of it as applied at all. (S) does not say that when we *establish* the pretense-worthiness of "there are these things," it *becomes* pretense-worthy that "they form a set." It says that if as a matter of fact (established or not) *there are these things,* then *there is the set of them.* If *there are the hereditarily finite sets*, then certainly *there are the von Neumann integers $(0 = \phi, n+1 = \{0,1,...n\})$*. And now (S) tells us that *there is the set $\{0, 1, 2, 3,...\}$,* in other words, *there is ω*. I believe (but will not try to prove) that similar reasoning shows we get all sets of rank α for each ordinal α. (S) yields in other words the full tower of sets: the full cumulative hierarchy.

Now, to say that (S) yields the full cumulative hierarchy might seem to suggest that (S) yields *a certain fixed bunch* of sets, viz. all of them. That is not the intention. There would be trouble if it were the intention, for (S) leaves no room for a totality of all sets. To see why, suppose for contradiction that *a, b, c,...* are all the sets*. (S) now tells us that *all the sets form a set V*. This set V must for familiar reasons be different from $a, b, c,...$. So the proposed totality is not all-encompassing. (I will continue to say that (S) yields the full cumulative hierarchy, on the understanding that the hierarchy is not a fixed bunch of sets, since any fixed bunch you might mention leaves something out. This does not prevent a truth-definition, and it does not prevent us from saying that some sentences are true of the hierarchy and the rest false.[12])

Conjuring up all these sets is a chore; why bother? The reason for bothering with numbers had to do with *cardinality*-type logical truths. Some of these truths are infinitely complicated, but with numbers you can formulate them in a single finite sentence. Something like that is the rationale for sets as well. The difference is that sets help us to deal with *combinatorial* logical truths— truths about what you get when you combine objects in various ways.

An example will give the flavor. It is a theorem of set theory that if $x = y$, then $\{x,u\} = \{y,v\}$ iff $u=v$. What combinatorial fact if any does this theorem encode? Start with "$\{x,u\} = \{y,v\}$." Its real content is that they$_{xu}$ are them$_{yv}$ —or, to dispense with the plurals, that $(x=y$ or $x=v)$ & $(u=y$ or $u=v)$ & $(y=x$ or $y=v)$ & $(v=x$ or $v=u)$. Thus what our theorem is really saying is that

If $x = y$, then

$$([(x=y \lor x=v) \land (u=y \lor u=v) \land (y=x \lor y=v) \land (v=x \lor v=u)] \text{ iff } u=v).$$

This is pretty simple as logical truths go. Even so it is not really comprehensible; I at least would have trouble explaining what it says. If truths as simple as this induce combinatorial bogglement, it should not be surprising that the set-theoretic formulations are found useful and eventually indispensable.

A second example is Cantor's Theorem. What is the logical truth here? One can express *parts* of it using the plural quantifier $\exists X$ ("There are some things such that..."). Numerical *plural* quantifiers are defined using the standard recursive trick:

$$\exists_0 X \; \phi(X) \text{ iff } \forall X \neg \phi(X)$$
$$\exists_{n+1} X \; \phi(X) \text{ iff } \exists Y \; (\phi(Y) \; \& \; \exists_n X \; (\phi(X) \; \& \; \neg X=Y))$$

Consider now $\exists_4 X \; \forall y \; (Xy \rightarrow Fy)$. I can't give this a *very* natural paraphrase, because English does not quantify over pluralities of pluralities. But roughly the claim is that there are four ways of making a selection from the Fs.[13] This lets us express part of what Cantor's Theorem is "really saying", viz. that if there are n Fs, then there are 2^n ways of selecting just some of the Fs, as follows:

$$\exists_n x \; Fx \rightarrow \exists_{2^n} X \; \forall y \; (Xy \rightarrow Fy).$$

This is a second-order logical truth, albeit a different such truth for each value of n. But we are still a long way from capturing the Theorem's real content, because it applies to infinite pluralities as well. There is (as far as I know) no way with the given resources to handle the infinite case.[14] It all becomes rather easy, though, if we are allowed to encode the content with sets. All we need say is that every set, finite or infinite, has more *subsets* than it has *members*. ($|P(X)| = 2^{|X|} > |X|$.)

Now let me try to give a general recipe for finding real contents. It will be simplest if we limit ourselves to talk of hereditarily finite sets; the procedure I think generalizes but that remains to be checked. Take first atomic sentences, that is, sentences of the form $x=y$ and $x \in z$. A reduction function **r** is defined:

(A_1) **r**$(x \in z)$ is

1. $\exists y \; ((\lor_{u \in z} \; y = u) \; \& \; x = y)$	if z has members
2. $\exists y \; (y \neq y \; \& \; x = y)$	if z is the empty set
3. $x \in z$	if z is not a set.[15]

Note that the first line simplifies to $\lor_{y \in z} \; x=y$; that is in practice what I will take the translation to be. (The reason for the quantified version is that it extends better to the case where z is the empty set.) The third line marks the one place where $\in$ is not eliminated. If z is not a set, then it is (literally) false to say that x belongs to it, which is the result we want. The rule for identity-statements is

(A$_2$) $\mathbf{r}(x=y)$ is

      1. $\forall u \ (u \in x \leftrightarrow u \in y)$ if x and y are sets
      2. $x=y$ if either is not a set.

In the "usual" case, x and y have members, and $\forall u \ (u \in x \leftrightarrow u \in y)$ reduces to $(\wedge_{u \in x} \vee_{v \in y} u = v) \wedge (\wedge_{v \in y} \vee_{u \in x} v = u)$. If x has members and y is the null set, it reduces to $\forall u \ (\vee_{z \in x} u = z \leftrightarrow u \neq u)$. If both x and y are the null set, we get $\forall u$ $(u \neq u \leftrightarrow u \neq u)$. Otherwise $\mathbf{r}$ leaves $x=y$ untouched. Non-atomic statements reduce to truth-functional combinations of atomic ones by the following rules:

(R$_1$) $\mathbf{r}(\neg \ \phi)$ is $\neg \ \mathbf{r}(\phi)$

(R$_2$) $\mathbf{r}(\wedge_i \ \phi_i)$ is $\wedge_i \ \mathbf{r}(\phi_i)$

(R$_3$) $\mathbf{r}(\vee_i \ \phi_i)$ is $\vee_i \ \mathbf{r}(\phi_i)$

(R$_4$) $\mathbf{r}(\forall x \ \phi(x))$ is $\wedge_{z=z} \ \mathbf{r}(\phi(z))$.

(R$_5$) $\mathbf{r}(\exists x \ \phi(x))$ is $\vee_{z=z} \ \mathbf{r}(\phi(z))$.

The real content of ϕ is found by repeatedly applying $\mathbf{r}$ until you reach a fixed point, that is, a statement ϕ^* such that $\mathbf{r}(\phi^*) = \phi^*$. This fixed point is a truth-functional combination of "ordinary" statements true or false for concrete (non-mathematical) reasons. These ordinary statements are to the effect that $x = y$, where x and y are concrete, or $x = y$, where one is concrete and the other is not, or $x \in z$, where z is concrete.[16]

How do we know that a fixed point will be reached? If ϕ is a generalization, the (R$_i$)s turn it into a truth-functional combination of atoms ψ. If ψ is an atom talking about sets, then the (A$_i$)s turn it into a generalization about sets of a lower rank, and/or non-sets. Now we apply the (R$_i$)s again. Given that ϕ contains only finitely many quantifiers, and all the sets are of finite rank, the process must eventually bottom out.[17] The question is how it bottoms out, that is, the character of the sentence ϕ^* that gives ϕ's real content.

I claim that if ϕ is a set-theoretic truth, then ϕ^* is, not quite a logical *truth*, but a logical *consequence* of basic facts about concreta: identity- and distinctness-facts, and facts to the effect that concreta have no members. To have a word for these logical consequences, let's call them *logically true over concrete combinatorics*, or for short *logically true$_{cc}$*. Three assumptions will be needed, analogous to the ones made above for arithmetic. First, the real content of a universal (existential) generalization is given by the countable conjunction (disjunction) of its instances. Second, conjunctions all of whose conjuncts are logically true$_{cc}$ are themselves logically true$_{cc}$. Third, disjunctions any of whose disjuncts are logically true$_{cc}$ are logically true$_{cc}$.

Every set-theoretic truth has a logically true$_{cc}$ real content.

The set-theoretic truths (recall that we are limiting ourselves to hereditarily finite sets) are the closure of the atomic and negated-atomic truths under four rules: (1) conjunctions of truths are true; (2) disjunctions with truths are true; (3) universal generalizations with only true instances are true; (4) existential generalizations with any true instances are true. The hard part is to show that atomic and negated-atomic truths are logically true$_{cc}$ at the level of real content. The proof is by induction on the ranks of x and y.

Basis Step

(a) If x and y are concrete, then the real content of $x = y$ is that $x = y$. This is logically true$_{cc}$ if true, because it's a consequence of itself. Its negation is logically true$_{cc}$ if true for the same reason.

(b) If x is concrete and y is a set, then $x \neq y$ is true. Its real content $x \neq y$ is logically true$_{cc}$, because a consequence of the fact that $x \neq y$.

(c) If x and y are the null set, then $x = y$ is true. Its real content $\forall u \, (u \neq u \leftrightarrow u \neq u)$ is a logical truth, hence logically true$_{cc}$.

(d) If x is a non-empty set and y is the null set, then $x \neq y$ is true. Its real content $\neg \forall u \, (\vee_{z \in x} u = z \leftrightarrow u \neq u)$ is logically true, hence logically true$_{cc}$.

(e) If y is a non-set then $x \notin y$ is true. Its real content $x \notin y$ is logically true$_{cc}$ because a consequence of itself.

(f) If y is the null set then $x \notin y$ is true. Its real content $\neg \exists z \, (z \neq z \, \& \, x = z)$ is logically true$_{cc}$ because logically true.

Recursion Step

(a) If and y are nonempty sets, then $\mathbf{r}(x = y)$ is $(\wedge_{u \in x} \vee_{v \in y} u = v) \wedge (\wedge_{v \in y} \vee_{u \in x} v = u)$. (a1) If it is true that $x = y$, then $\mathbf{r}(x = y)$ is a conjunction of disjunctions, each of which has a true disjunct $u = v$. By hypothesis of induction, these true disjuncts have logically true$_{cc}$ real contents. So $\mathbf{r}(x = y)$ has a logically true$_{cc}$ real content. And the real content of $\mathbf{r}(x = y)$ is also that of $x = y$. (a2) If it is true that $x \neq y$, then $\mathbf{r}(x \neq y)$ is a disjunction of conjunctions, each of which is built out of true conjuncts. By hypothesis of induction, these true conjuncts are logically true$_{cc}$ at the level of real content. So $\mathbf{r}(x \neq y)$ has a logically true$_{cc}$ real content. And the real content of $\mathbf{r}(x \neq y)$ is also that of $x \neq y$.

(b) If z is a nonempty set, then $\mathbf{r}(x \in z)$ is $\vee_{y \in z} x = y$. (b1) If it is true that $x \in z$, this has a true disjunct $x = y$. By hypothesis of induction, $x = y$ has a logically true$_{cc}$ real content. But then $\mathbf{r}(x \in z)$ is logically true$_{cc}$ at the level of real content, whence so is $x \in z$. (b2) If the truth is rather that $x \notin z$, then $\mathbf{r}(x \notin z)$ is a conjunction of true conjuncts. By hypothesis of induction, these conjuncts are logically true$_{cc}$ at the level of real content. So $\mathbf{r}(x \notin y)$ has a logically true$_{cc}$ real content, whence so also does $x \notin y$.

10. Summing Up

The view that is emerging takes something from Frege and something from Kant; one might call it "Kantian logicism." The view is Kantian because it sees mathematics as arising out of our representations. Numbers and sets are "there" because they are inscribed on the spectacles through which we see other things. It is logicist because the facts that we see through our numerical spectacles are facts of first-order logic.

And yet the view is in another way the opposite of Kantian. For Kant thinks necessity is imposed *by* our representations, and I am saying that necessity is imposed *on* our representations by the logical truths they encode. Another possible name then is "*anti*-Kantian logicism." I will stick with the original name, comforting myself with the notion that the "anti" in "Kantian" can be thought of as springing into semantic action when the occasion demands.

Back now to our three questions. Why does mathematics seem (metaphysically) necessary, and apriori, and absolute? The first and second of these we have answered, at least for the case of arithmetic and set theory. It seems necessary because the real contents of mathematical statements are logical truths. And logical truths really are necessary. It seems apriori because the real contents of mathematical statements are logical truths. And logical truths really are apriori.

That leaves absoluteness. It might seem enough to cite the absoluteness of logical truth; real contents are not logically true relative to this system or that, they are logically true period.

But there is an aspect of the absoluteness question that this fails to address. The absoluteness of logic does perhaps explain why individual arithmetical statements seem in a non-relative sense correct. It does not explain why Peano Arithmetic strikes us as superior to arithmetical theories that contradict it. It does not tell us why the Zermelo-Fraenkel theory of sets strikes us as superior to set theories that contradict it. For it could be that PA is not the only arithmetical theory—ZF is not the only set theory—with the property that its real content is logically true. AP and FZ could be (at the level of real content) just as logically true as PA and ZF. Let me say something about the ZF side of this problem.

If FZ has a logically true real content, it is *not* the content induced by the game sketched above: the game based on principle (S). (Remember, FZ proves some A such that ZF proves ¬A. Unless something has gone very wrong, A and ¬A will not come out assertible in the same game.) FZ can be "correct" only if real contents are judged relative to a *different* principle than

> if it is to be imagined that there are some things x, y, z,...., then it is to be imagined that there is a set of those things.

This gives us a way out of our difficulties. I said early on that you cannot accuse someone of changing the subject just because they deny some principle of ZF. *But principle (S) is a great deal more basic than anything found in ZF.* If someone has trouble with the idea behind (S)—the idea that when you have got a determinate bunch of things, you are entitled to the *set* of those things—then that person arguably *doesn't* mean the same thing by "set" as we do.[18]

Suppose we call a theory "ZF-like" if it represents the sets as forming a cumulative hierarchy. Then here is an argument that only ZF-like theories get the sets right. If FZ is not ZF-like, then by definition it does not represent sets as forming a cumulative hierarchy. But the cumulative hierarchy comes straight out of (S), the rule that says that if you've got the objects, you've got the set of them as well. So, whatever it is that FZ describes, it is not a system of entities emerging (S)-style out of their members. Emerging (S)-style out of your members is definitive, though, of the sets as we understand them. FZ may well get something right, but that something is not the sets.[19]

Notes

1. Although on the Frege-Russell definition of number, there is, arguably, intrinsic change. The empty set can change too, if as Lewis suggests it is definable as the sum of all concreta. But I am talking about what we *intuitively* expect, and no one would call these definitions intuitive.
2. Wright & Hale suggest in "Nominalism and the Contingency of Abstract Objects" that Field might not accept even that much. Field *does* say that numbers are conceptually contingent. But it would be hard to pin a metaphysical contingency thesis on him, for two reasons. (1) He is on record as having not much use for the notion of metaphysical necessity. (2) To the extent that he tolerates it, he understands it as conceptual entailment by contextually salient metaphysical truths. If salient truths include the fact that *everything is concrete*, then (assuming they are not concrete) numbers will come out metaphysically impossible.
3. Burge (2000) takes a different view (p. 28).
4. See Rayo and Yablo (2000) for an interpretation that (supposedly) frees the logic of these commitments.
5. See Balaguer (2001) for discussion.
6. Impure abstracta like singleton-Socrates are not thought to be necessarily existent. So really I should be talking about pure-abstractness. I'll stick to "abstract" and leave the qualification to be understood. (Thanks here to Marian David.)

7. Hale and Wright (1996).

8. Hale and Wright expect this objection, but think it can be met.

9. $\exists_0 x\ Fx =_{df} \forall x(Fx \rightarrow x \neq x)$, and $\exists_{n+1} x\ Fx =_{df} \exists y(Fy\ \&\ \exists_n x(Fx\ \&\ x \neq y))$

10. There is an analogy here with Hartry Field's views on "the reason" for having a truth-predicate, in the absence of any corresponding property.

11. Mario Gomez-Torrente pointed out that some atomic truths have not been fitted out with real contents, a fortiori not with logically true real contents. An example is $(3+2)+1 = 6$. This had me worried, until he pointed that these overlooked atomic truths were logically equivalent to non-atomic truths that hadn't been overlooked. For instance, $(3+2)+1 = 6$ is equivalent to $\exists y((3+2 = y)\ \&\ (y+1 = 6))$. A quick and dirty fix is to think of overlooked sentences as inheriting real content from their not overlooked logical equivalents. A cleaner fix would be desirable, but Mario hasn't provided one yet.

12. See the last few pages of Putnam (1967) and "Putnam Semantics" in Hellman (1989).

13. Alternatively, there are some things all of which are Fs, and some things not the same as the first things all of which are Fs, and etc. (Say there are two Fs. You can pick both of them, either taken alone, or neither of them. Note that "all the Fs" and "none of them" are treated here as limiting cases of "some of the Fs.")

14. You could do it with plural quantification over ordered pairs.

15. The idea is that '$x \in z$' describes x as one of the things satisfying the condition of membership in z. The condition for membership in $\{a, b, c,...\}$ is $x=a \vee x=b \vee x=c \vee ...$The condition for membership in the null set is $x \neq x$.

16. Statements of the first type are necessarily true or necessarily false, depending on whether x is indeed identical to y. Statements of the second and third types are necessarily false, since concreta cannot be sets or have members.

17. The same argument would seem to work with sets of infinite rank; there are no infinite descending chains starting from infinite ordinals either.

18. This might sound funny, given the widespread view that there are *some* things (the sets) that are too many to form a set. This widespread view is at odds with (**S**) only if it is supposed that there is some definite bunch of things including all and only the sets. If the sets are a definite bunch of things, it is very hard to understand what could be wrong with gathering them together into a further set. I agree with Putnam when he says that "no concrete model [of Zermelo set theory] could be maximal— nor any *non*concrete model either, as far as that goes. Even God could not make a model for Zermelo set theory that it would be *mathematically* impossible to extend, and no matter what 'stuff' He might use. ...it is not necessary to think of sets as one system of objects...in order to follow assertions about all sets" (1967, 21).

19. I am grateful to a number of people for criticism and advice; thanks above all to Gideon Rosen, Kit Fine, Gilbert Harman, Mario Gomez-Torrente, Marian David, Ted Sider, Paul Horwich, and Stephen Schiffer.

References

Balaguer, Mark. (1996) "A Fictionalist Account of the Indispensable Applications of Mathematics," *Philosophical Studies* 83: 291–314.

Balaguer, Mark. (2001) "A Theory of Mathematical Correctness and Mathematical Truth," *Pacific Philosophical Quarterly* 82: 87–114.

Burge, Tyler. (2000) "Frege on Apriority," in Paul Boghossian & Christopher Peacocke (eds.), *New Essays on the Apriori* (Oxford: Oxford University Press).

Burgess, John & Gideon Rosen. (1997) *A Subject with No Object* (Oxford: Clarendon).

Field, Hartry. (1980) *Science without Numbers* (Princeton: Princeton University Press).

Field, Hartry. (1989) *Realism, Mathematics, & Modality* (Oxford: Basil Blackwell).

Hale, Bob & Crispin Wright. (1996) "Nominalism and the Contingency of Abstract Objects," in M. Schirn (ed.), *Frege: Importance and Legacy* (de-Gruyter: Hawthorne).

Hellman, Geoffrey. (1989) *Mathematics without Numbers* (Oxford: Clarendon).

Putnam, Hilary. (1967) "Mathematics without Foundations," *The Journal of Philosophy* 64: 5–22.

Rayo, Agustin and Stephen Yablo. (2001) "Nominalism Through De-Nominalization," *Noûs* 35: 74–92.

Walton, Ken. (1993) "Metaphor and Prop Oriented Make-Believe," *European Journal of Philosophy* 1: 39–57.

Yablo, Stephen. (1996) "How in the World?" *Philosophical Topics* 24: 255–286.

Yablo, Stephen. (1998) "Does Ontology Rest on a Mistake?" *Proceedings of the Aristotelian Society*, supp. vol. 72: 229–262.

Yablo, Stephen. (2000) "Apriority and Existence," in Paul Boghossian & Christopher Peacocke (eds.), *New Essays on the Apriori* (Oxford: Oxford University Press).

Yablo, Stephen. (forthcoming) "Go Figure: A Path Through Fictionalism," *Midwest Studies in Philosophy*.

META-ETHICS AND NORMATIVE COMMITMENT

James Dreier
Brown University

Introduction

The inspiration for this paper is an article of Ronald Dworkin's: "Objectivity and Truth: You'd Better Believe It".[1] I will not dwell on the details of Dworkin's paper, but let me set out the issue broached there that I want to explore.

Dworkin's paper argues against what he calls an 'Archimedean' position about ethics, one which seeks a point outside ethics proper to pass external judgments on the status of ethical propositions, saying that they are not objective, or not really true, or the like, while avoiding taking a normative position of its own. Attempts to establish Archimedean positions are quite well known. For instance, Emotivism seeks such a position, and John Mackie's Error Theory, and various forms of Subjectivism. The point is that these are not theories of what to do at all. They are supposed to be theories of the nature of moral advice, what sort of a thing it is. And they all claim that it lacks a certain preferred status: it is not the sort of thing that can be objectively correct.

One of Dworkin's main strategies is to try to draw the Archimedean into making recognizably *ethical* judgments. For instance, if the Archimedean says that the judgment, that slavery is unjust, is not true, then Dworkin takes this to be a (very implausible) moral judgment, namely, the judgment that there is nothing unjust about slavery. Fair enough (I think). But Dworkin makes a sweeping claim. He says that there is no Archimedean position at all. There is no way to have a purely meta-ethical theory, one without any substantive normative implications.

Earlier in this century just about all of the better known meta-ethical theories were supposed to be 'pure' meta-ethical theories, carrying no normative moral implications. Besides the Archimedean theories (or, if Dworkin is right, the *would-be* Archimedean theories) I mentioned, there was also Moore's theory. Moore did, of course, include a lot of substantive normative ethics in *Principia Ethica*, but the meta-ethical theory there seems to be independent of any particular moral view. One could agree with Moore that goodness is a *sui generis*, simple, non-natural property, without agreeing with his broadly eudaimonistic consequentialism. Moore's theory was not Archimedean, in Dworkin's sense, since it in no way attempted to cast any doubt on the objectivity or reality of moral properties, but it was still 'pure'.

But nowadays one hears more and more doubts that there is such a bright line between meta-ethics and normative ethics, doubts that there are or could be any pure meta-ethical theories. In this paper I will investigate these doubts. I think they are ill-founded. I think there are meta-ethical theories that carry no normative moral commitments whatsoever.

Dworkin's paper considers explicitly a couple of the theories I think really are Archimedean. One of these theories (really a family of theories) is Expressivism. Dworkin argues that Expressivist theories, including Simon Blackburn's Quasi-realism and Allan Gibbard's Norm Expressivism, are failures as Archimedean theories. I will not pursue that particular matter.[2] The other family of theories sometimes goes by the name of Secondary Quality theory, and the particular version that seems to me most clearly Archimedean is one that says that a thing is morally wrong if and only if it tends to cause in us *as we actually are* a feeling of moral disapproval. Dworkin insists that this theory is not Archimedean at all. I will explain briefly what is in dispute. The bulk of my paper is devoted to developing enough theoretic understanding of the idea of a theory's carrying moral commitment to be able to address the dispute in a rigorous way, and I will return to this special form of Secondary Quality theory at the end of the paper.

Dworkin considers a Secondary Quality theory according to which moral wrongness is a disposition to 'outrage' normal observers. He writes,

> But someone who holds that moral properties are secondary properties does take sides in actual or potential substantive disputes. Suppose we discovered that, contrary to our expectations, contemplating genocide does not in fact outrage even most normal people. Genocide would not then be morally wrong on that dispositional account, though, of course, many people would think it was. [101]

It is not entirely clear which of two points Dworkin is making here. He might be suggesting that for all we know, most people are not outraged by the idea of genocide, so that the Secondary Quality theory entails that genocide is not *in fact* morally wrong. It is not easy to see what significance this suggestion has, since it is extremely implausible. Or he might be asking us to consider a mere possibility, a possible world in which most people would not be revolted by genocide. Then the point would be that the Secondary Quality theory has very implausible consequences, consequences that are themselves counterfactuals. The counterfactual consequence in point would be this one:

(1) If most normal people were not outraged by genocide, then genocide would not be morally wrong.

This counterfactual is not true. Since one version of the Secondary Quality theory entails it, that version cannot be true. I think this is a good argument against the version of the Secondary Quality theory in question.

However, there is another version that does better. It is the theory that identifies moral wrongness with the disposition, not to outrage whichever people happen to exist, but to outrage *us actual moralizers*, to outrage us as we actually are.[3] This version, which ties moral wrongness to our *actual* dispositions, is more plausible than the simpler version. When we consider a merely possible situation, asking whether genocide would be morally wrong in that situation, this 'actualized' Secondary Quality theory tells us to consider whether we ourselves, as we actually are, feel outrage at the genocidal acts, the merely possible ones. And of course we do, we find genocide morally horrible.

But Dworkin does consider this 'fix', and he rejects it. Here is what he says:

> The dispositional account might, it is true, take a different form. It might hold, for example, that what makes genocide wrong is the reaction, not of whichever kind of people happen to exist from time to time, but of us, that is, of people with the physiological structure, basic interests, and general mental dispositions that people actually have now. In that case, it would no longer follow that genocide would cease being wicked if human beings developed very different general interests or different neural wiring. But some plainly substantive and controversial claims would still follow: for instance, that genocide would not have been wicked if economic or other circumstances had been different as human reactions evolved, so that creatures with our general interests and attitudes had not been revolted by genocide. [102]

I find it difficult to interpret this objection. After all, 'creatures with our general interests and attitudes' would indeed be revolted by genocide, since revulsion at genocide *is* one of our general interests and attitudes. Creatures who shared many of our interests and attitudes but were not revolted by genocide would simply not be relevant, according to the 'actualized' Secondary Quality theory, to the determination of moral wrongness. So there is a dispute here, but it is hard to know what further can be said. At the most general level, it is a dispute over whether meta-ethical theories, and in particular Secondary Quality theories, carry normative moral implications. I would like to be able to resolve the dispute, but there is an obstacle. It is not easy to say what it is for a theory to carry normative moral implications. One difficulty is in saying which implications are normative moral implications, but this difficulty is not grave for our purposes, I think. More problematic is to explain the relevant notion of a commitment. One simple explication says that something carries normative commitments just in case its logical implications include some normative statements. But this turns out to be a useless explication. In the first section I will explain why it is useless. In the second and third sections I will suggest an alternative. Then I will examine one kind of theory that I will claim to be Archimedean, and finally I will return to Dworkin's claims.

I. Why the Normative Commitments of a Theory are Not Just Its Normative Implications

A. *Hume's Law*

To explain what a normative commitment is, what it means for a (meta-ethical) theory to carry normative commitments, we have to explain both what it is for something to be normative and what it is for a theory to carry something as a commitment. We could kill both birds with one stone if only we could rely on Hume's Law:[4]

(H) There is no logically valid argument with only non-moral premises and a normative moral conclusion.

If we could rely on Hume's Law, then we could suppose that a commitment of a theory was anything it logically entailed. And since we can identify with confidence at least certain normative statements, we could test others for normativity by checking to see whether they entailed any of the paradigmatically normative statements. If a meta-ethical theory turned out to logically entail a normative statement, then the theory itself would be a normative moral statement, by Hume's Law. Do we need to worry about what exactly a 'normative moral statement' is? Here we are interested in normative moral commitments, and there are plenty of paradigms. Rather than providing a list, I'll assume that basic, paradigmatically moral statements are predications of moral predicates, especially 'wrong', 'right', 'morally permissible', 'evil', 'good'. As long as we can rely on Hume's Law, we can check other statements for normative moral status by seeing whether they can be used as premises in arguments (all of whose other premises are clearly descriptive) with paradigmatically moral conclusions.

If we are going to answer the question about meta-ethical theories in a fully rigorous way, we need to characterize meta-ethical theories rigorously. I doubt that the common philosophical understanding of meta-ethical theory is capable of sharp definition, though, so I will focus on a certain central core of meta-ethical theories, which I will call 'Standard'. A Standard meta-ethical theory is an instance of the schema

(Standard)$\Box$ (x) $(Mx \leftrightarrow Dx)$

where 'Mx' stands in for a "moral formula" and 'Dx' for a "descriptive formula". By a "moral formula" I mean one whose instantiations with ordinary names (or other singular terms) are moral sentences. A descriptive formula is one that is not moral; typically a Standard theory will have a clearly descriptive, clearly non-moral component for 'Dx'.

For example, here is familiar sort of contractualism expressed in Standard form:

(Contract)□ (x) $(x$ is wrong $\leftrightarrow x$ would be disallowed by any set of rules which could be agreed to by all members of society)

Any instance of (Standard) logically implies some very good candidates for normative moral statements. For each instance implies an instance of

$$D \rightarrow M$$

I'll call such instances, $D \rightarrow M$ *conditionals*. These are typically very good candidates for normative moral statements just on intuitive grounds. For instance, consider

(2) If Peter eats meat, then he is morally reprehensible.

Hume's Law gives us another excellent reason to think of $D \rightarrow M$ conditionals as invariably normative moral statements, since together with a descriptive premise (D) they always entail a moral conclusion (M). Indeed, one might even say that this is the whole point and function of a $D \rightarrow M$ conditional: it is an inference ticket granting its bearer passage from a descriptive premise to a normative moral conclusion.

So if we could rely on Hume's Law, we would have a quick and satisfying argument to the conclusion that all Standard Theories carry normative commitments. Unfortunately, we cannot rely on Hume's Law.

B. Hume's Law Refuted

The following alarmingly simple refutation of Hume's Law is due to A. N. Prior (Prior 1960).

Let us suppose, as seems safe, that the negation of a non-moral proposition is itself non-moral.[5] At the very least, it seems reasonable to suppose that if a sentence contains no moral vocabulary at all, then it is non-moral. In the demonstration below, we may assume that D, a non-moral proposition, is chosen so as to contain no moral vocabulary; so neither does its negation; so its negation is also non-moral.

We show that Hume's Law is false by Cases.

Take some moral proposition, M, and some non-moral one, D. Consider their disjunction, $D \vee M$. Is it moral, or non-moral?

(i) Suppose it is moral. But it is logically entailed by D. So Hume's Law is false.

(ii) Suppose it is non-moral. But together with $\neg D$, it entails M. So Hume's Law is false.

We cannot rely on Hume's Law. So we cannot use it to decide whether a given complex statement is a normative moral statement, and in particular we cannot use it to decide whether a $D \rightarrow M$ conditional is a normative moral statement. We need another approach.

C. Hume's Kernel Salvaged?

We could try a conservative revision, fixing up Hume's Law to save the kernel of truth while avoiding Prior's refutation. One such revision is due to Toomas Karmo (Karmo 1988). Karmo suggests that we classify a sentence as moral ('ethical', he says) *at a possible world, w*, if and only if it is true at w according to one moral standard, and false at w according to another. For the notion of a 'moral standard', we consider the class of *uncontroversially moral sentences*. And for our purposes, this could just be the class of atomic sentences that are predications of moral predicates. (The characterization of moral predicates we leave open. While there are controversial examples, we will be concerned only with the uncontroversial ones, like 'is wrong', 'is morally good'.) A moral standard, then, is (or more intuitively, is determined by and determines) a consistent assignment of truth-values to uncontroversially moral sentences.

With Karmo, we classify sentences as moral only *at a world*. An example explains why.

Consider

(3) Benito is evil or New Zealand is a Communist Republic.

In our world, this sentence counts as moral, because it is true according to any moral standard that assigns the value True to "Benito is evil" and false according to any other moral standard. But in a possible world in which New Zealand is a Communist Republic, (3) is not moral, because it is true according to any moral standard. Intuitively, Karmo's scheme says that a proposition is non-moral (at a world) if and only if you can tell whether it is true (at that world) without any moral investigation.

A counterintuitive feature of Karmo's taxonomy is that it fails to close the class of moral sentences under converse entailment (and fails to close the class of non-moral statements under entailment). That is, it may happen that although a sentence is moral, it is entailed by a sentence which is not moral. How this can happen should be obvious; (3), counted as moral at our world, is entailed by "New Zealand is a Communist Republic", which is not moral. In our context this counterintuitive feature cannot be counted as an objection, though, since it amounts to the point that Karmo's taxonomy does not respect Hume's Law.

So, as Karmo organizes things, Hume's Law fails. But a relative succeeds:

(K) There is no sound argument with only non-moral premises and a moral conclusion.

Karmo's Law, together with his classification of statements, manages to avoid Prior's refutation by making sure that at least one true premise in any "bridge-crossing" valid argument will be false. For example, the valid argument from "New Zealand is a Communist Republic" to (3) has a false premise in this world. Bring the same argument over to a possible world in which New Zealand is a Communist Republic and the argument becomes sound, but the conclusion gets classified as non-moral relative to that world. If we consider instead the disjunctive syllogism from (3) and "New Zealand is not a Communist Republic" to the conclusion, "Benito is evil", we find that at our world it may be sound (it is sound just in case Benito is evil), but that (3), one of its premises, is counted as a moral statement. Bring the argument to a world in which New Zealand is a Communist Republic and the premises will all be non-moral, but the argument will no longer be sound.

This particular salvage does not seem very helpful for our purposes. For one thing, Karmo's classification counts Newtonian mechanics as having moral consequences, merely because Newtonian mechanics is false. (All false statements will have Karmo-moral consequences.) To see this, consider the following material conditional, which is a logical consequence of Newtonian mechanics:

(Y) If Newtonian mechanics is false, then eating yams is morally wrong.

(Y) is plainly a Karmo-moral implication of Newtonian mechanics.

We were hoping for a sense of carrying moral commitment in which meta-ethical theories do and Newtonian mechanics does not carry any. We won't get such a sense by letting moral commitments be Karmo-moral implications

There is another mismatch between the intuitive idea of something's carrying moral commitment and its Karmo classification. The idea of an assertion 'committing' one to something is not quite the same as the idea of a proposition's having the something as an implication. The examples I'm thinking of are relatives of Moore's Paradox.[6] They have nothing in particular to do with *moral* commitments, but they illustrate the more general phenomenon. Moore noticed that

(M) It is raining, but I don't believe that it is raining.

has the flavor of a contradiction, even though it is perfectly possible that it be true (on any occasion of utterance). I suggest that this flavor of contradiction has to do with the *commitments* carried by an assertion of (M). A contradiction *implies* every proposition, it is (maximally) too strong a claim to be true. (M) is not like that. But (M) over*commits* one, it commits one to too much, it is too strong to be asserted. The relative I want to consider is

(N) Either it is raining, or I don't believe that it is raining.

(N) stands to (M) roughly as a tautology stands to a contradiction. Where (M) is maximally overcommitting, (N) is so noncommittal as to be trivial. Anyone could assert (N), no matter what his beliefs. Suppose (following (Stalnaker 1978)) we think of a conversation as having the primary function of informing the various interlocutors about the beliefs of the others. Then (N) fails to inform. We start out, let's suppose, with no idea of what other conversants believe. My representation of George's beliefs is the big set of *all* the possible worlds—not that I take him to have such weak beliefs, but that I am leaving open all the belief sets he might have. I do not, from the beginning, eliminate any possibilities. When George makes an assertion I use it (assuming I take the assertion to be sincere) to whittle down the set of possible worlds that might be George's belief set. When he asserts that it is raining, I rule out all of those worlds in which it is not raining. But when he asserts (N), I can't rule anything out.

Can't I? Can I rule out this possibility: that George believes it is not raining, but believes that he believes that it is raining? Such a failure of transparency in belief is hard to imagine, but I don't mean to take a stand on the issue here. As will emerge in the remainder of the paper, what matters to the conception of a 'moral commitment' (of an assertion) is what a person's views must be in order for the person to be willing to make the assertion. So the point of the analogy is that George should be willing to assert (N) whether he believes that it is raining (since in that case he can infer (N) from its first disjunct) or not (since in that case he 'safely' asserts something true). George can recognize that (N) cannot commit him to anything false that he does not already believe. So (N) might be considered especially noncommittal, even though it does imply something substantial (namely, that George does not falsely believe that it is raining).

Moore's Paradox and its relative have to do with assertions about belief. The main groundwork that I want to lay, though, has to do with a different conception of the commitments of an assertion. The type of examples I'll focus on are drawn from a different philosophical literature, the literature on 'analytic contingencies'.

II. Assertions and Their Commitments

Let's start with this example.

(4) Jamie's first grade teacher is identical to Jamie's actual first grade teacher.

(4) certainly does not express a necessary truth. What it says is not true at every possible world. For there is a world at which Jamie's first grade teacher is Arnold Schwarzenegger, and Arnold Schwarzenegger is not identical to Jamie's actual first grade teacher (who was, for the record, Mrs. Proctor). So the proposition expressed by (4) is false at such a world. Of course, the proposition that *would* be expressed by (4) if it were uttered at such a world is true. Still, (4) actually expresses some proposition. Let's use sets of possible worlds as (to represent) propositions. Then (4) expresses a set containing all those worlds which are like the actual one in respect of who teaches me in first grade (that is, all those worlds in which Mrs. Proctor is my first grade teacher).

Now this proposition *implies*, in the sense of strict implication, that my first grade teacher is a woman (taking a person's sex as essential to her, controversially but harmlessly for illustration). But there is a fairly ordinary sense of an assertion's *committing* one to something in which asserting (4) does not at all commit anyone to the proposition that my first grade teacher is a woman. In fact, in this same fairly ordinary sense, asserting (4) is perfectly noncommittal. One might assert it, you could say, without fear of contradiction. How exactly do commitment and implication come apart?

We may appeal to some apparatus developed by theorists at the intersection of semantics and pragmatics. For many purposes we can represent propositions by sets of possible worlds: intuitively, a proposition is represented by the set of all worlds at which that proposition is true. Assuming (pretending, really) that we have a standard enumeration of the possible worlds, we can think of a proposition as a row of cells each containing a 'T' or an 'F', depending on whether the proposition in question is true or false at the world corresponding to that cell. Clearly, a row-style-proposition is recoverable from a set-style-proposition, and vice versa.

Some sentences express different propositions in different contexts. The sentence

(5) Yesterday was Wednesday.

expresses different propositions when asserted on different days. Some of these propositions are (timelessly) true, and others are false. If I utter the sentence on Tuesday, what I say is false, and *what I said* continues to be false in the days ahead. Of course, the very same sentence in some sense turns true two days later, but the proposition I expressed doesn't.

We can't represent the full semantic value of a *sentence* by a set of possible worlds. For compare:

(6) Jamie's first grade teacher is a woman.
(7) Jamie's actual first grade teacher is a woman.

The first of these sentences could be represented by the set of all worlds in which I have a woman for a first grade teacher. The second cannot, though. I suppose the proposition expressed by the second is the set of all worlds at which Mrs. Proctor exists. (As long as Mrs. Proctor had existed, she would have been a woman.) But this set of worlds cannot represent the semantic value of the sentence, for if that very same sentence had been uttered by me at a world in which Arnold Schwarzenegger were my first grade teacher, it would have expressed a proposition containing no worlds at all.

We may represent sentences containing indexicals, like 'actually', by two dimensional matrices. Each row in the matrix will be a proposition, so each column will be labeled by a world. A given row gets filled in with 'T's and 'F's depending on whether its proposition is true or false at the world labeling the column. The rows are labeled by *contexts* of utterance. A sentence expresses a proposition at one context, and maybe another at a different context. What are contexts? For our immediate purposes, we may include just worlds, again, as important features of context.

Then for simplicity let's restrict our attention to just three worlds. At world i, Jamie's first grade teacher is Mrs. Proctor. At world j, Jamie's first grade teacher is Arnold Schwarzenegger. At world k, Jamie's first grade teacher is David Kaplan. Here is the matrix representing (4).

	i	j	k
i	T	F	F
j	F	T	F
k	F	F	T

What is salient about this matrix is that its diagonal is full of T's. Following Stalnaker let's speak of the strip of T's and F's along the diagonal of a matrix as the *diagonal proposition* of the given sentence. The diagonal proposition of (4) is the necessary proposition. (Again, we are ignoring worlds at which I have no first grade teacher, for simplicity.) Since we'd decided that (4) is an especially noncommittal sentence to assert, we might speculate that its vacuity derives from the necessity of its diagonal. And I think this is correct.

Some theorists have said that we think of sentences as (expressing?) things knowable *a priori* exactly when those sentences have necessary diagonal propositions. Without going into subtleties, the reason for putting it this way is fairly simple. Without knowing anything about which world I am in (without knowing anything about the world that I don't already know about all possible worlds), I can deduce that such a sentence is true in my world. This is a bit odd, since I cannot deduce *a priori* the proposition that the sentence expresses. The suggestion is that it is really sentences that are knowable *a priori*, or perhaps a-proposition-relative-to-a-sentence (see (Wong 1996)). Whatever plausibility accrues to the proposal, I propose to commandeer it for a sense of an assertion's committing one to something. Think of it this way. Suppose I assert a sentence with this matrix:

	i	*j*	*k*
i	F	F	F
j	F	T	F
k	T	F	T

And suppose for a moment that we are in fact at world *k*; *k* is the actual world. One *might* think that my commitment is: we are at world *i* or world *k*. For those are the worlds at which the proposition I asserted is true. But this seems wrong. Am I really committed to our not being at world *j*? Is my commitment really fulfilled if we are at world *i*? If you could convince me that we are at world *i*, then I would be forced to withdraw my assertion. For if we were at world *i*, I would have just asserted something false. So in that sense, I am committed to our not being at world *i*. Suppose instead you were to convince me that we were at world *j*. I should not want to withdraw my assertion, then, for what I asserted would be true. And similarly if I become convinced that we are at world *k*, I will not withdraw my assertion. A reasonably natural way to put it is this: I would withdraw my assertion if and only if I came to believe that in my world, what I asserted was false. I would stand by my assertion if and only if I thought that in my world, what I asserted was true. (This way of putting it is ambiguous. The more formal way of putting it is univocal.) Formally, I would withdraw my assertion just in case I came to believe that I was at a world with an F at the diagonal proposition of the sentence I asserted, and stand by if I came to believe that I was at a world with a T at the diagonal. So it does seem right to say that my commitment is precisely to the set of worlds true along the diagonal of the sentence I assert.

III. Moral Commitment

A. Informally

Investigating the idea of 'moral commitments', we concluded that the notion of a statement's having moral implications was not really what we had in mind. We concluded, for example, that Newtonian mechanics has moral implications (merely by being false).

Though it is not entirely useless for us, Karmo's classification fails to capture a crucial sense of a statement's being moral, or having moral implications. Suppose that you hear me assert confidently:

(8) Either tea drinking is common in England, or all New Zealanders ought to be shot.[7]

Knowing me as you do, you won't jump to any hasty conclusions. You ask me my grounds for the outrageous assertion, and I explain that I know very well that tea drinking is common in England. Then you won't draw any conclusions about my moral views. You will take my assertion to carry no moral commitment; my ground for it is entirely non-moral. Of course, Karmo's scheme does count this statement as non-moral relative to our actual world. But now suppose you hear me assert:

(9) Either the senator is a Cherokee or all New Zealanders ought to be shot.

Again you inquire, and again I explain my grounds: I am extremely confident the senator is a Cherokee. Then again you take my assertion to carry no moral commitment. But this time Karmo's scheme classifies it as moral (since the senator is not, in fact, a Cherokee). The difference is that your assessment depends on what world you think I take us to be in, whereas Karmo's depends only on what world we *are* in. This is not to disparage Karmo's classification. Indeed, it has pointed us to a fairly satisfactory solution. Asserting a proposition, we might say, is committing oneself morally whenever that proposition counts as Karmo-moral *relative to the world the speaker believes he is in*.

There are a number of complications involved in filling out this account. For one thing, a speaker does not generally believe that he is in a particular world. To believe that I am in some particular world is to have unimaginably detailed beliefs. Rather, speakers' beliefs are better representable by a set of worlds. Then we might consider whether a sentence that is Karmo-moral relative to some of my belief worlds but not others is morally committing or not. But I will not consider that question. Second, we should admit that we are idealizing people's epistemic states by representing their total system of beliefs even by sets of possible worlds. Thinking of beliefs that way is taking them to be more systematic than real people's beliefs are. A person might believe two things which are incompossible; then we would represent his 'belief system' by the empty set. But this looks too crude. It just seems wrong to say of such a person that he believes everything. Again, I will ignore this problem, and continue to use the idealization.

Most important for our purposes, the proposition asserted does not seem to be quite right as the measure of a speaker's commitments, moral or otherwise. We have just seen why not. If someone asserts that Jamie's first grade teacher is identical to Jamie's actual first grade teacher, we should not take her to be committed to the proposition expressed, but to the diagonal proposition of the matrix of the sentence spoken. For, as we noted, the assertion does not seem to be at all committing. Under no circumstances would the speaker be required to withdraw it.

To measure moral commitment, we need something like the diagonal of our matrices. But the matrices are not exactly the ones we use to represent the semantic values of ordinary, non-moral sentences (those containing no moral vocabulary at all).

B. *Formally: Moral Systems in Place of Possible Worlds*

To begin with we dispense (for the time being) with possible worlds, focusing on a different aspect of context and a different index of truth evaluation. Remember that on Karmo's scheme, a statement is counted moral (relative to a world) iff it is true according to some moral standards and false according to others (at that world). This is the test that we'll use for a statement's being morally committing, too. The rough idea is that if I assert a statement that is true relative to some moral standards but not others, you will be able to draw some conclusions about my moral standards. I will have committed myself to standing by one or another of those moral standards that count the statement true. So as you listen to me make assertions, you will be able to narrow down the class of moral standards that could make my assertions true.

Since (to start with) we will ignore the plurality of possible worlds, we are really interested in another feature of contexts of assertion: the speaker. Here, of course, the idea is that the same sentence might express now one proposition, now another, depending on who utters it. We combine these two variable features (moral standards, delivering truth values from moral propositions, and contexts, delivering propositions from indexical sentences) in a matrix to represent the semantic value of a moral sentence. For example, here is the matrix for the sentence,

(10) Making fun of me is wrong.

	m_1	m_2	m_3
a_1	F	T	F
a_2	T	F	F
a_3	T	T	F

Here the a_i are speakers, and the m_i are moral standards. And in particular, we'll let a_1 be G. E. Moore, a_2 be Ray Charles, and a_3 be the Pope; and m_1 counts as wrong making fun of the blind and the Catholic, m_2 counts making fun of philosophers and Catholics wrong; m_3 permits making fun of anyone. We get a moral claim, something that is true or false according to various moral standards, given a context, and in particular the speaker in the context. The context supplies a referent for 'me'. The standards provide a truth valuation.

C. Morally Noncommittal Assertions Are True on the Diagonal

In the matrix above there was no particular connection between the indexing of the moral standards, the m_i, and the indexing of the persons. The subscript of the one was not particularly related to the subscript of another. We could have written the indices in any old order. But now I want to impose another restriction.

Let us arrange the matrices so that for each i, m_i is the moral standard held by a_i. What exactly does this mean? What determines what your moral standard is or mine? I don't want to give any developed theory.[8] The moral standard of the speaker is supposed to be analogous to her 'belief world'. In practice, a speaker hasn't any particular world in mind as the actual one, but a set of worlds; and in practice, we don't have full moral standards but only partial ones. But we are interested in the *commitments* of a speaker. We are interested in explaining in what way her assertions commit her to some subset of all the possible moral standards. We might think of a speaker's particular moral standard as being that standard which she would come to accept in reflective equilibrium.

Now consider the sentence:

(11) Abortion is wrong if and only if it is counted wrong by my moral standard.

The matrix for this sentence is:

	m_1	m_2	m_3
a_1	T	T	F
a_2	T	T	F
a_3	F	F	T

We'll specify only that a_1's moral standard (which is standard m_1) permits abortion, as does a_2's, and a_3's does not. So the first row is the moral proposition that abortion is wrong if and only if it is counted wrong by a_1's moral standard; this is counted true (because the right side simply is false and the left side is counted false) by both m_1 and m_2, and counted false (because the right side remains simply false, while the left side is counted true) by m_3. And similarly for the other two rows.

The diagonal of the matrix is all T's. So, I say (for the moment), the sentence itself (the assertion of it) is morally noncommittal. Why is this the proper criterion? A person may confidently assert a sentence whose diagonal moral proposition is true, no matter what her moral standard. Even if she is not quite settled about what her moral standard is, she can be sure that whatever it turns out to be, what she has said will be true according to that moral standard. She has incurred no unwanted moral commitment.

We could think of it this way. Suppose my moral standard is standard M, one which strictly forbids abortion. Then by uttering the sentence, I have said that abortion is wrong if and only if it is wrong according to standard M. (This is not quite right, but it is good enough for the moment, since we are ignoring the plurality of possible worlds.) Well, abortion *is* wrong according to standard M. So by committing myself to the biconditional, I am committing myself to abortion's being wrong. But since it is wrong, according to my moral standard, that is a commitment I am happy with. From the perspective of the audience, things are a bit complicated. Supposing that you don't know what my moral standard is, you don't know exactly what moral standards make the moral proposition I have uttered true and which ones make it false. Since in fact my moral standard permits abortion, all and only those moral standards which permit abortion make that moral proposition true. But you can't tell that just by hearing me. Now, if you learned more about my moral standard, you would discover that what I said is true according to just those moral standards according to which abortion is permissible. Then you could specify my moral commitment. You could narrow down the class of moral standards to which I am committed by pruning away all those standards that prohibit abortion. But of course, if you were able to learn that much about my moral standard, that is exactly what you would have learned! You would have been able to prune away all the abortion-prohibiting standards from my commitment set. So my assertion adds nothing. That is why it is perfectly noncommittal. Or in any case, it is perfectly noncommittal as long as we do not consider other possible worlds. The picture changes when we start to consider them. The next section explains how the picture changes.

D. Boggling Dimensions: Worlds and Moral Standards Together

We have (for a short while) been ignoring the plurality of worlds. Our matrix, the way we represent the semantic value of a moral proposition, includes no dimension for possible worlds. But we will want to represent modal moral sentences, things like

(12) Although capital punishment is wrong, it could have been permissible.

So now we have to complicate our model. We could add two dimensions, a dimension of possible worlds each for context and evaluation, and we would have four dimensional matrices. But we can just add one, with a simplifying trick that keeps the dimensionality of the matrices small enough to visualize.

We'll think of a moral proposition as delivering a proposition (a set of possible worlds, or an assignment of truth values at each world) given a moral standard. So it is a propositional function, taking moral standards as arguments. Then a moral proposition is itself a matrix, with worlds as one dimension and moral standards as the other. And for contexts we'll take not speakers, or worlds, but speakers-at-worlds (or if you prefer, ordered pairs of worlds and speakers at those worlds). Then a sentence containing moral terms gets represented by a three dimensional matrix. A cell in the matrix is specified by a context, a world, and a standard, and is filled in with a truth value. Though three dimensional matrices are not so easy to visualize, and the graphic value of using them as heuristics is thus smaller than that of two dimensional matrices, we can think of their dimensions as Height, Depth, and Length. Each horizontal row is a proposition, so the worlds (of evaluation) are arranged along the Length. Each row is a section of both a horizontal and a vertical *slab*; a slab is a two dimensional matrix. Vertical slabs are moral propositions. A moral proposition delivers a proposition given a moral standard; so the moral standards are arranged along the Depth. And contexts are arranged along the Height; each context picks out a slab, a moral proposition.

Next, ordering. Contexts are speakers-at-worlds. For each i, let w_i be the world in c_i, the ith context, and m_i be the moral standard of the person-at-world i. This means that the sequence of worlds along the Length contains repetitions of worlds. Worlds will occur at more than one position. For there will be many contexts containing the same world (one for each speaker, if we are to be complete). Formally there is no real objection to this feature, though it does prevent us from thinking naturally of the rows of cells as propositions in the most straightforward way. But the rows are still easily convertible to (and from) sets of possible worlds, which is all that matters technically. Moral standards recur, too, in their sequence, since two speakers-at-worlds might have the same moral standard.

Now, what is the formal characteristic of a sentence's matrix that marks it as morally noncommittal (to assert)? If any old speaker at any old world could assert the sentence sincerely, no matter what her moral system, then assertion of the sentence reveals nothing. So if, for each world w^* and speaker a^*, the moral proposition (a slab having Height and Depth but no Length) expressed by the sentence at the context a^*-at-w^* is true at w^*, according to the moral system held by a^* at w^*. Hard to parse. But not so hard to visualize; morally noncommittal sentences have T's all along their major diagonal. (Which diagonal is the major one? We haven't said which corner we start with. One corner is the origin, labeled by the first context, the first world, the first moral standard. The major diagonal runs from that corner and cuts all three dimensions.)

By way of illustration, here is a morally noncommittal sentence.

(13) Necessarily, abortion is wrong if and only if my actual moral standards count it wrong.

In a context (that is, relative to a speaker at a world), this sentence expresses a moral proposition (a slab, or a function from moral standards to plain old propositions). Suppose it is spoken by Karl at world w_k. Then it expresses the moral proposition that takes moral standards to the proposition that necessarily, abortion is wrong-according-to-the-given-standard iff Karl's moral standards at w_k count abortion wrong. Then this moral proposition takes Karl's own moral standards, m_k, to the proposition that necessarily, abortion is wrong according to m_k iff abortion is wrong according to m_k. Since the embedded biconditional is indeed true at every world, the proposition is true. We conclude that it is true independent of the choice of k (and independent of any facts about Karl); then the matrix for the sentence is true all along the major diagonal. So it is morally noncommittal. And intuitively this seems right, too. For no matter who uttered it, no matter what his moral standards, no matter which world he turns out to be in, under no circumstances would he be compelled to withdraw his assertion.

Although (13) is an example of a morally noncommittal sentence, it is not a theory. With technical apparatus in hand, we now return to meta-ethical theories, including some that are, by our criterion, morally noncommittal.

IV. Secondary Quality Theories

Here is a simple version of what we earlier called Secondary Quality theory.

(SQ) $\Box$ (x) (x is wrong $\leftrightarrow$ x tends to cause in us a feeling of moral disapproval)

I leave vague the terms 'us' and the expression 'feeling of moral disapproval'. Particular versions of the Secondary Quality theory will arise by specification. I believe that the assertion of a theory in the same family as (SQ) is not morally revealing. Let me start with a clearer case.

(SQ*) $\Box$ (x) (x is wrong $\leftrightarrow$ x is wrong according to my moral standards)

Here, one might think, is a standard meta-ethical theory whose assertion lacks moral commitment. For instantiations will yield biconditionals which in turn imply basic moral judgments *only* when the biconditionals are combined with propositions about my moral standards. All we could infer about a person's moral commitments, from the fact that she asserted (SQ*), would be that her moral standards say that a certain thing is wrong just in case it is wrong according to her moral standards. And this is a logical truth. Not to say that the instantiations are themselves logical truths! But the implications of her sincerely asserting (SQ*), or its instantiations, are vacuous.

One might think so. But only if one has ignored the necessity operator of (SQ*). In the previous section we went to some trouble to combine the moral with the modal, and found a way of characterizing the morally noncommittal modal assertions. We now apply the formalism.

Without harm, though not strictly correctly, let's call such sentences as the following 'instantiations of (SQ*)':

(SQ*i) □(eating meat is wrong ↔ eating meat is wrong according to my moral standards)

Suppose that according to my actual moral standards, eating meat is not wrong. Now consider a world, w, in which I have standards according to which eating meat *is* wrong. I assert (SQ*) in the actual world. I am thereby committed to (SQ*i). (SQ*i) is true if and only if

(14) Eating meat is wrong ↔ eating meat is wrong according to my moral standards.

is true in every world, including w. By hypothesis, the right hand side of (14) is true in w. So I am committed to the left hand side's being true in w, too. But this does appear to be a substantive moral commitment. To put the same point another way, consider

(15) If my moral standards prohibited eating meat, then eating meat would be wrong.

(SQ*) entails (15). If you discover that I am committed to (15), you have, intuitively, discovered something substantial about my moral standards. And this fits our formal characterization, for (15) is not true all along the (three dimensional) diagonal of its matrix. It is false, in particular, when the context is a speaker, Gilbert, at a world, the actual one, and it is evaluated at Gilbert's moral system and the actual world. For Gilbert's actual moral system permits eating meat in any nearby world, including those nearby worlds in which he would have a moral system that prohibited eating meat. (He regards such worlds as worlds in which he has a mistaken, or overly fastidious, moral view.)

Notice that (SQ*i) is itself false at some points along its diagonal. To see this, note that it will be false at any context and moral system at which (14) expresses a proposition that is not necessarily true. Take as a context, again, Gilbert at the actual world, and as a moral system Gilbert's actual moral system, M_G. Then the proposition expressed by (14) is true at just those worlds, w, in which Gilbert has a moral system that agrees with M_G on the morality of eating meat in w. And this means that it is false at any world at which Gilbert has a moral system that forbids the eating of meat. And there are, of course, many of these. So (14) does not express a necessary proposition, relative to the context and moral system in question. And that means that (SQ*i) is false at such a context and system, *necessarily* false; it expresses a proposition that is false everywhere. So its matrix is false at that spot on its diagonal.

We have just shown that contrary to first impressions, (SQ*) does carry normative commitment (it is morally revealing). But we can now remove that commitment by a simple device.[9] Consider

(ASQ) □ (x) (x is wrong $\leftrightarrow$ x is wrong according to my *actual* moral standards)

(ASQ) is the 'actualized' version of a Secondary Quality theory. The standards denoted on the right hand side of the biconditional formula are my actual ones. Even when we *evaluate* instantiations of this formula at other worlds, the standards we use are the ones to which I actually subscribe, not the ones to which I subscribe at the world of evaluation. And now the normative moral commitment of the theory has disappeared.

(ASQ) is true at every point of its matrix's diagonal. For, when evaluating its truth on the diagonal, we will always select the same moral system for both sides of the biconditional. For the left hand side, we will always use the system of the context (the speaker's system in the world of the context). And for the right hand side, we are also constrained to use that same system; because of the '*actual*' we will not go to the world of evaluation to find the speaker's system at that world. So for each choice of x and each world, the two sides of the biconditional will say the same thing, so the biconditional will be true everywhere, satisfied by every object.

To see in a more intuitive way that an assertion of (ASQ) lacks all moral commitment, ask what commitments are compatible with (ASQ). Take some arbitrary normative commitment I might have, to the effect that ϕ-ing is wrong in some possible world, w. So ϕ-ing is wrong in w, according to my moral standards. I accept (I believe, I am willing to assert) that in w, ϕ-ing is wrong; I believe also that it is wrong according to my moral standards. Since I accept both sides of the biconditional, "ϕ-ing is wrong $\leftrightarrow$ ϕ-ing is wrong according to my *actual* moral standards," I accept the biconditional. Given an arbitrary world, and an arbitrary ϕ, then, (ASQ) entails nothing incompatible with my normative view about ϕ-ing in w. But such entailments are the only implications that could conflict with my normative views. So my normative views do not conflict with (ASQ). No matter what my normative views, I should be willing to accept (ASQ). Then my acceptance of (ASQ) reveals nothing about my normative views; it rules nothing out. So it is not morally revealing.

(ASQ) is a standard meta-ethical theory whose assertion is not morally revealing. So, I say, there is a good sense in which it carries no normative moral commitment. True enough, there is also a perfectly good sense in which it has normative moral implications (Karmo's sense—there are certainly sentences it entails which are moral in this world). Nonetheless, it could not reasonably be called a normative moral theory, just because its assertion carries no normative moral commitment.

V. Dworkin on Dispositional Theories

We now return to Dworkin.

A. Dworkin's Mistake

Dworkin points out one fact we have noted above, namely, that (SQ*) does carry moral commitment. But he also insists that even (ASQ) is a substantive moral thesis. In this he is mistaken.

About a theory roughly equivalent to (SQ*), he writes,

> But someone who holds that moral properties are secondary properties does take sides in actual or potential substantive disputes. Suppose we discovered that, contrary to our expectations, contemplating genocide does not in fact outrage even most normal people. Genocide would not then be morally wrong on that dispositional account, though, of course, many people would think it was. [101]

We have already seen that Dworkin is right about this. But then he considers a theory roughly equivalent to (ASQ), and he writes,

> The dispositional account might, it is true, take a different form. It might hold, for example, that what makes genocide wrong is the reaction, not of whichever kind of people happen to exist from time to time, but of us, that is, of people with the physiological structure, basic interests, and general mental dispositions that people actually have now. In that case, it would no longer follow that genocide would cease being wicked if human beings developed very different general interests or different neural wiring. But some plainly substantive and controversial claims would still follow: for instance, that genocide would not have been wicked if economic or other circumstances had been different as human reactions evolved, so that creatures with our general interests and attitudes had not been revolted by genocide. [102]

But this is wrong. For imagine a possible world in which human beings evolved differently, so that human beings with our general interests and attitudes had not been revolted by genocide.[10] Would it be true, at that world, that genocide tends to cause in *us as we actually are* a feeling of moral disapproval? Of course. We can even do the experiment ourselves: don't you feel moral disapproval of any genocide that might occur in such a world? Of course; for according to your actual moral standards, genocide is morally wrong.

Dworkin continues,

> [J]ust as any philosophically illuminating account of what the disgustingness of rotten eggs consists in yields counterfactual claims about the circumstances in which rotten eggs would not be or have been disgusting, so any illuminating account of

moral properties as secondary entails counterfactuals that state substantive moral positions. [102–3]

I can't find any argument for this claim. So I think it is not supposed to be a claim that needs to be argued for at all, but rather a judgment about what would count as an "illuminating account". Dworkin is of the opinion that any theory that lacked substantive moral entailments would thereby fail to be illuminating. Maybe he can't quite believe that anyone would offer a theory like (ASQ), maybe he thinks it's just obviously unilluminating. If so, I think he's wrong about that.

B. How a Theory Could Be Illuminating

Let's add a typical clause to (ASQ). It's a weasely clause, notoriously so, but we'll add it anyway, and call the result a Weasely Actualized Secondary Quality theory:

(WASQ)   An act is wrong iff it tends to cause in standard perceivers *as we actually are* a feeling of moral disapproval.

The weasel: what makes a perceiver standard? We dodge this question.

Now, someone might say, "Of course, if a perceiver is 'standard', then he will certainly disapprove morally of all and only the wrong things. Otherwise he doesn't count as standard." And he might facetiously propose

(SQUARE)   An object is square iff it tends to cause in standard perceivers as we *actually are* an impression of squareness.

The idea, of course, is that there is little question but that we can rig 'standard' in such a way that (SQUARE) comes out true. But this obviously doesn't show that squareness is a projected property, that it is a feature contributed by our minds or perceptual abilities rather than by the properties that things have independently of us. (SQUARE) seems to explain nothing about the nature of squareness or squares. So why should (WASQ) be thought to explain anything about the nature of moral wrongness?

We might maintain that there is an important difference between (WASQ) and (SQUARE). For each is a biconditional, but there is a difference in the direction in which the biconditional is to be read; that is, the *explanation* runs in different directions in each case. In (SQUARE), most of us will agree that it is our being standard perceivers, along with the fact that the jewelbox is square, that explains why it tends to cause in us an impression of squareness. Whereas, it might be maintained, in the case of (WASQ), it is our being standard perceivers, along with extortion's tendency to cause in us a feeling of moral disapproval, that explains the wrongness of extortion, explains in virtue of what extortion is wrong. Or we could think of it this way. In the one case, we think there is some independent explanation of what squareness is, and then the notion of a standard perceiver of squares will just follow, empirically, from (SQUARE). Whereas in the other case, we might think that there is some independent explanation of what it is to be a standard moral perceiver, and then the notion of moral wrongness may be read off of (WASQ).

A theory of the nature of moral properties, even one which lacked altogether any substantive moral entailments, could be philosophically illuminating in just this way, that it would explain what moral properties are. It would say that they are dispositions. Moral properties, according to such a theory, would be disposition to affect *us as we actually are* in certain affective ways.

Dworkin is concerned in "Objectivity and Truth" to show that there are no Archimedean metaethical theories, perspectives from which one might pass unfavorable judgment on the objectivity of moral statements without oneself incurring any startling first order moral commitments. I have argued that he is mistaken. For (ASQ) looks to be a significant and (for all that's been shown) coherent Archimedean position. No doubt there are some serious objections to (ASQ). And perhaps it is not entirely clear or rigorous exactly in what sense it might be thought to imply that moral judgments are not 'objective'. But we cannot reject it as a failed attempt to establish an Archimedean theory. (ASQ) seems to say exactly what some Archimedeans want to say about moral properties and facts.[11]

Notes

1. (Dworkin 1996), hereafter cited only with page numbers in the body of the text.
2. See (Dreier 1996), especially comments by Blackburn and Zangwill and Dworkin's reply.
3. See (Davies 1980), where this sort of theory is discussed but not endorsed.
4. So-called by Arthur Prior (Prior 1960).
5. Though note that Humberstone's taxonomy does not support this supposition. See (Humberstone 1982) and (Humberstone 1996).
6. See (Moore 1942 p. 543), and also (Moore 1962 p. 277).
7. This is Prior's example.
8. See my (Dreier 1990) for details.
9. Due to (Davies 1980).
10. As I noted above, in the Introduction, Dworkin couldn't mean *all* of our attitudes. For one of our attitudes is the attitude of *revulsion at genocide*. Presumably Dworkin means to be imagining that human beings have the attitude of revulsion, but not toward genocide.
11. Thanks to audiences at Arizona State University and the New School's "Conference on Methods" where I read early versions of this paper, and also to Ronald Dworkin, who got me interested in the topic, and who will certainly disagree with the spirit of my position.

References

Davies, Martin, I. L. Humberstone. (1980) "Two Notions of Necessity," *Philosophical Studies*, 38 pp. 1–30.

Dreier, James. (1990) "Internalism and Speaker Relativism," *Ethics*, 101 pp. 6–26.

Dreier, James, David Estlund (eds.). (1996) "BEARS Symposium on Dworkin's 'Objectivity and Truth'," http://www.brown.edu/Departments/Philosophy/bears/symp-dworkin.html.

Dworkin, Ronald. (1996) "Objectivity and Truth: You'd Better Believe It," *Philosophy and Public Affairs*, 25 pp. 87–139.

Humberstone, I. L. (1982) "First Steps in a Philosophical Taxonomy," *Canadian Journal of Philosophy*, 12 pp. 467–478.

Humberstone, I. L. (1996) "A Study in Philosophical Taxonomy," *Philosophical Studies*, 83 pp. 121–169.

Karmo, Toomas. (1988) "Some Valid (but no Sound) Arguments Trivially Span the 'Is'-'Ought' Gap," *Mind*, 97 pp. 252–257.

Moore, G. E. (1942) "A Reply to my Critics," in *The Philosophy of G. E. Moore*, P. A. Schilpp (ed.). La Salle, Illinois: Open Court.

Moore, George Edward. (1962) *Commonplace Book*. New York: Macmillan.

Prior, A. N. (1960) "The Autonomy of Ethics," *Australasian Journal of Philosophy*, 38 pp. 199–206.

Stalnaker, Robert. (1978) "Assertion," in *Syntax and Semantics*, P. Cole (ed.). New York: Academic Press.

Wong, Kai-Yee. (1996) "Sentence Relativity and the Necessary A Posteriori," *Philosophical Studies*, 83 pp. 53–91.

Philosophical Issues, 12, Realism and Relativism, 2002

EARNING THE RIGHT TO REALISM
OR RELATIVISM IN ETHICS

Carol Rovane
Columbia University

For some twenty hundred years, the disjunction between realism and relativism has had Philosophy in its grip. It may be that we simply can't prove either realism or relativism, at least not if that means keeping to the high standard of providing a proof that could not possibly be regarded as question-begging by the other side.

Consider, for example, the following argument against relativism, which is likely to get raised early on in any discussion of the issue. The argument points out that we cannot state that all truths are relative without making the statement itself an exception, thereby repudiating relativism and supporting realism after all. The thought behind this argument seems to be the following one: unless we intend our statement of relativism to be true in the realist sense, we will have failed to express the fact that relativism stands opposed to realism. Prima facie, the thought seems a good one. But before we draw a realist conclusion, we need to view the thought from the relativist's perspective. The relativist will insist that the statement of her thesis should not be interpreted along realist lines, on the ground that doing so would beg the question against her. Apparently, the only way not to beg the question here is to allow that the statement of relativism itself is only relatively true. The realist may try to turn this allowance against relativism, by pointing out that it leaves us free, even by the relativist's lights, to re-assert realism. But a determined relativist can grant this point without regarding herself as refuted. By her lights, the realist's assertion of realism is only relatively true and, so, can hardly serve to rule out relativism. In response, the realist may echo the response that the relativist had earlier made to her, and insist that her statement of realism should not be interpreted along relativist lines—on the ground that doing so would just as clearly beg the question against her as she had earlier done against the relativist. And so on and on.

If these are the only terms in which we can argue about realism vs. relativism, the issue begins to look like a stand-off in which everyone must ultimately beg the question. Realists may want to point out that their position accords better with a classically conceived logic and with ordinary discourse. But it doesn't follow that they have more right to beg the question on their side. For, insofar as relativists can successfully beg the question on the other side, it is fair to ask that realists do more in order to earn the right to realism than just claim default status.

My aim in this paper is to explore the prospects of earning the right to realism or relativism in the ethical domain, insofar as reasons can be offered on either side that, though they do beg the question, don't *merely* beg the question. In section 1 I'll develop a positive conception of realism that I think is especially well suited to the ethical domain. The heart of this conception is a certain *realist ideal*, according to which there is a single and complete body of truths. I'll be arguing that this ideal constitutes the single most basic dividing point between realists and relativists. Regardless of how else they might want to characterize their respective positions and differences, realists are bound to embrace, while relativists are bound to reject, this realist ideal of a single and complete body of truths. If nothing else, identifying this basic dividing issue should help to clarify the terms of debate. But I will show that the realist ideal also points the way to a *pragmatic conception of realism*. So conceived, realism is a *practical stance* that we can bring to bear in *inquiry*. What makes this an essentially realist stance within an essentially realist project of inquiry is precisely that it is guided by the realist ideal of a single and complete body of truths. What I'm proposing, then, is this: that we frame the issue of realism vs. relativism in ethics in terms of the feasibility and point of this realist ideal, which would motivate a form of ethical inquiry that ethical relativists are fundamentally committed to rejecting. I'll elaborate and defend this proposal in section 1.

My proposal has the effect of transposing the metaphysical issue about realism into one that is also practical, more an issue about how inquirers should proceed, and less about the nature of reality and whether it is or is not epistemically constrained. As I see it, this transposition represents the best hope for realism in ethics. But I'm sure that many philosophers will disagree because, in their view, no position deserves to be called "realist" unless it provides for a conception of the world as it is in itself, independently of how we might take it to be. Bernard Williams calls this the "absolute conception of reality," Thomas Nagel calls it "the view from nowhere," and it is often called "metaphysical realism." On the metaphysical realist view, beliefs and judgments are true just in case they capture the ways things really are—that is, just in case they 'correspond' to the mind-independent facts. From this metaphysical realist perspective, no view deserves to be counted as a realist view unless it provides a positive account of these "truth-makers."

Let me briefly indicate at the start some of the reasons why I'm going to set aside the doctrine of metaphysical realism.

It is well known that the doctrine invites skepticism. Frankly, I don't see any point in going to the trouble of earning the right to realism in ethics if skepticism is the destination.

Not all metaphysical realists are skeptics. The best example we have of an attempt to earn the right to metaphysical realism without skepticism is scientific realism. And some ethical theorists propose to model ethical realism on scientific realism.[1] This approach deserves a full discussion that I hope to provide elsewhere. [2] For the purposes of this paper, I'm going to set it aside on the basis of a difficulty that Mackie has raised.[3] He points out that ethical realists would first have to posit mind-independent evaluative facts—which he calls "funny" facts. And, then, they would have to face the problem of explaining how we could possibly be in epistemic touch with them. We are able to do this in the case of science because the sort of mind-independent facts that science deals with are not "funny." They are physical facts that were initially introduced in the context of the theory of perception, in order to explain various aspects of perceptual appearances. All we have to do in order to explain how we are in epistemic touch with these physical facts is run the same explanation backwards: it is first via perception and, ultimately, via scientific theorizing, that we are in epistemic touch with them. But there is nothing comparable in the domain of ethics. Even if there are things that we might be inclined to call ethical appearances, there is no perceptual apparatus like vision or hearing or touch by which we are put into causal and epistemic touch with them. Because this is so, we have no explanatory framework that would allow us to see ethical appearances as systematic reflections of how things are in themselves, ethically speaking—at least, not if we have in mind something analogous to what we have in the case of sense perception. This is one of the main grounds on which Mackie rejects ethical realism altogether. But we needn't go so far as that. We can conclude more cautiously that scientific realism is a poor model for ethical realism.

It stands to reason that scientific realism is a poor model for ethical realism. After all, the aims of ethics are very different from the aims of science. While the aims of science are explanatory, the aims of ethics are evaluative. What one wants from an ethical theory is some sort of guidance concerning how one ought to conduct oneself, especially in relation to other people and, more broadly, in relation to anything that has a point of view from which it could be said to matter how we treat it. These different aims bring in train different approaches to the task of theoretical justification. In accordance with the explanatory aims of science, the task of justification there is primarily one of establishing the explanatory adequacy of a given theory with respect to various empirical data that stand in need of such explanation, where this task is closely associated with correct prediction. In contrast, ethical theories tend to look for "foundations" of certain ethical values. Although it could be said that these foundations "explain" why certain ethical values ought to be given priority in our lives, it is a quite different sense of explanation than we find in science. The task is not to predict or otherwise account for empirical data but, rather, to justify certain reasons for action, often in the form of a normative ideal of which our actions fall short.[4]

The favorite candidates for such a foundation in ethics are reason and human nature. The former has been claimed to ground Kantian ethics and some versions of utilitarianism, while the latter has been claimed to ground virtue ethics. Anyone who is convinced of any of these foundationalist ethical theories is thereby bound to regard ethical relativism as untenable. This is especially clear in the case of the rationalist theories proposed by Kantians and utilitarians. Each of these theories provides a single ethical principle that is supposed to determine the truth-value of all of our more specific judgments about what is ethically right or wrong, good or bad. That leaves no room for relativism. I want to urge, therefore, that the proponents of these theories be counted as ethical realists even if they can't satisfy the demands of metaphysical realists to provide a positive account of what the mind-independent ethical "truth-makers" are. However, I'm not going to assume that either Kantian ethics or utilitarianism—or, indeed, anything like these ethical theories—is true. This is partly because they are controversial. But it's also because I'm inclined to take value pluralism seriously. And ethical theories of the sort that would automatically vindicate ethical realism don't typically recognize a significant plurality of ethical values. Obviously, virtue ethics recognizes a greater plurality of ethical values than the Kantian and utilitarian theories do. But virtue ethics will not automatically rule out relativism unless it seeks a foundation for the virtues in human nature. And such a foundation would have a constricting effect on the number and range of virtues that it recognizes. The sort of value pluralism that I'm inclined to take seriously would be more broad-ranging than that. It would countenance virtues and other values that cannot be said to have a foundation in either reason or human nature. So I would not propose to earn the right to realism in ethics by defending any of the major ethical theories. It may seem that my determination to leave room for a broad-ranging value pluralism stacks the deck against ethical realism. But I don't see why this should be so. I don't see why there couldn't be just as much objectivity in connection with a plurality as there can be in connection with a unity. The evident plurality of natural facts all around us does nothing to undermine the idea that they are objective.

So far, I've explained that I'll be setting aside two strategies for earning the right to realism in ethics: the strategy of modeling ethical realism on scientific realism, and the strategy of establishing the truth of any foundationalist ethical theory. There is one last strategy that I'll be setting aside that also deserves mention, namely, the strategy of carrying Davidson's argument against conceptual relativism over to the case of ethics.[5] I myself have tried this strategy and failed. As it turns out, there is much to be learned even from the failed attempt. But I haven't the space to elaborate here. For the purposes of this paper, I'll just declare that we can't rule out ethical relativism by ruling out the intelligibility of alternative ethical schemes. There is too much intelligible ethical disagreement and too much actual diversity of ethical opinion.

By setting aside these three strategies, I'm left with the following point of departure. On the one hand, I've improved the prospects for earning the right to realism in ethics by relinquishing the metaphysical ambitions of scientific realism in the ethical domain. But, on the other hand, that gain has been offset by my decision to recognize both a significant plurality of ethical values and a significant diversity of ethical opinion. For that precludes our earning the right to realism in ethics by establishing one of the major ethical theories or by arguing in Davidsonian fashion that we all by and large agree in ethical matters. It may seem that there is no route from this point of departure to a realist conclusion. But this isn't so. The realist stance that I described above—that is, the commitment to a realist project of ethical inquiry in the light of the realist ideal of a single and complete body of ethical truths—is compatible with both a significant plurality of ethical values and a significant diversity of ethical opinion. And we shall see that it is highly resilient in the face of various arguments for ethical relativism.

In particular, the realist stance is not undermined by Gilbert Harman's argument for moral relativism. His argument rests on a particular account of the foundations of morality, in terms of what self-interested individuals have reason to agree to on the basis of moral bargaining. Harman is certainly right that this account provides for a certain kind of relativity in the ethical domain: some moral judgments have force only relative to specific moral agreements. But, at the same time, the account also provides scope for the sort of ethical inquiry that goes together with the realist stance. In fact, we can get a very clear picture of what a realist project of ethical inquiry might consist in by seeing how it could and should be conducted within Harman's framework. So, not only is it the case that Harman's argument does not undermine the realist stance; it positively invites it. This will emerge in section 2.

In section 3 I'll explore the extent to which Bernard Williams provides us with reasons to abandon the realist stance in favor of the relativist stance. Unfortunately, the reasons he officially gives presuppose that scientific realism is the only viable model for ethical realism. This leads him to overlook how the realist stance might yield a distinctive form of ethical inquiry. Yet, although he never discusses this realist project, there are aspects of his overall ethical vision that might be taken to pose difficulties for it—in fact, I think it is very likely that he himself would raise these difficulties if the matter were put to him. For he clearly holds that many attempts to make comparative evaluations of values drawn from different ethical systems will prove to be pointless. And the whole point of ethical inquiry as I'm envisaging it depends upon the meaningfulness and informativeness of such comparisons. I think Williams underestimates the extent to which such comparisons would be meaningful and informative. However, I'll also identify a specific condition in which no genuine ethical illumination could be gained in this way. In this condition, the realist stance in ethics would be pointless, just as Williams has claimed. So, one way to earn the right to relativism in ethics is to show that this condition is the one we're actually in. I'll close with some remarks about how to settle the hard question whether it is our condition.

1. Realism as a Practical Stance

Let me restate my point of departure. I'm going to take it for granted that we shouldn't try to earn the right to realism in ethics by any of the following strategies: modeling ethical realism on scientific realism; defending one of the major ethical theories; arguing against the very idea of an ethical scheme. The reasons why are, respectively: the aims of ethics are different from the aims of science; the major ethical theories are controversial and, also, they fail to recognize a significant plurality of values; there is too much diversity of ethical opinion to afford the Davidsonian conclusion that we all by and large agree in ethical matters.

It might seem that this point of departure is bound to preclude our earning the right to realism in ethics. For, once we've rejected all of these strategies it is not clear what other strategy might still be left to try. Yet there is one. It is striking that the three strategies I'm rejecting lay down very different sorts of requirements for realism. A metaphysical realist would not regard either the establishment of a particular ethical theory, or a Davidsonian argument against relativism, as a way of earning the right to realism in ethics. Similarly, a Davidsonian would reject the further requirements that metaphysical realists want to lay down as unintelligible. Given these divergences, it seems to me that we ought to step back and ask: What is the most basic and minimal commitment that is held in common by different sorts of realists, and that all relativists are committed to denying? If we could identify this basic and minimal realist commitment, then we could formulate a new strategy for settling the issue of realism vs. relativism. We could consider what reasons there are to embrace or reject this basic and minimal realist commitment.

I've already stated what I take this commitment to be, which most fundamentally distinguishes realists from relativists. It is their commitment to the realist ideal of a single and complete body of truths.

Let me now clarify what I take this ideal to consist in. When I say that a body of truths is *complete* I mean: for every well-formed proposition, either it or its negation figures in that body. This may remind readers of Dummett's formal characterization of realism in terms of the principle of bi-valence. [6] But I have something different in mind. I do not intend to characterize realism is such a way that realists cannot countenance truth-value gaps. Such gaps might well arise due to reference failure, vagueness, threatened paradox, etc., without prompting us to embrace any form of relativism. That is why I incorporate the idea of a *well-formed* proposition in my characterization of completeness. I mean well-formed in a very broad sense, according to which a proposition is well formed just in case it is capable of having a truth value. Thus, a body of truths is complete just in case, for every proposition that is capable of having a truth value, either it or its negation figures in it. This idea of completeness can be further qualified by restricting it to specific domains. For example, we can think of a complete body of truths within the domain of facts or within the domain of values, or within the more restricted domains of physical facts, psychological facts, mathematical facts, ethical values, aesthetic values, and so on. If we are prepared to distinguish domains, then we can raise the issue of realism vs. relativism separately in each domain. To embrace realism with respect to a given domain is to hold that there is a single and complete body of truths in that domain. And, if we embrace realism in more than one domain, then the various bodies of truths associated, respectively, with each domain, would together constitute a single and complete body of truths. In other words, they would not be *many* bodies of truths in the sense that interests the relativist. The whole point of relativism is to allow that there can be many bodies of truths that *cannot* be conjoined in accord with the realist ideal of a single and complete body of truths.

I've introduced the idea of a realist *stance*, because I want to draw attention to the fact that the realist ideal is something we can actively embrace and that, when we do so, we must *act* in accord with it. There are two fronts on which its practical implications need to be recognized, namely, inquiry and interpersonal relations.

Inquiring realists hold that there is a single and complete body of truths in the domain (or domains) into which they are inquiring. It follows that there is no well-formed proposition in that domain (or domains) concerning which the question of its truth value does not arise. Any such proposition is, therefore, an appropriate target of investigation. However, it would be wrong to infer that the realist ideal constitutes the proper goal of inquiry. For one thing, it is probably an incoherent goal, since it is probably impossible for finite beings like us to know all of the truths. But even if it were not an incoherent goal, there are many reasons why we might not embrace it. Take the domain of facts. There are certainly truths about the facts that it would be quite useless to know (how many grains of sand are there); indeed, many of these truths are too boring even to think about (this is what goes wrong with the game of counting road-signs and out-of-state license plates when the journey gets too long); other such truths might be useful or interesting, but too costly to discover (this, I take it, is a poignant fact that most working scientists face whenever they apply for funding); still other truths might be downright dangerous to know (some take this view of genetics). For all these reasons, a commitment to the ideal of a single and complete body of truths need not bring in train a commitment to knowing all of them. Later, we'll consider whether the case might be different in the ethical domain. Perhaps ethical truths are the sorts of things we should want to know. But my point here is an *in principle* one. All that the realist stance *per se* commits us to is the idea that there is a single and complete body of truths. And, in most domains, we can retain this commitment even if we happen not to be interested in knowing all of the truths in those domains. Yet even when this is our attitude, the commitment still has practical import. If we do embrace the realist ideal, we shall have to conceive inquiry—the business of acquiring knowledge of the truths in which we *are* interested—in relation to it. It will remain true that there is no well-formed proposition (in the domain of our inquiry) concerning which the question of its truth does not arise. And, insofar as we think our beliefs are true, we must think of them in accord with the realist ideal. That is, we must think of them as figuring in the single and complete body of truths. Likewise whenever we change our minds. Whenever we acquire new beliefs or correct mistaken beliefs, we must think of these epistemic activities as bringing us closer to that ideal.

The practical implications of the realist stance for interpersonal relations are as follows. Once we adopt the stance, we cannot ever be *wholly* indifferent to the views of others. We must always take a stand. If we find that others' views are not conjoinable with ours, then we must either reject theirs as false or change our own minds. (When we change our minds we have two options. Either we can reject our own view as false, or we can suspend belief on the matter. The point is that we are constrained by the realist ideal to do one of these things whenever we are unwilling to reject a conflicting view as false.) And if we find that others' views are different from ours but conjoinable, then we must allow that we may have something to learn from them. Of course, there is no presumption that others are right when they believe a proposition we haven't yet considered. There isn't, any more than there is a presumption that others are right when we disagree. Nor is there any general presumption that we should always be interested in the propositions that others believe but we don't (though, as I've already indicated, there may be reason to presume this in the specific case of ethics). What is presumed—actually that's too weak: what is *built into* the realist stance—is that there is a single ideal in the light of which all of the differences among believers could in principle be sorted out, namely, the one complete body of truths. The realist stance does not exhort us to actually resolve our differences with others (any more than it exhorts us to learn all of the truths). It only requires that we view our differences with others in the light of the realist ideal. As realists, we must hold that whenever disagreements do arise, at most one party can be right. And this, of course, is precisely what the relativist wants to deny.

It should already be clear that relativism can also be characterized as a stance that has significant practical implications. When I adopt the relativist stance, I am free to disregard epistemic differences between me and others in the deepest possible way: I can regard others as neither right nor wrong by my lights. And this is not because I regard myself as ignorant about whether they are right or wrong. It is rather because the sense in which they might be right or wrong has absolutely nothing to do with my own inquiry into what's true. I can view others as seeking something else, namely, *their* truths. Their truths are not conjoinable with mine at all. But I need not, for that reason, reject them as false. They are altogether out of the loop of consideration.

I want to emphasize that it is important not to exaggerate the practical implications of these stances. One very common mistake is to think that relativism instructs us to be tolerant of the views of others, while realism instructs us to be intolerant. But this is not so. Realism does provide the resources for one very common argument in favor of intolerance, which I'll call the argument from righteousness. This argument says that there is one truth and, if I take myself to know that truth, then I have a duty to spread it to everyone else whether they want it or not. But the realist stance doesn't require such an intolerant attitude toward the views of others. It is coherent to embrace the realist ideal of a single and complete body of truths and yet, also, embrace the sorts of moral values that would entail an obligation to be tolerant—values like self-determination and freedom from oppression. Similarly, it is coherent to adopt the relativist stance according to which different people may have different truths and yet, also, embrace the project of trying to stamp out alternative viewpoints. What is clear is that relativism lacks the resources to mount the righteous argument for intolerance that is available to realists. But, nevertheless, relativists have available less righteous grounds for intolerance, such as zeal to get everyone to be just like me.

I hope it is clear, then, that the practical differences between the realist and relativist stances cannot be cashed out in terms of the issue of tolerance. The difference turns on a less morally loaded and more purely epistemic issue. When I adopt the relativist stance, I am free to disregard the views of others as lying completely outside my pursuit of truth. They are utterly irrelevant—so irrelevant that even if they conflict with mine I needn't, for that reason, regard them as false. As I put it earlier, the views of others are simply out of the loop of consideration. But this is not so when I adopt the realist stance. If I'm pursuing truth in the sense that goes together with the realist ideal, then no one's views are ever wholly irrelevant. And this is so even if I am not particularly interested in them. Even so, my critical perspective on my own views must somehow comprehend theirs as well. If their views conflict with mine, I can't hold mine without deeming theirs false. Or, to put the point in its full generality, I must view myself and others as subject to a single standard in the light of which all of our epistemic differences could in principle be sorted out—the single and complete body of truths.

So, my proposal is that we address the issue of realism vs. relativism in the ethical domain by considering the respective merits of these two practical stances in that domain. This is why I call it a pragmatic approach to the issue.

Unsurprisingly, this pragmatic approach to the issue of realism vs. relativism allows for the possibility that card-carrying pragmatists might qualify as realists. Despite Rorty's insistence that pragmatism goes together with relativism,[7] there are other brands of pragmatism besides his that are consistent with embracing the realist ideal of a single and complete body of truths—Peirce's, for example.[8] This is not because the realist ideal can be equated with his ideal limit of inquiry. It is rather because the realist ideal satisfies his requirement of having practical meaning. I've already noted that finite beings like us probably can't coherently aim to know the whole truth that is articulated in that ideal. But we have seen that the ideal still has practical meaning, because we can always conceive inquiry in relation to it. Whenever we acquire new beliefs, and whenever we give up mistaken beliefs, we can conceive ourselves as doing so in order to get closer to the ideal. This does not mean that we should view our epistemic history over the millennia as a history of progress toward that ideal—toward knowing the single and complete body of truths. Whether such progress has actually occurred is an empirical question to which I do not know the answer. And, in any case, it will not compromise my point here if our epistemic history turns out to have been full of many false starts and even regress. My point is not about the overall progress of inquiry over time. My point is about how realists must view each moment of their inquiries from the inside, as they engage in them. Every time they change their minds, they must think of themselves as making some kind of epistemic improvement *then*. And, insofar as they are committed to the realist ideal of a single and complete body of truths, they will conceive each such attempt at improvement in relation to that ideal.

These last remarks may seem to be in some tension with my earlier claim that we needn't conceive the realist ideal as setting the goal for inquiry—that we needn't be committed to discovering the single and complete body of truths. But I don't see any real tension here. I can see myself as making progress toward an ideal while at the same time viewing the ideal itself as beyond my reach. I'm aware that many pragmatists would prefer to avoid any reference to such ideals. They would prefer to characterize our efforts at epistemic improvement in more myopic terms. Why, they might ask, can't I acquire a new belief, or revise a prior belief, without thinking of myself as getting closer to the ideal of the single and complete body of truths? In answer, I must confess that I myself can't make very much of the alleged distinction between "more" and "closer to an ideal limit or totality." But for the benefit of those who attach great importance to the distinction, perhaps I should say a bit more about why I include the idea of completeness in my characterization of the realist ideal. I want to bring out something that the realist is committed to and the relativist rejects. Here is one familiar way of bringing it out: for *any* disagreement (over well-formed propositions) that could arise (within a given domain) at most one party is right. It seems to me that anyone who rejects relativism—even a pragmatist—needs to frame such a universally quantified thought. Now, think of the sum of all of the possible disagreements and, then, think of the sum of the "right sides" of those disagreements. As far as I can see, that would be a single and complete body of truths. And also, as far as I can see, any pragmatist or, indeed, anyone, who rejects relativism is implicitly committed to there being such a thing.

There is another important respect in which my conception of realism as a practical stance is consistent with a more generally pragmatist outlook. It is consistent with the pragmatist eschewal of skepticism. I can consistently embrace the realist ideal and also regard my current beliefs as immune from skeptical doubt. In fact, to hold my beliefs is, precisely, to regard them as beliefs in truths that figure in the single, complete body of truths. If I didn't think they so figured, I would give them up. Given my larger aim in this paper, it is not a disadvantage that my proposal affords a conception of realism that is compatible with pragmatism. Of all the "isms" pragmatism is the least hospitable to drawing distinctions between belief and value. This is not because pragmatists are not interested in the sort of objectivity that science delivers; it is rather because they insist that there can be just as much objectivity in the domain of values as there is in the domain of facts into which scientists inquire.

On the other hand, the realist stance does not require us to embrace pragmatism. It is possible to embrace the realist ideal and also impose further conditions on realism. We might think that, in addition to embracing the ideal of a single and complete body of truths, we must conceive the ideal along metaphysical realist lines as a realm of mind-independent facts. Or we might think that the ideal should be construed along Davidsonian lines, as what we already by and large agree about. But the important point is this: no such additional conditions could ever undermine the connection between realism and the realist ideal of a single and complete body of truths. It would be incoherent to say that one is a realist because one believes that there are mind-independent "truthmakers" and, then, go on to reject the idea that there is a single and complete set of them. For, in rejecting that idea one would have lost the absolutist conception of truth that distinguishes realism from relativism. The same goes for the Davidsonian position. When he argued that we all by and large agree, his aim was to establish a condition in which we are justified in viewing all of our remaining differences as disagreements in which only one party can be right, rather than as conflicts in which each party is right relative to their conceptual scheme. And, to view them in this way is, precisely, to view them in the light of the realist ideal of a single and complete body of truths.

It seems to me that the real merit of conceiving realism in terms of a commitment to this ideal is that it allows us to pose the issue of realism vs. relativism in ethics *without* imposing any additional conditions on realism. For it probably doesn't make sense to impose them in the ethical domain. Doing so would require us to assimilate ethics to science in inappropriate ways, or overlook the existence of actual diversity of ethical opinion. I will be arguing in the next two sections that the realist stance allows us to frame a *realist project of ethical inquiry* in the face of all this—in the face of the fact that the enterprise of ethics is different from science and in the face of manifest ethical diversity.

Despite all I have said in this section, I expect I may still evoke the following complaint from many: to embrace the realist ideal in ethics without providing a positive account of the ethical "truth-makers" is not to embrace anything that deserves the label "realism." My concern isn't so much to keep the label. My concern is to see whether we can earn the right to a position in ethics that stands opposed to ethical relativism because it insists that, in all cases of ethical conflict, at most one party is right. It would be very reassuring to get that much objectivity in the ethical domain, even if we couldn't satisfy the metaphysical ambitions that enter into some philosophers' conception of realism.

And, in any case, there is at least one good reason to call this sort of objectivist position in ethics a kind of realism. It incorporates the idea that there is something to inquire *about* in the ethical domain—something to get right or wrong, something to know.

2. Harman's Defense of Moral Relativism

I want next to consider whether Gilbert Harman's defense of moral relativism gives us reason to abandon the realist stance in ethics in favor of the relativist stance.[9] We shall see that the reverse is true. Harman's conception of the foundations of morality positively invites the realist stance, along with all of its practical implications for ethical inquiry and interpersonal relations.

On Harman's account, moral rules are the result of moral bargaining. Such rules arise when individuals find self-interested reasons to enter into agreements with others to abide by certain common moral rules. It is undeniable that there are moral agreements in Harman's sense. And he is absolutely right that they provide an occasion for adopting the relativist stance. When we observe that other people subscribe to a different agreement, as outsiders to that agreement we are free to regard what's right or wrong within it as irrelevant to the question what would it be right or wrong for us to do. We can say to ourselves, that's just what they agreed to do and their agreement doesn't bind us in any way. Harman captures this relativist attitude with his notion of an "inner moral judgment," which he defines as a judgment about what it is right or wrong to do in the light of a specific moral agreement. Once we've mastered this notion, we're supposed to recognize that our inner moral judgments can't properly be extended to those who stand outside of the moral agreement(s) to which we are party. And, of course, we know that the same goes for parties to other agreements; they too must recognize that their inner moral judgments do not extend beyond their agreements. Harman illustrates this relativity of inner moral judgments with a rather unwinning example, in which he points out that it sounds odd to say that Hitler was "wrong" to do the various things he did. It doesn't sound nearly so odd to me as it apparently sounds to him. But I think I see what he means. Hitler does seem to be beyond the reach of a certain *sort* of moral judgment, namely, the sort of inner moral judgment that presupposes that he and we subscribe to the same moral agreement. It is not Harman's aim, however, to show that Hitler is immune from all ethical evaluation on our part. He allows that we can say of him that he was evil.

This allowance should give us pause. If we are capable of ethical responses that are *not* confined to our moral agreements, that should make us wonder whether Harman is right to locate the foundations of morality in such agreements, rather than in our capacity for such wider ethical responses. But, for the sake of argument, I'll assume that he is right to do so. For it will prove instructive to see what does and doesn't follow. It follows that every ethical concept that is now available to us began its life as a by-product of moral bargaining. (Self-interest is the one exception, for obvious reasons.) It also follows that the initial meaning of any given ethical concept incorporates a kind of implicit relativization to the specific moral agreement in which it was first introduced. However, no interesting form of relativism follows unless it can be shown that our ethical concepts are forever confined to their original contexts. And I don't see how this can be shown. More specifically, I don't see how we can rule out the possibility of extending the application of ethical concepts beyond the confines of the moral agreements that originally gave rise to them. It seems obvious to me that this has actually happened. It happened, for example, when we took notions of rights that were originally introduced in the context of the specific moral agreement that is articulated in the U.S. Constitution and, then, used those same notions as a standard for criticizing agreements arrived at in quite different political contexts. A defender of Harman-style relativism might point out that it is always within the rights of those who stand outside our moral agreements to protest that they should not be subjected to the standards of our agreements. This is certainly true; the relativist stance is always available. But that doesn't end the matter. For, as I shall now argue, Harman's highly rationalistic account of the foundations of morality invites us to frame and pursue a project of ethical inquiry that is essentially realist in spirit.

Agents who have the requisite rational capacities to devise and implement moral agreements in Harman's sense must surely also have general capacities for critical reflection. And, so, even if they begin by uncritically accepting the ethical concepts that figure in their own moral agreements, there is no reason why they couldn't or shouldn't subject them to critical scrutiny. Of course, within Harman's framework the only possible source of such critical insight is other moral agreements to which one is not a party. But this is a perfectly good source. There is nothing to stop us from learning about other moral agreements to which we are not a party, and thereby acquiring conceptual resources for adopting a critical perspective on our own moral agreements. And it is important to see that such a critical perspective would not coincide with the moral perspective that is supplied by the particular moral agreement to which one is a party. It is a more comprehensive critical perspective from which one can make comparative judgements about whether one's own moral agreement is better or worse than some others. It is also important to see that this more comprehensive critical perspective need not coincide with the perspective of self-interest that one occupies while contemplating whether to enter into a given moral agreement. I can certainly ask whether someone else's agreement would be better for me than the one to which I am a party. But there are other critical issues I can raise as well. To take a realistic example, consider a woman who is party to a moral agreement that systematically oppresses women. It is in her self-interest to abide by this agreement not because it is serves her interests so very well, but because she has no better option. After having made the agreement and lived by it, she comes to learn about a different moral agreement in which women are given the same rights to education, property and self-determination as men.

And she thinks to herself, that's a better agreement. Perhaps this thought begins as a self-interested wish that her agreement were more like that one, or that she were a party to that one rather than her own. But she also has the conceptual resources to think that that agreement is simply fairer. I've assumed for the sake of argument that the notion of fairness is itself a by-product of moral bargaining and, so, must have begun its life relativized to a particular moral agreement. But the point remains that it can also provide a perfectly reasonable standard by which we can make comparative judgments *about* moral agreements. When we make these comparative judgments, we are taking conceptual resources that, by assumption, have been supplied by *different* agreements and we are incorporating them into a *single* critical perspective. This constitutes a move away from the relativist stance, toward the sort of ethical inquiry that would go together with the realist stance.

It might be objected that this sort of ethical inquiry needn't be fully committed to the realist ideal according to which *all* ethical differences could in principle be sorted out. Perhaps it needn't be. But, once we've begun the task of critical reflection, it is unclear why we should ever bring it to a halt. That is, it is unclear why, once we've begun the process of comparative evaluation of different moral agreements and their different terms, we should regard any of the ethical differences we find as falling outside the constraints that are imposed by the realist ideal. Either they are the sorts of differences that are conjoinable, or they are conflicts that need to be resolved. We needn't be committed to the idea that we will always know how to resolve such conflicts in order to cleave to the realist stance. We need only be committed to the idea that there is something to resolve. And, it should be born in mind that there are more ways to resolve conflicts among evaluative attitudes than among beliefs. Instead of giving up one or other of the conflicting values, we can resolve the conflict by ranking them in relative importance. It should also be born in mind that some ethical conflicts aren't really significant from the point of view of the realist ideal. I'm thinking of the sort of conflict that arises when we rank several ethical values as equally important and yet, due to contingent practical limitations, we find that we can't pursue them all together. The fact that we must choose among them for this reason does not signify that they wouldn't all figure in the single and complete body of ethical truths. And, more generally, the fact that there are all of these ways to interpret and cope with ethical conflict should help to strengthen our confidence in the feasibility of the realist project of ethical inquiry.

The specific approach to this project that I've proposed as a response to Harman is not the only possible approach. I think that anyone working in the contractarian tradition of moral and political philosophy who doesn't share Harman's relativism is carrying out what is, essentially, a realist project of ethical inquiry. These contractarians seek an answer to the very same question that would guide the inquiry I just described, namely, what is the best moral agreement? The main difference is that they tend to give a narrow interpretation to the term "best" as meaning something like "serves everyone's interests in the most optimal way," and they tend to take a highly rationalistic approach to establishing what is best in this narrow sense. It is important to see that this familiar contractarian endeavor qualifies as ethical inquiry in the realist mode. But it is also important to see that the alternative approach that I've described here is also available. On this approach, ethical inquiry can be far more empirical, insofar as it undertakes to make many specific and substantive comparisons between actual moral agreements using their own terms.

3. Williams's "Truth" in Relativism

I turn now to Bernard Williams's defense of ethical relativism.[10]

My point of departure in this paper is virtually identical with his. He holds that we can't model ethical realism on scientific realism; he rejects the major ethical theories, thereby losing another possible ground for ethical realism; and he recognizes a diversity of ethical opinion sufficient to rule out the Davidsonian strategy against ethical relativism. There is one crucial difference, however. He takes for granted—wrongly in my view—that scientific realism is the only viable model for ethical realism. And, so, he never considers the possibility of a realist project of ethical inquiry along the lines I'm envisaging. But the question still arises, is it the case that his overall ethical vision should give us pause about that project? My aim in this section is to determine the extent to which this is so.

In order to accomplish this aim I'll need to spell out some of the details of Williams's defense of ethical relativism—what he calls "the conditions of the problem." First, there must be two or more systems of belief (Ss) that are to some extent self-contained. The issue of relativism concerns whether and how issues of preference can arise in connection with such Ss. Of course, issues of preference among different Ss cannot arise unless the Ss can be understood by the same parties—so that is another condition of the problem. Yet, although it must be the case that different Ss can be understood by a single party they must, nevertheless, be exclusive of one another—for, otherwise, they could be conjoined in accordance with the realist ideal of a single and complete body of ethical truths. One way of being exclusive is to have conflicting consequences. In the case of scientific theories, this usually means conflicting predictions. But this kind of conflict is symptomatic of realism rather than relativism, because it provides a basis for saying that one of the conflicting Ss is true while the other is false—and again we would have conformity with the realist ideal. There is a temptation to say that the relativist is looking for a kind of exclusivity that leaves both of the conflicting Ss standing as true. But Williams takes care not to characterize relativism in terms of truth, presumably in order to avoid some of the obvious formal difficulties that would otherwise ensue. In the ethical domain, these formal difficulties can be avoided by characterizing conflict in practical terms rather than logical terms. Thus, in ethics, two Ss have conflicting consequences insofar as they give conflicting answers to the question whether a given action should be performed. But in the interest of generality, Williams settles on a somewhat vaguer characterization of exclusivity that can apply to both science and ethics. He says that two Ss are mutually exclusive if it is impossible to *live* within both of them at the same time.

Having specified the conditions of the problem, Williams goes on to define two sorts of confrontation that can occur between two Ss, real confrontations and merely notional confrontations. Holders of S1 stand in real confrontation with S2 if it is a real option for them to abandon S1 in favor of S2. If S2 is to be a real option for holders of S1, then the two Ss must be comparable; that is, it must be possible for holders of S1 to view the transition to S2 as making sense in the light of a comparison between them. Furthermore, they must be able to go over to S2 without losing their grip on reality. Notional confrontations do not display these features. When holders of S1 are in merely notional confrontation with S2, S2 is not a real option for them. They do not find S1 and S2 comparable, and they could not go over to S2 while retaining their grip on reality.

With this distinction in hand, between real and notional confrontations, Williams is able to characterize relativism in the following terms: When we stand in a real confrontation with a real option, then we face the task of appraising it with the vocabulary of true/false, right/wrong, etc. When we don't face a real option—in other words, when we stand in merely notional confrontation with some alien system—then, although we *can* apply our vocabulary of appraisal, it may be pointless to do so. The system may be too alien to be relevant to our judgements. When this happens, it makes sense to take up what I've been calling the relativist stance.

Williams holds that the relativist stance is appropriate in ethics but not in science. But this is not because notional confrontations arise only in ethics and not in science. As he himself observes, phlogiston theory is not, at present, a real option for us. Yet we don't take a relativist stance toward that theory. That is, we don't find it pointless to bring our vocabulary of appraisal to bear on it. On the contrary. Precisely because the theory cannot be conjoined with theories we now hold true, we find it important to appraise it as false—a clear reflection of the fact that we embrace the realist stance in science. But Williams contends that the situation is different when we stand in notional confrontations with alternative ethical outlooks. He maintains that there is no particular point in appraising them. If he were right about this, then it would be pointless to take up the realist stance toward them. One might as well abandon it in favor of the relativist stance.

However, we need to consider very carefully whether it really is pointless to take up the realist stance in ethics, and why. Clearly, it won't suffice merely to point out the existence of notional confrontations in ethics. We've just seen that the existence of such confrontations in science is perfectly compatible with the realist stance there. Williams is moved by the fact that science provides a particular way of earning the right to realism that doesn't carry over to the case of ethics. But we shouldn't conclude to ethical relativism unless we are convinced that there is no other model for realism in ethics. And this means, in particular, that we need to uncover reasons for thinking that a realist project of ethical inquiry that is not modeled on science is either unfeasible, or unwarranted, or inappropriate.

The best way to uncover these reasons is by seeing what a realist project of ethical inquiry might amount to given the constraints that would be imposed by Williams's ethical vision and, then, assessing the merits of that project.

There are two main components of Williams's vision, both of which I find overwhelmingly plausible. First, he rejects the major ethical theories and, second, he conceives values as the products of social and historical and cultural forces. It follows that values are not typically chosen, either individually or collectively, in the way that the contractarian tradition portrays them but, rather, they evolve within particular forms of life that give them their point and meaning. Consequently, it also follows that, for Williams, the goal of ethical inquiry could not be the one that I considered in the last section in response to Harman. The goal cannot be to discover what the best moral agreement is, because most of the ethical issues we face have nothing to do with any such agreements. Yet there is one very basic ethical question that Williams thinks we all face, no matter what our social circumstances might be. This is the Socratic question, how shall I live? The question immediately suggests a very broad goal for ethical inquiry, which is simply to discover the best way of living. A realist project of ethical inquiry organized along these lines would be something like the project of an Ultra liberal arts education. The aim would be to discover what the best way of living is. And the method by which this aim would be achieved would be a comparative study of different forms of life.

So, here is my thought. If we assume the basic components of Williams's ethical vision, then we can assess the merits of the realist stance in ethics by assessing the merits of this form of ethical inquiry, construed as something like the project of an Ultra liberal arts education. I hope it is clear that my thought is very much in harmony with Williams's way of setting up the problem of relativism in ethics. For this form of ethical inquiry has a point only insofar as there is a point in appraising alternative ethical systems. To the extent that we find such appraisal pointless, so too is ethical inquiry. And, in that case, we may as well forsake the realist stance in ethics in favor of the relativist stance, which is exactly Williams's suggestion.

However, we need to consider very carefully whether this form of ethical inquiry, which consists in the appraisal of alternative ethical outlooks, really is pointless and why.

It may be tempting—and I think Williams himself may be tempted—to think that the mere fact that values are the products of culture and history already suffices to make such appraisal pointless. But I don't see why this should be so. Compare the case of science, where we clearly do see a point in making cross-cultural evaluations of theories that belong to different social and historical traditions. Such evaluations can serve our current scientific inquiries in various ways. At the very least, such comparisons can help to clarify our theoretical commitments, by showing us what they rule out, such as phlogiston theory. But the comparisons needn't always work in favor of currently prevailing theories. If it should turn out that phlogiston theory would help to solve certain unsolved problems, then the scientific attitude requires that we should resurrect it in something like the spirit in which Chomsky has resurrected certain themes from Cartesian philosophy in order to solve problems in contemporary linguistics. The ethical inquirer can do something similar, by embracing values that originated in other forms of life. Obviously, there are limits on the extent to which ethical values are transportable from one context to another. Sometimes, one context can be quite accommodating of values drawn from another—for example, the American context can fairly easily accommodate conversion to Buddhism. But, presumably, there are other values that the American context can't so easily accommodate. Williams's example of medieval samurai warrior ethics might be a good example, but I don't know enough about gangland life in the urban U.S. to be sure. In any event, even when we can't just start living by the values we learn about from other contexts, there are other avenues of action that may be open to us. We might immigrate to a place where it is possible to live by those values, or we might stay where we are and fight for social change.

I take it to be Williams's view that, very often, all three of these avenues are closed: our own context won't accommodate living by the values we learn about from other contexts; but we also can't move to those other contexts in order to live by them; nor can we realistically expect to change our own context so as to accommodate them. This is another way of seeing the difference between ethics and science. In general, scientific theories are exportable from one context to another. But not so with ethical values. Being the sorts of social and historical products they are, they are not, according to Williams, easily transportable. And very often, we can't make up for this fact by doing the travelling ourselves. We too are the products of social and historical forces that, like our values, are pretty much bound to our particular contexts.

I happen to take a more optimistic view than Williams, of the possibility that one or another of these three avenues will be open to us in a given case. But I want to grant for the sake of argument that he might be right. If he is right, then there is a danger that ethical inquiry in the realist mode might reduce us to nostalgia and wistfulness. Even so, I'm not at all sure that it follows that the inquiry would have been pointless. I do see that it may *seem* pointless. For, it is a fair constraint on ethical inquiry that it should yield some form of ethical illumination. And there is much to recommend the idea that such illumination should make a practical difference in our lives. The clearest case in which there would be such a practical difference is this: that the fruits of ethical inquiry consisted in implementable instructions about how to live. But, of course, the case we're now considering is precisely the case in which this isn't so. What other form might ethical illumination take in this case, where implementable instructions about how to live are not forthcoming from ethical inquiry? Well, suppose that when I study other forms of life, I discover values that I come to estimate very highly, even though it is not open to me to implement them. At the very least, this discovery would give me a kind of counterfactual knowledge about what I should do if I had the opportunity. And, with the acquisition of this counterfactual knowledge, I would learn something important about the values I currently live by. I would learn how conditional they are on my contingent circumstances. The opposite may happen as well. I may discover ethical attitudes and practices that I could never bring myself to share, no matter what my circumstances might be. And this discovery would show me certain respects in which my values are not conditional on my contingent circumstances. In both cases, I would learn something about the very *contents* of my standing evaluative commitments—something worth having, and something that I think qualifies as ethical illumination. So, I see a point in a realist project of ethical inquiry, even given the bleakest assumptions about how rare the opportunities are for implementing what we thereby learn.

These points that ethical inquiry might have, beyond delivering implementable knowledge, depend upon something that might be called into question. They depend on significant normative interaction between values drawn from different contexts. So, for example, I couldn't learn how conditional my values are on my actual context, unless I could see how those values would be outweighed in contexts where other values can be implemented. Similarly, I couldn't learn how unconditional my values are unless I could see how they outweigh values that might be acted upon in other contexts. So, one way to establish Williams's claim that it is often pointless to appraise values drawn from other contexts is by calling this normative interaction into question. Perhaps values drawn from different contexts don't speak to one another at all. Then it might, indeed, be pointless to engage in the form of ethical inquiry I've been discussing.

Notice that this sort of evaluative insularity will arise only if the following is true: When I pursue my Ultra liberal arts education I find that I am virtually indifferent to the values that others live by in their contexts. I don't mind that others act on those values, which shows that they're not entirely ruled out by my values. Yet they're not exactly ruled in either, except in the minimal sense that they're not ruled out. They simply go in at the very bottom of my preference ordering, as values I can't imagine ever pursuing so long as there is an alternative. This would engender a fairly deep experience of otherness. If ethical inquiry couldn't deliver anything else, besides such an experience of otherness, then it would make sense to abandon the realist stance in favor of the relativist stance. For, to repeat, the realist stance has a point in ethics only if it generates a project of ethical inquiry that can yield ethical illumination. And this outcome wouldn't be ethically illuminating. It wouldn't help me to settle any practical questions about how to live. Nor would it help me to clarify the contents of my current evaluative commitments—except to underscore how little they speak to most other values.

So, I've finally identified a condition in which the relativist stance would make more sense than the realist stance in ethics. Yet I'm not saying that the realist stance would be untenable in this condition. The realist stance is tenable come what may. I'm only saying that it would be pointless. By pursuing ethical inquiry in the light of the realist ideal of a single and complete body of ethical truths, all we would arrive at is a very long list of conditional claims about what is valuable in different contexts. I've already explained that knowledge of this list would not qualify as ethical illumination. It would never bear on the ethical questions we face as agents whose lives and values are, by hypothesis, context-bound. Indeed, it seems to me that the knowledge would be better characterized as sociological than as ethical. And again, the reason why is the insularity of the values that evolve in different contexts, their failure to speak to one another. If that really is the nature of ethical value, then we might as well abandon the realist project of ethical inquiry in favor of the relativist stance.

However, we would be warranted in this relativist conclusion only if we *knew* that we were in the condition I've identified. Think how many things we would have to know. We would have to know a) that we typically can't implement in our actual circumstances any values we learn about from other forms of life; b) we also can't implement those values through cultural emigration; c) we can't strive to get into a position to implement them by trying to foster social change; d) learning about such values could never give us reason to rethink our priorities; e) learning about such values could never serve to clarify the contents of our evaluative commitments, by revealing ways in which they are or are not conditional on our actual circumstances. I don't find a single one of these propositions plausible. I certainly don't think we know they obtain. But, on the other hand, I can imagine someone protesting that we don't know that they don't obtain either. For the sake of argument, then, and judiciousness, I propose that we suspend belief on this matter. That is, I recommend that we suspend belief about whether the condition in which ethical relativism would be warranted is our actual condition.

It may appear that, in saying this, I'm recommending that we shelve the whole issue about realism vs. relativism in ethics. But that isn't quite so. We're bound to come across ethical difference. And I don't see how we could possibly respond without adopting one stance or the other, the realist or the relativist. We will have to choose. Furthermore, when we choose, we should want to do more than *merely* beg the question on the side we prefer. We should want to earn the right to our chosen stance. Obviously, we can't do this without addressing the question on which I've recommended that we suspend belief: is our actual condition the condition in which the relativist stance would be warranted? This is an empirical question. And the only way to answer it is by pursuing the realist project of ethical inquiry. We need to learn about values that figure in other forms of life and try to make comparative evaluations. Of course, what the ethical realist hopes to gain from these comparisons is ethical illumination, perhaps in the form of learning about new practical possibilities that we might pursue, or in the form of a deeper understanding of (or even correction of) our evaluative commitments. But it may be that ethical inquiry will fail to deliver such illumination. If a sustained attempt at such inquiry failed to deliver anything of ethical interest, then we could in retrospect say that the realist stance had, after all, been pointless. This is important. It shows that the realist stance does not prejudge the central issue on which its warrant would ultimately depend. In contrast, the relativist stance does prejudge the issue—at least in fact, if not in intention. It would foreclose the realist project of ethical inquiry. And that would prevent us from discovering the extent to which the project does or does not have a point. This is something we need to discover and know. Because this is so, we have reason, at least at the present time, to prefer the realist stance in ethics over the relativist stance.

I have tried to transpose the virtues of realism as being those of the nature of inquiry rather than directly of a certain conception of epistemically unconstrained reality, and I have tried to do so in a way that, unlike Peirce, does not make any idealized end point of inquiry the licit surrogate of the idea of such an unconstrained conception of reality. It's not as if, by stressing inquiry and having criticized the contractarian tradition, I have tried to find a licit surrogate for their notion of a discoverable, contractable ideal in some Whiggish *consummation* of the *progress* that the path of ethical inquiry might take. No notions of progress, and no ideal consummation inform the realist project of ethical inquiry that I have tried to formulate. Nevertheless it is in inquiry, and its pursuit under the realist stance that I have elaborated and defended, that the doctrine of ethical realism will flourish, if it does.[11]

Notes

1. There is a large and varied literature on moral realism that is more or less sympathetic to this proposal. For two central examples, see Peter Railton, "Moral Realism," *Philosophical Review*, 95 (1986) and William Lycan, "Moral Facts and Moral Knowledge," *Southern Journal of Philosophy* 24, Supplement (1986: Spindel Conference).

2. For reasons of space, I must ignore the fact that there are rival accounts of scientific realism, as well as the fact that there are important objections to scientific realism. I must also forego any detailed account of attempts on the part of ethical theorists to extend the scientific realist position to ethics. The upshot, I fear, will be that I appear insufficiently critical of scientific realism in general and, yet, at the same time, overly critical of its particular bearing in ethics. As I've said, I hope to remedy these deficiencies elsewhere. Here I mean only to say enough to clarify the point of departure for my positive suggestions in this paper, which depart significantly from the scientific realist picture altogether.

3. See J. L. Mackie, *Ethics: Inventing Right and Wrong* (New York: Penguin, 1977).

4. I realize, of course, that those who propose to model ethical realism on scientific realism are aware of these obvious differences between ethics and science.

5. See his "On the Very Idea of a Conceptual Scheme," *Proceedings and Addresses of the American Philosophical Association* 67 (1973–74).

6. See his "What is a Theory of Meaning? (II)" in G. Evans and J. McDowells, eds., *Truth and Meaning: Essays in Semantics*, Oxford University Press (Oxford: 1976).

7. See his *Consequences of Pragmatism* (Minneapolis: Minnesota University Press, 1982).

8. See his "How to Make Our Ideas Clear" in *Philosophical Writings of Peirce*, ed. J. Buchler (New York: Dover Publications, 1955).

9. See his "Moral Relativism Defended," *Philosophical Review* 84 (1975).

10. I've assembled this defense mainly from two sources: "The Truth in Relativism" in his *Moral Luck* (New York: Cambridge University Press, 1981) and *Ethics and the Limits of Philosophy* (Cambridge, Mass.: Harvard University Press, 1985).

11. I'd like to thank Stefan Baumrin, Akeel Bilgrami, Patricia Blanchette, Donald Davidson, Michael Della Rocca, Jerrold Katz, Philip Kitcher, Isaac Levi, Achille Varzi, Stephen White, Meredith Williams, Michael Williams, and Susan Wolf for discussing the issues of this paper with me.

Philosophical Issues, 12, Realism and Relativism, 2002

MORAL REALISM AND INDETERMINACY

Stephen Schiffer
New York University

I'm going to argue for something that some of you will find repugnant but which I can't help thinking may be true—namely, that there are no determinate moral truths. As will become apparent, my interest in moral discourse as manifested in this paper derives more than a little from my interest in the theory of meaning. Moral discourse has always presented a puzzle for the theory of meaning and philosophical logic, and I take myself to be following the advice of Bertrand Russell when he recommended testing philosophical theories by their capacity to deal with puzzles, "since these serve much the same purpose as is served by experiments in physical science."[1]

Section (I) offers an epistemological argument for the claim that there are no determinate moral truths. This argument raises further questions, which subsequent sections try to answer. In the course of answering those further questions, another, non-epistemological, argument is offered for the claim that there are no determinate moral truths. In the end, I hope we see not only that there are no determinately true moral propositions, but what it is about moral concepts which makes that so.

I. An Epistemological Argument

The argument I have in mind begins with the following master argument (EA), whose interest lies in the arguments for its premises:

(1) If there are determinately true moral propositions, then there are moral principles that are knowable a priori.

(2) There are no such moral principles.

(3) ∴ There are no determinately true moral propositions.

A few clarifications. First, my use of 'determinately' in (EA) is pretheoretic and at this point in my exposition presupposes no account of how the notion should be explicated. This notion implies, *inter alia*, that if x is a borderline case of an F, then it's indeterminate whether x is an F. It may or may not transpire that being indeterminate entails being neither true nor false. I'll have more to say about this later. Second, by a "moral proposition" I mean a proposition that can be the content of a substantive moral judgment. This would exclude trivial truisms such as the proposition that one morally ought not to do what is morally wrong. If there is such a proposition as the proposition that eating animals is morally wrong, then that would count as a moral proposition, as would the proposition, should it exist, that your stepping on my blue suede shoes was a morally bad thing. If moral principles are things that can be known (as opposed to rules or injunctions of some kind), then they are general moral propositions, such as the proposition that slavery is wrong. Third, a priori knowledge is, at least to a first approximation, knowledge whose knowledge-making grounds include no empirical proposition believed to be evidence for what one knows. One reason this is a first approximation is as follows. Suppose I'm doing conceptual analysis and, after some labor, conclude that, necessarily, a speaker means p iff she intends to get her audience to believe p by means of the audience's recognition of her intention to get him to believe p. Suppose, too, that my philosophical exercise has been so well conducted that it actually results in my *knowing* the proposition to which it brought me. As most philosophers use 'a priori knowledge', my knowledge of the necessary truth about speaker-meaning would count as a priori. At the same time, these philosophers wouldn't deny that part of my justification for believing what I know is the *empirical* proposition that I have been unable to think of any counterexamples. I merely note this qualification to the standard gloss on a priori knowledge and won't try to achieve a more adequate gloss. Suffice it to say that I intend my use of 'a priori knowledge' to be on all fours with the use of most philosophers who believe the expression has application.

Returning to (EA), we see that it's plainly valid, thus reducing the issue it raises to that of the truth of its two premises.

Re premise (1): If there are determinately true moral propositions, then there are moral principles that are knowable a priori. To say there are moral truths may for present purposes be taken to mean that there are moral properties and that at least some of them are instantiated. For example, if it's true that my stepping on your blue suede shoes was morally wrong, then my act instantiates the property of being morally wrong. I assume—and assume no one would deny—that, for any x and any moral property M, if x has M, then there is some non-normative property Φ, however complex, such that x has Φ and having Φ minimally metaphysically entails having M—that is, having Φ metaphysically entails having M and nothing contained in Φ (so to say) is inessential to its metaphysically entailing having M. In the event, the proposition that whatever has Φ, has M is a necessarily true moral principle. It follows that if there are determinately true moral propositions, then there are necessarily true moral principles. Such moral principles would themselves be determinately true. I take it to be obvious and not in need of argument that if there are such moral principles, then at least some of them are knowable, indeed known. What reader will claim she has moral knowledge but deny that, e.g., she knows that it's wrong to torture children just for the fun of it? Now, if there are necessarily true moral principles that are knowable, then at least some of them are knowable a priori. This, too, I simply take to be obvious. I don't deny that some metaphysically necessary propositions can be known only a posteriori. This seems to be true, for example, of the necessarily true proposition that water is constituted of H_2O molecules. But I doubt that what explains the a posteriori status of these necessary propositions can apply to every necessarily true knowable moral principle. We couldn't with a straight face speculate that we know that prima facie it's morally wrong to inflict pain because someone made the empirical discovery that the property of inflicting pain was the hidden property that accounted for the superficial features of acts on the basis of which we ascribed the property of being morally wrong, or because it was discovered that the property of inflicting pain was the property that played such-and-such role in the moral theory that fixed the reference of moral terms. Just ask yourself why *you* believe that prima facie it's morally wrong to inflict pain and you'll find the a priori status of your belief written on its surface.

Re premise (2): No moral principles are knowable a priori. There are two related reasons for accepting this premise. The two reasons are related in that the first reason—which is apt to be perceived as somewhat tendentious when first presented on its own—sets up, and thus serves as a nice introduction to, the second reason, and the truth of the second reason explains the truth of the first reason. Because of this explanatory asymmetry, the second reason is the deeper reason for thinking that premise (2) is true.

The first reason may be put in the following way. If one person knows p a priori, then, platitudinously, so will any other person in the relevantly same epistemic situation with respect to p, which means that if one person knows p a priori and another doesn't, then this other person is epistemically lacking in some way with respect to p that the first person isn't. Perhaps the non-knower lacks complete mastery of one or more of the concepts needed to know p, or perhaps she hasn't reasoned as well as the first person, or been as imaginative, etc.[2] But now, as skeptics of moral realism have long claimed, whatever moral principle one believes a priori, it would seem to be possible that there is someone else who doesn't believe that principle but who does not differ in any relevant way as regards one's epistemic situation *vis-à-vis* the principle. The two of you agree about all relevant non-normative issues, have equal mastery of moral concepts, and are equally intelligent, sane, rational, imaginative and attentive, and have attended to and reasoned about the principle equally well (and so on). You take yourself to know a priori that a woman has the right to abort a three-week-old fetus if having a child would interfere with her career. But there are people just as intelligent and imaginative as you, with equal command of all relevant concepts and equal access to all relevant non-moral facts, who reason as well as you, and have reasoned on this issue as well as you, but who don't believe that a woman has the right to abort a three-week-old fetus just because bringing the fetus to term would interfere with the woman's career. There need be nothing you can do to get the other to share your belief, where the reason for this has nothing to do with that person's being prevented or disabled from believing the truth in some way that doesn't beg the question.

Perhaps, it might be countered, we can imagine a standoff over the principle about abortion, but what about the principle that it's morally wrong to torture children for the mere fun of it? Actually, it's not all that hard to think of people with not entirely outrageous moral views who wouldn't accept the principle in question. Consider someone who implicitly accepts what Derek Parfit calls the *Self-interest Theory* and has as her single ultimate moral principle that one ought to pursue those outcomes that would make one's life go as well as possible.[3] Such a person might be a sincere moral egoist in the cast of Ayn Rand who thinks that the only moral obligation anyone has is to achieve his or her potential and to satisfy whatever desires will give him or her the most accomplished, lucrative, and enjoyable life. This moralist might concede that only a monster would want to torture anyone but nevertheless stick to her guns about what is morally wrong (she can even allow that, while one can't assert without qualification that it's always wrong to torture children for the mere fun of it, in many cases such behavior would be wrong because of the way it interferes with other, more important ends one has). This seems entirely conceivable to me, and if the example is adequately described, there need be no flaw of reason or concept possession or imagination to explain this person's not believing the principle.[4] Yet if anyone has a priori knowledge of any moral principle, we could hardly find a better example of such knowledge than the a priori knowledge that it's morally wrong to torture children for the mere fun of it!

As I indicated above, I take the foregoing reason for accepting premise (2) of (EA) to be relatively superficial. Although I think it can stand (somewhat shakily) on its own, it's best viewed as a prolegomenon to a deeper reason, a reason for accepting premise (2) which accounts for why the first reason obtains. The deeper reason has to do with difficulties in explaining *how* one might have a priori knowledge of a moral principle, and may be elaborated in the following way.

If one has a priori knowledge of a moral principle, then there must be a correct explanation of how one has that knowledge, of what it is by virtue of which one's mental state constitutes a priori knowledge of the principle. I can think of five ways one might try to account for one's having a priori knowledge of a given moral principle, and none of them holds much promise.

First, it might seem that one possible explanation of one's a priori knowledge of a moral principle is that one knows it on the basis of one's having deduced it from more ultimate moral principles one knows a priori. Clearly, this couldn't account for all of one's a priori knowledge of moral principles, since the explanation presupposes a priori knowledge of a moral principle that one doesn't know on the basis of having deduced it from some other moral principle one knows a priori. But even apart from this point, it's not a promising account of *any* plausible candidate for a priori moral knowledge. It's not that one can't know a moral principle on the basis of knowing a more ultimate moral principle (or principles); it's just that if there are such cases, then the less ultimate principle will be derived from the more ultimate principle (or principles) together with some empirical proposition, thereby precluding one's knowledge of the less ultimate principle from being a priori.[5]

Second, it might seem that one's a priori knowledge of a given moral principle is *concept-based* where, intuitively put, one's knowing *p* is concept-based provided that part of the explanation of one's knowing *p* is that no one could have the concepts involved in thinking *p* unless one believed *p*. For example, Smith knows a priori that every widow was once married. If asked how he knows, Smith might not be able to say anything very helpful, because his belief that every widow was once married isn't based on other beliefs he has; if queried as to why he believes the proposition, he might say that it's obvious, or that he can't imagine how it could be false. But whatever Smith might say, we might explain his a priori knowledge (at least in large part) by saying that Smith has the concept of a widow, and no one can be in full possession of that concept and not believe the conceptual truth that every widow was once married. Now, we evidently have concept-based a priori knowledge of the proposition that it's morally wrong to do what one morally ought not to do, but is it plausible that one has concept-based a priori knowledge of any substantive moral principle? I think not. Substantive moral principles link moral concepts with non-normative concepts, but our moral concepts float free of the non-normative concepts with which they're linked in substantive moral principles in that it's never the case that a person who possesses both concepts can't believe one applies unless she believes the other also applies. It's always possible for one to believe that something falls under a moral concept without also believing that it falls under a particular non-normative concept with which it may be linked in some plausible moral principle. There is no substantive moral principle such that it's impossible for there to be someone who fails to find its negation inconceivable. This, of course, is precisely the intuition that lies behind G. E. Moore's "Naturalistic Fallacy" and his claim that "propositions about the good are all of them synthetic and never analytic";[6] it's an intuition that isn't usually contested by either side in the debate between moral realists and their skeptics. For any non-normative concept Φ, it's always possible for some rational person who has command of the concept of moral wrongness not to believe that Φ acts are morally wrong, however her intuitions about the concept of moral wrongness are suitably tweaked, and likewise, *mutatis mutandis*, for every other moral concept. This wouldn't be so if one could have concept-based a priori knowledge of substantive moral principles.

(There is an ancillary point to be made in this connection. The discussion of a couple of paragraphs back showed how a rational person with full command of moral concepts might nevertheless not accept the principle that it's morally wrong to torture children for the mere fun of it. This illustrates the point just made about concept-based a priori moral knowledge, for if that's not a conceptual truth, then it's highly unlikely that any other moral principle can make a better claim to being a conceptual truth. Christopher Peacocke in effect claims that we have concept-based a priori knowledge of the principle that prima facie it's morally wrong to inflict avoidable pain,[7] but that hardly trumps the prohibition about torturing children. Suppose, however, I'm wrong and that Peacocke's example, or the one about torturing children, is an example of a substantive moral principle that is also a conceptual truth. Even so, my skepticism would be scarcely touched were I to concede that certain moral principles, such as the ones just cited, couldn't be denied by anyone in full possession of the concept of moral wrongness. For there would be so few such principles that any moral system having them as their only axioms would be useless as a guide to what to do. We don't need morality to keep us from torturing children for the fun of it. But what *useful* moral principle is there of which we might have concept-based a priori knowledge? If the only moral truths we could know were ones backed by principles for which it's possible to have concept-based underived a priori knowledge, then morality would be useless in helping us decide what to do.)

A third way of explaining a priori knowledge of a moral principle is suggested by a certain "reflective-equilibrium" way of gaining a priori knowledge. This would be the way philosophical analysis typically yields a priori knowledge, when it succeeds in yielding knowledge. A philosopher starts his inquiry not knowing the answer to a certain question. After much hard work, he concludes that the answer he seeks is p, where p is a necessary truth, if true at all. Earlier I imagined a philosopher arriving in this way, rather improbably, at the a priori knowledge that, necessarily, a speaker means p iff she intends to get her audience to believe p by means of his recognition of her intention to get him to believe p. The philosopher's knowledge won't be based on a more ultimate principle about speaker meaning. The philosopher's justification for believing his new theory will be a story about how nicely it accounts for the known facts about speaker meaning, integrates in an illuminating way with other semantic notions, and, crucially, is resistant to the attempt to find counterexamples. No doubt something very much like this also applies to certain kinds of mathematical and logical inquiry. Might one have a priori knowledge of a moral principle that was of this sort? I doubt it. First of all, if one could know an ultimate moral principle that wasn't stated in terms of problematic expressions like 'prima facie' or 'ceteris paribus', it would arguably be of this sort, unless it was like the principle that it's wrong to torture children merely for the fun of it. But it's hardly how one knows, if one does know, that principle or the principle that it's prima facie morally wrong to inflict avoidable pain. So even if the analytical exercise of reason could result in knowledge of some moral principles, it wouldn't explain all such knowledge one might take oneself to have. Second of all—and this is the more important point—the following consideration seems to preclude one's gaining a priori knowledge of a moral principle via the analytical route in question. Crucial to the idea that any sort of conceptual analysis might justify one in believing a necessarily true proposition is the ability of that proposition to resist the search for counterexamples by others like one in relevant respects. Yet such immunity can't be guaranteed for moral principles if, as I argued, moral concepts float free of the substantial non-normative concepts with which they're joined in candidate moral principles. Perhaps *you* can't find a counterexample to the claim that acts of such-and-such kind are wrong, but the guy with whom you're locked in irresoluble dispute finds them all over the place. Just think of the situation of a person who can't find a counterexample to the claim that it's morally permissible for a healthy woman to abort a healthy one-month-old fetus because it would interfere with her career.

Are there other ways of explaining a priori knowledge of a moral principle that are worth considering? One thing that comes to mind is something like G. E. Moore's "moral intuition." But if that doesn't fall under what has already been discussed, then I doubt it's worth discussing. Another possible suggestion is that we have certain underived a priori beliefs as a result of natural selection, which could account for those beliefs' constituting knowledge if we assume, as seems reasonable, that beliefs produced by natural selection enjoy a reliability that is knowledge inducing.[8] But it seems to me that there are two things that make this suggestion problematic. First, I doubt that we've had moral concepts long enough for natural selection to make any moral beliefs a priori, and second, since there is actual or nomically possible disagreement among otherwise normal humans on just about every moral principle, it's bound to be difficult to explain why Mother Nature favors some but not others.

Finally, there is this to notice about premise (2) of (EA). Whether or not being indeterminate entails not being true, it is a mere platitude that a proposition is knowable only if it is determinately true. Thus, although (EA) ventures to show that there are no determinately true moral propositions via a premise which asserts that no moral principle is knowable a priori, the conclusion of the argument, if true, would in turn *explain* why it is that the premise is true. This reflection reveals no circularity in my argumentation, for although there being no a priori knowable moral principles is explained by there being no determinate moral truths, the reasons initially offered for the claim that there are no a priori knowable moral principles in no way presupposed the conclusion the claim was being used to support. At the same, to foreshadow a little, any argument for the indeterminacy of moral propositions that didn't presuppose premise (2) of (EA) would itself be an independent argument for the truth of that premise.

II. Cognitivism

Suppose, as I've just argued, that there are no determinately true moral propositions. What explains this? Are there no determinately true moral propositions because *non*cognitivism is true and there are no moral propositions, or are there no determinately true moral propositions notwithstanding the truth of cognitivism?

The two sentences

(a) Eating animals is a source of protein
(b) Eating animals is wrong

appear to be semantically on a par. The noncognitivist agrees but adds that in this case appearances are misleading. Normative sentences like (b) are masqueraders; the kind of meaning they actually have is different from the kind they appear to have—namely, the kind of meaning (a) in fact has. Whatever kind of meaning sentences like (a) have, it's what defines cognitivism. So what kind of meaning do sentences like (a) have? Well, the meaning of any sentence is determined by two things: the kind of speech act the literal speaker must perform in uttering the sentence on its own, and the kind of propositional content those speech acts must have. If we assume that stating and believing are relations to propositions, then, as regards (a), the literal speaker who utters it on its own must be *stating (saying/asserting) that eating animals is a source of protein*, where the proposition *that eating animals is a source of protein* is both truth-evaluable and something one might believe. It's truth-evaluable in that it's true iff eating animals is a source of protein, and false iff eating animals isn't a source of protein. By the criterion this implies, cognitivism is true if the meaning of (b) is determined by its being the case that the literal speaker uttering it on its own must be *stating (saying/asserting) that eating animals is wrong*, where the proposition *that eating animals is wrong* is both truth-evaluable and something one might believe (and believe in exactly the sense in which one believes that eating animals is a source of protein). What should we say about cognitivism, if we assume that there are no determinate moral truths?

The most common response of those who deny, implicitly or explicitly, that there are determinate moral truths is to deny cognitivism. For one thing, it may be difficult to see how one could account for there being no determinate moral truths if cognitivism were true. If there really is an objective property of being morally wrong, what on earth would explain why nothing can determinately instantiate it? Another reason is that the moral skeptic typically also holds that moral judgments have a certain conative force, in that, roughly speaking, if one fully accepts that one morally ought not to do acts of a certain kind, then to some non-negligible degree one will want to live in a world in which no one does acts of that kind. But if cognitivism is true, then to believe that acts of a certain kind are wrong is just to believe that acts of that kind have a certain objective property, and, to voice the familiar Humean worry, such a belief would be consistent with one's feeling any way at all about whether anything has that property. Because of these two concerns, noncognitivists are typically *expressivists* of one kind or another: moral judgments are just ways of emoting; they're prescriptions to act in a certain way; they express whatever package of non-normative beliefs and desires is constitutive of a moral opinion; we can speak of "stating" and "believing" moral "propositions," but these notions must now be understood in certain expressivist ways; and so on.

In my opinion, noncognitivism is determinately false. No one can coherently deny that each of the following may be true:

> It's true that eating animals is wrong iff eating animals is wrong
> Jane believes that eating animals is wrong
> Herbert stated that eating animals was wrong.

The noncognitivist must therefore argue that, while there are uses of 'true', 'believes', and 'states' on which the displayed sentences are, or may be, true, there are also uses on which they are not true, and it's in terms of these uses that cognitivism must be defined.

It's plausible these other senses exist only if it's plausible that *the proposition that eating animals is wrong* (the referent of the that-clause in 'Jane believes that eating animals is wrong') can't be truth-evaluable or believed/stated in precisely the way *the proposition that eating animals is a source of protein* (the referent of the that-clause in 'Jane believes that eating animals is a source of protein') is. Otherwise the sentences just displayed would suffer from a quite inexplicable ambiguity. Now, certain presently irrelevant qualifications aside, every sentence of the form 'α is F' is pleonastically equivalent to 'α has the property of being F', wherein 'the property of being F' refers to the property of being F, and every indicative sentence 'S' is pleonastically equivalent to 'That S is true' (more colloquially, 'It's true that S'), wherein 'that S' refers to the proposition that S. Thus, it's a conceptual truth that if α is a dog, then α has the property of being a dog and the proposition that α is a dog is true; and it's a conceptual truth that if α is wrong, then α has the property of being wrong and the proposition that α is wrong is true. It's trivial that 'dog' expresses the property of being a dog and that there are propositions that ascribe that property to things, and it's trivial that 'wrong' expresses the property of being wrong and that there are propositions that ascribe that property to actions. There are no other relevant senses of 'property', 'proposition', or 'true'. Cognitivism, in the stipulated sense, is easily obtained—which, as we'll presently see (in section IV), isn't to say that the cognitivism that obtains isn't in a certain way something less than full-blooded. It obtains in that moral sentences, like other indicative sentences, are in the semantic business of stating truth-evaluable propositions; they don't need to be assimilated to 'Yuk!' or to 'Let no one ever have an abortion!' As regards meaning, 'Eating animals is wrong' is on all fours with 'Eating animals is a source of protein'.

So it's not the case that there are no determinately true moral propositions because there are no moral propositions. There are moral propositions in the same sense there are any other propositions. Why, then, can't any of these truth-evaluable propositions be determinately true? Is it because none can be true *tout court*, and therefore not determinately true? Or is it that none can be *determinately* true, however this might affect the further question of their being true? Something needs to be said about being determinately true.

III. Indeterminacy and Moral Propositions

The master argument (EA) concludes that there are no determinate moral truths, not, with the traditional moral skeptic, that there simply are no moral truths. Some moral propositions are determinately false, but only those whose negations are not moral propositions, such as the proposition that a certain earthquake was morally wrong, it being false because only the actions of intentional agents can be morally wrong, so that the determinately true proposition that the earthquake wasn't morally wrong isn't a moral proposition in that it doesn't entail that the earthquake was morally right. As regards those infinitely many moral propositions whose negations are also moral propositions, (EA) tells us that every one of those moral propositions is *indeterminate*—neither determinately true nor determinately false. If being indeterminate entailed being neither true nor false, then there would be no gap between my conclusion and the traditional skeptic's. But it isn't my view that being indeterminate entails being neither true nor false; for what it's worth, it's my view that it's indeterminate whether being indeterminate entails being neither true nor false, since it's indeterminate whether the principle of bivalence applies to indeterminate propositions.[9] I therefore have an obvious reason for concluding that there are no determinately true moral propositions instead of that there are no true moral propositions. Nothing about the knowability of a proposition can be inferred from the assumption that it's true unless we can conclude that no indeterminate proposition can be true, since it's a platitude accepted by virtually every theorist, regardless of his or her account of indeterminacy, that indeterminate propositions are unknowable. The direct link with any kind of knowability is with *determinate* truth, not truth *tout court*. Since I hold that it's at best indeterminate whether indeterminate propositions have truth-values, I'm in no position to reach the traditional skeptic's conclusion.[10]

What explains why moral propositions can't be determinately true? Why is it that, though there are moral properties, nothing determinately instantiates any of them? I'm going to put off trying to answer this question until after I propose a new line of argument for the view that there are no determinately true moral propositions, an argument that also both provides a third reason for accepting premise (2) of (EA) and explains the truth in the other two reasons for accepting that premise. To state this argument I need first to say something about my own account of indeterminacy.[11] Since I can't hope to do any more here than summarize what I have published elsewhere, the conclusions reached in this section will be implicitly conditional in nature: *if* my account of indeterminacy is correct, *then* ....

My account of indeterminacy turns on a distinction between two kinds of partial belief. Although we philosophers often suppress the point, we know that believing is a matter of degree having to do with how firmly—the degree to which—one accepts a proposition. One can believe a proposition more or less firmly, and to say that someone believes *p tout court* really means that she believes *p* to some contextually relevant high degree. What is less well known is that there are two distinct kinds of partial belief. One kind is what philosophers usually have in mind when they think about partial belief; I call this kind of partial belief *standard partial belief* (SPB). This is the kind of partial belief which can under suitable idealization be identified with subjective probability in that under suitable idealization SPBs satisfy the standard axioms of probability theory. Pretend that degrees of belief can be measured by real numbers from 0 (unqualified disbelief) to 1 (unqualified belief). Then examples of SPBs might be your believing to degree .7 that it will rain tonight and your believing to degree .16 that your nephew will pass his logic course. So, if you take these two partially believed propositions to be unrelated, then you, rational person that you are, will believe to degree .112 the conjunction that [it will rain tonight and your nephew will pass his logic course]. The following points also characterize SPB.

> SPB is the kind of partial belief we would have even if, *per impossibile*, there were no indeterminate propositions.

> SPB is a measure of *uncertainty*. If one s-believes *p* to a degree less than 1 and greater than 0, then one takes *p* to be uncertain and oneself to be in a state of partial *ignorance* in that one doesn't know for certain what truth-value *p* determinately has (as we'll presently see, one can only s-believe propositions one takes to be determinately true or determinately false).

> SPBs generate corresponding likelihood beliefs. Thus, if Renata s-believes to degree .5 that she left her glasses in her office, then she thinks it's just as likely that she left them there as that she didn't. She's apt to say that she thinks that there's a fifty-fifty chance she left her glasses in her office. If she believes to degree .01 that Mexico will win the World Cup, then she thinks it's extremely unlikely that Mexico will win the World Cup.

> In every, or virtually every, case in which one s-believes *p* to some degree between 0 and 1, one doesn't take oneself to be in the best possible position to pronounce on the truth of *p*, even if one has complete confidence in the integrity of the evidence one has for or against *p*'s being true. Sometimes one thinks there's a better epistemic position available to oneself, as, for example, Renata believes she can find out for certain whether her glasses are in her office by looking for them there. And even if one thinks one can't get into a better epistemic position oneself, one will think there's a better position others might occupy, or

might have occupied. Thus, there's nothing I can do to improve my opinion about the color of Thales' eyes, but a contemporary of his could have satisfied herself on that score.

The other kind of partial belief is what I have elsewhere called *vagueness-related partial belief* (VPB).[12] I called it that because it was introduced in work whose primary concern was the kind of indeterminacy manifested in borderline vague propositions. If I were introducing the notion now I might have called it *indeterminacy-related partial belief*. VPBs, whatever we call them, are those partial beliefs that can't under any idealization be identified with subjective probability. Moreover, the just-displayed points that characterize SPB don't characterize VPB. Thus, as we'll presently see:

> ➤ We couldn't have VPBs if our language could express only determinate propositions. VPBs go hand-in-hand with indeterminacy. Our language couldn't express indeterminate propositions if we didn't have VPBs, and our having VPBs secures our ability to express indeterminate propositions.
> ➤ VPB is *not* a measure of uncertainty. VPB is the kind of partial belief we have when confronted with a proposition we take to be neither determinately true nor determinately false. In such a case, we have some temptation to judge *p* true and some temptation to judge *p* false, but we don't feel *uncertain* about the proposition's truth-value, as though we're in the dark about something hidden.
> ➤ VPBs don't give rise to corresponding likelihood beliefs. If, for example, you v-believe to degree .5 that borderline Harry is bald, then you *won't* think there's a fifty-fifty chance that he's bald.
> ➤ If one v-believes *p* to any degree and one's epistemic circumstances are known to be ideal in a certain way, then one won't think that one, or anyone else, can get into a better epistemic position with respect to *p*.

Now for an example, admittedly somewhat artificial, which I've used before.

Sally is a rational speaker of English, and we're going to monitor her belief states throughout the following experiment. Tom Cruise has consented to have his hairs plucked from his scalp one by one until none are left. Sally is to witness this, and will judge Tom's baldness after each plucking. The conditions for making baldness judgments are ideal and known by Sally to be such. For simplicity of exposition I'll assume both that Sally's degrees of belief can be measured by real numbers from 0 to 1 and that Sally's partial beliefs are always of some determinate degree.

Sally starts out believing to degree 1 that Tom is not bald and to degree 0 that he is bald. This state of affairs persists through quite a few pluckings. At some point, however, Sally's judgment that Tom isn't bald will have an ever-so-slightly-diminished confidence, reflecting that she believes Tom not to be bald to some degree barely less than 1. The plucking continues and as it does the degree to which she believes Tom not to be bald diminishes while the degree to which she believes him to be bald increases. At some point, we may pretend, the degree to which Sally believes both that Tom is bald and that he isn't bald is .5, and Tom thereby represents for Sally a solid borderline case of baldness. Having reached .5, Sally's degrees of belief that Tom is bald will gradually increase as the plucking continues, until she believes to degree 1 that he is bald.[13]

Although there's more to be said, and more that I've written, on the matter, I believe, and will assume, that Sally's qualified judgments express partial beliefs. My claim is that Sally's partial beliefs that Tom is bald are VPBs. For consider her at the point in the plucking when she believes to degree .5 that Tom is bald:

- ✔ Sally *won't* believe that there's a fifty-fifty chance that Tom is bald. She won't wonder how the issue of Tom's baldness might turn out, or what the underlying reality of it *really* is.
- ✔ If Sally's .5 partial belief that Tom is bald were a SPB, then she'd believe to degree 1 that he's bald or not-bald. But Sally won't believe to degree 1 that Tom is bald or not bald. Sally, a non-philosopher, has no views about excluded middle *per se*, and she's apt to react to the question whether Tom is bald or not bald the same way she reacts to the question whether he's bald.
- ✔ Suppose that in addition to having his hairs plucked one-by-one from his scalp, Tom has also suffered the indignity of being entirely nude throughout the process, and that he is a paradigm borderline case of a thin man. Suppose further that at the point in the plucking when Sally believes to degree .5 that Tom is bald, she also believes to degree .5 that he is thin, and that, pretheoretically speaking, she takes the two propositions to be completely unrelated: the truth of neither proposition would give her any reason to believe or to disbelieve the other. Now, to what degree does Sally believe the conjunction that Tom is bald and thin? It's intuitively clear, I submit, that Sally, confronted with what she would say are "all the facts," will believe the conjunction to the same degree she believes each conjunct, viz., .5. If her partial beliefs were SPBs, she would s-believe the conjunction to degree .25.

Now, what is it for Tom to be a borderline case of baldness? *Semanticists*, such as supervaluationists, deny that bivalence applies to borderline propositions. For them, being indeterminate is a matter of being neither true nor false, or of having some other kind of alternative status. *Epistemicists* accept bivalence, so for them the proposition that Tom is bald at *t*, a time when he's determinately a borderline case of baldness, is determinately true or false (albeit, of course, not determinately true or determinately false), although it's impossible for anyone to know which. Indeterminacy, at least in the case of vagueness, is a kind of ignorance.

I believe both positions to be flawed. Crispin Wright put his finger on the problem with the semanticist's position. For the semanticist, he wrote, "indeterminacy consists ... in some kind of status other than truth or falsity—a *lack* of a truth-value, perhaps, or the possession of some other truth-value," and to such "*third-possibility views* of indeterminacy" he objected that "it is quite unsatisfactory in general to represent *in*determinacy as any kind of determinate truth-status—any kind of middle situation, contrasting with both the poles (truth and falsity)—since one cannot thereby do justice to the absolutely basic datum that in general borderline cases come across as hard cases: as cases where we are baffled to choose between conflicting verdicts about which polar verdict applies, rather than as cases which we recognize as enjoying a status inconsistent with both."[14] The main problem with epistemic theories is that they can't adequately explain how it is that every predicate expresses an absolutely precise property, let alone an absolutely precise property that it's impossible for anyone to know is the precise property the predicate expresses.[15]

My view is that indeterminacy, whether or not it turns on typical cases of vagueness, is neither a semantic notion nor an epistemic notion but rather a *psychological* notion. Let a VPB* be a VPB formed under epistemically ideal conditions (and see my "Vagueness and Partial Belief" for how that vague notion is to be understood). I propose, for present purposes, the following sufficient (though not necessary) condition for a proposition's being indeterminate:

[D] p is indeterminate if someone could v*-believe p to degree .5[16]

Since I can't hope to give this any real defense or further elaboration here, I shall assume it as a working hypothesis and see how it affects moral propositions.

A priori moral beliefs also come in degrees. Suppose Sally is undecided about the status of P as an ultimate moral principle—that is, as a moral principle she takes to be ungrounded in any other moral principle—and that she believes P a priori to degree .5; she's really torn, even though she takes herself to have access to all relevant non-normative and normative facts. I think it's clear that Sally's partial belief that P is a VPB, not an SPB. She won't think there's a fifty-fifty chance that P is true, and if she s-believes to degree .5 the independent proposition that it will rain tonight, then the degree to which she believes the conjunction that [P and it'll rain tonight] will be .5. If her partial moral belief were an SPB, she would believe the conjunction to degree .25. And if, as we may suppose, Sally is in ideal epistemic circumstances with respect to P, then she v*-believes P to degree .5, and that together with [D] entails that P is indeterminate. Since P is any moral principle, we have a new argument for there being no determinately true moral propositions:

(1) If there are no determinately true moral principles, then there are no determinately true moral propositions.[17]

(2) [D]

(3) For any moral principle P, someone can v*-believe P to degree .5.

(4) ∴ There are no determinately true moral propositions.

This argument from indeterminacy not only gives a new argument for the claim that there are no determinate moral truths; it also, as I earlier hinted (p. 292), offers still another reason to accept premise (2) of (EA) (the claim that no moral principles are knowable a priori), a reason that also accounts for why the premise is true. For if every moral principle whose negation is a moral principle is indeterminate in the sense of [D], then that explains why none of them is knowable a priori.

But even if we're persuaded of the soundness of this argument, we should still want to know what it is about moral concepts that accounts for the truth of premise (3) of the argument just displayed.

IV. Why Moral Propositions Are Indeterminate: The Peculiar Nature of Moral Concepts

A little indirection will help. In Bob's conceptual scheme, the concept W is governed by the following two conditions.

a. In order for Bob to believe that α is W, there must be some non-normative concept N such that Bob also believes both that α is N and that being N entails being W.

b. It isn't required that N be any particular concept; N can be anything, provided certain conditions are met. These conditions pertain to what Bob *wants*; for example, Bob should want not to live in a world in which people do anything that is N.

Given this we should expect *two* kinds of indeterminacy to be manifested in Bob's beliefs involving W.

The first kind is simply the sort of indeterminacy manifested in borderline vague propositions. Thus, suppose that the value of 'N' Bob settles on entails the property of being a lie. Then the proposition that Jane's calling Bob a Republican was W may be indeterminate simply because Jane's utterance was a borderline case of a lie and thus, by Bob's lights, a borderline case of a W act.

The second kind of indeterminacy is that, for any given relevant non-normative concept N,[18] it may be indeterminate whether being N entails being W, where this isn't a matter in any ordinary sense of the *vagueness* of N or W. Indeed, independently of any account of indeterminacy it ought to be intuitively clear given the setup that, for any N, the proposition that being N entails being W *must* be indeterminate. For suppose that the operative non-normative concept for Bob is $N*$, whereas for Carla, whose concept W is also governed by (a) and (b), the operative non-normative concept requires her to believe that being $N*$ does *not* entail being W. Given the conditions governing the role of W, it's patently absurd to suppose that either Bob or Carla has the determinately true belief in their dispute about whether being $N*$ entails being W. And this is just the verdict [D] yields. For any non-normative concept N, Bob may, even under epistemically ideal conditions, believe to any degree that being N entails being W, and these beliefs will perforce be VPBs. Thus, for any non-normative concept N, someone can $v*$-believe to degree .5 that being N entails being W, and therefore the proposition that being N entails being W is indeterminate.

You won't be surprised to learn that it's my view that what goes for Bob's W isn't all that far removed from what goes for our moral concepts. There are differences, of course, but what makes it impossible for any substantive W proposition to be determinately true also makes it impossible for any substantive moral proposition to be determinately true. The differences are that:

- It belongs to our moral concepts that their application must supervene on the application of some non-normative concept, but, unlike Bob, an ordinary person needn't have complete non-normative sufficient conditions *explicitly* in mind when she applies a moral concept. If, for example, she judges an act to be wrong, she will believe that it has a certain defeasible, but undefeated, wrong-making property. What she typically won't be able to do with any great confidence is reel off the possible defeaters that don't obtain. If she's to be confident that no defeater obtains, then she must believe she can recognize a defeater when she sees one, and, if that's so, then she would evidently have some sort of tacit belief about the non-normative property on which she takes the moral property she's ascribing to supervene.

- I earlier implied that, while cognitivism (in the sense stipulated) was true, it wasn't true in an entirely full-blooded sense. I was alluding to what must be an important concession to the expressivist—viz., that one's conative attitudes enter into the determinants of the non-normative notions on which the application of one's moral concepts will be taken to supervene. Since these conative attitudes are essential to one's having moral concepts, it further follows that the meaning of 'wrong' in one's *lingua mentis* (as it were) is unlike that of predicates which express non-normative concepts in that the former supervenes partly on *conative* facts.[19] This is the principle ingredient that distinguishes moral concepts from "naturalistic" concepts that enjoy determinate application and that accounts for their not having determinate applications of the kind in question. At the same time, the conative requirements on our actual moral concepts are considerably vaguer than the conative requirement on Bob's W. The concept of having a certain moral concept, such as the concept of moral wrongness, is extremely vague, and it's even a cheat to speak of *the* concept of, say, moral wrongness. As with any concept, there will be significant individual differences. The paradigm possessor of a moral concept has a strong conative component in the underived conceptual role of her concept, but the vagueness inherent in the concept of possessing the concept no doubt allows for R. M. Hare's inverted-commas guy who makes moral judgments not caring who does what.[20] Still, the conative component is what gives cohesiveness to the concept, and is why we speak of substantial disagreements on moral issues, rather than supposing that people who accept different underived moral principles are employing different concepts, so that ostensibly irresoluble disputes about ultimate moral principles are really just verbal disputes, like a debate about whether whales are fish when one party's use makes it true that they are and the other party's use makes it false.[21]

Yet the resemblances that remain with Bob's use of *W* give to our moral concepts a conceptual role that explains the truth of premise (3) in the argument last displayed. Given the peculiar conceptual role common to all our moral concepts, it will always be possible for someone in ideal epistemic circumstances to believe a moral principle to degree .5, and such a belief will perforce be a VPB*. And given [D], my sufficient condition for indeterminacy, it follows that no moral principle is determinately true. Accepting this doesn't preclude anyone from having ultimate and underived desires about the kind of world he or she wants to live in, nor does it preclude using moral language in an instrumental way, as in the rearing of one's children. That may have been the point of moral language in the first place.[22]

V. Indeterminacy and the Argument from the Rational Irresolubility of Moral Disputes

Skeptics about moral realism nearly always appeal to some form of the argument from irresolubility. David Hume was making such an appeal when he wrote:

> But when I reflect, that ... yet men still dispute concerning the foundation of their moral duties: When I reflect on this I say, I fall back into diffidence and skepticism, and suspect, that an hypothesis, so obvious, had it been a true one, would, long ere now, have been received by the unanimous suffrage and consent of mankind.[23]

Such skeptics may be construed as making the following two-part claim:

A. If moral judgments assert moral propositions, then it's always possible for two people to disagree about the truth-value of any moral proposition, even when they agree about all relevant non-normative issues, have

equal mastery of moral concepts, and are equally intelligent, rational, imaginative and attentive (please feel free to insert whatever I left out).
B. If (A), then there are no true moral propositions.

The position advanced in this paper, if correct, explains the truth in the traditional moral skeptic's argument from irresolubility as formulated in (A) and (B), but we should be clear what that truth is.

My position implies an important disagreement with (A). My position is that if one person fully believes a moral proposition, then it's always possible in principle for there to be another person who doesn't believe the moral proposition but is nevertheless, as regards epistemic justification and knowledge, on a par with the believer. That is the truth contained in (A); but (A) goes further in holding that rationally irresoluble dispute about moral propositions is always in principle possible, and the opposite is implied by my position. For if, as I claim, the moral proposition is neither determinately true nor determinately false, then the two disputants may, at least in theory, be brought to believe just that—provided they have enough free time and philosophical ability (and, unlike you, my readers, are unencumbered by commitments to incompatible philosophical positions). My disagreement with (B) is that it overreaches itself, both as regards (A) as it is and as regards the truth contained in it. Either way, the most that one is entitled to conclude is that there are no *determinately* true moral propositions, not that there are no *true* moral propositions.

In this way, the truth in the traditional moral skeptic's argument from the rational irresolubility of moral disputes is explained—albeit explained in a way that shows it to be a mistake to use this argument in the aid of noncognitivism.[24]

Notes

1. "On Denoting," in R. C. Marsh, *Bertrand Russell: Logic and Knowledge, Essays 1901–1950* (George Allen & Unwin, 1956), p. 47.
2. Cf. Crispin Wright's notion of *Cognitive Command* in his *Truth and Objectivity* (Harvard University Press, 1992), pp. 92–93.
3. *Reasons and Persons* (Oxford University Press, 1984).
4. But doesn't Parfit go on to refute the Self-interest Theory in Part II of his book? Not when it's construed as a moral theory, since his argument then begs the question, as it presupposes a conception of morality that is incompatible with the Self-interest Theory. To this one might want to protest that morality *is* inconsistent with the Self-interest Theory, and this is a question I'm about to address.
5. Perhaps a trivial exception is when one comes to know an unobvious restriction of a moral principle one knows a priori by deductive reasoning, as a dull thinker might come to realize that it's morally wrong to torture all children born out of wedlock for the mere fun of it since it's morally wrong to torture any child for the mere fun of it.
6. *Principia Ethica* (Cambridge University Press, 1903), p. 7. This sentence is quoted in Ralph Wedgwood, "Conceptual-Role Semantics for Moral Terms," *The Philosophical Review* 110 (January 2001): 1–30, n. 35, p. 26.

7. "Moral Rationalism," a draft of work in progress, given as a lecture at the GAP conference in Bielefeld, Germany, in September 2000. This work was part of his William James Lectures given in spring 2001 at Harvard.

8. Paul Horwich offered this suggestion.

9. "Vagueness and Partial Belief," *Philosophical Issues* 10 (2000): 220–257.

10. Crispin Wright, "On Being in a Quandary," *Mind* 110 (January 2001): 45–98, also argues that moral propositions are indeterminate, and his particular appeal to intuitionistic logic seems to imply his commitment to the indeterminacy of bivalence. Although my position and Wright's were developed independently, there are some striking parallels.

11. My most recent statement of this account is in "Vagueness and Partial Belief," but see also my "Two Issues of Vagueness," *The Monist* 81 (1998): 193–214.

12. I first called it that in "Two Issues of Vagueness."

13. Schiffer, "Vagueness and Partial Belief," p. 224.

14. "On Being in a Quandary: Relativism, Vagueness, Logical Revisionism," *Mind* 110 (January 2001): 45–98; the quotations are from pp. 69–70.

15. See my "The Epistemic Theory of Vagueness," *Philosophical Perspectives*, 13 (1999): 481–503. Timothy Williamson has a reply in the same issue.

16. To say that someone could v*-believe *p* to degree .5 is to say that there is some possible world such that it's similar in relevant respects to the actual world and in which someone v*-believes to degree .5 that Tom is bald. In the case of Tom's baldness, the relevant respect of similarity is the exact hair situation on Tom's scalp—the number, size, distribution, etc., of the hairs on his scalp.

17. This is intended to be true when a moral proposition is true by virtue of its being true under every candidate moral system, it being indeterminate which system is correct. For even then there will be a (possibly disjunctive) sufficient condition for the proposition's being true, and that sufficient condition counts as a moral principle.

18. "Relevant" non-normative concepts are such that it's not impossible for anything to fall under them and such that it's not trivially true that they don't entail being *W*, as for example, the concept of photosynthesis makes it trivially false that photosynthesis is *W*.

19. The idea that the conative component in what fixes the meaning of a moral predicate yields a less than full-blooded cognitivism was suggested by a reading of Kit Fine's "The Question of Realism," forthcoming.

20. See, e.g., Hare's *The Language of Morals* (Oxford University Press, 1952).

21. See my "Meaning and Value," *The Journal of Philosophy*, Vol. LXXXVII, 11 (November 1990): 602–614, especially pp. 609–610.

22. See "Meaning and Value," pp. 610–611.

23. *An Enquiry Concerning the Principles of Morals* (The Liberal Arts Press, 1957), p. 98.

24. An earlier version of this paper was read at the 2001 SOFIA conference, in Oaxaca, Mexico. I'm grateful for the comments of my two commentators at the conference, James Dreier and Michael Lynch, and to the participants in the discussion of my talk, especially Paul Horwich. I'm also indebted to Cian Dorr, David Enoch, Christopher Peacocke, and Josh Schechter for their comments on or pertaining to a first draft of this paper.

Philosophical Issues, 12, Realism and Relativism, 2002

MORAL RELATIVITY AND INTUITIONISM

Walter Sinnott-Armstrong
Dartmouth College

Many people jump straight from a descriptive premise of moral relativity to a substantive conclusion of moral relativism, a semantic/ontological conclusion of moral anti-realism, or an epistemological conclusion of moral skepticism. All such simple arguments fail, as critics have shown repeatedly.

Still, most common folk retain some sense that somehow the extent of disagreements about morality is relevant to the question of whether and how we can attain knowledge or justified belief about what is morally right or wrong or good or bad.[1] This paper will support that common sense by tracing a less direct path from one version of moral relativity to one kind of skepticism about moral intuitions.

Similar paths to the same conclusion start elsewhere. If this form of argument works, some psychological facts can also affect when we are epistemically justified in our moral beliefs. So can some claims in sociobiology, cultural history, and so on. The larger issue concerns the relevance of descriptive premises to normative epistemological conclusions, although here I will focus on descriptive premises about moral disagreements.

1—Moral Intuitionism

My target is a particular version of moral intuitionism. It is best understood in light of the problems that it is supposed to solve.

One central problem in moral epistemology, as in general epistemology, is the skeptical regress argument.[2] It seems that, if a person is justified in holding a certain moral belief, that person must have some reason to believe it. That reason must be expressible in some argument. That argument must have some premises. If the person is not justified in believing its premises, that argument cannot make that person justified in believing its conclusion. But, if the person is to be justified in believing those new premises, then the believer needs another argument for those premises. That argument must itself have further premises. And so on.

The easiest way to stop this regress is simply to stop. If a believer can work back to a premise that the believer is justified in believing without being able to infer that premise from anything else, then there is no new premise to justify, so the regress goes no further. That is how moral intuitionists stop the regress, and many moral intuitionists see it as the only way to stop.

Appeals to moral intuitions also seem unavoidable in practice. Even those who officially disdain moral intuitions often criticize utilitarianism or Kantianism for implying counter-intuitive moral conclusions. Then they use moral intuitions again to argue for some contrary moral theory. Applied ethicists also argue from moral intuitions on a regular basis, as do common folk when they need to make moral decisions and justify their decisions to others. It is hard to see how to justify any substantive moral view without appealing to some moral intuition at some point.

Such considerations make moral intuitionism attractive. These attractions do not, however, require all of the claims that have been shared by moral intuitionists.[3] Many moral intuitionists are non-naturalists about the metaphysics of moral properties and pluralists about the structure of morality. No such claims are needed to stop the regress or to use moral intuitions to justify moral decisions. These attractions of moral intuitionism are, instead, due to its moral epistemology.

The epistemological thesis of moral intuitionism claims that some people are justified in holding some moral beliefs independently of whether those people can infer those moral beliefs from any other beliefs. This independence claim does not require that such justified moral believers actually are not able to infer those moral beliefs from any other beliefs. The point instead is that, regardless of whether they happen to have that ability, such justified moral believers would remain justified even if they were not able to infer those moral beliefs from any other beliefs.

It is natural to state this thesis in terms of a *need* for inferential ability.[4] A believer needs an inferential ability (to make a belief justified) when the believer would not be justified in holding the belief if the believer were not able to justify that belief by inferring it from some other belief. The defining claim of moral intuitionism is then that some moral believers sometimes do not need any inferential ability (to make them justified in holding some moral beliefs).

This broad definition includes some views, such as moral sense theories and externalisms, that are often distinguished from moral intuitionism. I group these views together because my argument will apply to them all.

To treat such theories fairly, it is essential to notice what they do *not* claim. Moral intuitionists do not claim that every moral belief can be justified without any inferential ability. Their view applies only to relatively simple beliefs that are understood and held with confidence after reflection on relevant facts. Nonetheless, to call them justified is not to say that the believer has gone through any process of reflection or justification. It is only to say that the belief has a certain status.

The relevant status is *epistemic* rather than instrumental. Some beliefs are justified instrumentally, because they serve some interests; but this shows nothing about the truth of those beliefs. Moral intuitionists, in contrast, claim that certain moral beliefs are justified in some way that is related to their truth.[5]

Moral intuitionists need not claim certainty for any moral beliefs. They can admit fallibility. Still, moral intuitionists must claim that some such moral beliefs are justified *adequately*. If those beliefs were justified in a way that was inadequate because it was overridden or undermined, that weaker status would not be enough to stop the skeptical regress.

What needs to be justified is a person's belief *state*. Moral intuitionists need not go on to say anything about whether a certain belief content is itself justified impersonally, that is, apart from who it is that has a belief state with that content. For simplicity, I will sometimes call beliefs justified (or not), but this will always mean that a believer is justified (or not) in being in a belief state with that content.

Some belief states result from inferences. To say that I *infer* a belief is just to say that I go through a reasoning process of which the belief is the (or a) conclusion and other beliefs are premises. Inferences come in many kinds. Some are deductively valid, but others are inductively strong. Inductive inferences include inferences to the best explanation, arguments from analogies, statistical generalizations, applications of statistics, and others. Any reasoning process that is supposed to provide a justification for belief in its conclusion counts as an inference.

A believer is *able* to draw such an inference when the person already has enough information to go through a reasoning process that results in this belief if he had enough incentive to do so. This ability does not require the person to be currently self-conscious or reflective about their beliefs or their abilities. All that is needed, other than general intelligence, is for the requisite information to be encoded somehow in the correct brain at the correct time.

When a believer is able in this thin way to infer a belief somehow from another belief, then I will call that belief *inferable* for that believer. In contrast, a belief is *inferred* by that believer only when the believer actually does infer it somehow from another belief. Inferable beliefs need not be inferred, because believers do not bother to run through all of the inferences that they could.

Inferred beliefs are not *inference-based* if the believer does not hold those beliefs because of the inference (that is, if the reasoning process is not what causes the believer to continue believing rather than disbelieving or suspending belief). Similarly, inferable beliefs are *inferability-based* only if an ability to infer sustains the belief. Nonetheless, for simplicity, I will assume that inferred and inferable beliefs are based on the relevant inferences and inferential abilities.

These classifications are relative to a particular believer. One person might infer or be able to infer some belief that another person does not or cannot infer. What is non-inferable for one person might be inferred and inferable for another. Thus, it would be more precise to talk about whether a belief is inferred or inferable (or not) for a particular believer. Nonetheless, I will drop this qualification for simplicity when the context should make the point clear.

Having defined these categories, the next question asks whether they, especially the negative ones, are empty. Some non-moral beliefs do seem to be neither inferred nor inferable (for some persons). Consider "I feel pain now." I can believe this without inferring, or being able to infer, this belief from anything. This might be controversial, but I will assume it for the sake of argument.

More important here is whether any *moral* beliefs fall into these categories. Many people believe that lying is morally wrong (*pro tanto*, that is, in the absence of any defeater), even though they do not seem to infer this belief from any other beliefs. Some of these people *could* infer this moral belief from other beliefs, such as that lying is harmful and harmful acts are morally wrong (*pro tanto*); but others do not seem to believe any premises from which they could infer this moral conclusion. Then this moral belief seems neither inferred nor inferable for them.

Such believers might draw inferences among non-moral beliefs to determine facts about the act, such as that it is a lie. They might even apply a definition of lying. Then the moral belief is not completely independent of all theory, but it still might not be inferred in the relevant way, since these inferences conclude only that the act is lying, not that it is morally wrong. What determines whether a moral belief is inferred or inferable is whether the believer does or could draw an inference with that moral belief as its conclusion.

Other people still might be able to infer the moral belief, but the person who matters is the believer at the time. Maybe this person could infer the belief in the future after studying moral philosophy, but this would not make the belief inferable for this person at this time.

In this sense, at least some people do seem to lack the ability to support some of their moral beliefs with inferences. I could infer that lying is morally wrong (*pro tanto*) from the premises that lying is harmful and harmful acts are morally wrong (*pro tanto*) only if I believe these premises. If I believe that some lies are harmless or that some harmful acts are not morally wrong (even *pro tanto*), then I cannot use these beliefs as premises in an inference to justify my belief that lying is morally wrong (*pro tanto*). Similarly, I can cite Kant's categorical imperative only if I accept that principle. If I believe that lying is morally wrong (*pro tanto*), but I do not believe anything else from which I could infer this belief, then my moral belief is not inferable in the relevant way.

The psychological claim that some people do in fact form beliefs in this way might be controversial. If this psychological claim is not true, then moral intuitionism is in even more trouble than I imagine. Nonetheless, I will grant this psychological claim here, so that we can focus on other issues.

Epistemology enters the picture when one asks normative questions about whether beliefs of these kinds can be justified beliefs or knowledge. Moral intuitionism claims that some strongly-held non-inferable moral beliefs are justified. Since such believers are justified but lack the ability to infer, they are justified *non-inferentially*. A belief is justified *inferentially* only when an ability to draw some inference of some kind is needed to make that belief justified. What moral intuitionists claim, then, is that some believers are justified non-inferentially in believing some moral beliefs.

Some self-styled moral intuitionists do not claim so much. They claim only that some moral beliefs are justified without being *inferred*. They do not go so far as to claim that any moral beliefs are justified without being *inferable*. I will call this position *weak* moral intuitionism.

It is crucial to see how weak this position is. Suppose I believe that torture is morally wrong. I have the ability to infer this belief from my beliefs that torture intentionally causes pain and expresses disrespect and that any act that does so is morally wrong. I might also apply other principles. But suppose I don't bother to infer my moral belief from anything, because it seems so obvious to me that an inference would waste time. If this belief (or another like it) is justified, that is enough to validate weak moral intuitionism.

Many people are willing to accept this weak form of moral intuitionism. If someone could justify a moral belief by an inference (and bases his belief on that ability), then his lack of actual performance does not seem to make his belief unjustified. There is no point in criticizing someone for not doing what there was no need to do, if he could and would have done it if there had been any need. In such cases, the lack of actual inference does not make the belief unjustified. This is all that weak moral intuitionists claim.

The stronger view that I defined as moral intuitionism (proper) is more controversial. If I do not justify my moral belief by inference because I *cannot* infer it from anything, then more people would view my moral belief as unjustified. After all, a need for justification might arise, such as if someone questioned my moral belief, and then I would not be able to fulfill that need.

Since this strong version of moral intuitionism is controversial, it might be nice to avoid it. Unfortunately, that is not possible. The weak version of moral intuitionism is not enough to stop the skeptical regress. Even if weak moral intuitionism is correct, the status of moral beliefs as justified still might depend on the believer's ability to infer them from other beliefs. But then the skeptical regress arises for that inference that the believer must be able to draw. The ability to draw an inference cannot make a belief justified if beliefs in its premises are not justified themselves. The reason is that I could be justified in believing any absurdity if my belief could be made justified by an ability to infer that belief from other unjustified beliefs. Imagine that I believe that there are ghosts in my bedroom. I do not infer this belief from anything, but I could infer it from other beliefs that I hold, such as that there are ghosts in every room of my house. If such an ability were enough to make a belief justified regardless of whether the inference depends on beliefs in premises that are themselves unjustified, then my ability to draw this inference would make me justified in believing that there are ghosts in my bedroom. But this belief in bedroom ghosts is not justified, and that is not changed by my ability to infer it from my unjustified belief in ghosts all over my house. Consequently, a mere ability to infer a belief from other beliefs is not enough to make the conclusion justified unless those other beliefs in the premises are themselves justified. This is enough to restart the same old skeptical regress or another one very much like it. The skeptical challenge cannot, then, be met by weak moral intuitionism alone.

In contrast, the stronger view that I defined as moral intuitionism would be enough to stop the regress. If a belief can be justified independent of any actual inference and also independent of any ability to draw any inference, then there is no dependence on any inference with any new premise that needs to be justified. That would bring the regress to a screeching halt. So it is only the stronger version of moral intuitionism that moral skeptics need to deny.

Another traditional opponent of moral intuitionism is moral coherentism. Coherentists maintain that a believer is justified in holding a belief when and only when that belief coheres with the believer's other beliefs. The relations that constitute coherence make that believer able in my thin sense to infer the belief, even if no actual inference is drawn. Thus, moral coherentists claim in effect that some moral beliefs are justified by virtue of an ability to infer. They do not deny that some moral beliefs are justified without being actually inferred, so moral coherentists do not deny weak moral intuitionism.

Other opponents of moral intuitionism claim that moral beliefs are justified when they can be derived from non-moral premises, such as premises about the nature of action.[6] On this view, believers are justified if they can give such derivations of moral beliefs, even if they do not bother to do so in some actual situations. So these opponents also do not deny weak moral intuitionism.

Thus, to capture its opposition to its traditional opponents and its claim to stop the skeptical regress, moral intuitionism must be defined in terms of an ability to infer rather than by actual inference. I will bring up weak moral intuitionism when the contrast is relevant, but henceforth I will refer to strong moral intuitionism unless otherwise indicated.

I still have not defined what a moral intuition is. The reason is that this noun phrase causes countless confusions. Some people use "moral intuition" for an ability or tendency to form non-inferred moral beliefs. Others use it to refer to the non-inferred beliefs. Others include only non-inferable beliefs. Others refuse to call beliefs intuitions unless they are true or highly probable. Still others build epistemology into the definition so that beliefs are intuitions only if they are justified non-inferentially. Because its multiple uses engender misunderstandings, I will avoid the noun "intuition" unless necessary for simple phrasing. When I do refer to a moral intuition, I will mean a strongly-held non-inferable moral belief, regardless of whether it is true or justified. It is then a substantive claim that some moral intuitions are justified.

2—When Does the Need Arise?

To determine whether moral intuitionism is true, we need to determine when there is a need for inferential justification. How can we ascertain that?

We might cite particular examples of justified moral beliefs. Or we might cite general principles that certain conditions are sufficient for moral beliefs to be justified. However, such direct methods would risk begging the question. Our method should be acceptable to both sides.

Hence, we must resort to analogies. In areas other than morality, some beliefs seem to need inferential justification. Others do not. If we can isolate factors that create a need for justification in these other areas, then we can return to morality and ask when those factors are present in moral judgments. I will use analogies to perception and mathematics, because these are the most common models for moral intuition proposed by moral intuitionists themselves.

2.1—Disagreement in Perception

Imagine star gazing in Hollywood.[7] You and I are driving down Rodeo Drive looking for stars, when we stop at a light. I see a man walk across the street right in front of our car. He takes off his sunglasses and looks at me. I believe him to be Tom Cruise. I do not infer this belief from any premise such as that nobody else wears clothes like that. Instead, my belief that it is Tom Cruise seems to result directly from my visual experience without being inferred from anything. He just looks like Tom Cruise.

Am I justified in believing that it is Tom Cruise? Apparently. To deny that I am justified would be or suggest some criticism of my belief or my method of forming belief, at least in these circumstances. However, there is nothing wrong with any of these, if we suppose that my belief is true, my vision is 20/20, and the circumstances are daylight, short distance, and so on.

What makes me justified still might be an ability to draw some inference that I do not actually draw. Maybe I would not be justified if I did not have the ability to infer my belief from a general premise such as "I am good at identifying people under such circumstances" or from a particular premise such as "This man's face resembles the face that I saw in the movie last night." I will discuss the role of such inferential abilities later. The point here is just that I do seem justified so far.

But now suppose that you look at the same person, believe that it is not Tom Cruise (or any other star), and tell me so. You and I are looking at the same person at the same time from almost the same angle after similar movie experiences, but we still disagree about whether this is Tom Cruise. Our disagreement seems to make me unjustified in continuing to believe that it is Tom Cruise, at least until I have further evidence.

Even if I am correct, so you are mistaken, that doesn't make me justified. After all, you used the same method of belief formation but reached a different conclusion. Admittedly, I used my eyes, but you used your eyes. Still, if I have no reason to believe that my visual identifications are more reliable than yours, then I am not justified in trusting mine after I learn that you disagree with me.

Externalists might object that I am justified if I am good at identifying stars even if I have no reason to believe that I am. This view seems plausible only because we, like all normal adults, have identified many people before and have often received confirmation of our accuracy. Someone who has never made any personal identifications or confirmed their accuracy would not be justified in trusting their own identifications in the face of disagreement without additional evidence.

To become justified in believing that this is Tom Cruise, I might look for some reason to discount your eyes (such as that you are wearing sunglasses) or your experiences (such as that you have never seen a Tom Cruise movie) or your beliefs (such as that you think Tom Cruise is bald). If I can discount your belief, this will allow me to remain justified. But let's suppose that you are not wearing sunglasses, have seen Tom Cruise in many movies, and have no false beliefs about Tom Cruise; so I have no reason to discount your eyes or beliefs.

Then how could I become justified again? One method would be to run out and get an autograph from this person. If it reads "Tom Cruise", then I could infer that he is Tom Cruise, because most people sign their own names (although he might be a great pretender). Another possibility would be to ask someone else. If a third passenger in our car also believes that it is Tom Cruise, then I could infer that I am probably correct, since there are two of us and only one of you, and two people are correct more often than one (and more often than not), other things being equal. Alternatively, I could cite past experience. If I know that I have often correctly identified stars in similar circumstances, then I can infer that I am probably correct again. This might justify me in my belief.

These methods all use inferences of one kind or another. Other forms of inference also might make me justified despite our disagreement. However, it is hard to imagine any method that did not involve any kind of inference which could make me justified in holding my belief despite our disagreement.

The point is not that I must consciously run through all of the steps in any inference. Even if I do not bother to infer explicitly, I can be justified if I have enough information encoded in my brain as a result of past experience to make me able to draw some inference to support my belief or undermine yours. This thin kind of ability to infer can be enough to justify beliefs despite disagreement. Still, if I am not even able to draw any inference of any kind to support my belief against yours, then I do not seem justified in believing that the person I see is Tom Cruise.

This instance generalizes: If I know that others hold beliefs contrary to mine, then I need to be able to draw some kind of inference to support my belief or undermine theirs before I can be justified in believing that I am correct and they are incorrect. In short, disagreement creates a need for inferential justification.

Moral intuitionists might respond that, even if actual and known disagreement undermines and thereby defeats the status of my belief as justified, I am still justified when there is no disagreement or when I do not know of any disagreement. However, enough disagreement in a general area of belief also seems to create a need for inferential justification, even without known actual disagreement about the specific belief content. Just consider how often people disagree in identifying stars on Rodeo Drive. We don't know exactly why, but it probably has something to do with their desire to see stars. Suppose that I know this general fact. I also know that I desire to see a star. Then I see someone whom I believe to be Tom Cruise. This time there is nobody in the car with me, so I know of no actual disagreement. Indeed, there is no actual disagreement, since nobody denies that this person is Tom Cruise. Nonetheless, since I know the general fact that people often do disagree about identifications like these in circumstances like these, then I seem to need some reason to believe that my particular identification does not fall into that pattern of misidentification. That reason will introduce some inference, as before. Thus, an awareness of widespread disagreement in a general area is also enough to create a need for inferential justification.

My point can be supported and extended by a common counterexample to the traditional definition of knowledge as justified true belief. Imagine that you are driving through the countryside and see what looks exactly like a barn, so you think it is a barn, and it is. Unbeknownst to you, the surrounding area is filled with fake barns made of papier-mâché. You were just lucky. That is why you do not know that it is a barn, even though you do have justified true belief.

Now suppose that you find out that there are lots of fake barns in the area, but you still believe that what you see from the road is a barn without checking at all to see whether it is fake. Since you are aware of the danger but ignore it, you are not even justified in this case.

The intermediate case is when you do not know but *should* know about the fake barns. Maybe you know that people around here often try to trick tourists or build elaborate film sets. Or maybe a guide warned you about fake buildings, then you forgot. Somehow you have lots of evidence that should lead you to believe that there are fake barns in the area. Nonetheless, you don't bother to put together the evidence or formulate the belief, either because you are lazy or because you have some desire to see a real barn which motivates you to overlook evidence to the contrary. In this case, like the second, you do not seem justified in believing that what you see is a real barn. Thus, whether you are justified depends on what you should believe.

This case suggests that you need inferential justification not only when you are aware of disagreement, but also when you should be aware of disagreement. If disagreement is widespread and well-known to others, you should be aware of disagreement or at least the likelihood of disagreement. That is how widespread disagreement can create a need for inferential justification in perception.

2.2—Disagreement in Mathematics

Similar points apply to mathematics, the other common model for moral intuition. There is not much disagreement about simple arithmetic. More advanced mathematics usually rests on calculations, which are inferences. So let's consider probability, where more disagreement and less calculation are common in many contexts.

Imagine that you and I just took a Scholastic Aptitude Test (SAT). On the way out, I tell you that I think I did pretty well overall, and I felt very confident about some answers. For example, I was confident that the answer to question #66 about probability was 0.66. I did not even have to calculate it, I say, because the answer was obvious. "Oh yeah!", you respond, "I was confident that the answer was 0.5, so I didn't calculate it either. One of us got fooled!"

Before I found out that you disagree, I did seem justified in believing that the answer to #66 was 0.66. I seemed justified without inference, because I thought carefully, was confident, and knew about probability in general. In contrast, after I discover that you disagree, I am no longer justified in believing that the answer to #66 is 0.66. At that time, I am unjustified in trusting my instincts, if I have no reason to think that my instincts are better than yours.

To become justified again, I could calculate the probabilities. I could appeal to my past experience, if it shows that my instincts about probability are reliable. I could also ask a third party who did calculate or is more reliable. These methods all involve inference. Other kinds of inference might be useful as well. However, no method that does not use any kind of inference could make me justified again. I might not have to run through any inference consciously, but I cannot become justified in trusting my belief instead of yours if I do not at least have enough information encoded in my brain that I could draw some inference to support my belief or undermine yours if called upon to do so.

As with perception, then, if I know that someone else uses a similar non-inferential method but reaches contrary beliefs, then I need to be able to support my belief with some kind of inference in order to be justified in believing that I am correct and the other believer is not. Moreover, even if I am not aware of any actual disagreement, I still need this ability to be justified, if I am aware that many people get tricked by probability puzzles, as psychologists have shown.[8] Here, again, an awareness of widespread disagreement in a general area is enough to create a need for inferential justification, even without any known actual disagreement about the specific case.

2.3—Generalization

The examples so far suggest that disagreements create needs for justification in perception and mathematics or, at least, identifications and probabilities. It's possible that this need arises from something special about these areas.

If so, it might not extend to moral beliefs. However, moral intuitionists themselves use perception and mathematics as models for moral beliefs. Those models suggest that moral beliefs are justified under conditions similar to those for perceptual and mathematical beliefs. The need in perception and mathematics at least shifts the burden of proof, so that anyone who claims that moral beliefs are different in this respect owes us some reason why. I know of no such reason. I conclude that disagreements about morality also create needs for inferential justification of moral beliefs.

What is needed is some inferential ability. Careful reflection without any inferential ability can't be enough, because that much was already finished before the disagreement in my examples (such as during the SAT). The result would not be affected if the example were changed to include any non-inferential way of being justified. Since more confirmation is needed when disagreements arise after all non-inferential methods have been used up, only inference or inferential ability can provide the confirmation that is needed.

Foundationalists might object that this standard requires too much, because it leaves too few people justified. However, all normal adults and even children have the required abilities, because their past experiences taught them when they are reliable. This standard actually requires very little. No actual or self-conscious inference is required. No particular kind of justification is specified. All that is needed is a thin ability to draw some inference of some kind (deductive or inductive, first-order or second-order). Still, that much is required in the face of disagreement. This standard is suggested by the cases of perception and mathematics, and there is no reason not to extend it to moral beliefs.

3—Moral Relativity

For this standard to imply that inferential justification is needed in morality, there must be enough disagreement about morality to trigger the need. This makes it crucial to ask how much people do in fact disagree about morality.

One popular answer is a strong version of moral relativity, which claims that every moral principle and judgment is or would be denied by someone. This descriptive claim about actual moral beliefs must be distinguished from the normative view called moral relativism. I take moral relativism to be the claim that what is morally right or wrong varies in certain ways from society to society or from person to person. Moral relativism is then about what is morally right or wrong, whereas moral relativity is about moral beliefs.

Moral relativity is supported by a wide variety of disputes. Anthologies on applied ethics include thoughtful articles on both sides of abortion, euthanasia, capital punishment, terror bombing, animal rights, famine relief, pornography, homosexuality, and affirmative action. Even more disagreement occurs when we look beyond modern Western societies:

[S]ome people are cannibals, others find cannibalism abhorrent.... In some [societies], a man is permitted to have several wives, in others bigamy is forbidden. More generally, the moral status of women varies greatly from one society to another in many different ways. Some societies allow slavery, some have caste systems which they take to be morally satisfactory, others reject both slavery and caste systems as grossly unjust.... Infanticide is considered acceptable in some societies.... .[9]

And so on. No limited set of examples could prove that people disagree about everything in morality, but the range (and vehemence) of disagreements is surely impressive.

Some of these disagreements are not fundamentally moral, because they result only from disagreements over non-moral facts. If one person supports capital punishment only because she believes that it deters murder, and another person opposes capital punishment because he believes that it does not deter murder, then they might not disagree at all about whether capital punishment would be immoral if it did not deter murder. Different cultures also often hold different religious and (pseudo-)scientific beliefs that lead them to different moral conclusions even when the cultures share basic moral principles.

Other apparent disagreements are due to conceptual confusions. Consider one society that prohibits adultery (or bigamy) and another society that allows husbands to have sex with mistresses (or additional wives). If the concept of "marriage" in the first society requires a commitment to sexual exclusivity, but the "husbands" in the second society never made any such commitment, then they do not count as "married" in terms of the first society, so their sexual relations can't be "adultery" in the sense that the first society condemns. Thus, it is not clear that these societies really disagree at all.

When disagreements about moral issues arise solely from non-moral disagreements and conceptual confusions that could be removed by further inquiry and reflection, informed and rational people would not disagree. Such disputes are resolvable in principle. Disagreements that are resolvable in principle cause less trouble for those moral intuitionists who claim only that believers are justified in strong non-inferable beliefs when they are informed, rational, and not confused.

Still, many moral disagreements do not seem resolvable in such ways. They do not result from factual disagreements or conceptual confusions. Like many negative claims, this can't be proven, but there is substantial evidence for it.[10] Sometimes people who are discussing the same case do agree about all important non-moral facts of the case. Their beliefs might be false, unjustified, and/or incomplete, but they share all relevant non-moral beliefs. Nonetheless, they continue to hold contrary moral beliefs.

People also make moral judgments about imagined situations. Suppose two people stipulate facts about a hypothetical society, including the effects of capital punishment on murder rates, its costs relative to life imprisonment, the chances of parole and escape, recidivism rates for convicted murders who are not executed, relative rates of death sentences for different races, sexes, classes, and so on. They agree about all of these non-moral facts because those facts are simply accepted for the sake of argument in this fictional case. Nonetheless, they still disagree about whether capital punishment is morally permissible in these circumstances, because one person sees it as inhumane, whereas the other sees it as just retribution. Numerous moral disagreements like this cannot be explained away by non-moral disagreements, because there are none, by hypothesis.

Admittedly, people's intuitions about stipulated cases might be affected by prior beliefs about the real world. If I believe that capital punishment deters murder in the real world, this belief might incline me to accept capital punishment even in an imaginary world where it is stipulated that capital punishment does not deter murder. This mechanism, however, hardly seems adequate to explain away all or even most such moral disagreements, because the grounds that people cite often include factors like inhumanity and retribution, which do not depend on deterrence. Such principles often make people disagree morally while agreeing on stipulated non-moral facts.

Unresolvable moral disagreements also seem likely because of the sources of moral beliefs. Cultural training affects moral beliefs about what is inhumane, deserved, and so on. Differences between cultures (even within a single society) then cause moral disagreements. These disagreements probably cannot all be resolved by getting straight on the facts and concepts, since inclinations from early enculturation are too tenacious.

Admittedly, cultures also display commonalities, but they are too thin to resolve many common disagreements about morality. If everyone agrees that we should not be inhumane, this won't resolve a dispute on capital punishment, if people still disagree about whether capital punishment is inhumane. Then it is not even clear that everyone agrees substantially, since people might use different concepts of inhumanity. Similarly, even if we agree that killing is morally wrong (*pro tanto*), this agreement seems superficial if we still disagree about what counts as killing (euthanasia? abortion?), about who should not be killed (fetuses? animals?), and about which benefits could justify killing (the goals of vigilantes or terrorists?). If people and cultures agree on so little, then there is little reason to suspect that all moral disagreements will disappear once we agree on the facts.[11]

It is still possible that everyone would agree about morality if they had been exposed to the same cultural influences, and that humanity will converge on such agreement someday. That possibility, however, cannot show that people today are justified in their moral beliefs, since we do not find ourselves at that point yet. Today many moral disagreements persist among careful, rational, informed people who feel confident about their beliefs. Conflicts can occur even when such moral beliefs are non-inferred and non-inferable for both believers. Thus, strongly-held, non-inferable moral beliefs do sometimes conflict in ways that seem irresolvable.

We cannot conclude that disagreement always occurs, as moral relativity claims. That position seems false, because everyone does seem to agree on some trivial claims, such as that it is morally wrong to torture babies just for fun.

Since unresolvable moral disagreements occur sometimes but not always, we need to ask how often they occur. No precise answer is possible. We cannot specify a percentage of moral issues that are subject to disagreement, much less unresolvable disagreement. Luckily, exact numbers do not matter. The crucial issue here is whether the frequency, kinds, and circumstances of existing moral disagreements are enough to create a need for inferential justification.

To determine how much is enough, suppose that you are given a hundred old thermometers. You know that many of them are inaccurate, but you don't know how many. It might be eighty or fifty or ten. You pick one at random, put it in a tub of water, which you have not felt. It reads ninety degrees. Nothing about this thermometer in particular gives you any reason to doubt its accuracy. You feel lucky, so you become confident that the water is ninety degrees. Are you justified? No. Since you believe that a significant number of the thermometers are unreliable, you are not justified in trusting the one that you pick. You need to check it. One way to check it would be to feel the water or to calibrate this thermometer against another thermometer that you have more reason to trust. Both of these methods involve inference, so again what you need is inferential justification.

Believers with non-inferable moral beliefs are like thermometers (in relevant respects). Some believers are more reliable than others in that a higher percentage of their non-inferable moral beliefs are true. If we know that a large number of such believers are unreliable, then we are not justified in trusting any one believer without confirmation. We do know that a large number of such believers are unreliable, because of moral disagreements. If two people hold contrary beliefs about a moral issue, at most fifty percent can be correct. When each of five people disagree with the other four, at most twenty percent can be correct. The range of disagreements among strongly-held non-inferable moral beliefs, thus, shows that many moral believers are unreliable. It doesn't matter that we do not know how many are unreliable or whether any particular one is unreliable. The fact that moral disagreements are widespread still reveals enough unreliability to create a need for inferential justification of moral beliefs, contrary to moral intuitionism.

It also does not matter whether most or all of these moral disagreements are resolvable in principle. If we are not yet justified in believing that the moral disagreement will be resolved in favor of a certain moral belief, then we cannot be justified in holding that moral belief any more than we can be justified in trusting one thermometer in the above situation without checking its accuracy. The only way to check the accuracy of moral beliefs is by inference. Thus, moral disagreements that are resolvable in principle still create a need for inferential justification. Once resolvable disagreements are included, there are plenty of moral disagreements to create a need for inferential justification of moral beliefs.

4—Responses

Moral intuitionists might respond in several ways.

4.1—Moral Blindness

When strongly-held, non-inferable moral beliefs conflict, a classic move is for one side to accuse the other side of being "morally-blind", just as some people are color-blind. This charge is supposed to explain how one side can be justified, when the other is not.

Such analogies are misleading. We can trace color-blindness to the absence or failure of certain cells. We can also show that color-blind people lack abilities to discriminate between different colors. These abilities are valuable, for example, when looking for a car in a parking lot.

What is lacking in people with deviant moral intuitions is different. If a supposedly morally-blind person knows a supposedly morally-sighted person's beliefs about the non-moral properties of an act and its circumstances, as well as that person's antecedent moral beliefs and training, then the supposedly morally-blind person can usually predict whether the supposedly morally-sighted person will believe that act is morally wrong. No analogous prediction is possible by color-blind people, because normal color ascriptions do not follow from antecedent beliefs about color in general or about subvenient facts. Color-blind people cannot see colors, but they do not deny the existence or importance of colors; whereas supposedly morally-blind people do deny the existence or importance of the moral properties that others claim to see.

Moreover, drawing distinctions is often not praiseworthy in morality. Suppose someone calls one marriage wrong but another right, because only the former is interracial. This person claims to see a morally important difference. Most people today see none. But then it is most people today who are analogous to color-blind people, since they draw fewer distinctions than people who are not color-blind. Yet this does not show that most people today have defective moral vision.

Suppose someone distinguishes two colors when most people see no difference. This might show that this person has better vision than most people. That could be confirmed by instruments, such as spectrometers. The situation is very different with so-called moral vision. If someone draws a distinction, such as between interracial marriage and intraracial marriage, which we and most of our peers do not see as morally important, then we would not be impressed at all, even if he could consistently continue to classify cases as morally right or wrong on this basis. Thus, drawing more distinctions is not always valuable in morality as in color vision. This makes it misleading at best for one side in a disagreement to accuse opponents of moral-blindness.

4.2—Externalism

Some other difference between conflicting strongly-held non-inferable moral beliefs still might make one justified when the other is not. In particular, if one side's mechanism is reliable, but the other's is not, this difference could make the former justified but not the latter, according to reliabilists. Of course, if either side could show that they are reliable or their opponent is unreliable, that could make them justified. But showing this would require inference. To avoid depending on inference, moral intuitionists need a strong version of reliabilism, which holds that reliability by itself is sufficient to make believers justified even when those believers have no access at all to their reliability or any evidence for their reliability.

This extreme version of externalism is not plausible.[12] One reason arises in a blind wine-tasting. Suppose Frances never tasted any wine before today. She knows nothing about how or where wine is made. She has no reason at all to think that she is able to identify any wines. We set ten unidentified glasses of red wine in front of her. She tastes the first. We ask her where it comes from. She has no idea why, but it reminds her of California, where she traveled years ago. As a result, she forms the belief and tells us that this wine comes from California. She is right. Moreover, she is reliable at this task. Maybe her reaction is caused by some chemical combination in the wine peculiar to California. But nobody there has any evidence at all of her reliability. In this situation, almost everyone (except reliabilists trying to defend their theories) would admit that Frances is not justified in this belief.

What if she keeps trying? The second glass reminds her of Australia, so she believes that it comes from Australia. Right again! And so on down the line. If Frances knew that she got the first nine wines right, then she might be justified in believing what she does about the tenth wine. However, we never give her any reason at all to think that she gets any of the wines right. As far as she knows, she might have missed all of them. Her lack of any reason to believe that she is reliable as a detector of wine origins then continues to make her beliefs about wine origins seem unjustified.

This is not to say that Frances is not epistemically permitted to hold her beliefs. She also has no reason to believe that she gets the origins wrong. She need not even be epistemically irresponsible. Maybe she cannot stop believing or find any other evidence. She does the best she can. Still, she does not seem to have that positive epistemic status that is usually signaled by calling her justified. The explanation seems to be that she lacks any reason to trust her beliefs in these circumstances.

This situation is analogous to non-inferable moral beliefs. Frances is no worse epistemically than George who believes that a certain act is morally wrong, if George has no second-order reason at all to believe that his moral beliefs of this kind are reliable and also no way to test his belief with any first-order inference from other first-order beliefs. George bases his moral belief solely on what seems true to him, just like Frances. If George seems more justified than Frances, that is probably only because one assumes that George has run into moral problems before, so he has enough stored information to be justified in believing that his moral beliefs are reliable. But that is cheating. To test whether an ability to draw a second-order inference is necessary in the absence of any other inference, we need a case where the moral believer has no reason to believe that his non-inferable moral beliefs are reliable. Then the case is analogous to Frances. And then George's moral beliefs seems no more justified than were Frances's beliefs about wine origins.

But I need not claim that much here. Suppose other people taste the same wines but reach different beliefs than Frances. Surely, if Frances is aware of those others, then Frances is not justified. The bare external fact that she is reliable cannot be enough to make her justified when she is aware that others disagree and she has no reason to believe that they are any less reliable than she is. She needs to have some awareness of some feature that distinguishes her beliefs from the others. Otherwise she is just guessing that she is right instead of them. She might get lucky, just as she might pick an accurate thermometer out of the inaccurate thermometers described above. However, lucky guesses like this cannot be justified in the face of disagreement. These standards apply to moral beliefs as much as to beliefs about wine origins, so externalists cannot avoid my argument.

4.3—Defeasibility

Another response might be that, when strongly-held non-inferable beliefs conflict, even if neither believer is justified *adequately*, both believers still might be justified *defeasibly*. Defeasible justification is often explained by analogy with Ross's notion of *prima facie* duties. When I must break a promise to avoid killing, I do not have an actual duty to keep my promise, but I still have a *prima facie* duty to keep my promise. Analogously, my belief that I see a crow might be defeasibly justified even if it is not justified adequately because the fog is too thick between me and what I see. What makes this belief defeasibly justified is that it would be justified adequately if its status as justified were not defeated by the fog. Some moral intuitionists then claim that strongly-held non-inferable moral beliefs are justified defeasibly, even if moral disagreements are defeaters that keep them from being justified adequately.

To assess this response, we need to distinguish two kinds of defeaters. Some defeaters are reasons to believe something contrary. If a friend tells me that there is a sale at the bookstore today, then I might be justified in believing her until I read in the newspaper that the sale starts tomorrow, at which point my original evidence is overridden. That original evidence is not canceled, since I still have some evidence that the sale is today. After all, my friend might have more recent information than the newspaper. But the newspaper normally gives me more evidence to the contrary (in which case my friend's testimony is overridden) or as much evidence to the contrary (in which case my friend's testimony is counterbalanced). The situation is different if my friend later tells me, "I lied, because I wanted to get you to the bookstore today for a surprise party." After this revelation, I no longer have any reason at all to believe that the sale is today. This defeater does not just override or counterbalance my reason to believe that the sale is today. Instead, it cancels or undermines that evidence.[13]

When evidence is overridden or counterbalanced but not undermined, I will say that there is still *pro tanto* evidence or reason to believe.[14] In contrast, when evidence is undermined or canceled, I will say that there is no *pro tanto* evidence or reason, but merely a *prima facie* reason. A merely *prima facie* reason is then no real reason but at most the misleading appearance of a reason. A merely *pro tanto* reason is a real reason, although weaker than a conflicting reason. To call a reason *defeasible* is to say that it might be defeated by being either overridden or counterbalanced or undermined, so it might be a *pro tanto* reason, but it also might be a merely *prima facie* reason and, hence, no reason at all.

The crucial question then is this: Does the fact that I know that someone with equal epistemic claim disagrees with me undermine my reason to trust my own belief? If so, my reason is merely *prima facie* and, hence, not really a reason at all. If not, my reason is counterbalanced, which might show that I am not adequately justified, but I still have some real (*pro tanto*) reason to believe.

The answer is unclear in cases of vision. The fact that a car looks red to my friend next to me seems to be a reason to believe that it is red, at least when I have no other evidence. This makes it seem like an overrider. On the other hand, if we were looking into a desert, and I seemed to see a lake, but my friend did not seem to see anything from his slightly different angle, I would conclude that it is probably a mirage, and then I would have no reason at all to believe that there is a lake. This seems more like an underminer.

Similarly for moral disagreements. The fact that someone who is as reliable as me has an intuition that a certain act is morally wrong might seem to be a reason to believe that the act is morally wrong, at least when I have no other evidence. This makes it seem like a counterbalancer or overrider. On the other hand, my friend's conflicting moral intuition might make mine seem like an illusion, in which case our disagreement seems more like an underminer.

Maybe such disagreements among strong non-inferable moral beliefs both undermine and counterbalance. In any case, if such moral disagreements do undermine, among other things, then moral intuition does not yield any real evidence at all in the face of moral disagreement. It yields at most a *prima facie* reason, not a *pro tanto* reason, and so no real reason.

Of course, defenders of moral intuitionism can respond that moral disagreement provides only a counterbalancing reason and does not undermine or cancel my reason to trust my own moral intuition. If so, moral intuition yields a *pro tanto* reason with some epistemic force. But that remains to be shown. In the absence of any argument that moral disagreements just counterbalance without undermining moral intuition, it is not clear that moral intuitionists can escape the problem of moral disagreement in this way.

Moreover, the fact that disagreements are common in the general area seems unlike an overrider or counterbalancer, because it does not give me any reason to believe anything contrary to my own strongly-held non-inferable moral belief. Such a pattern of disagreement includes beliefs that agree with mine as well as others that disagree, so it seems like a reason to suspend belief rather than to hold any of the beliefs under dispute. The prevalence of disagreements, thus, seems to function more like an underminer. If so, then strongly-held non-inferable moral beliefs in the face of disagreement provide no *pro tanto* reasons but at most merely *prima facie* reasons, which are no real reasons at all.

In any case, strongly-held non-inferable moral beliefs still would not be justified *adequately*. Even if moral disagreements operate as counterbalancers rather than cancellers, believers retain at most some weaker reason to hold onto their beliefs. Their weaker reasons are inadequate because the conflicting reasons are at least as strong. To believe what we know to be defeated by equal or better reasons is to take the road to dupedom. If moral intuitionists claim only that moral intuitions are justified but inadequately, then it is not clear why their position has to be denied by their traditional opponents, such as moral skeptics and moral coherentists. This might suggest that the traditional dichotomies are confused, but moral intuitionists are at least in trouble if they claim to have refuted or denied what their traditional opponents claim.

4.4—Ignorance

Yet another possible response is that some people who strongly hold non-inferable moral beliefs are not aware that anyone disagrees with them. These believers might be justified non-inferentially in their moral beliefs, even if known disagreement creates a need for inferential justification.

In response, we need to distinguish those who cannot know that others disagree with them from those who do not know but should know better, because the evidence of disagreements is easily available to them. Consider a medieval peasant farmer who strongly and non-inferably believes that his wife has a moral duty as his wife to cook all of his meals. Suppose that this farmer has never met anyone or had the opportunity to meet anyone with different moral beliefs. Even his wife accepts her role. Since this farmer is not aware of any disagreement, he might have no reason to doubt the reliability of his strong non-inferable moral beliefs, and then he might seem not to have any need for inferential justification of this moral belief. If so, this moral believer is justified non-inferentially. This seems implausible to me, but others find it plausible, so let's grant it for now and ask whether it matters.

It would not follow that any people like us are justified non-inferentially in moral beliefs. Every educated adult in the modern world should have evidence of moral disagreements. Consequently, educated modern adults are not justified in holding their moral beliefs independent of inference, even if medieval farmers were so justified. I am concerned here with informed modern adults, so it would not bother me much if I had to concede that medieval peasants were non-inferentially justified in their moral beliefs.

If moral intuitions are justified only for believers who do not know that others disagree, their epistemic status will be exceedingly fragile, especially in the modern world, where discussants are usually able to cite real disagreements. Moreover, most moral intuitionists would hardly be satisfied by a way of being justified that depends on ignorance of other people's moral beliefs and disappears as soon as the believer becomes informed. The point is not that ignorance would increase knowledge. That happens whenever unknown evidence would be misleading. My point, instead, is that, once we learn how pervasive moral disagreements are, we can never recover innocence, so we cannot be justified in the way medieval peasants are. Thus, even if some beliefs were justified noninferentially in this way, these cases would be trivial and would not show that moral intuitionism holds for any moral beliefs of educated modern adults.

4.5—Some Agreement

The final response admits that conflicting moral beliefs are never justified non-inferentially but insists that some strong non-inferable moral beliefs are not subject to any disagreement at all.

There does seem to be no disagreement about some moral beliefs. One way to achieve agreement is to cite extreme cases and make defeasible claims. Everyone seems to agree that torturing babies is defeasibly morally wrong, since this means only that it is morally wrong to torture a baby without at least some counterbalancing or undermining reason. People still disagree about which reasons are adequate and about whether it would be morally wrong to torture a baby to save the world. However, (almost?) nobody would deny that it is morally wrong for a father to put out cigarettes on his baby's arm just because he gets slight sexual pleasure from watching his baby squirm in pain. As far as I know, no cultures allow this kind of act. It is hard to imagine how any culture that did allow it would last very long.

Once this pattern is seen, more examples flow easily. It is morally wrong to kill ten people just because you dislike them. It is morally wrong to break a solemn promise to a friend just because you feel like fishing. Such cases seem subject to no disagreement, or no reasonable disagreement, because the word "just" rules out any adequate reason for an act that seems defeasibly immoral.

Thus, even if *almost* every moral belief is subject to disagreement, and even if moral disagreement always creates a need for inferential justification, there still might be a few moral beliefs that are justified non-inferentially. Their status as justified might even be undefeated and, hence, adequate. Such uncontroversial cases are hardly enough for a complete moral system, but they might refute moral skepticism and moral coherentism, if those views deny that *any* moral belief is non-inferentially justified. Such cases also might be enough to establish moral intuitionism if that view claims only that *some* moral beliefs are justified non-inferentially.

However, no matter how obvious, the status of such moral beliefs as justified does not show that they are justified *non-inferentially*. Most people who believe that torturing babies is immoral can give at least some reason why it is immoral, either that torture hurts or violates rights or disrespects humanity or something. Others believe that what seems obviously immoral to them is usually immoral, and they also believe that torturing babies seems obviously immoral to them, so they are able to give a second-order inference to the conclusion that torturing babies is immoral. If some believers are not able to give any such inference, that must be because they do not trust their own moral beliefs and have no views about what makes torture immoral. Since such moral believers do not seem justified, the rest of us are justified only because we are able to draw some such inferences.[15]

The same conclusion arises from a dilemma: A moral believer either knows or does not know that there is no disagreement about a certain moral claim, P. Suppose the believer does not know that there is no disagreement about P. Assuming she is an educated modern adult, she should know that moral disagreement is widespread. But then, if she does not know that her belief in P is an exception to the trend, then she should know that there probably is disagreement about P. So this believer is not justified, for reasons given above.

Alternatively, if the believer knows that there is no disagreement about P, then the believer probably has enough information to draw an inference like this: Nobody disagrees with P. Most moral claims with which nobody disagrees are correct. Therefore, (probably) P. The first premise is true and known, by hypothesis, but the believer still might not believe the second premise. However, if a believer does not believe that most moral claims subject to no disagreement are correct, then it is hard to see how that believer could be justified in trusting his own moral intuitions when nobody disagrees. If someone does not believe that everyone's moral intuitions together are justified, how can he believe that his own intuition in particular is justified? Such a believer would not seem justified adequately, so this case could not establish moral intuitionism.

Moral intuitionists still might deny all of this. Nonetheless, at least the claims that everyone does agree in certain moral beliefs and that they are justified do not show that those believers are justified non-inferentially. For moral intuitionists merely to announce that they are justified non-inferentially is not an adequate response to my arguments, since common standards keep other beliefs from being justified non-inferentially in similar circumstances.

5—Conclusion

My conclusion is that moral intuitionism is false, because we need to be able in a weak way to draw some kind of inference for us to be justified in holding any moral belief. This conclusion follows from standards of when inferential justification is needed along with descriptive claims about the pervasiveness of moral disagreement.

As I said, this same conclusion could also be supported by findings from psychology, sociobiology, or cultural history. If central moral intuitions can be explained as framing effects, and if such effects depend on arbitrary assumptions, then this psychological explanation would seem to create a need for inferential justification.[16] Similarly, if central moral intuitions can be shown to depend causally on aspects of culture that are morally disreputable, then again this would seem to create a need for inferential justification.[17] However, to develop such supporting arguments would take another essay.

I will close, instead, by returning to the attractions of moral intuitionism. Moral theorists, applied ethicists, and everyday people do have to take some assumptions for granted without *actually* inferring those beliefs from anything. Otherwise, they could never get anywhere. Moreover, it is hard to see why discussants must look for reasons behind agreed assumptions.

Nonetheless, this is not enough to show that we are justified in holding such assumptions without any *ability* to infer them from any other beliefs. What we do not need to do is actually and consciously form any beliefs from which we can infer our moral beliefs. We still might have to be able to infer them in order to be justified in believing them. So these arguments might support weak moral intuitionism, but they cannot support moral intuitionism in any version that is strong enough to stop the regress of justification.

The same point applies elsewhere. Suppose a scientist tests the water of a lake and finds that its pH is 3. On this basis she infers that there are no live fish in that lake. In normal circumstances that is enough to justify her in believing that there are no live fish in that lake. But that justification is superficial. She assumes without inference that fish cannot live in a lake with a pH of 3. This seems reasonable. But this superficial justification is adequate only because she has enough expertise to be able to infer her assumptions from other beliefs if she needed to. Science works as it does because such deep justifications are available, even if scientists do not always formulate them explicitly. Moral beliefs are similar. One can give superficial justifications that rely on uninferred assumptions because one could go deeper if need be. The fact that there is usually no need to go deeper does not show that one's justification does not depend on one's ability to go deeper. If it does so depend, then our actual practices of superficial justification cannot do anything to support any kind of moral intuitionism that is strong enough to stop the regress.

The other common argument is that moral intuitionism is the only way to stop the skeptical regress discussed above. The moral intuitionist agrees with the moral skeptic about the failure of all other methods of moral justification, including coherentism, naturalism, contractarianism, and so on. Moral intuitionism is the only position left to show how we could ever be justified in any moral belief. The moral intuitionist assumes that some moral beliefs are justified, so moral skepticism is implausible. This is supposed to show that moral intuitionism must be correct.

To back up this argument, moral intuitionists would have to refute all positions other than moral intuitionism and moral skepticism. That won't be easy. Even if that task were accomplished, this argument would still run into another problem: This argument begs the question if moral intuitionists give no independent reason to reject moral skepticism. Many people find moral skepticism implausible or even outrageous, but that is often because they misunderstand moral skepticism. When properly understood, moral skepticism is not easy to refute or even dismiss.[18]

Moreover, even if moral intuitionists did find serious problems in moral skepticism and every other moral epistemology, this still would not provide any reason to accept moral intuitionism. Maybe no theory in this area is any good. To rule out that possibility, moral intuitionism at least needs to be defended against objections by its opponents. I have been arguing that moral intuitionism cannot be defended adequately against a certain objection based on moral disagreements.[19]

Notes

1. Although I will write about moral beliefs, I intend a minimal notion of belief that should be acceptable to any moral anti-realist who grants that moral claims can be true in some minimal way. I do think that moral realism better captures the content of common moral assertions and beliefs. See my "Expressivism and Embedding", *Philosophy and Phenomenological Research* LXI (2000), pp. 677–93. However, my argument here will not depend on moral realism, even if my way of speaking requires a bit of translation by moral anti-realists.

2. For more detail, see my "Moral Skepticism and Justification", in *Moral Knowledge? New Readings in Moral Epistemology*, ed. Walter Sinnott-Armstrong and Mark Timmons (New York; Oxford University Press, 1996), pp. 3–48 at 9–14.

3. For more detail, see my entry "Intuitionism" in *The Encyclopedia of Ethics*, ed. Lawrence C. Becker (New York; Garland, 1992), pp. 628–30.

4. As many moral intuitionists recognize, such as W. D. Ross, *The Right and the Good* (Oxford; Oxford University Press, 1930), p. 29: "without any need of proof."

5. For more detail on ways to be justified, see my "Moral Skepticism and Justification", pp. 18–19. There I also distinguish what is justified relative to different contrast classes, but here I will assume an everyday contrast class. This assumption makes my argument more forceful, since moral intuitionists might not claim any moral beliefs to be philosophically justified, and it would be easier for me to show that appeals to moral intuitions cannot rule out moral nihilism without begging the question.

6. See, for example, Alan Gewirth, "The 'Is-Ought' Problem Resolved" reprinted in *Human Rights; Essays on Justification and Application*, by Alan Gewirth (Chicago; University of Chicago Press, 1982), pp. 100–127.

7. A more common analogy is with color beliefs, but this is too simple, because colors do not supervene on other properties of objects in the way that moral properties are

supposed to supervene on other properties of acts. See my "Moral Experience and Justification", *Southern Journal of Philosophy*, Supplement to Volume XXIX (1991), pp. 89–96 at 90–91.

8. See Daniel Kahneman, Paul Slovic, and Amos Tversky, editors, *Judgment Under Uncertainty: Heuristics and Biases* (Cambridge; Cambridge University Press, 1982).

9. Gilbert Harman, "Moral Relativism", in *Moral Relativism and Moral Objectivity*, by Gilbert Harman and Judith Jarvis Thomson (Oxford; Blackwell, 1996), pp. 8–9. Similar conflicts occur inside a single person at different times, but I will focus on interpersonal disagreements.

10. For a contrasting position, see David Brink, *Moral Realism and the Foundations of Ethics* (New York; Cambridge University Press, 1989), pp. 110–13, 142–43, and 197–209. However, Brink wants to show that moral relativity does not refute moral realism, whereas my argument concerns moral epistemology.

11. For more detail, see Francis Snare, "Moral Relativity", *Mind* 89 (1980), pp. 353–69.

12. Examples like the following are given in Lawrence BonJour, *The Structure of Empirical Knowledge* (Cambridge; Harvard University Press, 1985), pp. 37–57; Keith Lehrer, *Theory of Knowledge* (Boulder; Westview Press, 1990), p. 163; and my "Moral Skepticism and Justification". pp. 28–29. For a different kind of criticism, see Earl Conee and Richard Feldman, "The Generality Problem for Reliabilism," *Philosophical Studies* 89 (1998), pp. 1–29.

13. For an analogous distinction with regard to Ross on *prima facie* moral duties, see my *Moral Dilemmas* (Oxford; Basil Blackwell, 1988), pp. 97–102.

14. This useful terminology is adapted from Shelly Kagan, *The Limits of Morality* (Oxford; Clarendon Press, 1989). p. 17.

15. This point might not generalize. I am normally able to draw a similar second-order inference when I hold an obvious non-moral belief, such as "I feel pain now". This belief still might be justified non-inferentially, as foundationalists claim, if no such inferential ability is needed to make it justified. My point about moral beliefs is that an inferential ability is needed to make even obvious moral beliefs justified, but there might be no such need with obvious non-moral beliefs.

16. Such an argument is suggested by Tamara Horowitz, "Philosophical Intuitions and Psychological Theory," *Ethics* 108 (1998), pp. 367–85. If Horowitz's argument is understood in this way, then it avoids the criticisms in Mark van Roojen, "Reflective Moral Equilibrium and Psychological Theory," *Ethics* 109 (1999), pp. 846–57. See also Frances Kamm, "Moral Intuitions, Cognitive Psychology, and the Harming-versus-Not-Aiding Distinction," *Ethics* 108 (1998), pp. 463–88.

17. See Gilbert Harman, *The Nature of Morality* (New York; Oxford University Press, 1977), p. 110. Some argument in this ballpark might also lie behind Friedrich Nietzsche, *On the Genealogy of Morals*.

18. See my "Moral Skepticism and Justification".

19. Thanks to Jack Hanson for helpful comments on an earlier draft and to Robert Audi and others at the University of Nebraska at Lincoln for insightful discussion of an even earlier oral presentation.

Philosophical Issues, 12, Realism and Relativism, 2002

EXPLORING THE IMPLICATIONS OF THE DISPOSITIONAL THEORY OF VALUE

Michael Smith
Australian National University

Suppose, just for the sake of argument, that the version of the dispositional theory of value that I myself prefer is correct (see, for example, Smith 1989, 1994a, 1997; compare Lewis 1989, Johnston 1989): when a subject judges it desirable for p to be the case in certain circumstances C, this is a matter of her believing that she would want p to be the case in C if she were in a state that eludes all forms of criticism from the point of view of reason—or, for short, and perhaps somewhat misleadingly (Copp 1997), if she were fully rational.[1] More precisely, if still somewhat misleadingly, let's suppose that when a subject judges it desirable that p in C this is a matter of her believing that, in those nearby possible worlds in which she is fully rational—let's call these the 'evaluating possible worlds'—she wants that, in those possible worlds in which C obtains—let's call these the 'evaluated possible worlds'—p obtains.

Once we have supposed this to be so it is, I think, extremely tempting to suppose that we have thereby either explicitly or implicitly taken a stand on certain crucial debates in meta-ethics: tempting to suppose that we must be cognitivists as opposed to non-cognitivists; relativists as opposed to non-relativists; and realists as opposed to irrealists. We must be cognitivists because we have supposed that evaluative judgement is a species of belief. We must be relativists because we have supposed that the truth conditions of a subject's evaluative beliefs are fixed by whatever that subject would want if she were fully rational, and hence are relative to what that subject herself actually desires: the contents of different subjects' evaluative beliefs must be different from each other simply because they are beliefs of different subjects. And we must be realists because there is every reason to suppose that there are facts about what different subjects want in possible worlds like the evaluating world, possible worlds in which they are fully rational; every reason to suppose, in other words, that some such beliefs are true. The realism that is thus implied contrasts not with the kind of irrealism defended by non-cognitivists, but with that defended by cognitivists like John Mackie who thinks that we should all be error theorists about value (Mackie 1997).

Notwithstanding the very understandable temptation to think that all of this is so, I will argue that the implications of the dispositional theory are either different or, at the very least, much less clear. Though the dispositional theory does give us grounds on which to make a case for cognitivism, I will argue that making that case requires that we appeal to certain controversial supplementary premises (§1). As regards relativism, I will argue that the dispositional theory not only has no such implication, but that, on its face, it commits us, if anything, to non-relativism (§2). And as regards realism, I will argue that the dispositional theory leaves it very much an open question whether realism or irrealism is true. That debate, too, turns on the truth of certain supplementary, and highly controversial, premises (§3).

1. The Dispositional Theory and Cognitivism

Since the issue that divides cognitivists from non-cognitivists is, by definition, whether evaluative judgements are expressions of belief (the cognitivists' view) or some non-belief state, a state of desire or whatever (the non-cognitivists' view), it may seem inevitable that, having taken it as given that a subject's judging desirable is a matter of her believing that she would have certain desires if she were fully rational, we must be cognitivists. Inevitable though it might appear, however, it seems to me this line of reasoning is mistaken.

Consider the following, much shorter, argument for cognitivism, by way of comparison.

Premise: When a subject judges it desirable for p to be the case in certain circumstances C, this is a matter of her believing that it is desirable for p to be the case in C.

Conclusion: A cognitivist theory of desirability judgements is correct.

Now I take it that no-one will find this argument convincing. The problem is not that the premise is false. The premise, being simply a correct report of the way in which we use the English word 'belief', is true. The problem is rather that, precisely because this is why the premise is true, it is too weak to establish the truth of the desired conclusion. Moreover the reason why this is so should be evident. Quite generally, the mere fact that we ordinarily describe things in certain ways does nothing to show that those descriptions apply to those things strictly speaking. The mere fact that we ordinarily describe certain people as 'pigs', for example, does nothing to show that they are pigs strictly speaking. It shows, at most, that they are like pigs in certain respects. Likewise, then, the mere fact that we ordinarily describe people as having evaluative beliefs does nothing to show that the attitudes thus described are beliefs strictly speaking either. It shows, at most, that the attitudes are like beliefs in certain respects. This is something that can be agreed by cognitivists and non-cognitivists alike.

The question that naturally arises is what more we need to establish in order to show that evaluative judgements express beliefs strictly speaking. In order for the attitudes that people have when we ordinarily describe them as having evaluative beliefs to be beliefs strictly speaking, the sentences that we use to give the 'contents' of these attitudes—sentences like 'It is desirable for p to be the case in C'—must be truth-apt. Belief is, after all, the attitude of taking something to be a certain way, and specifying one of the ways that something could be is the distinctive role of a truth-apt sentence (Jackson, Oppy and Smith 1994). It is this that cognitivists and non-cognitivists disagree about. Non-cognitivists think that there is a compelling reason to think that these sentences do not purport to say how things are (Hare 1952; Blackburn 1984). Non-cognitivists insist that those who use these sentences properly must, at least absent practical irrationality, be in some sort of non-cognitive state—a motivational state, or a state of approval—and the only way in which this could be so is if the function of these sentences wasn't to say how things are, but was rather to express that very non-cognitive state. It follows, at least as the non-cognitivists see things, that though we do not violate any rules of English usage when we describe those who are disposed to make evaluative judgements as having 'evaluative beliefs', this must be understood as loose talk (Smith 1994b; Blackburn 1998). The attitudes in question, though like beliefs in certain respects, are not beliefs strictly speaking.

Let's now return to the original argument. If what we have just said is right then the mere fact that we would ordinarily describe a subject as 'believing' that she would want p to be the case in certain circumstances C if she were fully rational does nothing to show that this attitude is a belief strictly speaking either. This too is so only if the sentence we use to give the 'content' of this attitude—the sentence 'Subject S would want p to be the case in circumstances C if she were fully rational'—is truth-apt; in other words, only if the function of the sentence is to specify a way that things could be. Here too cognitivists and non-cognitivists might therefore disagree. Non-cognitivists might insist that the very same consideration that shows that the sentence 'It is desirable for p to be the case in C' is not truth-apt shows that the sentence 'Subject S would want p to be the case in circumstances C if she were fully rational' is not truth-apt either (Blackburn 1998). In other words, they might argue that the connection between the state that one is in when one is disposed to make that judgement and some sort of non-cognitive state—a motivation, or a state of approval—shows that the role of the sentence is to express that non-cognitive state. If they were right about this we would once again have to conclude that we only speak loosely when we say that subjects believe that they would want p to be the case in C if they were fully rational. Strictly speaking they would not be in a state of belief at all. They would be in a non-cognitive state.

The upshot is thus that, even if we grant that a subject's judging desirable is a matter of her believing that she would have certain desires if she were fully rational, it simply doesn't follow that we thereby commit ourselves to the truth of cognitivism. In order to establish the truth of cognitivism we must establish the truth of further supplementary premises. Specifically, we must establish that the function of the sentence 'Subject S would want p to be the case in circumstances C if she were fully rational' is to specify a way that that subject could be. Moreover, in order to do this without begging the question against the non-cognitivists we must establish something else as well, namely, that when subjects have beliefs about themselves being that way, whatever that way is, their beliefs have the kind of connection with non-cognitive attitudes—with motivating attitudes, or attitudes of approval—that non-cognitivists say no belief can have.

Can these supplementary premises be provided? It seems to me that they can, but this is of course all very controversial. As I see things, the claim that a subject is fully rational—where, remember, in the present context this is just to say that the subject is in a state that eludes all forms of criticism from the point of view of reason—entails a set of quite specific claims about the way that that subject is.

For example, following Bernard Williams's lead, we must suppose that the fact that a subject's desires are based on ignorance or error is, at one and the same time, a determinate way that those desires are and, for that very reason, a criticism of those desires from the point of view of reason (Williams 1980). This is because someone who was perfect, from the point of view of reason, would be omniscient and make no mistakes. But, if this is right, then it follows that there is at least one counterexample to the quite general non-cognitivist suggestion that to say that a subject's desires are liable to criticism from the point of view of reason is not to specify a way that those desires are, but is rather to express a desire about, or some other non-belief attitude towards, those desires being a certain way. Indeed, it would seem to be completely irrelevant whether those who use the term 'fully rational' happen to desire people not to have desires that are based on ignorance or error, or whether they happen to have any other non-cognitive attitude towards them. Instead it seems to be analytic that desires based on ignorance and error are liable to criticism from the point of view of reason.

Once we see that this is so an obvious question presents itself. Are there other ways a subject's desires can be which, as such, make those desires criticizable from the point of view of reason? And the answer, as I see things, is that there most certainly are. To say that a subject has a desire set that, as a whole, exhibits incoherence, for example, or to say that she has a desire set which, as a whole, exhibits a lack of unity, is equally a specification of a way that that desire set can be and a criticism of that desire set from the point of view of reason. Again, it would seem to be completely irrelevant whether those who use the term 'fully rational' happen to desire people to have desires that are coherent and unified, or whether they have any other non-cognitive attitude towards them. Someone who claimed that, according to their usage of the words 'rational criticism', to say of a set of desires that they lack coherence and unity isn't a form of rational criticism is someone who simply doesn't understand what rational criticism is. It would therefore seem once again to be analytic that a desire set that lacks coherence or unity is, as such, a desire set that is liable to criticism from the point of view of reason.[2]

How might non-cognitivists try to resist this line of argument? Following a suggestion made by Geoffrey Sayre-McCord, they might profess not to understand what is meant by the terms 'coherence' and 'unity' when these terms are applied to sets of desires (Sayre-McCord 1997). Alternatively, following a suggestion made to me by Sigrún Svavarsdóttir in conversation, they might agree that they can understand what is meant, but only if the terms 'coherent and unified' as applied to sets of desires are taken to mean something like 'co-satisfiable', an interpretation which is of little help given that desires that do not form a coherent and unified set in this sense—that is, desires that do not constitute a co-satisfiable set—are hardly, as such, criticizable from the point of view of reason.

But neither of these responses seems to me to be very plausible. When applied to sets of beliefs the terms 'coherence' and 'unity' are plainly comprehensible as specifying ways that those sets of beliefs can be. The relations that hold between desires when the terms 'coherence' and 'unity' are applied to them are, as I will go on to argue, plainly relations of exactly the same kind as these. As such it is, I think, hard to take seriously the objections of both those who profess not to understand what is meant by the terms 'coherence' and 'unity' when these terms are applied to sets of desires, and those who wish to offer an idiosyncratic interpretation of the terms, an interpretation that has nothing to do with the possibility of criticism from the point of view of reason.

In order to see that the terms 'coherent' and 'unified' really do specify ways that sets of beliefs can be, consider various sets of beliefs that combine, on the one hand, ordinary observational beliefs together with, on the other, beliefs about the behaviour of theoretical entities, theoretical entities whose behaviour is supposed to explain those observations. It is, I take it, completely uncontroversial that some of these sets of beliefs will exhibit more or less in the way of coherence and unity than other sets. Moreover I take it that when we so describe sets of beliefs we plainly specify a way that these beliefs are. We would perhaps have difficulty specifying in terms other than 'coherent' and 'unified' what that way is—the concepts of coherence and unity are perhaps, in this respect, rather like recognitional concepts—and the classifications might be vague at the borders, but, at least after allowing for these peculiarities, it seems to me that we would have little difficulty in principle in providing an interpersonally agreed ordering of the various sets of beliefs from those that exhibit most in the way of coherence and unity to those that exhibit least. To this extent being coherent and being unified would seem to be ways that these sets of beliefs can be. Moreover, to say that a set of beliefs is a way such that it exhibits less rather than more in the way of coherence and unity is simultaneously a criticism of that set of beliefs from the point of view of reason. It is analytic that, at least other things being equal, a more coherent set of beliefs is less liable to criticism from the point of view of reason, and the same goes for a set of beliefs that is more unified.

If this is right, however, then it seems plain that much the same can be said about sets of evaluative judgements. Consider the variety of sets of judgements that combine what Rawls calls our considered evaluative judgements—these are evaluative judgements about rather specific situations in which we have the greatest confidence—together with various alternative sets of judgements that we might make about general evaluative principles, general evaluative principles which are supposed to justify these considered judgements (Rawls 1951). In this case, too, it seems that we can order the sets from those that exhibit most in the way of coherence and unity to those that exhibit least. There is, in other words, nothing about the nature of the relations that exist between the judgements themselves, whether those judgements are best thought of as expressing beliefs or desires, that requires us to suppose that these relations aren't of the very same kind as the relations that exist between the sets of beliefs just considered. In this case too, then, it seems that being coherent and being unified specify ways that these sets of judgements can be. Moreover in this case, too, to say of a set of evaluative judgements that it exhibits less rather than more in the way of coherence and unity is simultaneously a criticism of that set of judgements from the point of view of reason. It is analytic that, at least other things being equal, a more coherent set of evaluative judgements is less liable to criticism from the point of view of reason, and the same goes for a set of evaluative judgements that is more unified.

Finally, consider the relations that exist between the various sets of desires that we get if, for each set of evaluative judgements of the kind just mentioned we substitute a specific desire that A Φs in circumstances C for each specific evaluative judgement of the form 'It is desirable that A Φs in circumstances C', and we substitute a general desire that (x) (x Ψs in circumstances C') for each general evaluative judgement expressible in the form '(x) (It is desirable that x Ψs in circumstances C')'. Once we have granted that the various sets of evaluative judgements of the kind just mentioned exhibit relations of coherence and unity, it seems to me that there is no alternative but to suppose that the isomorphic sets of desires just described exhibit those same relations of coherence and unity. In this case, too, it seems that we must suppose that being coherent and unified specify ways that these sets of desires can be. In this case, too, to say of a set of desires that it is a way such that it exhibits less rather than more coherence and unity is simultaneously a criticism of that set of desires from the point of view of reason.

The upshot is that those who deny that claims of the form 'Subject S would want that p be the case in circumstances C if she were fully rational' specify a way that things could be look to be on very shaky ground. To say that S would have certain desires if she were fully rational is to say that she would have those desires if she had a set of desires that eludes all forms of criticism from the point of view of reason, and, so far, we have seen that this entails that her desire set would have to be certain quite specific ways: maximally informed, coherent, and unified. Though we haven't yet been given any reason to suppose that this provides an exhaustive account of the ways that S's desire set would have to be to be fully rational, we have so far been given no reason to suppose that such further conditions as we might add wouldn't simply be further specifications of ways that sets of desires have to be in order for them to count as fully rational. Though this does not constitute a decisive proof of cognitivism, it should at least be agreed that a cognitivist account of subjects' judgements about what they would want if they were fully rational looks to be on the cards. Pro tem, then, we should suppose that such judgements express not just beliefs loosely speaking, but beliefs strictly speaking.

I said above that if we aren't to beg the question against the non-cognitivists then, in order to show that evaluative judgements really do express beliefs strictly speaking, we would have to show not just that there is a way that someone takes things to be when they believe that they would desire p to be the case if they were fully rational, but also that their taking things to be that way has the kind of necessary connection with motivation that non-cognitivists insist evaluative judgements have. We must show, in other words, that, absent practical irrationality, a subject who believes that she would desire p to be the case in C if she were fully rational does indeed desire that p in C. Can this argument be given? Though this too is controversial (Shafer-Landau 1999), it seems to me that the argument can indeed be given (Smith 2001).

Imagine a case in which a subject comes to believe that (say) she would desire that she abstains from eating sweets in the circumstances of action that she presently faces if she had a maximally informed and coherent and unified set of desires, but that she doesn't have any desire at all to abstain. She desires to eat sweets instead. Now consider the pair of psychological states that comprises her belief that she would desire that she abstains from eating sweets in the circumstances of action that she presently faces if she had a maximally informed and coherent and unified set of desires, and which also comprises the desire that she abstains from eating sweets, and compare this pair of psychological states with the pair that comprises her belief that she would desire that she abstains from eating sweets in the circumstances of action that she presently faces if she had a maximally informed and coherent and unified set of desires, but which also comprises instead a desire to eat sweets. Which of these pairs of psychological states is more coherent?

The answer would seem to be plain enough. The first pair is much more coherent than the second. There is disequilibrium or dissonance or failure of fit involved in believing that you would desire yourself to act in a certain way in certain circumstances if you had a maximally informed and coherent and unified desire set, and yet not desiring to act in that way. The failure to desire to act in that way is, after all, something that you yourself disown; from your perspective it makes no sense, given the rest of your desires; by your own lights it is a state that you would not be in if you were in various ways better than you actually are: more informed, more coherent, more unified in your desiderative outlook.[3] There would therefore seem to be more than a passing family resemblance between the relation that holds between the first pair of psychological states and more familiar examples of coherence relations that hold between psychological states. Coherence would thus seem to be on the side of the pair that comprises both the subject's belief that she would desire that she abstains from eating sweets in the circumstances of action that she presently faces and the desire that she abstains from eating sweets.

If this is right, however, then it follows immediately that if the subject is rational, in the relatively mundane sense of having and exercising a capacity to have the psychological states that coherence demands of her, then, at least abstracting away from such other dynamic changes in her beliefs as might occur for evidential reasons (Arpaly 2000), that subject will end up having a desire that matches her belief about what she would want herself to do if she had a maximally informed and coherent and unified desire set. In other words, in the particular case under discussion, she will end up losing her desire to eat sweets and acquiring a desire to abstain from eating sweets instead. Subjects' beliefs about what they would want if they were fully rational thus seem both to be beliefs strictly speaking and to be beliefs which have the kind of necessary connection with motivation that non-cognitivists insist evaluative judgements have. Absent practical irrationality—that is to say, absent a failure either to have or to exercise the capacity to have the psychological states that coherence demands of her—a subject who believes that she would want p to be the case in C if she had a maximally informed and coherent and unified desire set will indeed desire p to be the case in C. The non-cognitivists' reasons for supposing that evaluative judgements are not beliefs strictly speaking therefore seem, in the end, to be unconvincing.[4]

2. The Dispositional Theory and Relativism

Let's now suppose not just that when a subject judges it desirable that p be the case in certain circumstances, C, this is a matter of her believing that she would want that p be the case in C if she were fully rational, but also that, for the reasons just given (§1), these states are beliefs strictly speaking. Once we grant this it is, I think, extremely tempting to suppose that we thereby commit ourselves to the truth of relativism (Johnston 1989). Here is why.

Consider two people, A and B, who appear to have the same evaluative belief, the belief that it is desirable that p. Given the equivalence, what A believes is that she, A, would desire that p if she, A, had a set of desires that is maximally informed and coherent and unified. But what B believes, by contrast, is that he, B, would desire that p if he, B, had a set of desires that is maximally informed and coherent and unified. A's and B's beliefs thus have quite different truth conditions. A's belief is made true by the desires that she would have, never mind about B's, and B's by the desires he would have, never mind about A's. If this is right, though—that is, if A's and B's beliefs do indeed have different truth conditions—then the appearance that they have the same belief, when they each believe that it is desirable that p, is misleading. A is more accurately represented as believing that it is desirable$_A$ that p, and B as believing that it is desirable$_B$ that p. The suggested equivalence thus seems to imply the truth of relativism.

Tempting though this line of thought is, we should, I think, resist it. In order to see why, it will be helpful to work through an example of a particular substituend for 'p' in the belief that it is desirable that p. To anticipate, my argument will be that once we pay due regard to three facts about values—the fact that value is universalizable, the fact that value can be either neutral or egocentric, and the fact that some neutral values and egocentric values are commensurable—it becomes plain that evaluations not only are not, but that they could not be, relative in the way that has just been suggested. If anything, these considerations suggest that we are committed to a non-relativist conception of value.

Imagine someone, A, with a belief whose content we might initially think she should express in the following sentence:

It is desirable that my$_A$ children fare well.

where the subscript to the 'my' simply serves to make it explicit whose children are being referred to. Given the equivalence, this amounts to A's having a belief whose content she could express in the following sentence:

I$_A$ would want that my$_A$ children fare well if I$_A$ had a set of desires that is maximally informed and coherent and unified.

Complications immediately arise, however.

It is, after all, a conceptual truth that evaluations are one and all universalizable. It therefore follows that specific evaluations, like this one, must be derivable from more universal beliefs to which agents are committed. We must therefore ask which universal evaluation A is committed to simply in virtue of having the belief that it is desirable that her own children fare well. In other words—and, remember, we are supposing equivalently—we must ask which universal evaluation A is committed to simply in virtue of having the belief that she would want that her children fare well if she had a set of desires that is maximally informed and coherent and unified.

One possibility is that A is committed to a universal evaluative belief with the following content:

(x) (It is desirable that x's children fare well)

or, perhaps equivalently:

(x) (I_A would want that x's children fare well if I_A had a set of desires that is maximally informed and coherent and unified)

But while this might be one possibility, it certainly isn't the only possibility. It simply assumes that A assigns neutral, or non-egocentric, value to the welfare of people's children—assumes, in other words, that A believes it equally desirable that her own children fare well and that other people's children fare well; assumes, in terms of the equivalence, that she would desire equally that her own children fare well and that other people's children fare well if she had a set of desires that is maximally informed and coherent and unified—whereas the original belief is plainly ambiguous between that possibility and the quite different possibility that she assigns egocentric value to the welfare of her children, and hence that the desires she would have if she had a set of desires that is maximally informed and coherent and unified would be quite specifically desires about the welfare of her own children. This, in turn, suggests that we went wrong in trying to give the content of her original belief. We should have noted that that belief is ambiguous, and insisted that it be disambiguated before we give its equivalent. Let's therefore start again.

The content of A's original belief, the belief that it is desirable that her children fare well, is ambiguous. What she has is either a belief the content of which she could express in the following sentence:

It is desirable$_A$ that my$_A$ children fare well

—this is what she believes if she assigns the welfare of her children egocentric value—or, alternatively, it might be suggested, she has a belief the content of which she could best express in the following sentence:

It is desirable that my$_A$ children fare well

which is what she believes if she assigns the welfare of her children neutral value. Because evaluations are one and all universalizable, these beliefs might then be thought to commit A to universal beliefs that she could best express in one or another of the following sentences:

(x) (It is desirable$_x$ that x's children fare well)

—this is the content of the universal belief to which she is committed if she assigns the welfare of her children egocentric value—or, alternatively,

(x) (It is desirable that x's children fare well)

which is the content of the universal belief to which she is committed if she assigns the welfare of her children neutral value.

But this can't be quite right either. If it were it would follow, implausibly, that such assignments of neutral and egocentric value to the welfare of children are radically incommensurable. Neutral value would, after all, be a completely different property from egocentric value—egocentric value would be an indexed property, whereas neutral value an unindexed property—and this in turn would mean that we couldn't sensibly ask someone who assigns both neutral value to the welfare of people's children and egocentric value to the welfare of her own children whether the egocentric value that she assigns to her own children's welfare was greater than or less than the neutral value that she assigns to their welfare. The comparative concept of desirability would, after all, have to be the comparative form of either the indexed property or the unindexed property. We could only ask A questions such as whether her own children's welfare has more *egocentric* value than the egocentric value possessed by other people's children (a question the answer to which is that it plainly does, since other people's children have no such egocentric value), or whether the welfare of other people's children has more *neutral* value than that possessed by her own children (the answer to which is plainly that it doesn't, since other people's children's welfare has the same neutral value as that possessed by her own).

As I said, it seems to me that the idea that assignments of neutral and egocentric value are radically incommensurable in this way is manifestly implausible. Those who assign neutral value to the welfare of people's children and egocentric value to the welfare of their own children have no problem at all comparing these two values. Indeed, I think that most people would insist that the egocentric value that they assign to their own children's welfare is greater than the neutral value they assign to their own children's welfare, and to the welfare of the children of others. This is why they feel totally justified in giving benefits to their own children over comparable benefits to strangers. We are, however, yet to find an account of the logical form of evaluations that makes it plain just what it might mean when we make such comparative evaluative claims.

Returning to the example we have been working through so far, what this suggests, I think, is that A should express the content of her original belief in the following sentence:

It is desirable$_A$ that my$_A$ children fare well

and that in order to disambiguate this belief we must say whether it, in turn, is derived from a universal belief with the following content:

(x) (It is desirable$_x$ that x's children fare well)

—this is the content of the universal belief to which A is committed if she assigns the welfare of her children egocentric value—or, alternatively, in a universal belief with the following content:

$(x)(y)$ (It is desirable$_x$ that y's children fare well)

This is the content of the universal belief to which she is committed if she assigns the welfare of her children neutral value. In other words, and rather naturally I think, the difference between a neutral evaluation of the welfare of a subject's children and an egocentric evaluation is that whereas the egocentric evaluation is an evaluation from that subject's own point of view, the neutral evaluation is an evaluation from everyone's point of view. Moreover, though the subscript on the desirability predicate in the neutral evaluation might look completely idle when neutral evaluations are considered in isolation from egocentric evaluations, the fact that there is such an index on the desirability predicate in the neutral evaluation is absolutely crucial when it comes to an understanding of how comparisons of neutral and egocentric value are possible. Much as I suggested above, for example, A might be committed to a comparative universal evaluative belief with the following content:

$(x)(y)$ ((It is desirable$_x$ that x's children fare well) & (It is desirable$_x$ that y's children fare well) & (It is more desirable$_x$ that x's children fare well than that y's children fare well))

This might be why the egocentric value that A assigns to the welfare of her own children is greater than the neutral value that she assigns to the welfare of people's children quite generally, including even her own children.

Note what we have done so far. So far we have simply focussed on evaluations themselves—particular substituends for the 'p' in the proposition 'It is desirable that p'—and asked how, in the light of three facts about values—the facts that evaluations are universalizable, that evaluations can be assignments of either neutral value or assignments of egocentric value, and that it is at least possible for neutral value and egocentric value to commensurate—a particular subject, A, should express the content of the evaluations to which she is committed when she believes that it is desirable that her own children fare well. We are now in a position to ask what the contents of A's beliefs are, given the equivalence postulated by the dispositional theory of value.

We have seen that A's belief that it is desirable that her own children fare well is ambiguous. In terms of the equivalence, how should she express the content of the universal evaluative beliefs to which she is committed under the various disambiguations? Disambiguating in favour of the possibility that she assigns her children's welfare egocentric value, it turns out that she is committed to a universal belief with the following content:

(x) (It is desirable$_x$ that x's children fare well)

which, given the equivalence, suggests that she is committed to a belief with the following content:

> (x) (x would want that x's children fare well if x had a set of desires that is maximally informed and coherent and unified)

Alternatively, disambiguating in favour of the possibility that she assigns her children's welfare neutral value, it turns out that she is committed to a universal belief with the following content:

> (x)(y) (It is desirable$_x$ that y's children fare well)

which, given the equivalence, means that she is committed to a belief with the following content:

> (x)(y) (x would want that y's children fare well if x had a set of desires that is maximally informed and coherent and unified)

A subject committed to a comparative evaluative belief with the following content:

> (x)(y) ((It is desirable$_x$ that x's children fare well) & (It is desirable$_x$ that y's children fare well) & (It is more desirable$_x$ that x's children fare well than that y's children fare well))

is, given the equivalence, committed to a comparative belief with the following content:

> (x)(y) ((x would want that x's children fare well if x had a set of desires that is maximally informed and coherent and unified) & (x would want that y's children fare well if x had a set of desires that is maximally informed and coherent and unified) & (the desire x has that x's children fare well would be stronger than the desire x has that y's children fare well))

As is perhaps already plain, when it comes to the issue of relativism, the conclusion is therefore exactly the opposite of the one that we were tempted by at the outset.

Imagine, once again, two people, A and B, both of whom believe that it is desirable that their own children fare well. Do their beliefs have the same truth conditions or different truth conditions? Since, as we have seen, A's and B's beliefs are ambiguous, the truth conditions of their beliefs depend on how we disambiguate them. Contrary to the suggestion made at the outset, however, and notwithstanding the fact that A's and B's beliefs are ambiguous, it turns out that, so long as we disambiguate them in the same way, their beliefs have the very same truth conditions. For, given universalizability, they must either both be committed to a belief with the following content:

(x) (x would want that x's children fare well if x had a set of desires that is maximally informed and coherent and unified)

—this is the belief to which they are committed if their original beliefs were about the egocentric value of their children's welfare—or, alternatively, to a belief with the following content:

(x)(y) (x would want that y's children fare well if x had a set of desires that is maximally informed and coherent and unified)

—this is the belief to which they are committed if their original beliefs were about the neutral value of their children's welfare.

On the assumption that we can generalize on the basis of this example, it would thus seem to follow that, contrary to the suggestion made at the outset, one subject's evaluative beliefs are made true not just by the desires that she would have if she had a set of desires that was maximally informed and coherent and unified, but also by the desires that every other subject would have if they had a set of desires that was maximally informed and coherent and unified. Far from the suggested equivalence committing us to relativism, then, it appears that it commits us if anything to non-relativism. The truth of a subject's evaluative beliefs requires that all subjects converge in the desires they would have if they had a set of desires that was maximally informed and coherent and unified.[5]

3. The Dispositional Theory and Realism

I said at the outset that the dispositional theory would seem to commit us not just to relativism, but also to realism. The connection between these two commitments should be plain.

We suggested initially that a subject's judgements about the desirability of p's being the case in circumstances C were made true by whether or not that subject herself would want p to be the case in C if she had a set of desires that was maximally informed and coherent and unified, never mind about what other subjects would want if they had a set of desires that was maximally informed and coherent and unified. If this were right then, since it is so plausible to think that there are some things that a particular subject would want if she had such a set of desires—this only requires that we be able to give determinate content to the relevant counterfactuals, after all—it follows that it would likewise be plausible to suppose that, since some such judgements are true, realism must be true. In other words, we could reject the possibility of an error theory of the kind argued for by John Mackie (1977). However, now that we have seen that the dispositional theory commits us not to relativism, but, if anything, to the rejection of relativism, we must reevaluate this commitment to realism.

If a subject's judgements about the desirability of p's being the case in certain circumstances C are made true not just by whether or not that subject herself would want that p be the case in C if she had a set of desires that was maximally informed and coherent and unified, but also by whether everyone else would want that p in C if they had a set of desires that was maximally informed and coherent and unified, then should we suppose that some such judgements are true? In other words, is it plausible to suppose that there are some desires that all subjects would converge upon if they had desire sets that are maximally informed and coherent and unified? Many will insist that that there are no such desires (Sobel 1999). If they are right then we must conclude that realism is false. The dispositional theory, since it entails non-relativism, entails irrealism. My own view, however, is that this is all far too quick. It is unclear whether there are any desires that all subjects would converge upon if they had desire sets that are maximally informed and coherent and unified, but it is equally unclear that there are no such desires. It therefore seems to me best to suppose that the debate between realists and irrealists is yet to be resolved.

Those who think that the dispositional theory entails irrealism are, I think, impressed by a chain of reasoning much like the following. We can surely imagine two subjects, D and E, each of whom, in actuality, has a single intrinsic desire—that is, a desire that they haven't derived from some further desire that they have plus a belief about means—but a different one: let's suppose, for example, that D has an intrinsic desire that p, whereas E an intrinsic desire that q. Furthermore, since their respective desires are intrinsic, we can also imagine that each of them would retain their single intrinsic desire no matter what further information they acquired. But since there is no reason to suppose that the acquisition of any further information would lead D and E to acquire additional intrinsic desires, and since D's and E's desire sets, comprising as they do just one desire each, are already as coherent and unified as they could possibly be, it follows that D and E would not converge in their intrinsic desires even if they did have a maximally informed and coherent and unified desire set. They would still diverge. Indeed, they would still just have their respective intrinsic desires that p and that q. It therefore follows that there are no desires that everyone would converge upon if they had a maximally informed and coherent and unified desire set. The hypothetical D and E constitute the decisive counterexample. If realism requires such convergence, then realism is false.

What is wrong with this chain of reasoning? The problem lies in the premise that there is no reason to suppose that the acquisition of further information would lead D and E to acquire any additional intrinsic desires beyond their respective intrinsic desires that p and that q. To begin, let's be clear what this premise says. It says, inter alia, that there is no information that D and E could acquire such that, having acquired that information, they would be rationally required to acquire intrinsic desires beyond their respective intrinsic desires that p and that q. But it seems to me that the only reason we would have to accept this premise is if we were to assume, quite generally, that there are no rational principles of the following form:

It is rationally required that subjects who believe that r either give up their belief that r or acquire an intrinsic desire that s.

Yet, as we have already seen, this quite general assumption is false.

This is, in effect, what we discovered earlier when we saw that coherence requires subjects who believe that they would want p to be the case in circumstances C if they had a desire set that was maximally informed and coherent and unified to desire that p be the case in C (§1). We saw, in other words, that the following—an instance of the rational principle we would have to assume quite generally to be false—is in fact true:

It is rationally required that an agent who believes that she would have an intrinsic desire that p be the case in circumstances C if she had a maximally informed and coherent and unified desire set either gives up her belief or acquires an intrinsic desire that p be the case in C.

Now, to be sure, this particular claim connecting the acquisition of information with intrinsic desiring is not sufficient all by itself to show that D and E would converge in their desires. But nor is that required at this stage of the argument. All that is required is that we show what is wrong with the chain of reasoning described above that purports to prove that two hypothetical subjects, D and E, would not converge in their intrinsic desires. The crucial point, to repeat, is that once we see that the quite general assumption that there are no rational principles of the form 'It is rationally required that an agent who believes that r either gives up his belief that r or acquires an intrinsic desire that s' is false—once we remind ourselves, in other words, that reflection can lead us to accept the surprising conclusion that certain instances of that principle are in fact true—then it is hard to see what, beyond dogmatic commitment, would lead anyone to think that *further* reflection won't lead us to the surprising conclusion that *more* instances of that principle are true (compare Korsgaard 1986). In particular, it is hard to see what, beyond dogmatic commitment, would lead anyone to think that further reflection won't lead us to discover that further instances of that principle, instances sufficient to show that D and E would converge in their desires, are true.[6]

At this stage it therefore seems to me that we would be wise to suspend judgement on the debate over realism versus anti-realism. Perhaps further reflection will reveal that such further instances of rational principles of the form 'It is rationally required that an agent who believes that r either gives up his belief that r or acquires an intrinsic desire that s' as are required in order to undergird a convergence in the desires of subjects with a maximally informed and coherent and unified desire set are true; perhaps it will not. We have little choice but to do the required reflection and see.[7]

NOTES

1. This is somewhat misleading because whereas non-culpable ignorance plausibly constitutes a failure to achieve an ideal of reason, and so something that is in this sense criticizable from that point of view, it may not constitute what we would ordinarily call a failure of rationality. For reasons that will become plain shortly I will, however, ignore these differences of meaning in what follows.

2. It should now be plain why we were right to ignore the fact that the shorthand term 'being fully rational' does not mean exactly the same as 'being in a state that eludes all forms of criticism from the point of view of reason' (see footnote 1 above). All that is crucial is that we can give an account of the way that subjects are when they are in the latter state. The term 'being fully rational' really is just convenient, if misleading, shorthand.

3. I have just said that a subject who believes that she would desire that she acts in a certain way if she had a maximally informed and coherent and unified desire set, but who does not desire to act in that way, is in a state that she would not be in if she were in various ways *better* than she actually is: more informed, more coherent, more unified in her desiderative outlook. It is important to note that this use of the term 'better' trades on an understanding of value that cannot be analysed in the way suggested by the dispositional theory, an understanding according to which it is simply analytic that a subject with a maximally informed and coherent and unified desire set is as good as she can be, and that subjects with desire sets that fall ever shorter of being maximally informed and coherent and unified are subjects who are correspondingly less good. This should perhaps come as no surprise given that being good as can be, in this sense, is simply a matter of being perfect from the point of view of reason. Hallvard Lillehammer suggests that dispositional theories that define value in terms of such a non-dispositional conception of the good give up on any claim to metaphysical modesty (Lillehammer 2000). For more on this see footnote 6 below.

4. Another way of putting the conclusion just reached is that it is in the nature of desires that they are psychological states that are rationally sensitive to our beliefs about what we would desire that we do if we had a set of desires that was maximally informed and coherent and unified, 'rationally sensitive' in the sense of being psychological states that we would acquire in the light of such beliefs given that we have a capacity to have the psychological states that coherence demands of us. As we will see later (§3), this is an important conclusion to draw, not just because it undermines one of the main arguments for non-cognitivism, but also because it undermines one of the main arguments for relativism.

5. Though I have argued for this conclusion elsewhere (Smith 1994a, 1997, 1999), note that the argument given in the text is completely new. To repeat, the argument given in the text is that the natural interpretation of the dispositional theory, given three facts about values—the fact that values are universalizable, that values can be either neutral or egocentric, and that at least some neutral values and some egocentric values are commensurable—is a non-relativist interpretation. The argument I have given in the past for the conclusion that we must give a non-relative interpretation of the

dispositional theory has been that only so can we capture the non-arbitrariness of values. The argument given in the text might well prompt the question whether it is so much as possible to formulate a relativist version of the dispositional theory. Would any such formulation have to assume, implausibly, either that values are not universalizable, or that values cannot be both neutral and egocentric, or that neutral values and egocentric values are radically incommensurable? Though I will not spell out the formulation here, let me say, for the record, that I do not think that this is so. It seems to me that it is possible to formulate a relativist version of the dispositional theory, albeit a very unintuitive and ad hoc version, that is consistent with the three claims about values just mentioned. Unsurprisingly, however, it also seems to me that when we spell out the relativist version of the dispositional theory that is consistent with these three claims it becomes manifest just how arbitrary value is, on such a relativist conception.

6. Hallvard Lillehammer (2000) suggests that dispositional theories that define value in terms of a non-dispositional conception of the good give up on any claim to metaphysical modesty. But there would seem to be nothing metaphysically immodest about the claims about the good made in footnote 3 above, and nor would there seem to be anything metaphysically immodest about principles of reason of the form 'It is rationally required that an agent who believes that r either gives up his belief that r or acquires an intrinsic desire that s'. What is true, of course, is that we do indeed find it surprising that there are true instances of a general principle of that form. But, as the argument given in §2 illustrates, perhaps the real surprise lies in the fact that the argument for that conclusion relies on such uncontroversial premises. It remains to be seen whether the arguments given for any further instances that we might discover rely on such similarly uncontroversial premises.

7. I would like to thank John Broome, David Estlund and Philip Pettit for helpful conversations while I was writing this paper.

References

Arpaly, Nomy 2000: 'On Acting Rationally against One's Best Judgment' in *Ethics*, pp. 488–513.
Blackburn, Simon 1984: *Spreading the Word* (Oxford: Oxford University Press).
———— 1998: *Ruling Passions* (Oxford: Clarendon Press).
Copp, David 1997: "Belief, Reason and Motivation: Michael Smith's, *The Moral Problem*" in *Ethics* October 1997, pp. 33–54.
Hare, R.M. 1952: *The Language of Morals* (Oxford: Oxford University Press).
Jackson, Frank, Graham Oppy and Michael Smith 1994: 'Minimalism and Truth-Aptness', *Mind*, pp. 287–302.
Johnston, Mark 1989: 'Dispositional Theories of Value', *Proceedings of the Aristotelian Society* Supplementary Volume, pp. 139–174.
Korsgaard, Christine 1986: 'Skepticism about Practical Reason', *Journal of Philosophy*, pp. 5–25.
Lewis, David 1989: 'Dispositional Theories of Value', *Proceedings of the Aristotelian Society* Supplementary Volume, pp. 113–137.
Lillehammer, Hallvard 2000: 'Revisionary Dispositionalism and Metaphysical Modesty' in *The Journal of Ethics*, pp. 173–190.
Mackie, J.L. 1977: *Ethics: Inventing Right and Wrong* (Harmondsworth: Penguin).
Rawls, John 1951: 'Outline of a Decision Procedure for Ethics', *Philosophical Review*, pp. 177–197.
Sayre-McCord, Geoffrey 1997: 'The Meta-Ethical Problem: a discussion of Michael Smith's *The Moral Problem*' in *Ethics*, pp. 55–83.

Schafer-Landau, Russ 1999: 'Moral judgement and normative reasons' *Analysis*, pp. 33–40.

Smith, Michael 1989: 'Dispositional Theories of Value' in *Proceedings of the Aristotelian Society* Supplementary Volume, pp. 89–111.

———— 1994a: *The Moral Problem* (Oxford: Blackwell).

———— 1994b: 'Why Expressivists About Value Should Love Minimalism About Truth' in *Analysis*, pp. 1–12.

———— 1997: 'In Defence of *The Moral Problem*: A Reply to Brink, Copp and Sayre-McCord' in *Ethics*, pp. 84–119.

———— 1999: 'The Non-Arbitrariness of Reasons: Reply to Lenman' in *Utilitas*, pp. 178–193

———— 2001: 'The Incoherence Argument: Reply to Shafer-Landau' in *Analysis*, pp. 254–266.

Sobel, David 1999: 'Do the Desires of Rational Agents Converge?' in *Analysis*, pp. 137–147.

Williams, Bernard 1980: 'Internal and External Reasons' reprinted in his *Moral Luck* (Cambridge: Cambridge University Press, 1981), pp. 101–113.

Contributors

Akeel Bilgrami, Johnsonian Professor of Philosophy, Columbia University

Michael Devitt, Distinguished Professor of Philosophy, The Graduate Center, The City University of New York

James Dreier, Associate Professor of Philosophy, Brown University

Eli Hirsch, Professor of Philosophy, Brandeis University

Terry Horgan, Professor of Philosophy, University of Arizona

Frank Jackson, Professor of Philosophy, Philosophy Program, Research School of Social Sciences, Australian National University

Philip Pettit, currently Professor of Politics, Princeton University (formerly Professor of Social and Political Theory, Australian National University)

Carol Rovane, Associate Professor of Philosophy, Columbia University

Stephen Schiffer, Professor of Philosophy, New York University

Alan Sidelle, Professor of Philosophy, University of Wisconsin-Madison

Walter Sinnott-Armstrong, Professor of Philosophy, Dartmouth College

Michael Smith, Professor of Philosophy and Head of the Philosophy Program, Research School of Social Sciences, Australian National University

Galen Strawson, Professor of Philosophy, University of Reading

Mark Timmons, Professor of Philosophy, University of Memphis

Peter van Inwagen, John Cardinal O'Hara Professor of Philosophy, University of Notre Dame

Achille C. Varzi, Assistant Professor of Philosophy, Columbia University

Stephen Yablo, Professor of Philosophy, Massachusetts Institute of Technology